# UNDERSTANDING CIVIL WAR

VOLUME 2: Europe, Central Asia, and Other Regions

# UNDERSTANDING CIVIL WAR

## Evidence and Analysis

Edited by
Paul Collier
Nicholas Sambanis

**THE WORLD BANK**

✳ 603 12030

This volume is a product of the staff of the International Bank for Reconstruction and Development / The World Bank. The findings, interpretations, and conclusions expressed in this paper do not necessarily reflect the views of the Executive Directors of The World Bank or the governments they represent.

The World Bank does not guarantee the accuracy of the data included in this work. The boundaries, colors, denominations, and other information shown on any map in this work do not imply any judgement on the part of The World Bank concerning the legal status of any territory or the endorsement or acceptance of such boundaries.

**Rights and Permissions**

Cover photo: ©Roger M. Richards

ISBN-10: 0-8213-6049-3
ISBN-13: 978-0-8213-6049-1
eISBN: 0-8213-6050-7
DOI: 10.1596/978-0-8213-6049-1

Library of Congress Cataloging-in-Publication Data

Understanding civil war: evidence and analysis / Paul Collier & Nicholas Sambanis, editors.
    p. cm
Includes bibliographical references and index.
Contents: v. 1. Africa – v. 2. Europe, Central Asia, and other regions.
ISBN 0-8213-6047-7 (v. 1: pbk.) – ISBN 0-8213-6049-3 (v. 2: pbk.)
    1. Civil war-Economic aspects–Case studies. 2. War–Causes–Case studies. I. Collier, Paul. II. Sambanis, Nicholas, 1967-

HB195.U43 2005  V. 2
330.9–dc22                                    2005047813

# Contents

FIGURES

TABLES

# Foreword

The World Bank's role in addressing the ravages caused by violent conflict is historical—its first loans were made to support the reconstruction of Western European countries devastated by the Second World War. Over the following five decades, as most of the world's conflicts amounted to proxy wars between the superpowers or postcolonial independence struggles, the Bank limited its involvement in conflict-affected countries to providing financial capital and rebuilding infrastructure after conflicts had ended. However, in a post-Cold War era marked by an increase in the number and severity of civil conflicts, the Bank found it had to adapt to different and more complex challenges. Two events in the mid-1990s marked a turning point in the Bank's approach to conflict. The first occurred in 1994, when the Bank was asked to administer the multidonor Holst Fund for the West Bank and Gaza; the second occurred in 1995, when the Bank was asked to take the lead with the European Commission in planning and coordinating international support for postconflict recovery in Bosnia-Herzegovina. The Bosnia-Herzegovina program, in particular, broke the mold and formed the basis for a new postconflict framework that was to become a Bank operational policy within a few years.

Realizing that it faced a far more difficult postconflict environment and growing expectations on the part of the international community, in 1997 the Bank created a small locus of expertise in postconflict reconstruction, the Post-Conflict Unit, and defined the parameters for Bank engagement in countries affected by conflict, firmly focused on the Bank's reconstruction role after the conflict ended. To complement this expertise, in August 1997 the Bank created the Post-Conflict Fund, a grant facility to support countries in transition from conflict to sustainable development and encourage innovation and external partnerships in dealing with conflict-affected countries.

Because poverty has proven to be both a cause and a consequence of conflict, toward the late 1990s the Bank sought to redefine its role more broadly in the context of a more comprehensive approach to development, in line with evolving international initiatives to explore the potential role of development assistance and conflict prevention. The Bank shifted its focus from an approach based on rebuilding infrastructure to one that seeks to understand the root causes and drivers of conflict, to integrate a sensitivity to conflict in Bank activities and to promote development assistance that minimizes the potential causes of conflict. In line with this shift in focus, and following a process of discussion and consultation inside and outside the organization, in January 2001 the Executive Directors of the World Bank approved a new and broader operational policy on Development Cooperation and Conflict. To signal this shift in emphasis toward a broader approach to conflict, the Post-Conflict Unit was renamed the Conflict Prevention and Reconstruction Unit.

At the same time that the Bank sought to redefine its operational role more comprehensively in the conflict and development nexus, findings from the Bank's research arm, headed by Paul Collier, opened up the global debate on the economic causes and consequences of conflict. For an institution well stocked with economists, there had been surprisingly little economic analysis or explanations of conflict in the Bank's research and analytical work. Bank economists were inclined to think of conflict as an exogenous shock, akin to a natural disaster or an adverse swing in the terms of trade—an adverse and unfortunate event that happened from time to time, which was not within the confines of the Bank's analytical arsenal and about which little could be done.

As the Bank broadened its approach to conflict, it also sought to gain a better understanding of the causes of conflict, recognizing, as pointed out in its operational policy on Development Cooperation and Conflict, that important knowledge gaps remained on the links between development assistance and conflict. With stronger intellectual underpinnings, the Bank could more effectively design strategies and programs that were sensitive to conflict and thus begin to realize the objective of viewing development through a conflict lens. To this end, in 1999 Paul Collier and his colleagues in the Development Economics Research Group began a major research effort, partly funded by the Post-Conflict Fund, to study the economics of conflict and violence. The approach, which became known as the Collier-Hoeffler model, confirmed the link between poverty and conflict, but some of its other findings were more controversial and sparked a lively international debate, which came to be known as the "greed versus grievance" debate. The main point of contention centered around whether the Collier-Hoeffler model was too narrowly focused on economic explanations and thus ignored genuine grievances, or other causes of conflict suggested in the political science and international relations literatures. Many critics argued that the statistical and econometric techniques used to try to untangle causality, while perhaps helpful in identifying patterns and risk factors, obscured or disregarded the insights and explanations of conflict that can only emerge from the detailed study of individual conflicts.

Partly in response to these concerns, a second and complementary phase of the research on the economics of conflict and violence sought to adopt a comparative case study approach to refine and expand the economics of conflict model. This second phase, also partly funded by the Post-Conflict Fund, is part of the "Political Economy of Civil Wars" project, a collaborative research undertaking between the World Bank and Yale University. The results of the case studies presented in this volume add considerably to our understanding of conflict. Through these case studies, we gain a more nuanced understanding of conflict and the conditions under which different variables influence the outbreak of violence. In addition, a number of important improvements to the Collier-Hoeffler model have been proposed. An important additional benefit of this research is that it may lay to rest the "greed versus grievance" caricature. The research presented here makes it clear that greed and grievances should not be seen as competing explanations of conflict—they are often shades of the same problem.

Ian Bannon
*Manager*
*Conflict Prevention and Reconstruction Unit*
*World Bank*

# Preface

C ivil wars around the world since 1945 have killed approximately 20 million people and displaced at least 67 million. Despite this massive scale of human misery associated with civil war, the academic community had not concentrated much attention on the problem of civil war until very recently. A major catalyst for increased academic and policy work aimed at understanding civil war and reducing its prevalence was the World Bank project on the "Economics of Political and Criminal Violence." The World Bank research team conceptualized civil war as a development problem and applied economic models to explain the occurrence, duration, and consequences of civil war. This approach seemed appropriate, given that civil wars occur disproportionately in poor countries and retard economic development in entire regions. If poor economic conditions cause civil wars, then we may be able to design economic policy interventions that reduce their occurrence, mitigating the human suffering that they cause.

The World Bank project made important strides in understanding civil war. Quantitative studies by the project's researchers identified a set of statistically significant correlates of civil war. The project's flagship article, "The Collier-Hoeffler Model of Civil War Onset," has been especially prominent in the literature and has inspired much additional research on the relationship between political conflict and economic development. The project's many empirical findings and theoretical arguments were summarized in a Policy Research Report, *Breaking the Conflict Trap: Civil War and Development Policy,* written by Paul Collier and his research team.

Collier and Hoeffler have put forward an economic model of civil war, arguing convincingly that it is not political and social grievance per se that leads to civil war, but rather, for given levels of grievance, it is the opportunity to organize and finance a rebellion that determines if a civil war will occur or not. The determinants of such opportunity in their model are mainly economic. Their model identifies conditions that make rebellion financially viable. This analysis was based on econometric tests using data that cover all countries for about 40 years (from 1960 to 1999).

Ultimately, the results of the Collier-Hoeffler model should be useful for the design of policy. For the moment, we can only draw very broad policy guidelines from the Collier-Hoeffler model. For example, the model (and related empirical results) demonstrates that by increasing the gross domestic product per capita in developing countries, we will be reducing the risk of civil war. But we clearly need more fine-grained, policy-relevant research on civil war before we can design appropriate interventions. Quantitative studies alone are unlikely to pinpoint specific policies that can reduce war risk in different countries at different stages of a conflict's cycle. To design targeted policy interventions, but also to develop further our theoretical understanding of civil war, we need to understand *how* and *when* the explanatory variables in the Collier-Hoeffler model will lead to civil war. An understanding of the *how* and *when* will improve our ability to identify countries at greater risk of an outbreak of civil war, and the more we understand the process of conflict escalation, the better we will become at designing time-sensitive policy interventions. This two-volume book takes the next step in that direction, by systematically applying the Collier-Hoeffler model to several countries, using a comparative case study design to draw lessons that can help us refine and expand the theory of civil war. The book also makes a methodological contribution as it illustrates a useful way to combine quantitative and qualitative research in political science.

This book is the product of collaborative research involving dozens of scholars, who worked together over a number of years. We thank the authors of the case studies most of all, for their contributions to this book. Ibrahim Elbadawi and Norman Loayza, both of whom had been involved in the World Bank project on the "Economics of Political and Criminal Violence," helped select countries, identify the case study authors, and draft the first set of guidelines that were distributed to authors at the Oslo conference, where the project was launched in June 2001. Ian Bannon and Colin Scott of the World Bank deserve special thanks. Without their help, financial support for this project would not have been available. Both of them made sure that the Bank's research on conflict maintained a clear policy perspective, and they were sources of encouragement and advice throughout the project. We also gratefully acknowledge financial assistance offered by the Yale Center for International and Area Studies. Funds from the Coca-Cola Fund were used to host the April 2002 conference in New Haven, where first drafts of the case studies were presented. We also received useful comments and suggestions from several colleagues, including Anna Grzymala-Busse, Keith Darden, Jennifer Hochschild, Stathis Kalyvas, Jack Snyder, and Sidney Tarrow, most of whom commented on earlier versions of the Introduction and Conclusion (parts of which were camouflaged as an article published in *Perspectives on Politics*). Ian Bannon, Robert Bates, William Foltz, Nils Petter Gleditsch, Anke Hoeffler, Norman Loayza, and Bruce Russett commented on first drafts of the case studies at the Yale conference. Three anonymous referees read through both volumes and offered useful suggestions for revisions. Susan Hennigan did an expert job in helping us organize the Yale Conference in April 2002 and administering the budget for the World Bank grant that financed this project. She and David Hennigan helped edit some of the case studies. The research and administrative staff at the Peace Research Institute, Oslo, helped organize the first conference that launched the project in June 2001.

Paul Collier
*Oxford, England*

Nicholas Sambanis
*New Haven, Connecticut*

# The Collier-Hoeffler Model of Civil War Onset and the Case Study Project Research Design

1

PAUL COLLIER, ANKE HOEFFLER,
AND NICHOLAS SAMBANIS

I n this book, we use a comparative case study design to develop the theory of
civil war. We do so by applying a well-known quantitative model of civil war
onset—the Collier-Hoeffler (henceforth, CH) model—to several countries,
using the model as a guide to conduct systematic case studies of the occurrence or
absence of war. Although we apply well-known methods from comparative politics, such as a "most similar systems" design in comparing the cases of Senegal and
Mali in volume 1 and civil wars in several states in the Caucasus in volume 2, our
book also presents narratives based on a new, innovative design that blends quantitative and qualitative analysis. Our innovation consists of selecting cases based
on a formal economic model of civil war and using the cases to develop the theory
further and to add context and texture to the basic insights of the CH model. We,
therefore, structure a design in which qualitative and quantitative research methods
are well integrated, leading to better theory development and, ultimately, to better
empirical testing as well.

We draw on 22 case studies of more than 30 civil wars to explore the fit of the
CH model to each case.[1] By "fit" we mean several things. We use the cases to see
if the empirical measures (often called proxies) in the CH model actually measure
the theoretically significant variables. We also use the cases to see if important
explanations of civil war are omitted from the CH model. The case studies have
several other uses; most important is their ability to track sequences of events leading to civil war. "Thick" (i.e., rich, detailed) descriptions of such sequences help
identify the causal mechanisms through which the independent variables in the
CH model influence the risk of civil war onset, leading to a deeper understanding
of civil war and suggesting possible revisions of the CH model. Some case studies
suggest potentially generalizable hypotheses about civil war that the CH model has

not considered. These hypotheses could, in another iteration, be incorporated in the model, by adding new measures for all countries and years in the data and by performing new empirical tests of an expanded model. The cases also help us identify similarities or differences across groups of countries and periods, which allows us to evaluate the assumption of unit homogeneity that underlies the empirical tests of the CH model and most quantitative other studies of civil war.

Even if the CH model predicted all cases of civil war onset perfectly, it would still not be able to tell us much about the process through which these outcomes (war or peace) are generated. By contrast, analyzing the process—the sequence of events and the interaction of variables in the CH model over time—is the comparative advantage of case study designs. Quantitative and qualitative research designs are often (mistakenly) considered as substitutes rather than complements in political science. Our book should suggest that there is much to learn by combining the two approaches. Quantitative analysis is the best way to analyze the covariance between civil war and many potentially important determinants of a process leading to war. Qualitative analysis can tell us how these determinants influence war outcomes over time and can help sort out the endogenous from the exogenous variables in the model. Also nontrivially, case studies offer a more textured and nuanced view of civil war and show that the distinction between "greed" and "grievance" in the CH model should be abandoned for a more complex model that considers greed and grievance as inextricably fused motives for civil war.

In this introductory chapter, we offer an abbreviated version of the CH model and empirical results. We omit the most technical parts of the CH article so as to make the chapter accessible to a broader audience. Experts might wish to review the original article for a more technical discussion. We focus here on the April 2000 and October 2001 versions of the CH model, which the case study authors used to structure their analyses. Although there have been slight revisions and improvements to the model since then, we must focus on the earlier versions for the sake of coherence between the theoretical model that guided the case studies and the discussion of the model in the case studies.[2] The published version of the article can be found in Collier and Hoeffler (2004). The data for all quantitative analyses referred to in this book can also be accessed online or by contacting the chapter authors.[3]

Following the presentation of the model in the next section, we turn to the research design for the case study project. We describe the project's aims and guidelines, and discuss important methodological issues in selecting and developing the case studies.[4] The case studies are presented in nine chapters in each volume. The final chapter synthesizes the main findings of the cases and suggests possible revisions and extensions to the CH model, based on the findings of the case study project.

## The Collier-Hoeffler Model of Civil War Onset[5]

Civil war is now far more common than international war. Most new outbreaks of large-scale armed conflict occur within the boundaries of sovereign states and pit the government against one or more groups challenging the government's sovereignty.[6]

Our model analyzes civil war and rebellion in terms of both motive and opportunity, but focuses on opportunity as the determining factor of rebellion.[7] In an econometric model of civil war onset, we use measurable variables to test the difference between motive and opportunity in 78 civil wars between 1960 and 1999 (constituting 750 five-year episodes from 1960 to 1999).

## Preferences, Perceptions, and Opportunities

In accordance with a small body of economic literature typified by Grossman (1991, 1999), we model rebellion as an industry that generates profits from looting, so that "the insurgents are indistinguishable from bandits or pirates" (Grossman 1999, 269). Such rebellions are motivated by greed, which is presumably sufficiently common that profitable opportunities for rebellion will not be overlooked. Hence, the incidence of rebellion is not explained by motive, but by the atypical circumstances that generate profitable opportunities (Collier 2000). The political science literature focuses on grievance (the demand for rebellion) while economists focus on a different motivation—greed—and explain rebellion as a result of atypical opportunities.

Hirshleifer (1995, 2001) provides an important refinement on the motive-opportunity dichotomy. He classifies the possible causes of conflict into preferences, opportunities, and perceptions. The introduction of perceptions allows for the possibility that both opportunities and grievances might be wrongly perceived. If the perceived opportunity for rebellion is illusory—analogous to the "winners' curse"—unprofitability will cause collapse, perhaps before turning into a civil war. By contrast, when exaggerated grievances trigger rebellion, fighting does not dispel the misperception and indeed may generate genuine grievances.

Misperceptions of grievances may be very common; all societies may have groups with exaggerated grievances. In this case, as with greed-driven rebellion, motive would not explain war. Societies that experienced civil war would be distinguished by the atypical viability of rebellion. In such societies, rebellions would be conducted by viable not-for-profit organizations, pursuing misperceived agendas by violent means. Greed and misperceived grievance provide a common explanation—"opportunity" and "viability" describe the common conditions sufficient for profit-seeking, or not-for-profit, rebel organizations to exist. They can jointly be contrasted with the political account of conflict in which the grievances that both motivate and explain rebellion are assumed to be well-grounded in objective circumstances such as unusually high inequality, or unusually weak political rights. We now turn to the proxies for opportunities and objective grievances.

## Proxies for Opportunity

Using and expanding war data from Small and Singer (1982) and Singer and Small (1994), we created a list of civil war occurrence and nonoccurrence for 161 countries covering the period 1960–99 (table 1.1 includes all wars in the data set). Our model tries to explain the initiation of civil war (using the Singer and Small definition).

## Table 1.1 Outbreaks of War in the CH Model

| Country | Start of the war | End of the war | Previous war | GDP sample | Secondary schooling sample |
|---|---|---|---|---|---|
| Afghanistan | 04/78 | 02/92 | | | |
| | 05/92 | Ongoing | * | | |
| Algeria | 07/62 | 12/62 | * | | |
| | 05/91 | Ongoing | * | * | * |
| Angola | 02/61 | 11/75 | | | |
| | 11/75 | 05/91 | * | * | * |
| | 09/92 | Ongoing | * | * | * |
| Azerbaijan | 04/91 | 10/94 | | | |
| Bosnia | 03/92 | 11/95 | | | |
| Burma/Myanmar | 68 | 10/80 | * | * | * |
| | 02/83 | 07/95 | * | * | * |
| Burundi | 04/72 | 12/73 | | * | * |
| | 08/88 | 08/88 | * | * | * |
| | 11/91 | Ongoing | * | * | * |
| Cambodia | 03/70 | 10/91 | * | | |
| Chad | 03/80 | 08/88 | | * | |
| China | 01/67 | 09/68 | * | * | |
| Colombia | 04/84 | Ongoing | * | * | * |
| Congo, Republic of | 97 | 10/97 | | * | * |
| Cyprus | 07/74 | 08/74 | | * | |
| Dominican Rep. | 04/65 | 09/65 | | * | * |
| El Salvador | 10/79 | 01/92 | | * | * |
| Ethiopia | 07/74 | 05/91 | | * | * |
| Georgia | 06/91 | 12/93 | | | |
| Guatemala | 07/66 | 07/72 | * | * | * |
| | 03/78 | 03/84 | * | * | * |
| Guinea-Bissau | 12/62 | 12/74 | | | |
| India | 08/65 | 08/65 | * | * | * |
| | 84 | 94 | * | * | * |
| Indonesia | 06/75 | 09/82 | * | * | * |
| | 03/74 | 03/75 | | * | * |
| | 09/78 | 12/79 | * | * | * |
| | 06/81 | 05/82 | * | * | * |
| Iraq | 09/61 | 11/63 | * | | |
| | 07/74 | 03/75 | * | * | * |
| | 01/85 | 12/92 | * | * | * |
| Jordan | 09/70 | 09/70 | | * | |
| Laos | 07/60 | 02/73 | * | | |
| Lebanon | 05/75 | 09/92 | * | | |
| Liberia | 12/89 | 11/91 | | * | |
| | 10/92 | 11/96 | * | | |
| Morocco | 10/75 | 11/89 | * | * | * |

(*Continued*)

# Table 1.1 Outbreaks of War in the CH Model (*Continued*)

| Country | Start of the war | End of the war | Previous war | GDP sample | Secondary schooling sample |
|---|---|---|---|---|---|
| Mozambique | 10/64 | 11/75 | | | |
| | 07/76 | 10/92 | * | * | * |
| Nicaragua | 10/78 | 07/79 | | * | * |
| | 03/82 | 04/90 | | | |
| Nigeria | 01/66 | 01/70 | | * | * |
| | 12/80 | 08/84 | * | * | * |
| Pakistan | 03/71 | 12/71 | | * | * |
| | 01/73 | 07/77 | | | |
| Peru | 03/82 | 12/96 | | * | * |
| Philippines | 09/72 | 12/96 | * | * | * |
| Romania | 12/89 | 12/89 | | * | * |
| Russia | 12/94 | 08/96 | | | |
| | 09/99 | Ongoing | * | | |
| Rwanda | 11/63 | 02/64 | | | |
| | 10/90 | 07/94 | * | * | * |
| Sierra Leone | 03/91 | 11/96 | | * | * |
| | 05/97 | 07/99 | * | * | |
| Somalia | 04/82 | 05/88 | | * | * |
| | 05/88 | 12/92 | * | * | * |
| Sri Lanka | 04/71 | 05/71 | | * | * |
| | 07/83 | Ongoing | * | * | * |
| Sudan | 10/63 | 02/72 | | | |
| | 07/83 | Ongoing | * | * | * |
| Tajikistan | 04/92 | 12/94 | | | |
| Turkey | 07/91 | Ongoing | | * | * |
| Uganda | 05/66 | 06/66 | | * | * |
| | 10/80 | 04/88 | * | * | * |
| Vietnam | 01/60 | 04/75 | * | | |
| Yemen, Rep. of | 05/90 | 10/94 | | | |
| Yemen, Arab Rep. of | 11/62 | 09/69 | * | | |
| Yemen, People's Dem. Rep. of | 01/86 | 01/86 | * | | |
| Yugoslavia | 04/90 | 01/92 | | | |
| | 10/98 | 04/99 | * | | |
| Zaïre/Congo, Dem. Rep. of | 07/60 | 09/65 | | | |
| | 09/91 | 12/96 | * | * | * |
| | 09/97 | 09/99 | * | * | * |
| Zimbabwe | 12/72 | 12/79 | | * | * |

*Note:* The "Previous war" column includes war starts from 1945 to 1994. The "GDP sample" and "Secondary schooling sample" indicate which cases are included in estimations using either of those two explanatory variables. This war list is from the March 2003 version of the CH article. The list included in the draft that was circulated to case study authors might have been slightly different.

5

The model is tested using quantitative indicators of opportunity and grievance. Financing for the rebels comes from three sources: extortion of natural resources, donations from diasporas, and subventions from hostile governments. Natural resources are proxied by the ratio of primary commodity exports to the gross domestic product (GDP), measured (as all variables are) at intervals of five years, starting in 1960 and ending in 1995. They then consider the subsequent five years as an "episode" and compare those in which a civil war broke out ("conflict episodes") with those that were conflict-free ("peace episodes"). We collected data for all country five-year periods in our data set and present descriptive statistics for all variables in table 1.2.[8]

A second source of rebel finance is from diasporas. We proxy the size of a country's diaspora by its emigrants living in the United States.[9] In our econometric

## *Table 1.2* Descriptive Statistics: CH Variables

| Variable | Sample (n = 1,167) | No civil war (n = 1,089) | Civil war (n = 78) |
|---|---|---|---|
| War starts | 0.067 | 0 | 1 |
| Primary commodity exports/GDP | 0.168 | 0.169 | 0.149 |
| GDP per capita (const. US$) | 4,061 | 4,219 | 1,645 |
| Diaspora (relative to population of country of origin) | 0.017 | 0.018 | 0.004 |
| Male secondary schooling (% in school) | 43.42 | 44.39 | 30.3 |
| GDP per capita growth (average for previous 5 years) | 1.62 | 1.74 | −0.23 |
| Previous war (% with war since 1945) | 20.8 | 18.5 | 53.8 |
| Peace duration (months since last conflict) | 327 | 334 | 221 |
| Forest cover (%) | 31.11 | 31.33 | 27.81 |
| Mountainous terrain (%) | 15.82 | 15.17 | 24.93 |
| Geographic dispersion of the population (Gini) | 0.571 | 0.569 | 0.603 |
| Population density (inhabitants per km²) | 150 | 156 | 62 |
| Population in urban areas (%) | 45.11 | 46.00 | 32.7 |
| Ethnic fractionalization (index, 0–100) | 39.57 | 38.64 | 52.63 |
| Religious fractionalization (index, 0–100) | 36.09 | 35.98 | 37.70 |
| Polarization $\alpha = 1.6$ (index, 0–0.165) | 0.077 | 0.077 | 0.076 |
| Democracy (index, 0–10) | 3.91 | 4.07 | 1.821 |
| Ethnic dominance (% with main ethnic group 45–90%) | 0.465 | 0.465 | 0.452 |
| Income inequality (Gini) | 0.406 | 0.406 | 0.410 |
| Land inequality (Gini) | 0.641 | 0.641 | 0.631 |

analysis, we also use predicted values for the diaspora variable, to account for the fact that part of the diaspora is caused by civil war in the country of origin (thus we control for endogeneity).

A third source of rebel finance is from hostile governments. Our proxy for the willingness of foreign governments to finance military opposition to the incumbent government is the Cold War. During the Cold War, each great power supported rebellions in countries allied to the opposing power. There is some support for the opportunity thesis: Only 11 of the 78 wars broke out during the 1990s.

Opportunities for rebellion can also arise from atypically low cost. Recruits must be paid, and their cost may be related to the income foregone by enlisting as a rebel. Rebellions may occur when foregone income is unusually low. We try three proxies for foregone income: mean income per capita, male secondary schooling, and the growth rate of the economy.[10] As shown in table 1.2, the conflict episodes started from less than half the mean income of the peace episodes.[11] The second proxy, male secondary school enrollment, has the advantage of being focused on young males—the group from whom rebels are recruited.[12] The third measure, the growth rate of the economy in the preceding period, is intended to proxy new income opportunities. Conflict episodes were preceded by lower growth rates.

The opportunity for rebellion may be that conflict-specific capital (such as military equipment) is unusually cheap. We proxy the cost of such capital by the time since the most recent previous conflict; the legacy of weapon stocks, skills, and organizational capital will gradually depreciate. Empirically, peace episodes are preceded by far longer periods of peace than conflict episodes (see table 1.2). While this supports the opportunity thesis, it could also be interpreted as reflecting the gradual decay of conflict-induced grievances.

Another dimension of opportunity is an atypically weak government military capability. An unambiguous indicator is whether the terrain is favorable to rebels: Forests and mountains provide rebels with a safe haven. We measured the proportion of a country's terrain that is forested[13] and also created equivalent data on mountainous terrain.[14] Geographic dispersion of the population may also inhibit government capability: Herbst (2000) suggests that Zaire is prone to rebellion because its population lives around the edges of the country. We measure dispersion by calculating a Gini coefficient of population dispersion.[15] Similarly, low population density and low urbanization may inhibit government capability. Before war episodes, both population density and urbanization are low (table 1.2).

A final source of rebel military opportunity may be social cohesion. Ethnic and religious diversity within organizations tends to reduce their ability to function (Alesina Bagir, and Easterly 1999; Collier 2001; Easterly and Levine 1997). A newly formed rebel army may be in particular need of social cohesion, constraining recruitment to a single ethnic or religious group. A diverse society might in this case reduce the opportunity for rebellion by limiting the recruitment pool. The most widely used measure of ethnic diversity is the index of ethnolinguistic fractionalization. This index measures the probability that two randomly drawn people will be from different ethnic groups. We constructed a similar measure of religious fractionalization using data from Barrett (1982) and interacted the two measures to construct a proxy that measures the maximum potential social fractionalization.[16]

## Proxying Objective Grievances

We considered four objective measures of grievance: ethnic or religious hatred, political repression, political exclusion, and economic inequality. Ethnic and religious hatreds cannot be easily quantified, but they evidently can only occur in societies that are multiethnic or multireligious, and so our proxies measure various dimensions of diversity. The previously discussed measures of fractionalization are pertinent: intergroup hatreds must be greater in societies that are fractionalized than in those that are homogeneous. However, arguably the source of intergroup tension is not diversity but polarization, which we measured by adapting a measure created by Esteban and Ray (1994). The descriptive data do not suggest that polarization is important; conflict and peace episodes have very similar mean values (table 1.2).

We measure political repression using the Polity III data set (see Jaggers and Gurr 1995). Our index of political rights ranges 0–10 on an ascending ordinal scale. Political rights differ considerably between conflict and peace episodes. We also investigated the Polity III measure of autocracy and a measure of political openness published by Freedom House (the Gastil Index). The quantitative political science literature has already applied these measures to analyze conflict risk. Hegre et al. (2001) find that repression increases conflict except when it is severe.

Even in democracies, a small group may fear permanent exclusion. A potentially important instance is when political allegiance is based on ethnicity and one ethnic group has a majority. The incentive to exploit the minority increases when the minority is larger, since there is more to extract (Collier 2001). Hence, a minority may be most vulnerable if the largest ethnic group constitutes a small majority. We term this "ethnic dominance" and measure it as a binary variable coded "1" if the largest ethnic group in a country constitutes 45 to 90 percent of the population.

Inequality may also drive civil war. The poor may rebel to induce redistribution and rich regions may mount secessionist rebellions to preempt redistribution. We measured income inequality by the Gini coefficient and by the ratio of the top-to-bottom quintiles of income. We also measured asset inequality by the Gini coefficient of land ownership. The data are from Deininger and Squire (1996, 1998).

Finally, we should point out that these measures of opportunity (such as primary commodity exports, income, and school enrollment) are scaled by measures of country size. For given values of these variables, opportunities should be approximately proportional to size. Grievance might also increase with size: public choices diverge more from the preferences of the average individual as heterogeneity increases. We are, however, able to control for three aspects of heterogeneity: ethnic, religious, and income diversity. Empirically, the conflict episodes had markedly larger populations than the peace episodes.

## Regression Analysis

The proxies for opportunity and objective grievances are largely distinct and so can be compared as two nonnested econometric models. There is, however, no reason for the accounts to be exclusive, and the aim of our econometric tests is to arrive at an integrated model that gives an account of conflict risk in terms of all those opportunities and grievances that are significant. We use logistic regression to predict the risk that a civil war will start during a five-year episode. We consider only those countries that were at peace at the start of the episode (e.g., January 1965) and predict whether the peace was sustained through to its end (e.g., December 1969).

We start with the opportunity model (see table 1.3). The first regression (column 1) excludes per capita income and diasporas. Because per capita income and enrollment in secondary schooling are highly correlated, they cannot be used in the same regression. The diaspora measure is available only for 29 war episodes, so we explore it as an addendum. The variables included in the first regression permit a sample of 688 episodes, including 46 wars.

Primary commodity exports are highly significant. Although their effect is nonlinear, the risk of conflict peaks when they constitute around 32% of GDP, which is a high level of dependence. The other proxy for finance, the end of the Cold War, has the expected sign but is insignificant. The foregone earnings proxies are also both significant with the expected sign: Secondary schooling and growth both reduce conflict risk. Our proxy for the cost of conflict-specific capital is the number of months since any previous conflict (back to 1945), which is highly significant (column 2). The proxies for military advantage also have the expected sign and are marginally significant: mountainous terrain, population dispersion, and social fractionalization. Finally, the coefficient on population is positive and highly significant.

The third column replaces secondary schooling with per capita income. This permits a larger sample—750 episodes including 52 wars. Per capita income is highly significant with the expected negative sign. The change of specification and the expansion of sample make social fractionalization significant and population dispersion nonsignificant.

In the last two columns of table 1.3, we introduce the diaspora variable and retreat to a more parsimonious model to preserve observations (since several of our variables have many missing values). All the included explanatory variables remain significant. The size of the diaspora is not directly significant in the initiation of conflict. However, it is significant when interacted with the number of months since the previous conflict. "Diaspora/peace" divides the size of the diaspora by the time since a previous conflict. The variable is positive and significant; a large diaspora considerably increases the risk of repeat conflict. We control for the potential endogeneity of diasporas in the final column of table 1.3 (see our article for the technical details). Diasporas remain significant and the size of the coefficient is only slightly altered (it is not significantly different from that on the endogenous diaspora measure). This suggests that there is indeed a substantial causal effect of the diaspora on the risk of conflict renewal. The result also guides our interpretation of why the risk of conflict repetition declines as peace is maintained. Recall that in

**Table 1.3** Opportunity Model

| Variable | 1 | 2 | 3 | 4 | 5 |
|---|---|---|---|---|---|
| Primary commodity exports/GDP | 18.149 | 18.900 | 16.476 | 17.567 | 17.404 |
|  | (6.006)*** | (5.948)*** | (5.207)*** | (6.744)*** | (6.750)*** |
| (Primary commodity exports/GDP)$^2$ | −27.445 | −29.123 | −23.017 | −28.81 | −28.456 |
|  | (11.996)*** | (11.905)*** | (9.972)** | (15.351)* | (15.366)* |
| Post-Cold War | −0.326 | −0.207 | −0.454 |  |  |
|  | (0.469) | (0.450) | (0.416) |  |  |
| Male secondary schooling | −0.025 | −0.024 |  |  |  |
|  | (0.010)** | (0.010)** |  |  |  |
| Ln GDP per capita |  |  | −0.837 | −1.237 | −1.243 |
|  |  |  | (0.253)*** | (0.283)*** | (0.284)*** |
| GDP growth | −0.117 | −0.118 | −0.105 |  |  |
|  | (0.044)*** | (0.044)*** | (0.042)*** |  |  |
| Peace duration | −0.003 | −0.004*** | −0.004 | −0.00 | −0.002 |
|  | (0.002)$p$ = .128 | (0.001) | (0.001)*** | (0.001) | (0.001) |
| Previous war | 0.464 |  |  |  |  |
|  | (0.547)$p$ = .396 |  |  |  |  |
| Mountainous terrain | 0.013 | 0.014 | 0.008 |  |  |
|  | (0.009)$p$ = .164 | (0.009) | (0.008) |  |  |

| | (1) | (2) | (3) | (4) | (5) |
|---|---|---|---|---|---|
| Geographic dispersion | -2.211 | -2.129 | -0.865 | | |
| | (1.038)** | (1.032)** | (0.948) | | |
| Social fractionalization | -0.0002 | -0.0002 | -0.0002 | | |
| | (0.0001)p = .109 | (0.0001)p = .122 | (0.0001)** | | |
| Ln population | 0.669 | 0.686 | 0.493 | 0.295 | 0.296 |
| | (0.163)*** | (0.162)*** | (0.129)*** | (0.141)** | (0.141)** |
| Diaspora/peace | | | | 700.931 | |
| | | | | (363.29)** | |
| Diaspora corrected/peace | | | | | 741.168 |
| | | | | | (387.635)* |
| (Diaspora-diaspora corrected)/peace | | | | | 82.798 |
| | | | | | (287.192) |
| N | 688 | 688 | 750 | 595 | 595 |
| No. of wars | 46 | 46 | 52 | 29 | 29 |
| Pseudo-$R^2$ | 0.24 | 0.24 | 0.22 | 0.25 | 0.25 |
| Log-likelihood | -128.49 | -128.85 | -146.86 | -93.2 | -93.23 |

*Note*: All regressions include a constant. Standard errors are in parentheses.

***, **, * indicate significance at the 1, 5, and 10 percent level, respectively.

principle this could be either because hatreds gradually fade, or because "rebellion-specific capital" gradually depreciates. How might diasporas slow these processes? Diasporas preserve their own hatreds, which is why they finance rebellion. However, it is unlikely that the diaspora's hatreds significantly influence attitudes among the much larger population in the country of origin. By contrast, the finance provided by the diaspora can offset the depreciation of rebellion-specific capital, thereby sustaining conflict risk.

In table 1.4 we turn to objective grievance as the explanation of rebellion, dropping all the economic measures of opportunity and retaining the number of months since a previous conflict, because this can be interpreted as a proxy of fading hatreds.

## *Table 1.4* Grievance Model

| Variable | 1 | 2 | 3 |
|---|---|---|---|
| Ethnic fractionalization | 0.010 | 0.011 | 0.012 |
| | (0.006)* | (0.007)* | (0.008) |
| Religious fractionalization | −0.003 | −0.006 | −0.004 |
| | (0.007) | (0.008) | (0.009) |
| Polarization $\alpha = 1.6$ | −3.067 | −4.682 | −6.536 |
| | (7.021) | (8.267) | (8.579) |
| Ethnic dominance (45–90%) | 0.414 | 0.575 | 1.084 |
| | (0.496) | (0.586) | (0.629)* |
| Democracy | −0.109 | −0.083 | −0.121 |
| | (0.044)*** | (0.051)* | (0.053)** |
| Peace duration | −0.004 | −0.003 | −0.004 |
| | (0.001)*** | (0.001)*** | (0.001)*** |
| Mountainous terrain | 0.011 | 0.007 | −0.0001 |
| | (0.007) | (0.009) | (0.009) |
| Geographic dispersion | −0.509 | −0.763 | −1.293 |
| | (0.856) | (1.053) | (0.102) |
| Ln population | 0.221 | 0.246 | 0.300 |
| | (0.096)** | (0.119)** | (1.133)** |
| Income inequality | | 0.015 | |
| | | (0.018) | |
| Land inequality | | | 0.461 |
| | | | (1.305) |
| N | 850 | 604 | 603 |
| No. of wars | 59 | 41 | 38 |
| Pseudo-$R^2$ | 0.13 | 0.11 | 0.17 |
| Log-likelihood | −185.57 | −133.46 | −117.12 |

*Note:* All regressions include a constant. Standard errors are in parentheses.
***, **, * indicate significance at the 1, 5, and 10 percent level, respectively. In column 1, the two measures of fractionalization and ethnic dominance are not jointly significant.

In the first column, we also exclude the inequality measures because of considerations of sample size. This enables a very large sample of 850 episodes and 59 civil wars.

The four proxies for ethnic and religious tension are surprisingly unimportant. Ethnic fractionalization is significant at 10 percent with the expected sign. Religious fractionalization and polarization are insignificant with the wrong sign, and ethnic dominance is insignificant. These three measures are also not jointly significant.[17] Democracy is highly significant with the expected sign—repression increases conflict risk. The time since the previous conflict is again highly significant, but we have suggested that this is more likely to be proxying rebellion-specific capital than grievance. In the second and third columns, we introduce income inequality and land inequality, respectively. Although the sample size is reduced, it is still substantial—more than 600 episodes with a minimum of 38 wars. Neither variable is close to significance. All three grievance models have very low explanatory power (the pseudo-$R^2$ is 0.17 or lower).

We now turn to the question of which model—opportunity or grievance—provides a better explanation of the risk of civil war. Because the two models are nonnested (i.e., one model is not a special case of the other), we use the $J$ test as suggested by Davidson and MacKinnon (1981). As shown in the first two columns of table 1.5, we find that we cannot reject one model in favor of the other. Thus, we conclude that while the opportunity model is superior, some elements of the grievance model are likely to add to its explanatory power. We, therefore, investigate a combined model in column 3 of table 1.5.

Since this combined model includes income inequality and a lagged term, our sample size is much reduced (479 observations). In column 4, we drop inequality (which is consistently insignificant). Omitting inequality increases the sample size to 665. In this combined model, neither democracy, ethnic and religious fractionalization, nor the post-Cold War dummy is significant. Other variables are statistically significant or close to significance and the overall fit is reasonable (pseudo-$R^2$ of 0.26). Since both the grievance and opportunity models are nested in the combined model, we can use a likelihood ratio test to determine whether the combined model is superior. We can reject the validity of the restrictions proposed by the grievance model, but not by the opportunity model.

Although the combined model is superior to the opportunity and grievance models, several variables are completely insignificant and we drop them sequentially. First, we exclude the post-Cold War dummy, then religious fractionalization, then democracy, then polarization, then ethnic fractionalization, and, finally, mountainous terrain, yielding the baseline model of column 5 and its variant with per capita income replacing secondary enrollment in column 6. No further reduction in the model is accepted and no additions of variables included in our previous models are accepted. The baseline model and its variant yield very similar results, although the variant has less explanatory power and two variables lose significance (ethnic dominance and geographic dispersion).

Our baseline model allows us to calculate the change in the probability of war starts for different values of the explanatory variables. This model was used to generate

**Table 1.5 Combined Opportunity and Grievance Model**

| Variable | 1 | 2 | 3 | 4 | 5 | 6 | 7 |
|---|---|---|---|---|---|---|---|
| Primary commodity exports/GDP | 19.096 | | 37.072 | 23.385 | 18.937 | 16.773 | 50.608 |
| | (5.993)*** | | (10.293)*** | (6.692)*** | (5.865)*** | (5.206)*** | (14.09)*** |
| (Primary commodity exports/GDP)$^2$ | -30.423 | | -69.267 | -36.33 | -29.443 | -23.800 | -131.00 |
| | (12.008)*** | | (21.697)*** | (12.998)*** | (11.781)*** | (10.040)** | (42.93)*** |
| Post-Cold War | | | -0.873 | -0.281 | | | |
| | | | (0.644) | (0.459) | | | |
| Male secondary schooling | -0.021 | | -0.029 | -0.022 | -0.031 | | -0.034 |
| | (0.011)** | | (0.013)** | (0.011)** | (0.010)*** | | (0.011)*** |
| Ln GDP per capita | | | | | | -0.950 | |
| | | | | | | (0.245)*** | |
| (GDP growth)t – 1 | -0.108 | | -0.045 | -0.108 | -0.115 | -0.098 | -0.113 |
| | (0.044)*** | | (0.062) | (0.045)** | (0.043)*** | (0.042)** | (0.046)*** |
| Peace duration | -0.0003 | 0.0005 | -0.0003 | -0.003 | -0.004 | -0.004 | -0.003 |
| | (0.002) | (0.0014) | (0.0015) | (0.001)*** | (0.001)*** | (0.001)*** | (0.001)*** |
| Mountainous terrain | 0.005 | 0.001 | 0.005 | 0.015 | | | |
| | (0.010) | (0.008) | (0.012) | (0.009) | | | |
| | | | | $p = .11$ | | | |
| Geographic dispersion | -1.978 | 0.135 | -4.032 | -1.962 | -2.487 | -0.992 | -2.871 |
| | (1.049)* | (1.106) | (1.490)*** | (1.149)* | (1.005)** | (0.909) | (1.130)*** |
| Ln population | | -0.014 | 0.927 | 0.697 | 0.768 | 0.510 | 1.123 |
| | | (0.136) | (0.250)*** | (0.181)*** | (0.166)*** | (0.128)*** | (0.226)*** |
| Social fractionalization | -0.0002 | | -0.0008 | -0.000 | -0.0002 | -0.0002 | -0.0003 |
| | (0.0001)*** | | (0.0003)** | (0.0003) | (0.0001)*** | (0.0001)*** | (0.0001)*** |
| | | | | $p = .11$ | | | |

| | (1) | (2) | (3) | (4) | (5) | (6) | (7) |
|---|---|---|---|---|---|---|---|
| Ethnic fractionalization | | 0.008 (0.007) | 0.041 (0.019)** | 0.023 (0.015) | | | |
| Religious fractionalization | | −0.005 (0.008) | 0.015 (0.020) | 0.014 (0.019) | | | |
| Polarization | | −9.358 (8.735) | −25.276 (13.390)* | −15.992 (10.518) | | | |
| Ethnic dominance (45–90%) | | 1.212 (0.648)** | 2.020 (0.915)** | 1.592 (0.746)** | 0.670 (0.354)* | 0.480 (0.328) | 0.769 (0.369)** |
| Democracy | | −0.036 (0.054) | −0.018 (0.062) | −0.042 (0.054) | | $p = .14$ | |
| Income inequality | | | 0.025 (0.024) | | | | |
| Grievance predicted value | 0.767 (0.413)** | | | | | | |
| Opportunity predicted value | 1.052 (0.212)*** | | | | | | |
| Primary commodity exports/GDP × oil dummy | | | | | | | −28.275 (9.351)*** |
| (Primary commodity exports/GDP)$^2$ × oil dummy | | | | | | | 106.459 (38.704)*** |
| $N$ | 665 | 665 | 479 | 665 | 688 | 750 | 654 |
| No. of wars | 46 | 46 | 32 | 46 | 46 | 52 | 45 |
| Pseudo-$R^2$ | 0.24 | 0.25 | 0.24 | 0.26 | 0.24 | 0.22 | 0.30 |
| Log-likelihood | −126.69 | −125.29 | −89.55 | −124.6 | −128.21 | −146.84 | −114.20 |

*Note:* All regressions include a constant. Standard errors are in parentheses.
***, **, * indicate significance at the 1, 5, and 10 percent level, respectively.

probability estimates for the case studies and probability estimates for each case are discussed in each chapter. At the mean of all variables the risk of a war start is about 11.5 percent.[18] Our model predicts that a hypothetical country with all the worst characteristics found in our sample would have a near-certain risk of war, whereas one with all the best characteristics would have a negligible risk.

The effect of primary commodity exports on conflict risk is both highly significant and considerable. At peak danger (primary commodity exports being 32 percent of GDP), the risk of civil war is about 22 percent, whereas a country with no such exports has a risk of only 1 percent. The effect is sufficiently important to warrant disaggregation into different types of commodities. We categorized primary commodity exports according to which type of product was dominant: food, nonfood agriculture, oil, other raw materials, and a residual category of "mixed." Of the many potential disaggregations of primary commodity exports permitted by these data, only one was significant when introduced into our baseline regression, namely oil versus nonoil. The results are reported in column 7 of table 1.5. We add variables that interact the primary commodity export share and its square with a dummy variable that takes the value of unity if the exports are predominantly oil. Both variables are significant: Oil exports have a distinct effect on the risk of conflict. However, the effect is modest. At the average value of primary commodity exports, oil has the same effect as other commodities. Low levels of oil dependence are somewhat less risky than other commodities and high levels of dependence are somewhat more risky. The disaggregation slightly reduces the sample size, does not change the significance of any of the other variables, and substantially improves the overall fit of the model.

Recall that the other proxies for financial opportunities, the Cold War and diasporas, are not included in this baseline. The end of the Cold War does not have a significant effect. Diasporas are excluded from the baseline purely for considerations of sample size. In the parsimonious variant in which they are included, their effect on the risk of repeat conflict is substantial. After five years of peace, switching the size of the diaspora from the smallest to the largest found in postconflict episodes increases the risk of conflict sixfold.

The proxies for foregone earnings have substantial effects. If the enrollment rate for secondary schooling is 10 percentage points higher than the average, the risk of war is reduced by about 3 percentage points (a decline in the risk from 11.5 percent to 8.6 percent). An additional percentage point on the growth rate reduces the risk of war by about 1 percentage point (a decline from 11.5 percent to 10.4 percent). Our other proxy for the cost of rebellion is also highly significant and substantial. Directly after a civil war, there is a high probability of a restart, the risk being about 32 percent. This risk declines over time at around 1 percentage point per year.

The only measures of rebel military advantage that survive into the baseline are population dispersion and social fractionalization. Consistent with Herbst's hypothesis, countries with a highly concentrated population have a very low risk of conflict, whereas those with a highly dispersed population have a very high risk (about 37 percent). Consistent with the hypothesis that cohesion is important for rebel effectiveness, social fractionalization makes a society substantially safer. A maximally fractionalized society has a conflict risk only one quarter that of a homogeneous society.

Only one of the proxies for grievance survives into the baseline regression, namely ethnic dominance. If a country is characterized by ethnic dominance, its risk of conflict is nearly doubled. Thus, the net effect of increased social diversity is the sum of its effect on social fractionalization and its effect on ethnic dominance. Starting from homogeneity, as diversity increases, the society is likely to become ethnically dominated, although this will be reversed by further increases in diversity. The risk of conflict would first rise and then fall.

Finally, the coefficient on the scale variable, population, is highly significant and close to unity; risk is approximately proportional to size. We have suggested that proportionality is more likely if conflict is generated by opportunities than by grievances.

These results are generally immune to several tests for robustness. We considered the sensitivity both to data and to method, investigating the effect of outlying observations and of different definitions of the dependent and independent variables. With respect to method, we investigated random effects, fixed effects, and rare events bias. The reader can review the results of these alternative estimations in the original article.

## Interpretation and Summary

Using a comprehensive data set of civil wars over the period 1960–99 and estimating logit regressions, we predicted the risk of the outbreak of war in each five-year episode. We find that a model that focuses on the opportunities for rebellion performs well, whereas objective indicators of grievance add little explanatory power. The model is robust to a range of tests for outliers, redefinitions, and alternative specifications.

One factor influencing the opportunity for rebellion is the availability of finance. We have shown that primary commodity exports substantially increase conflict risk. We have interpreted this as being the result of the opportunities for extortion that such commodities provide, making rebellion feasible and perhaps even attractive. Another source of finance is diasporas, which substantially increase the risk of conflict renewal.

A second factor influencing opportunity is the cost of rebellion. Male secondary education enrollment, per capita income, and the growth rate all have statistically significant and substantial effects that reduce conflict risk. We have interpreted them as proxying earnings foregone in rebellion; low foregone earnings facilitate conflict. Even if this is correct, low earnings might matter because they are a source of grievance rather than because they make rebellion cheap. However, if rebellion were a protest against low income, we might expect inequality to have strong effects, which we do not find.

A third aspect of opportunity is military advantage. We have found that a dispersed population increases the risk of conflict and there is weaker evidence that mountainous terrain might also be an advantage to rebels.

Most proxies for grievance were insignificant: inequality, political rights, ethnic polarization, and religious fractionalization. Only ethnic dominance had adverse effects. Even this has to be considered in combination with the benign effects of social fractionalization. Societies characterized by ethnic and religious diversity are safer than homogeneous societies as long as they avoid dominance. We have suggested that diversity makes rebellion harder because it makes rebel cohesion more costly.

Finally, the risk of conflict is proportional to a country's population. Both opportunities and grievances increase with population size, so this result is compatible with both the opportunity and grievance accounts. Grievances increase with population because of rising heterogeneity. Yet those aspects of heterogeneity that we are able to measure are not associated with an increased risk of conflict. Hence, a grievance account of the effect of population would need to explain why unobserved, but not observed, heterogeneity increases conflict risk.

One variable—time since a previous conflict—has substantial effects: Time "heals." Potentially, this can be interpreted either as opportunity or grievance. It may reflect the gradual depreciation of rebellion-specific capital, and hence an increasing cost of rebellion, or the gradual erosion of hatred. However, we have found that a large diaspora slows the "healing" process. The known proclivity of diasporas to finance rebel groups offsets the depreciation of rebellion-specific capital, and so would be predicted to delay "healing." The diaspora effect thus lends support to the opportunity interpretation.

Opportunity as an explanation of conflict risk is consistent with the economic interpretation of rebellion as greed motivated. However, it is also consistent with grievance motivation as long as perceived grievances are sufficiently widespread to be common across societies and time. Opportunity can account for the existence of either for-profit or not-for-profit rebel organizations. Our evidence does not imply, therefore, that rebels are necessarily criminals. But the grievances that motivate rebels may be substantially disconnected from the large social concerns of inequality, political rights, and ethnic or religious identity.

## Building on the Collier-Hoeffler Model Using Case Studies[19]

Having presented the core elements of the CH model and all major empirical results, we now turn to the research design for the case study project. We address a number of methodological questions: How were cases selected? Do they represent the population of cases? Can the cases help us develop hypotheses about civil war onset? Do they provide sufficient historical detail to support counterfactual analysis? Do the cases constitute independent, homogeneous observations?[20] We address these and other methodological questions that explain how we use case studies in this project.

### Goals of the Case Study Project

The main purpose of the case study project was to supplement the quantitative analysis, develop theory, and improve the causal inferences drawn from the CH model.

Causal theories should explain *how* a particular outcome (in this case, civil war) occurs—*how* and *under what conditions* different explanatory variables lead to that outcome. The CH model suggests a plausible microlevel theory of civil war, but it is tested empirically with macrolevel data that describe conditions under which individual decision making takes place.[21] The empirical findings of the CH model, therefore, do not necessarily test a microlevel theory of civil war.[22] Given that the CH model and the literature on civil war generally suffer from such a "missing link" between microlevel theories and macrolevel data, case studies can be used to improve our understanding of *how* the variables used in the empirical tests influence the probability of civil war. Context-rich narratives of historical processes can provide insight into the causal paths linking independent variables in the CH model to civil war outbreak and can help disentangle complicated multicausal relationships.

To understand better these "how" questions, we asked case study authors to do process tracing[23] and write narratives of individual cases by focusing on a set of common questions.[24] The list of questions structured their research and allowed us to treat their narratives as structured-focused comparisons. Authors were asked to focus on the mechanisms through which the right-hand-side variables (the $X$'s) influence the dependent variable ($Y$) and were encouraged to explore interrelationships among the $X$'s (interaction effects). The fact that such a large number of case studies systematically addressed the same questions implies that this project was better suited than most other comparative case study projects to test a theoretical model. But, since the CH model had already been tested using large-$N$ statistical methods, we did not need to retest it using case studies. We, therefore, gave the case study project different priorities, such as theory building and exposition of the mechanisms through which the variables in the CH model influenced civil war onset. We also sought to develop alternative explanations of war, given the large amount of variance in civil war outcomes that is left unexplained by the CH model.[25] Moreover, by exploring microlevel processes and tracing their linkages to macrolevel analysis in the CH model, case studies provided us with a better sense of which variables in the CH model are endogenous and which are exogenous.[26] Close attention to country context also allows us to improve the CH model and its empirical tests by refining our empirical proxies and reducing measurement error.

The case study project has value-added because it teaches us about the *process* that leads to war, rather than focusing only on underlying "structural" characteristics of countries that experience civil war (or not). Process matters if different policy interventions can be designed to reduce the risk of war at various stages of conflict. In most cases, quantitative studies that present correlations between $X$ and $Y$ do not demonstrate causality and several competing explanations can be imposed on the same correlation. In other words, statistical methods can perform hypotheses tests, but they cannot necessarily distinguish among rival theories with closely related observable implications.[27] Case studies give us a "feel" for the data that allows us to develop better judgment in discriminating among possible explanations.

Case studies can also help us understand why the model fits some data points well and others poorly. If the statistical analysis identifies outliers (i.e., predictions that are two or more standard deviations from the mean predicted value of $Y$), case studies can help us understand if this prediction failure is due to systematic variation that is not captured by the model or to idiosyncratic reasons that the model should not try to explain. If several case studies point to a few potentially significant variables that are missing from the model, we could adjust the model and see if these variables can be incorporated in it. Coding these variables for all observations in the CH data set would allow us to test their fit to the data using statistical methods.[28] This approach offers a truly interactive way to blend quantitative and qualitative research and can help us develop better causal theories of civil war.

Our preferred approach of moving back and forth between case study and quantitative research designs reflects the view that case studies alone cannot easily develop generalizable theory and they do not offer the ideal environment for hypothesis testing. For any single case, there is potentially an inordinate amount of historical detail that the analyst must sort through to explain an outcome. Hypotheses about causes of that outcome are generally purely inductive in case studies. No amount of historical detail can be sufficient to recreate past events and the analyst's decision of which events to discuss reflects a prior belief in a plausible explanation for the event in question. Moreover, trying to fit a multivariate explanation of war to a single case runs into the familiar problem of indeterminacy (due to negative degrees of freedom). Our case study project gains degrees of freedom by virtue of the large number of cases (wars and periods of no war) considered and because authors focus on a specified set of variables and do not consider an arbitrarily large number of possible explanations. But even so, the degrees-of-freedom problem is hard to avoid entirely, which is another reason that we use the cases primarily for theory building. We did ask authors to suggest additional explanations for peace or war in their countries, if their narratives would have been incomplete without them. But, ultimately, to see if these explanations can be generalized, we must add them to the CH model and test them using statistical methods.

## Case Selection

The fact that case analysis serves a secondary function in this project has implications for case selection. If we had relied primarily on the case studies to test the CH model, then the cases should have been selected so as to provide a representative sample of countries (with and without wars). But the large number of causal relationships implied by the CH model makes it increasingly difficult to use case study methods for empirical tests (Ragin 1987, 49). To avoid problems of identification and multicollinearity, we would have needed many more cases to test the model. With only a few cases, we would have had limited degrees of freedom and high uncertainty surrounding our inferences.

In both qualitative and quantitative research designs, random selection and assignment is typically the best way to reduce the risk of endogeneity, selection, and omitted variable bias. But random selection of countries to include in our study would have resulted in a sample that predominantly included cases of no war, given that civil war occurs relatively rarely. It could also result in a sample with no significant varia-tion in the independent variables (IVs). We could have avoided the first (but not the second) problem by sampling more heavily on cases of war, but nonlinearities that may be present in the data could have complicated the sampling process.[29]

With these constraints in mind, we could select cases from the universe of cases. We selected partly on the dependent variable (DV) and partly on the independent variables.[30] We included mostly countries that had experienced at least one civil war, but also high-risk countries that did not have a war.[31] We can find useful infor-mation both in those cases that the CH model explains well (i.e., cases on the regression line) and in those cases that the model predicts poorly (type I and type II errors). Given that in all cases we knew the values of the DV (i.e., we knew when and where civil wars had taken place), our research design could not legitimately aim to predict values of the DV. By selecting cases with different predicted values of the DV, our project avoids the problem of no variance in the DV, which is some-times encountered in case study research.[32]

The selection of negative cases resembles Mill's "indirect method of difference" in that it "uses negative cases to reinforce conclusions drawn from positive cases. . . . The examination of negative cases presupposes a theory allowing the investigator to identify the set of observations that embraces *possible* instances of the phenome-non of interest" (Ragin 1987, 41).[33] Typically, case studies have difficulty in identi-fying such negative cases "in the absence of strong theoretical or substantive guidelines" (Ragin 1987, 42). Our project makes the application of this method eas-ier, because we identify negative cases on the basis of (theoretically based) predic-tions from the core model.

We did not focus exclusively on the DV in selecting our cases. We also wanted to ensure sufficient variation in some key IVs. Thus, we partly selected cases accord-ing to IVs in the CH model, including a country's history of political violence, level of ethnic fractionalization, degree of dependence on natural resources, type of regime, and so forth. Selection on IVs alone has been described as "the best intentional" research design (King, Keohane, and Verba 1994, 140).[34] We knew the values of the explanatory variables ahead of time, so we could pick countries to ensure that there was sufficient variation.[35] But, since the CH model controlled for these IVs in the regressions, selecting cases to ensure variation in the IVs did not create any inference problems.[36] A matched-case selection might have been a bet-ter research design if we wanted to develop a theory "from scratch." However, the purpose of this project was to build on and refine existing theories of civil war by identifying the causal mechanisms underlying these theories and exploring the fit of the CH model to particular contexts/countries. Case selection proceeded with that purpose in mind.

Case studies of war onset and avoidance in the following countries were finally drafted: Algeria, Azerbaijan, Bosnia, Burundi, Colombia, Georgia, the Democratic Republic of Congo, Jamaica, Indonesia, Côte d'Ivoire, Kenya, Lebanon, Macedonia, Mali, Mozambique, Nigeria, Russia (focusing on Chechnya, Dagestan, and other regions), Senegal, Sierra Leone, Sudan, and the United Kingdom (Northern Ireland).[37]

We include a large subset of these cases in this volume. The geographical distribution of countries roughly corresponds to the prevalence of civil war in different regions of the world, although there is perhaps a greater emphasis on African wars in the selection of cases. Because our selection rules were based on the CH quantitative model, which controls for the variables that might make Africa "special" (such as high ethnic fractionalization, low levels of democracy, and high levels of poverty), we believe that the fact that there is sufficient variation along these dimensions should remove any bias in our case selection.

Authors were asked to focus on the country or the civil war as their unit of observation. Most case studies focus on the country and analyze both periods of peace and war in that country. If a country had recurrent wars, we asked authors to analyze all or most of them and to explore the linkages across episodes of war (see, e.g., the chapters on the Democratic Republic of Congo and Nigeria). If a country had not experienced civil war (Macedonia, Côte d'Ivoire, Jamaica), authors were asked to analyze periods of high risk for war and discuss why war did not occur. In effect, each case study provides us with several observations of peace and war. For example, the Indonesia study focuses on patterns of war and peace in Aceh over eight five-year periods and can, therefore, be considered a study of eight observations (two observations of war and six of no war). The Nigeria study analyzes the politics of several regions over several periods and traces the development of false-positive and false-negative predictions of the CH model in two different regions of the country in the late 1960s and 1980s. This approach actually makes it difficult to establish clearly how many observations we have in each case study and we often end up with many more observations for some countries than for others (some authors made a more conscious effort than others to analyze patterns of war and peace in their country over different periods). The uncertainty about the precise number of observations would have presented more problems if we had wanted to use the case studies to test the CH model rather than as a way to complement, rather than replace, quantitative tests.

Ultimately, it may be impossible for any single case study design to present a compelling and historically accurate test of a theory or to articulate an exhaustive set of hypotheses about the relationship between an antecedent and a consequent. However, we do not rely on the case studies for our theory—at least not all of our theory. Our set of structured, focused comparisons provides rich context against which to evaluate the soundness of the CH economic model and to refine that model.[38] In addition to illuminating the causes of onset of civil war, each chapter in our book offers a perspective on other aspects of civil war, such as the organization of rebel groups, the dynamics of violence during civil war, and the link between intercommunal violence and civil war, or crime and political violence.

## Identifying Causal Mechanisms

One of the main contributions of any case study project is that it can explain *how* the antecedent is connected to the consequent. King et al. (1994) argue that many case studies do not achieve this goal because of three frequently encountered methodological problems: endogeneity, selection, and omitted variable bias.[39] These problems, however, are also commonly found in quantitative studies.[40] In fact, rather than being more susceptible to these problems, case study methods can grapple better with endogeneity and selection by constructing a "thick description" of the events leading up to civil war. Reconstructing the chronology of a conflict helps us deal with endogeneity and identifies interactions between pairs of explanatory variables that might have been undertheorized in the original model.

Case studies can also help us distinguish among several competing mechanisms. We probably cannot know all the mechanisms that link the $X$'s to the $Y$ in the CH model, but we can and should identify some central ones. For example, liberal democracy may facilitate conflict resolution in one country by ensuring minority representation and, in another country, by guaranteeing the independence of the judiciary. In a third country, democracy may be a precondition of economic stability, if it ensures property rights. Identifying causal mechanisms shifts the focus of inquiry from the outcome to the process. Some authors would argue that understanding the process is more important than explaining a specific outcome. In their new research project on the "dynamics of contention," McAdam, Tarrow, and Tilly (2001, 4) aim to show "how different forms of contention—social movements, revolutions, strike waves, nationalism, democratization, and more—result from similar mechanisms and processes" . . . and "explore combinations of mechanisms and processes to discover recurring causal sequences of contentious politics." In their work and the work of other political scientists, social processes are understood as sequences and combinations of causal mechanisms. Mechanisms are defined (2001, 24) as a "delimited class of events that alter relations among specified sets of elements in identical or closely similar ways over a variety of situations." So, for example, in explaining resource mobilization in the classic social movement literature, authors would focus on "environmental, cognitive, and relational mechanisms" (p. 25) such as the "significance of organizational bases," "resource accumulation," and the "collective coordination for popular actors" (2001, 17). McAdam et al. point out an important problem, separating mechanisms from correlations, and a more difficult problem, distinguishing between a mechanism and a process (a family of mechanisms).

Ethnic mobilization, for example, can be considered as both a mechanism and a process, and so can political identity formation. Another example of a mechanism is the "sons of the soil" argument that Fearon and Laitin (2003) make to explain political violence as the result of conflict between migrant communities and autochthonous populations in peripheral regions of countries. But how can we be certain that migration is the mechanism through which we get ethnic violence in these cases? If we look "upstream," we can locate an earlier mechanism in the government's decision to reduce the strength of peripheral ethnicities. Migration of other ethnic groups in their areas is one of several possible mechanisms through which violent conflict between peripheral communities and the state can develop. Although we cannot hope to identify all possible mechanisms or establish a hierarchy among them, we can use our case study project to go beyond the statistical analysis in explaining how each $X$ influences $Y$. The task for the case study authors is to provide a sufficiently detailed process tracing, that is, a narrative of the way in which civil war erupts.

## Unit Heterogeneity

Several of our case studies note that ethnic mobilization increases the risk of civil war. A possibility that the CH model does not consider is that wars that are fought by ethnic groups might have different antecedents than wars fought across nonethnic (or nonracial, nonreligious) cleavages. Most of the literature seems to discard this possibility as it treats civil war as an aggregate category, implicitly assuming that a typology of civil war that distinguishes, for example, secession from revolution would not be meaningful. This assumption of unit homogeneity has not yet been proven in the literature. Is there sufficient evidence in the cases to support a typology of political violence? Can we observe differences between types of civil war and between civil war and other forms of political violence? We say more about this issue in the conclusion, where we review the evidence from the cases.

The data set used to test the CH model assumes unit homogeneity. According to King et al. (1994, 91), "two units are homogeneous when the expected values of the dependent variables from each unit are the same when our explanatory variable takes on a particular value." In the CH model, as in most of the quantitative literature on civil war, "civil war" is considered a homogeneous category. However, if the CH model predicts or explains civil war and other violence (e.g., genocides or criminal homicides) equally well (or equally poorly), then either the model has omitted variables that could help differentiate between the causes of these different forms of violence, or differences across forms of violence are small and the model might be better tested by combining violent events of different forms. For the moment, quantitative studies of civil war are not able to distinguish clearly between civil war and other forms of violence, such as genocide, riots, or coups. The case studies can help us better understand what forms of violence the CH model might be able to explain and can highlight some differences both between civil war and other violence and among different types of civil war.

The assumption of homogeneity implies constant effects across countries and time periods. Most of the influential models of civil war onset (Collier and Hoeffler 2000; Fearon and Laitin 2003; Hegre et al. 2001) assume constant effects. However, if this assumption is wrong, it is likely to bias our causal inferences (King et al. 1994, 94). Case studies allow us to explore the homogeneity of our observations and not to assume that a priori (Ragin 1987, 49). If we suspected substantial unit heterogeneity, an alternative approach would have been to utilize a "most similar systems" design—for example, we could choose only cases from Sub-Saharan Africa or some other region so as to "control" for several explanatory variables and isolate the "treatment" variable, in an effort to create a research design as close as possible to an experimental design (Przeworski and Teune 1970; Ragin 1987, 48). Such an approach, however, would have resulted in exploring only "within-systems relationships" (Przeworski and Teune 1970, 57–59) and might not have allowed us to develop further the CH model, which is not region-specific. Early results from the quantitative literature (Collier and Hoeffler 2002b) also point to no statistically significant differences across regions (e.g., Africa versus the rest of the world) with respect to the fit of the CH model. This suggests that we can forego a most similar systems approach in the case study design.

But other nonlinearities might exist in the data. Recent research suggests that some of the variables in the CH model behave differently in rich and poor countries. For example, democracy is correlated with peace only in highly developed countries (Hegre 2003). This is a question that most studies of civil war have not addressed.[41] Case studies can help us identify the different institutional pathways through which democracy may prevent civil war outbreak in rich countries, but not in poor countries. Other interesting interactive effects are also explored, as between economic growth and democracy, and ethnic heterogeneity and political institutions.

## From Statistics to Cases and Back to Statistics

In sum, the case study project has several uses. It helps us establish the internal validity of the logic that underlies the CH model of civil war onset; it identifies problems with data measurement and suggests solutions for it; it helps resolve the endogeneity and selection problems in the statistical analysis of civil war occurrence through detailed historical narratives and a chronological sequence of events; it identifies and selects among causal mechanisms that explain the process of getting to civil war; and it identifies potentially omitted variables that might be usefully incorporated in a model of the causes of civil war.

At the same time, all this is possible because a first attempt at theory building and empirical testing is available through the CH model. Case selection was guided by the statistical analysis and the narratives were structured around questions that referred to the way in which independent variables from the model were connected, or addressed questions that were generated by the statistical analysis. The case studies can then feed back into the statistical analysis, as new candidate variables are identified to expand the theory of civil war onset, and these variables are coded so that they can be integrated in the data set. With the new, refined proxies added to the data set, the new and expanded CH model can be reestimated in another "iteration" of this research. In the conclusion to this volume, we focus much more on the lessons learned from the case studies and on possible expansions of the theory of civil war.

## Organization of the Volume

All of the cases that we have chosen to include in this book are rich and engaging accounts of war or, sometimes, of how war was avoided. To help the reader digest the large quantities of facts, conclusions, and conjectures in this book, a synthesis of the cases is presented in the conclusion. We have organized the cases in two volumes. The first volume includes case studies of African civil wars (including Algeria, even though Algeria is often lumped together with the Middle East). The second volume includes cases from all other regions. There is no substantive rationale behind this organization of cases—we do not think that African civil wars are different. This is simply a device to present the material effectively, given the considerable length of the book. The introduction (the model and research design) and the conclusion (the synthesis of the findings of the case studies) are repeated in each volume. The conclusion draws on all cases and relates them back to the CH model. The CH model is not region-specific, so it is appropriate to draw on all cases in the conclusion. This also allows readers who have more geographically defined interests and who will not read both volumes to see how cases from other regions compare to cases from "their" region.

There are some "natural" comparisons across the two volumes. Indonesia and Nigeria are both oil-rich states with much violence throughout their history. Both cases illustrate complex pathways linking oil to violence. Burundi and the Democratic Republic of Congo put in perspective CH's arguments on the impact of resource-dependence and ethnic diversity. Both highlight the importance of the territorial concentration of resources and, in Burundi, the territorial concentration of political power. Bosnia and Indonesia also deal with the issue of regional inequality and ethnic differences across regions. Algeria and Kenya are two cases that force us to think harder about the concept of ethnic war. In both cases the violence took an ethnic hue, but ethnic divisions may not have been the deciding factor underlying that violence. Several cases in both volumes highlight the role of external intervention in inciting and supporting civil war. Civil wars in Lebanon, Mozambique, and Sudan cannot be understood without a close look at the role of external military or economic intervention.

Some of the cases consider the links between political and criminal violence. Not only are there important spatial effects (diffusion and contagion) that explain violence in Russia and Colombia, but there is also a dynamic relationship between the organization of criminal networks and the pursuit of political agendas in civil wars (see the cases on civil wars in the Caucasus as well as Algeria). These cases lead us to consider the effects of state capacity. In Northern Ireland, extreme violence was avoided largely as a result of substantial state capacity. By contrast, in Kenya, war might have been avoided because of substantial state capacity to repress opposition (though the state has caused much intercommunal violence). Those cases push us to think harder about the mechanisms through which state capacity operates to reduce the risk of civil war, because those mechanisms may be different in economically developed and underdeveloped states. In Macedonia, although state capacity was low, a war was averted largely as a result of substantial external assistance and a generally open regime.

Each volume ends with a regional comparison (in chapter 9) between cases that share considerable similarities. Volume 1 includes an analysis of the civil wars in

Mali and Senegal. Volume 2 includes an analysis of civil wars in South Ossetia (Georgia), Abkhazia (Georgia), and Chechnya (Russia), comparing them to cases of war avoidance in Adjaria (Georgia) and Dagestan (Russia). The chapters on Bosnia and Macedonia also offer useful comparisons, as those cases share many of the same underlying conditions and were similarly affected by the collapse of the Yugoslav state.

In chapter 10, the conclusion, we draw out the main lessons from all the cases and suggest ways to use those lessons to modify, refine, or expand the theory of civil war. Now, we turn to the cases.

# Notes

1. We do not present all the cases in this book. Drafts of those cases that are mentioned in the introduction or conclusion, but not included in the book, are available from the editors. Some of the chapters/cases cover more than one episode of civil war.
2. See Collier and Hoeffler (2000, 2001, 2002a, 2004).
3. Data, codebooks, and other replication information for the chapters included in this book can be accessed online at: http://pantheon.yale.edu/~ns237/.
4. We offer more details in a supplement posted online (it includes the original set of guidelines given to authors): http://www.yale.edu/unsy/civilwars/guidelines.htm. Our guidelines changed somewhat over time, as we moved away from the idea of using cases to test the theory and toward the idea of using the cases to develop theory and explore other issues, such as mechanisms, sequences, measurement, and unit homogeneity. This shift in focus was communicated to authors during and after the second conference (April 2002 in New Haven), where authors presented first drafts of their case studies.
5. This section draws heavily on Collier and Hoeffler (2001, 2004). Tables with statistical results and excerpts from the article are reproduced with permission from Oxford University Press.
6. Civil war involves such an armed conflict between the government and local rebels with the ability to mount some resistance. The violence must kill a substantial number of people (more than 1,000). See Sambanis (2004b) for a discussion of the definition and measurement of civil war.
7. We use "rebellion," "insurgency," and "civil war" interchangeably.
8. Only brief descriptions of the data and sources are included here. For more details, see Collier and Hoeffler (2001, 2004).
9. The source for the data is the U.S. Bureau of the Census. CH divided these numbers by the total population in the country of origin.
10. *Source:* GDP World Development Indicators.
11. The CH model measures income as real purchasing power parity (PPP)-adjusted GDP per capital. The primary data set is the Penn World Tables 5.6 (Summers and Heston 1991). Because the data are only available from 1960 to 1992 we used the growth rates of real PPP-adjusted GDP per capita data from the World Bank's World Development Indicators 1998 in order to obtain income data for the 1990s. These GDP per capita data were used to calculate the average annual growth rate over the previous five years.

12. We measure male secondary school enrollment rates as gross enrollment ratios, that is, the ratio of total enrollment, regardless of age, to the population of the age group that officially corresponds to the level of education shown. Secondary education completes the provision of basic education that began at the primary level, and aims at laying the foundations for lifelong learning and human development, by offering more subject- or skill-oriented instruction using more specialized teachers. *Source:* World Bank Development Indicators 1998.

13. We used data from the Food and Agriculture Organization to measure the proportion of a country's terrain which is covered in woods and forest. *Source:* http://www.fao.org/forestry.

14. The proportion of a country's terrain that is mountainous was measured by Gerrard (2000), a physical geographer who specializes in mountainous terrain. His measure is based not just on altitude but takes into account plateaus and rugged uplands.

15. We constructed a dispersion index of the population on a country-by-country basis. Based on population data for 400-km² cells, we generated a Gini coefficient of population dispersion for each country. A value of 0 indicates that the population is evenly distributed across the country and a value of 1 indicates that the total population is concentrated in one area. Data are available for 1990 and 1995. *Data sources:* Center for International Earth Science Information Network (CIESIN), Columbia University; International Food Policy Research Institute (IFPRI); and World Resources Institute (WRI). 2000. *Gridded Population of the World (GPW), Version 2*. Palisades, NY: IESIN, Columbia University. Available at http://sedac.ciesin.org/plue/gpw.

16. Ethnic fractionalization data are only available for 1960. The source for the data is *Atlas Narodov Mira* (USSR 1964). Using data from Barrett (1982) on religious affiliations, we constructed an analogous religious fractionalization index. The fractionalization indices range from 0 to 100. A value of 0 indicates that the society is completely homogeneous, whereas a value of 100 would characterize a completely heterogeneous society. Social fractionalization is the product of the ethnolinguistic fractionalization and the religious fractionalization index plus the ethnolinguistic or the religious fractionalization index, whichever is the greater. By adding either index, we avoid classifying a country as homogeneous (a value of 0) if the country is ethnically homogeneous but religiously diverse, or vice versa.

17. We measure polarization with $\alpha = 1.6$ and define ethnic dominance as occurring when the largest ethnic group constitutes 45 to 90 percent of the population. For a discussion of religious polarization and its effect on civil war, see Reynal-Querol (2000, 2002).

18. Data and modeling changes were made to the version of the CH analysis that we use here, resulting in different average probability estimates of civil war than the figures reported in several of the case studies. The case studies drew upon an earlier version of the model and data with an average war risk around 6 percent. Probability estimates are slightly dependent on whether GDP or education is used to proxy opportunity cost.

19. This section draws heavily on Sambanis (2004a). Excerpts from that article are reprinted with permission of Cambridge University Press.

20. These are issues that apply equally to qualitative and quantitative studies.

21. In this book, the distinction between micro- and macrolevels is used to reflect the difference between individual-level preferences and actions (the microlevel) and systemwide or country-level opportunity structures and processes (the macrolevel).

22. Green and Seher (2002) identify this as a general problem in the literature on ethnic conflict. The literature clearly suffers from a disjuncture between an abundance of macrohistorical evidence and macropolitical explanations of violence, on the one hand, and a scarcity of individual-level or group-level data and theories of violent conflict on the other hand.

23. Process tracing is a method of making historical arguments about causal processes. It explains the "process by which initial conditions are transformed into outcomes . . . [and] uncovers what stimuli the actors attend to: the decision process that makes use of these stimuli to arrive at decisions; the actual behavior that then occurs; the effect of various institutional arrangements on attention, processing, and behavior; and the effect of other variables of interest on attention, processing, and behavior" (George and McKeown 1985, 35). See, also, George (1979).

24. A set of questions was developed in collaboration with Ibrahim Elbadawi and Norman Loayza. We gave the list to all authors at a conference held in Oslo, Norway, where we launched the project. All authors had read and discussed a set of core papers, including the CH model that they would apply to their cases. Authors were also briefed on the specific targets of the project. Research design refinements were communicated to the authors in a second conference, held in New Haven, CT, where authors presented first drafts of their papers. The editors sent detailed comments and instructions for revisions to all authors after the New Haven conference and, again, after second drafts were submitted. Final drafts were reviewed by the editors and submitted to an external review.

25. In the quantitative literature, the goal of statistical analysis is usually not to maximize the $R^2$ of a regression, because this can be done by adding nonstatistically significant variables to the model. But if most of the variance is left unexplained, the risk of omitted variable bias should also be greater. If the cases can help develop a model that explains more of the variance while also identifying significant variables, that should also reduce the risk of omitted variable bias.

26. Endogeneity could be caused both by nonrecursiveness in the model (i.e., if a variable such as economic growth influences civil war risk and civil war, in turn, influences economic growth) and by jointly determined explanatory variables (as would be the case, for example, if income level or growth caused the level of democracy and all three variables were included in the model). See Sambanis (2002) for a discussion of problems of endogeneity in quantitative studies of civil war.

27. An example is the interpretation of the statistically significant negative relationship between per capita GDP and civil war onset in Collier and Hoeffler (2000, 2004) and in Fearon and Laitin (2003). Collier and Hoeffler interpret this finding as evidence of their "economic opportunity cost" theory of civil war, whereas Fearon and Laitin argue that GDP measures state capacity and interpret the finding differently. Thus, the same hypothesis test can be used to inform two very different theories with different causal mechanisms leading to civil war.

28. If the model predicts a high risk of civil war for a given country-year and war does not occur, this could be seen as a prediction failure that can be usefully analyzed. Some might say that, even though there was no war, the model is technically still "right" since it only predicts the risk of war, not actual war. Thus, war might have been avoided for random reasons. This is always true with probabilistic models, but the argument can be turned around: War occurrence in countries with a high predicted risk of war might also happen for reasons that are outside the model. The case studies' ability to uncover spurious correlations and detect measurement error helps us improve the model. If we expand the model using theoretical insights derived from the case studies as suggested here and then test the expanded model by taking it back to the quantitative data, we will be able to test formally the significance of the theoretical differences between the old and new versions of the model by formally comparing the models' explanatory power.

29. Nonlinearities imply that the theorized linear relationship between the DV and IV does not apply to the entire data. If ethnic identity matters in different ways in developed and less developed countries (cf. Horowitz 1985), then adding interaction terms is one way to explore conditional effects properly. If such effects are present, then a stratified sampling method should be used, if cases are used for hypotheses testing. Even a case-control design would have resulted in the inclusion of far too many middle-to-high-income countries in our sample. Those countries might well be different from poor countries and they might have less to teach us about civil war.

30. According to King et al. (1994, 141), selecting "observations across a range of values of the dependent variable" is a legitimate "alternative to choosing observations on the explanatory variable." Some of our cases are not included in the CH estimations of civil war risk because of missing data. We select such cases on the basis of IVs and of general interest in the case. Where possible (see Bosnia chapter), we filled in those missing data points and reestimated the CH model, obtaining predictions for those cases. Then we compared those predictions to actual events and to the model's average predictions for the population of cases.

31. In each chapter, authors refer to the estimated civil war risk for each period in their country, according to the CH model. In several cases, authors reestimate that risk after making small changes to the CH model and data, or after filling in missing data. These probability estimates are often different from the CH estimates, if the CH estimates have miscoded some variables or if they have not coded some episodes of civil war.

32. The risk of civil war varies over time. Each case in our project offers several observations, as it includes both periods of war and periods of no war (or, alternatively, periods of both high and low risk of civil war).

33. By contrast, Mill's "method of agreement" identifies necessary conditions that are linked to the observation of a positive outcome.

34. Selecting on the independent variables does not introduce any bias, but may reduce efficiency of parameter estimates. See KKV (1994, 137).

35. We did not use a research design that depended entirely on categories of the explanatory variables because the aim of such a design is to "find out the values of the dependent variable." See King et al. (1994, 139). As mentioned earlier, we already knew where the civil wars had happened.

36.  King et al. (1994, 94) write that "If the process by which the values of the explanatory variables are 'assigned' is not independent of the dependent variables, we can still meet the conditional independence assumption if we learn about this process and include a measure of it among our control variables." They also write that, if cases are selected on the basis of values of a given variable, that variable must be controlled for in the model. Thus, we only selected cases on the basis of variables from the CH model.

37.  Studies on the following countries were commissioned, but not completed: Afghanistan, El Salvador, Moldova, Somalia, Sri Lanka, Uganda.

38.  Thus, we agree with Huber (1996, 141) that case studies illuminate "the logic of the argument rather than the validity of its empirical claims . . . [they] yield a story about *why* . . . variables should be related to each other."

39.  Omitted variable bias occurs when a variable is omitted that is correlated with the dependent variable and one or more of the included explanatory variables (King et al. 1994, 169). Endogeneity, in its purest form, refers to simultaneous causation between $Y$ and one or more of the $X$'s. Selection bias refers to the problem of observing an outcome only as a function of an unobserved variable, though there can also be selection on observables.

40.  See Elbadawi and Sambanis (2002) and Sambanis (2002) for a discussion of endogeneity and selection problems in the quantitative literature on civil war.

41.  Another reason to forego a random sampling rule is that, if there is heterogeneity in the data, random sampling would not result in a representative sample.

# References

Alesina, A., R. Baqir, and W. Easterly. 1999. "Public Goods And Ethnic Divisions." *Quarterly Journal of Economics* 114 (4): 1243–84.

Barrett, D. B., ed. 1982. *World Christian Encyclopedia.* Oxford: Oxford University Press.

Collier, Paul. 2000. "Rebellion as a Quasi-Criminal Activity." *Journal of Conflict Resolution* 44: 839–53.

———. 2001. "Ethnic Diversity: An Economic Analysis of its Implications." *Economic Policy* 32: 129–66.

Collier, Paul, and Anke Hoeffler. 2000. "Greed and Grievance in Civil War." Mimeo, DECRG, World Bank, Washington, DC.

———. 2001. "Greed and Grievance in Civil War." Policy Research Working Paper 2355, World Bank, Washington, DC.

———. 2002a. "Greed and Grievance in Civil War." CSAE Working Paper, WPS 2002-01. http://www.economics.ox.ac.uk/CSAEadmin/workingpapers/pdfs/2002-01text.pdf.

———. 2002b. "On the Incidence of Civil War in Africa." *Journal of Conflict Resolution* 46 (1): 13–28.

———. 2004. "Greed and Grievance in Civil War." *Oxford Economic Papers* 56: 563–595.

Davidson, R., and J. G. MacKinnon. 1981. "Several Tests for model specification in the presence of alternative hypotheses." *Econometrica* 49: 781–93.

Deininger, K., and L. Squire. 1996. "A New Data Set Measuring Income Inequality." *World Bank Economic Review* 10: 565–91.

———. 1998. "New Ways of Looking at Old Issues: Inequality and Growth." *Journal of Development Economics* 57: 249–87.

Easterly, W., and R. Levine. 1997. "Africa's Growth Tragedy: Policies and Ethnic Divisions." *Quarterly Journal of Economics* 113: 1203–49.

Elbadawi, Ibrahim A., and Nicholas Sambanis. 2002. "How Much War Will We See? Explaining the Prevalence of Civil War." *Journal of Conflict Resolution* 46 (3): 307–34.

Esteban, J., and D. Ray. 1994. "On the Measurement of Polarization." *Econometrica* 62 (4): 819–51.

Fearon, James D., and David Laitin. 2003. "Ethnicity, Insurgency, and Civil War." *American Political Science Review* 97 (1): 91–106.

George, Alexander L. 1979. "Case Studies and Theory Development: The Method of Structured, Focused Comparison." In *Diplomacy: New Approaches in History, Theory, and Policy*, ed. Paul Gordon Lauren. New York: Free Press.

George, Alexander L., and Timothy J. McKeown. 1985. "Case Studies and Theories of Organizational Decision Making." *Advances in Information Processing in Organizations* 2: 21–58.

Gerrard, A. J. W. 2000. "*What Is a Mountain?*" Mimeo, DECRG, World Bank, Washington, DC.

Green, Donald P., and Rachel L. Seher. 2002. "What Role Does Prejudice Play in Ethnic Conflict?" Unpublished paper, Yale University (September 5 version).

Grossman, Herschel I. 1991. "A General Equilibrium Model of Insurrections." *American Economic Review* 81: 912–21.

———. 1999. "Kleptocracy and Revolutions." *Oxford Economic Papers* 51: 267–83.

Hegre, Håvard. 2003. "Disentangling Democracy and Development as Determinants of Armed Conflict." Paper presented at the Annual Meeting of International Studies Association, Portland, OR, February 27.

Hegre, H., T. Ellingsen, S. Gates, and N.-P. Gleditsch. 2001. "Toward a Democratic Civil Peace? Democracy, Political Change, and Civil War, 1816–1992." *American Political Science Review* 95: 33–48.

Herbst, Jeffrey. 2000. *States and Power in Africa*. Princeton, NJ: Princeton University Press.

Hirshleifer, Jack. 1995. "Theorizing About Conflict." In *Handbook of Defense Economics*, ed. K. Hartley and T. Sandler, Vol.1, 165–89. Amsterdam: Elsevier Science.

———. 2001. *The Dark Side of the Force: Economic Foundations of Conflict Theory*. Cambridge, UK: Cambridge University Press.

Horowitz, Donald L. 1985. *Ethnic Groups in Conflict*. Berkeley and Los Angeles: University of California Press.

Huber, John D. 1996. *Rationalizing Parliament: Legislative Institutions and Party Politics in France*. New York: Cambridge University Press.

Jaggers, K., and T. R. Gurr. 1995. "Tracking Democracy's Third Wave with the Polity III Data." *Journal of Peace Research* 32: 469–82.

King, Gary, Robert O. Keohane, and Sidney Verba. 1994. *Designing Social Inquiry: Scientific Inference in Qualitative Research*. Princeton, NJ: Princeton University Press.

McAdam, Doug, Sidney Tarrow, and Charles Tilly. 2001. *Dynamics of Contention*. Cambridge: Cambridge University Press.

Przeworski, Adam, and Henry Teune. 1970. *Logic of Comparative Social Inquiry*. Malabar, FL: Krieger Publishing.

Ragin, Charles. 1987. *The Comparative Method: Moving Beyond Qualitative and Quantitative Strategies.* Berkeley: University of California Press.

Reynal-Querol, Marta. 2000. "Religious Conflict and Growth: Theory and Evidence." Ph.D. thesis, London School of Economics and Political Science.

———. 2002. "Ethnicity, Political Systems and Civil War." *Journal of Conflict Resolution* 46 (1): 29–54.

Sambanis, Nicholas. 2002. "A Review of Recent Advances and Future Directions in the Literature on Civil War." *Defense and Peace Economics* 13 (2): 215–43.

———. 2004a. "Expanding Economic Models of Civil War Using Case Studies." *Perspectives on Politics* 2 (2): 259–80.

———. 2004b. "What Is a Civil War? Conceptual and Empirical Complexities of an Operational Definition." *Journal of Conflict Resolution* 48 (6): 814–58.

Singer, D. J., and M. Small. 1994. *Correlates of War Project: International and Civil War Data, 1816–1992.* Ann Arbor, MI: Inter-University Consortium for Political and Social Research.

Small, M., and J. D. Singer. 1982. *Resort to Arms: International and Civil War, 1816–1980.* Beverly Hills, CA: Sage.

Summers, R., and A. Heston. 1991. "The Penn World Table (Mark 5): An Expanded Set of International Comparisons, 1950–1988." *The Quarterly Journal of Economics* 99: 327–68.

USSR. 1964. *Atlas Narodov Mira.* Moscow: Department of Geodesy and Cartography of the State Geological Committee of the USSR.

World Bank. 2000. *World Development Indicators.* Washington, DC: World Bank.

# Resources and Rebellion in Aceh, Indonesia

2

MICHAEL L. ROSS

Indonesia is large, poor, and resource abundant, and has had a history of political violence. It should be no surprise that it suffered from a civil war in 1989–91 and then again at the start of 1999. Both of these conflicts took place in the westernmost province of Aceh. How well does the Collier-Hoeffler (CH) model explain the Aceh conflicts?

To answer this question this study focuses on the rise of Aceh's rebel organization, known as GAM (*Gerakan Aceh Merdeka,* Aceh Freedom Movement).[1] GAM has had three incarnations: the first in 1976–79, when it was small and ill-equipped, and was easily suppressed by the military; the second in 1989–91, when it was larger, better trained, and better equipped, and was only put down through harsh security measures; and the third beginning in 1999, when it became larger and better funded than ever before, challenging the Indonesian government's control of the province (see table 2.1). This chapter explains why GAM arose at each of these times, and why, between 1976 and 2002, it steadily grew larger and more powerful.

Although Indonesia has frequently suffered from violent conflict, the civil wars in Aceh have been the country's only civil wars since 1960, if the standard definition of civil wars is applied.[2] A government-sponsored slaughter in 1965–66 killed between 100,000 and 1 million people, but this was a one-sided massacre in which government forces suffered few casualties, and the victims were civilians, not a rebel army. The Indonesian government invaded the Dutch colony of Netherlands New Guinea in 1962, and the Portuguese colony of East Timor in 1975, causing many thousands of deaths in each territory. Since these were invasions of foreign territory, however, they cannot be classified as "internal" conflicts.[3] In 1999–2000, there were bloody clashes between Christians and Muslims in Indonesia's Molucca Islands; these too do not qualify as civil wars, since the parties fought each other, not the government. Only the conflicts between the Indonesian government and GAM—which resulted in over 1,000 deaths in 1990, 1991, 2000, 2001, 2002, and possibly several other years—qualify as civil wars.

This chapter makes several arguments. The first is that the civil war in Aceh can be largely explained by the central insights of the CH model, particularly its stress on

*Table 2.1* The Three Incarnations of GAM

| Organization | Years | Active members | Casualties |
|---|---|---|---|
| GAM I | 1976–79 | 25–200 | >100 |
| GAM II | 1989–91 | 200–750 | 1990–92: 2,000–10,000 |
| GAM III | 1999– | 15–27,000 | 1999: 393 |
| | | | 2000: 1,041 |
| | | | 2001: 1,700 |
| | | | 2002: 1,230 |

the importance of rebel financing, poverty, and the effects of past conflict. The second argument is that to provide a more complete explanation of Indonesia's civil wars, it is useful to include four additional factors: charismatic leadership, which appeared in the form of GAM's founder, Hasan di Tiro; popular grievances, which influenced the willingness of the Acehnese to support GAM; demonstration effects, which came from the referendum for independence in another Indonesian province, East Timor; and government credibility, which dropped sharply between 1987 and 1999 and made it virtually impossible for the Indonesian government to placate the Acehnese people with an offer of local autonomy.

The third argument is that even though Aceh's abundance of primary commodities had an important influence on the civil war (as Collier and Hoeffler predict), this effect occurred through different causal mechanisms than the one that they suggest. Collier and Hoeffler suggest that commodities increase the risk of civil war because they offer rebels an easy source of start-up funding. Even though Aceh is rich in natural resources, it provided the rebels with no start-up funding; yet it did contribute to the onset of the war in three other ways: by creating grievances over the distribution of resource revenues; by introducing a larger and more aggressive military presence into the province; and possibly by making the government's offer of regional autonomy less credible.[4]

This study is organized into three sections and a brief conclusion. The first section examines the rise and fall of GAM between 1976 and 1979; the second, GAM's rise and fall between 1989 and 1991; and the third, GAM's return and growth between 1999 and 2003. Each of these sections looks at the factors that influenced the risk of civil war in Indonesia as a whole, and in Aceh as a region, on the eve of GAM's incarnation and describes GAM's organization, funding, strategies, and activities, and the government's response. The conclusion summarizes the analysis and examines in greater detail the role of Aceh's natural resource wealth.

## Conflict Risk in Indonesia and Aceh, 1976

### Indonesia

In 1976, Indonesia faced a relatively high risk of civil war because of a combination of ethnic, geographical, economic, political, and historical factors. Indonesia's ethnic composition had, and still has, both positive and negative implications for the country's risk of civil war. It is among the most ethnically diverse countries in the world, home to perhaps 300 distinct language groups. In at least some instances, this extraordinary level of diversity has probably reduced the risk of civil war by making it more difficult for aggrieved groups to form large alliances against the state. In West Papua, for example, members of the long-standing pro-separatist organization *Organisasi Papua Merdeka* have had difficulty forming a united front, because of animosity among the province's tribes.

Indonesia's ethnic composition poses a civil war risk, however, because of the dominance of the largest "ethnic" group, the Javanese. In 1976, the ethnic Javanese constituted 45 percent of the population; the Sundanese, who are often grouped with the Javanese because they, like the Javanese, are concentrated on the island of Java, constituted another 15 percent of the population. Whether they are treated as 45 percent or 60 percent of the population, the size of this group has often contributed to antagonism between Indonesians who are indigenous to Java, and those from other islands. Non-Javanese people see Indonesia's government and military as Javanese-controlled.

Viewed along religious lines, Indonesia suffers from a second type of ethnic dominance: close to 90 percent of the population is Muslim. In Indonesia's predominantly non-Muslim areas—East Timor, Nusa Tenggara, and West Papua—this has at times produced a profound fear of Muslim supremacy. Although Indonesia is not an Islamic state, and Indonesia's governments have generally supported the religious rights of minorities, the rebellions in East Timor and West Papua have both been partly motivated by a fear of Muslim dominance.

Indonesia's economic status in the mid-1970s also produced a significant conflict risk. Indonesia is a low-income country, and per capita in 1976 was just $395 (in constant 1995 dollars) (World Bank 2001). Moreover, in 1976 Indonesia was highly dependent on the export of natural resources, with a resource export-to-gross domestic product (GDP) ratio of 19.4 percent. This was due to a boom in both oil and timber exports in the early 1970s.[5]

At the same time, there were several economic factors that mitigated this risk. Economic growth was steady and high, averaging 7.8 percent from 1970 to 1979 and never falling below 6 percent. Income inequality has been, and remains, relatively low: its Gini coefficient was 34.6, which is relatively favorable for a low-income country. A 1987 survey found that the poorest 20 percent of households had 8.8 percent of national income. This is a greater share than in all but one low-income state and two lower-middle-income states for which data were available (World Bank 1992).

By 1976, Indonesia had suffered from a history of violent conflict, although that conflict is usually not coded by scholars as a "civil war." In 1965–66, between 100,000 and 1 million Indonesians were killed by the military and citizen groups supported by the military, as part of an effort to eradicate the influence of the Indonesian Communist Party (PKI). The slaughter was touched off by a coup and countercoup that eventually toppled President Sukarno, and replaced him with Major General

Suharto. Because these killings took the form of a massacre of mostly unarmed civilians, scholars generally do not treat this event as a civil war. Nevertheless, if a recent prior conflict raises the danger of a future conflict by producing unresolved grievances, the 1965–66 slaughter may have heightened the risk of subsequent conflict.

Finally, the absence of a large diaspora may have reduced Indonesia's civil war risk. Although most adjacent countries provide no data on Indonesian migrants, Indonesians commonly migrate to other islands within the archipelago, not to other countries. The largest populations of overseas Indonesians are almost certainly found in Malaysia, Singapore, and Thailand.

## Aceh

While Indonesia's 1976 conflict risk was high, it was not equally high across the country's 26 provinces and 13,000 islands. Within Indonesia, the conflict risk may have been atypically high in the westernmost province of Aceh.

Even though Indonesia as a whole is ethnically diverse, Aceh is relatively homogeneous. Virtually all of Aceh's 2.26 million people in 1976 were Muslim; and 21 percent belonged to ethnic minority groups, including the Gayonese (10 percent), the Tamiang Malays (9 percent), and the Alas (2 percent). However, these groups posed no obstacles to the formation of a separatist movement (Central Bureau of Statistics 1971; King and Rasjid, 1988). Indeed, one report suggested that members of the largest minority group, the Gayonese, had joined the Acehnese separatists in attacking Javanese settlers (*Tempo* 2001b).[6]

Aceh's geography is also a risk factor: 53 percent of the land is "steep" (having more than 25 percent slope) and 36 percent is "very steep" (more than 45 percent slope) (Dawood and Sjafrizal 1989). Mountainous terrain can help provide a safe haven for a guerrilla army that is outnumbered by government forces.

In general, Aceh's economy did not pose any special risk.[7] According to a national survey in 1971 (which predates the development of major energy resources on Aceh), Aceh's per capita GDP was 97 percent of the national average. Between 1971 and 1975, Aceh's real annual growth rate averaged 5.2 percent; this was below the national average but still robust (Hill and Weidemann 1989).

Although there is no reliable information on inequality in Aceh in the mid-1970s, there is substantial evidence that poverty rates were low, due in part to a large surplus of rice, the staple food crop. In 1980, just 1.8 percent of the rural population and 1.7 percent of the urban population were below the poverty line; these were among the lowest rates in the country. Health standards were also relatively high and improved substantially during the 1970s: in 1969, infant mortality rates were 131 per 1,000, slightly below the national rate of 141 per 1,000. By 1977, Aceh's rates had dropped to 91 per 1,000, while national rates fell to 108 per 1,000. Life expectancy was also better than the national average and improved sharply between 1969 and 1977 (Hill and Weidemann 1989).

Even before the rise of GAM, Aceh had a long history of violent conflict. In the 19th century, the independent sultanate of Aceh offered the fiercest resistance to

Dutch colonial rule in Indonesia, and was only subjugated after 30 years of brutal warfare (1873–1903). Although the Acehnese people broadly supported the creation of the Indonesian Republic in the late 1940s, Aceh was the site of a 1953–62 rebellion led by Teungku Daud Beureueh. Importantly, the rebellion did *not* call for Acehnese independence, but rather, greater local autonomy and a stronger role for Islam in the national government.[8] After several years of negotiations, the rebellion ended when the government offered Aceh status as a "special region" (*Daerah Istimewa*) with autonomy over religious, cultural, and educational affairs. But in 1968, shortly after Suharto came to power, the Acehnese government's special autonomy was effectively revoked.

Aceh's history as an independent sultanate, and the revocation of special autonomy, contributed to a sense of political grievance toward Jakarta, and was reflected in the national elections of 1971 and 1977. The Suharto regime used myriad forms of coercion to produce a large majority at the national level for its own party (known as *Golkar*); but in Aceh, a rival, Muslim-oriented party (the Development Unity Party, or PPP) enjoyed unique popularity. In 1971, Golkar won 49.7 of Aceh's votes, versus 48.9 percent for the group of parties that later became the PPP. In 1977 Golkar won just 41.0 percent of the vote, while the PPP won 57.5 percent; Aceh was one of just two provinces that did not give Golkar at least a plurality (King and Rasjid 1988).

Finally, there was a small but notable Acehnese diaspora in 1976. Aceh lies along the Malacca Straits, which has long been a migration route to mainland Southeast Asia. Although no figures are available from adjacent countries for the 1970s, in 1991 an estimated 10,000 Acehnese were living in Malaysia (Vatikiotis 1991).

## The Rise and Fall of GAM I

In the mid-1970s, these factors contributed to the foundation of GAM, a separatist rebel movement. During its 1976–79 incarnation, GAM was small and underfinanced and was easily suppressed by the government. Still, the brief 1976–79 incarnation of GAM would contribute to the resurgence of GAM in 1989–91, which in turn led to GAM's return in 1999.

It is hard to imagine the foundation of GAM without the efforts of Hasan Muhammad di Tiro. di Tiro came from a prominent Acehnese family in the Acehnese district of Pidie; he was the grandson of Teungku Chik di Tiro, a renowned hero of Aceh's war against Dutch colonial rule. In the early 1950s, di Tiro lived in New York City and worked at the Indonesian Mission to the United Nations. In 1953, he quit to support the Daud Beureueh rebellion.

In early 1976, di Tiro secretly returned to Indonesia to build a new guerrilla movement dedicated to Acehnese independence. He recruited a cadre of young intellectuals, tried but failed to gain Daud Beureueh's endorsement, and issued a "Declaration of Independence of Acheh-Sumatra."[9] The declaration offers a glimpse of di Tiro's rationales: It presents a romantic account of Aceh's history as an independent state; it denounces the "illegal transfer of sovereignty over our fatherland by the old, Dutch, colonialists to the new, Javanese colonialists"; it claims that Aceh has been impoverished by Javanese rule, stating that "the life-expectancy of our people is 34 years and is decreasing"; and it blames these economic hardships on the central government's appropriation of revenue from Aceh's new natural gas facility: "Acheh, Sumatra, has been producing a revenue of over 15 billion US dollars yearly for the Javanese neo-colonialists, which they used totally for the benefit of Java and the Javanese."

Some of the declaration's assertions had little empirical basis. Life expectancy in Aceh rose from 48.5 years in 1969 to 55.5 years in 1977; by contrast, life expectancy in Indonesia as a whole was 46.5 years in 1969 and 52.5 years in 1977 (Hill and Weidemann 1989). Aceh was also not yet producing the $15 billion for "the Javanese" as the declaration claimed, but the allusion to Aceh's mineral wealth fore-shadowed GAM's preoccupation with the province's natural resources.

The declaration is notable for what it does not say: It makes no mention of Islam, an issue that was central to the Daud Beureueh rebellion and a major source of dis-satisfaction with Jakarta. Acehnese tend to be more devout than their fellow Indonesians, and at the polls favored the Islamic PPP over the secular Golkar. The declaration also fails to mention the Suharto government's authoritarian rule and does not call for a federal Indonesia with greater autonomy for Aceh, a position pre-viously advocated by di Tiro (di Tiro [1958] 1999).

di Tiro's decision to back independence, not federalism, was influenced by his efforts to find a message that appealed to both the Acehnese people, and to foreign governments that could fund the movement. After quitting his United Nations post in 1953, di Tiro had tried to raise funds and purchase arms for the Daud Beureueh rebellion. Therefore, he must have been acutely aware of the need to appeal to for-eign funders.

di Tiro believed that foreign governments would not support a movement that called for Aceh's autonomy within an Indonesian federation, since this would be regarded as a purely domestic affair. If the movement called for Acehnese independ-ence, he reasoned, foreign governments would be more likely to lend their support. He may have also chosen independence as a goal for a second reason: the Daud Beureueh rebellion—which the young di Tiro passionately supported—ended in 1962 when the central government agreed to grant Aceh a special level of autonomy within the Indonesian state. Jakarta never fulfilled its promise, and Aceh remained a "special aera" in name only. Any future pledges of autonomy would have little cred-ibility in di Tiro's mind, and were pointless to pursue.

He apparently decided not to make appeals based on Islam, for fear it would alien-ate potential foreign backers. This was a critical decision, because it apparently cost di Tiro the support of Daud Beureueh himself, along with his energetic and experi-enced supporters (Sjamsuddin 1984).[10] di Tiro solicited aid from the CIA, but with-out success.

Instead of raising the issues of Islam or democracy, di Tiro focused on Aceh's new status as an exporter of liquefied natural gas (LNG). Mobil Oil had discovered immense deposits of gas in Aceh in 1971, near the town of Lhokseumawe; there was enough to generate $2–$3 billion annually in export revenues over a 20- to 30-year period.[11] To exploit these reserves, Mobil entered into a joint venture with Pertamina, the Indonesian oil parastatal, and Jilco, a Japanese consortium. Production began in 1977, reaching maximum capacity in 1988 (Dawood and Sjafrizal 1989).

There were considerable economic benefits for Aceh from the LNG boom. During construction, the new facility employed 8,000–12,000 people; during the peak years of production, it employed between 5,000 and 6,000. Since local infrastructure was poor, Mobil also built new roads, schools, medical facilities, and 4,000–5,000 new houses. Along with the processing facility came several downstream industries, including a fertilizer plant and a chemicals plant (Dawood and Sjafrizal 1989).

There can be little doubt that the new LNG complex was welcomed in Aceh. The government initially planned to extract the gas and ship it to North Sumatra, an adjacent province with a more quiescent reputation, for processing. After strong Acehnese protests, they agreed to build the industrial complex in Aceh (Sjamsuddin 1984).

Still, the LNG complex also produced resentments. Locals believed that the project employed too few Acehnese, and that local firms were unfairly excluded from consideration. Mobil officials suggested that they employed as many Acehnese as they could, but were often forced to rely on Indonesians from other parts of the country who had more skills and experience.[12] Hasan di Tiro was personally familiar with these resentments. In 1974, he had lost to Bechtel, a U.S. firm, in a bidding competition to build one of the pipelines (Robinson 1998). GAM was not opposed to the LNG facility itself, but it did object to the payment of royalties to the central government.[13]

In its 1976–79 incarnation, GAM was small and engaged in few military activities. It never controlled any territory, and it was forced to move on as soon as its presence was discovered by the Indonesian army. Estimates of its active membership range from two dozen to 200. Some of its fighters were apparently forced to join the movement. Much of GAM's activity consisted of distributing pamphlets and raising an Acehnese flag. They possessed only a "few old guns and remnants from World War II," and extorted money from townspeople to support their efforts. At times, di Tiro and his men went for days without food (Hiorth 1986; Sjamsuddin 1984).

Several of their most significant actions were directed against the LNG facility. Around 1977, GAM guerrillas stole the facility's payroll. In December 1977, GAM shot two American workers at the plant, killing one. The shootings occurred when GAM rebels tried to arrange a secret meeting with an Acehnese manager for the LNG plant, to "discuss ways and means to protect the LNG plant . . . from possible damage from the raging guerrilla warfare around it" (di Tiro 1984). di Tiro's description implies that GAM may have been trying to extort protection money from the facility.

The government responded to GAM's emergence with a combination of military force and economic programs. Suspects were arrested and tortured; women and children were held as hostages by the government when their husbands evaded arrest; and between August 1977 and August 1980, 30 men in Aceh were shot dead in public without due process. At the same time, the government initiated new road projects, installed new television relay stations in remote rural areas, and persuaded civic leaders, including some who had been involved in the Daud Beureueh rebellion to oppose GAM. Daud Beureueh himself was flown to Jakarta to make sure he would not throw his support behind di Tiro. In 1979, di Tiro was forced to leave the country, and most of his followers either fled with him or were killed by the military. The military's operations against GAM continued until 1982, and trials of suspected GAM supporters continued until 1984 (Kell 1995; Sjamsuddin 1984).

By the early 1980s, GAM had effectively disappeared. Its activities lasted barely two years and attracted only a handful of backers. It was chronically short of funds and arms and was easily extinguished by government forces. Although Aceh was the site of an earlier rebellion, GAM was unable to attract the support of key backers of the previous movement. The LNG facility was just starting production, and had not yet generated the resentments and disappointments that would later provide GAM with widespread sympathy. It was not a time well suited to rebellion.

## Conflict Risk in Aceh, 1989

Between 1979 and 1989, Aceh enjoyed swift economic growth, yet the province's risk of conflict escalated as a boom in LNG production created new grievances. The late 1970s and the 1980s were a period of exceptional economic performance in Aceh, characterized by strong growth across all sectors. Aceh's agricultural GDP grew, in real terms, at an average annual rate of 7.6 percent from 1975 to 1984, and at just under 5 percent from 1984 to 1989. Aceh's manufacturing sector did even better, growing at an average rate of 13.7 percent between 1975 and 1984, and at almost 8 percent annually from 1984 to 1989. But the economy's most striking feature was the LNG boom. In 1976, oil and gas accounted for less than 17 percent of the province's GDP; by 1989, it accounted for 69.5 percent. Thanks to these trends, Aceh's per capita GDP (excluding the value of oil and gas) kept pace with Indonesia's quickly rising incomes.[14]

This rapid growth, ironically, may have caused social disruptions that eventually contributed to the 1989 return of GAM. Between 1974 and 1987, the district of North Aceh, which included P. T. Arun, Mobil's natural gas facility, rose in population from 490,000 to 755,000; social amenities and infrastructure for workers and job seekers were severely overstretched. Some 50,000 migrants from other parts of Indonesia had also come to Aceh, largely attracted by the oil and gas boom (Hiorth 1986). Rapid urbanization, the incursion of the non–Acehnese, land seizures, pollution, and competition for jobs in the industrial sector all contributed to tensions that facilitated GAM's 1989 re-emergence (Kell 1995).

There were also several political developments that appeared to *increase* popular support for the central government, at least through 1987; however, from 1987 to 1989, this trend may have reversed. In 1984, top officials in the ruling Golkar party began a strategy to increase the party's popularity in Aceh by appointing a popular figure as governor, launching new development projects, and obtaining the endorsement of religious leaders (including Daud Beureueh himself) who had formerly supported the opposition PPP. These efforts led to a jump in Golkar's share of the popular vote, from 37 percent in 1982 to 51.8 percent in 1987. But the boost was temporary. Shortly after the election, Aceh's development budget dropped by 36 percent, and many campaign promises went unfulfilled (King and Rasjid 1988; Liddle 1988).

## The Rise and Fall of GAM II

GAM's second coming in 1989 was aided by three factors: support from a foreign government, assistance from local Indonesian security officers, and grievances among the population. Even though GAM was larger and better equipped in 1989 than it had been a decade earlier, it still failed to win widespread support, perhaps because of the region's strong economic performance.

After slipping out of Indonesia in 1979, Hasan di Tiro and some of his top advisors moved to Sweden, where they set up an Acehnese government-in-exile. Around 1986, GAM made contact with the Libyan government. In 1986 or 1987, GAM began to receive Libyan support, as part of dictator Muammar Qaddafi's efforts to promote insurgencies worldwide (Kell 1995). Between 250 and 2,000 GAM recruits, drawn primarily from the Acehnese population in Malaysia, received military and ideological training in Libya in the late 1980s.[15] In 1989, between 150 and 800 Libya-trained fighters slipped into Aceh from Malaysia and Singapore (Vatikiotis 1991).

There is also evidence that GAM received a boost from defecting government troops. Amnesty International (1993) notes that in early 1989 at least 47 military officers based in Aceh were dismissed, possibly because of an antinarcotics campaign. Around the same time, "dozens" of ex-military and police officers joined GAM and began to attack military installations and personnel. These defections may help explain both the timing of GAM's re-emergence and its surprising strength (Vatikiotis 1990).

Grievances against the corruption, gambling, and prostitution associated with the transmigrants who were drawn to Aceh by the LNG boom were another factor. In 1988–89, these grievances produced a series of local protests.

> In May 1988, for example, villagers of Idi Cut, Aceh Timur, burned down the local police station following reports that a police officer had sexually assaulted a local woman. In August, a hotel in Lhokseumawe, Aceh Utara, was bombed following repeated complaints by the local community that it was being used as a prostitution centre. In March 1989, an estimated 8,000 people rioted in the same town destroying a military-owned building in which a circus, considered offensive by local Islamic leaders, was due to perform. (AI 1993, 8)

GAM was far more aggressive in 1989 than it had been in 1977, both as a result of its larger size and better training. From early 1989 to early 1990, it attacked only

Indonesian police and army units, killing about two dozen officers.[16] In mid-1990, it began targeting civil authorities, commercial property, suspected government informers, and non-Acehnese settlers in the Lhokseumawe area (AI 1993).

GAM's activities were more widespread geographically than they had been a decade earlier, but they were still concentrated along Aceh's northeastern coast, in the districts of Pidie, North Aceh, and East Aceh. Although GAM controlled no territory, it had a rudimentary command structure in these districts, and could mobilize guerrillas for hit-and-run attacks and ambushes (Vatikiotis 1991). North Aceh was also the home of the LNG complex, and both North Aceh and East Aceh had been sites of the 1988–89 protests. Many observers connected the rebellion to grievances caused by the LNG boom, including disputes over the distribution of high-paying jobs and revenues, official corruption, and the un-Islamic behavior of non-Acehnese migrants (Kell 1995; Robinson 1998; Vatikiotis 1990, 1991).

Estimates of GAM's strength in 1989–91 range from 200 to 750 active members. Although Libya had provided training, it did not offer GAM any additional funds or weaponry. Some money was apparently raised among the Acehnese living in Malaysia. GAM also stole (or, perhaps, purchased) weapons from Indonesian security forces, obtaining some 200 automatic rifles and light machine guns by June 1990. Still, guns were scarce, and guerillas were reportedly forced to share their arms (Kell 1995).

Until mid-1990, the government responded to the attacks on its forces in a relatively low-key manner. But in June 1990, President Suharto ordered 6,000 additional troops to Aceh, including special counterinsurgency units. From this point forward, Aceh was regarded as a "DOM" (*Daerah Operasi Militar,* "area of military operations"), a designation that has no fixed definition or legal status but implies that the military can conduct its operations with impunity.[17]

The government's response was successful in the short term. By the end of 1991, many of GAM's field commanders had been captured or killed. But the government's brutality produced a deep-seated antipathy toward Jakarta and ultimately contributed to GAM's third incarnation in 1999.

Independent estimates of the death toll during the 1990–92 period range from just under 2,000 to 10,000. The vast majority of deaths were caused by the government (AI 1993; ICG 2001a). Although human rights violations continued after 1993, only a handful of additional deaths were recorded.

## Conflict Risk in Aceh, 1999

By 1999, Aceh's conflict risk had risen sharply, due to five developments: an economic crisis, a transition from authoritarian rule to partial democracy, the demonstration effect from a successful referendum for independence in the province of East Timor, the proximity of the 1989–91 carnage, and a decline in the credibility of the central government.

From 1989 to 1996, the economy in Aceh, as in Indonesia as a whole, continued its rapid growth. But in mid-1997, a currency crisis in Thailand triggered a run on the Indonesian rupiah, leading to a banking crisis, capital flight, and a sudden economic collapse. The economy contracted by 17.8 percent in 1998 and grew just 0.4 percent in 1999. The crisis was less severe in Aceh than it was in the rest of the country. Nevertheless, Aceh's non-oil and gas GDP declined by 5.9 percent in 1998 and 2.9 percent in 1999. This produced a jump in unemployment and underemployment: In 1998 alone, the size of the official labor force dropped 37.3 percent. Aceh remained overwhelmingly dependent on natural resources. In 1998, oil and gas accounted for 65 percent of Aceh's GDP and 92.7 percent of its exports, although it employed only one-third of 1 percent of the province's labor force (BPS Aceh 1999, 2000).

In May 1998, President Suharto was forced to resign after 32 years in power; he was replaced by Indonesia's vice president, B. J. Habibie. After parliamentary elections, Habibie was succeeded in October 1999 by Abdurrahman Wahid, who headed a new coalition government. The move from authoritarian rule to partial democracy appeared to raise the likelihood of conflict. Many cross-national studies suggest that partial democracies face an unusually high risk of civil war, since aggrieved constituencies may be able to organize, but their grievances cannot be adequately addressed through the electoral system (DeNardo 1985; Hegre et al. 2001). This would prove to be true in Aceh: People became free to express their grievances toward Jakarta, but the electoral system was too weak to facilitate a peaceful solution.[18]

Suharto's fall led to a pair of developments that further raised the conflict risk in Aceh: the independence referendum in East Timor and the loss of government credibility. In January 1999, President Habibie announced that East Timor would be allowed to secede from the Indonesian Republic, if its citizens voted to do so in a province-wide referendum. Within weeks, student groups in Aceh had formed organizations calling for a similar referendum. East Timor's referendum was held in September 1999, and produced an overwhelming vote for independence. The following month there were massive marches across Aceh in support of a similar referendum. In November 1999, hundreds of thousands of people—and according to some estimates, as many as 1 million people—gathered in the Acehnese capital, Banda Aceh, to hold a rally in support of the referendum. According to polls taken by a leading pro-referendum nongovernmental organization and the virtually unanimous perception of outside observers, a freely held referendum would have produced a strong vote for independence.

Political leaders in Jakarta were keenly aware of growing support for independence in Aceh and took a series of measures to defuse it. In late July 1998, a fact-finding team from the national parliament admitted that serious human rights violations had occurred in Aceh between 1990 and 1998. In early August 1998, armed forces chief Wiranto visited Aceh to announce a withdrawal of combat forces and an end to the DOM, and to apologize for the army's human rights abuses. In March 1999, President Habibie visited Aceh himself and pledged to aid the region's economy, to help children orphaned by the conflict, and to establish a commission to examine human rights abuses by the security forces (Robinson 1998).

The government also adopted new legislation to address Aehnese grievances. In late April 1999, the parliament adopted a pair of decentralization laws (Nos. 22 and 25 of 1999) that gave all of Indonesia's regional and local governments extensive powers, and enabled them to retain much of the income from the extraction of natural resources in their own regions—including 15 percent of the net public income from oil, 30 percent from natural gas, and 80 percent from timber (which is also abundant in Aceh). The parliament adopted a third law (No. 44 of 1999) that affirmed Aceh's right to control its own cultural, religious, and educational affairs.

These developments should have made Aceh's status as a member of the Indonesian republic *more* attractive and independence *less* attractive for Aceh's citizens and politicians. They should have thereby reduced the likelihood that a new civil war would break out. The fact that they failed points to another critical development: a deterioration in the credibility of the government's commitments toward Aceh.

If the government's pledges in 1998 and 1999 were credible, the notion of independence, a risky option that appeared to have little popular support before the late 1980s,[19] should have been unappealing to most Aehnese. But if these commitments were not credible, then the only way that the Aehnese people could be certain they would no longer suffer from the Indonesian military's brutality, and would retain control of the province's resource wealth, was to secede from the rest of the country.

The central government's poor credibility in Aceh could be traced back to several events: the founding of the republic, when the government refused to make Aceh a separate province, despite Aceh's history as an independent state; actions in 1968 when the Suharto government effectively abrogated the 1963 agreement that granted Aceh special autonomy; and the failure of the Suharto government to fulfill the promises it made to Aceh during the 1987 election campaign.

However low it was initially, the government's credibility seemed to fall even further beginning in 1998 because of a series of events: the revelations about the government's human rights abuses in Aceh, which followed years of denials; President Habibie's failure to keep his pledge to bring human rights violators to justice; President Wahid's failure to fulfill his promises to support the Aceh referendum, prosecute human rights violators at all ranks, and withdraw nonlocal troops from the province; armed forces chief Wiranto's reversal of his August 1998 promise to withdraw combat forces from Aceh; and the government's failure to stop the military's attacks on civilians. The most notably of these were the May 1999 massacre of some 40 peaceful demonstrators near Lhokseumawe, and the July 1999 massacre of between 57 and 70 people at an Islamic boarding school in Beutong Ateuh.

In March 2000, historian Anthony Reid wrote that "During the past year, the overwhelming evidence of military atrocities has rapidly eroded" the belief in national unity formerly held by many Aehnese (Reid 2000). Political scientist Harold Crouch concluded in June 2001:

> The credibility of the central government in Aceh is close to zero, amongst all sections of the population. Given a history of promises made and broken since the 1950s, even the minority of Aehnese who see autonomy as the best solution have little trust in Jakarta's good faith. (ICG 2001b)

The Acehnese people, hence, had little reason to believe that the government's offer of regional autonomy, and freedom from further atrocities, would be kept. The central government's reliance on natural gas revenues from Aceh, which in 1998 were worth $1.2 billion, and provided the government with 9 percent of its total government revenues, may have made these promises even less credible because it convinced the Acehnese that the government would not be financially able to fulfill its promise to allow the province to retain more of its resource revenues.[20] The belief that Jakarta would not give Aceh true autonomy—and that its promises could not be trusted—helped make independence seem like the most practical solution.

Finally, the proximity of the 1989–91 civil war made a renewal of conflict more likely, as grievances toward the military grew. Soon after Suharto was removed from office, Aceh's newly freed media publicized reports of summary executions, torture, rape, and theft committed by the military over the previous decade. When combat troops started to pull out of Lhokseumawe in August 1998, crowds stoned departing trucks and attacked the provincial office of the ruling Golkar party. In Guempang Minyek, villagers destroyed a Special Forces interrogation center where suspects were allegedly tortured. According to a foreign journalist, "In Aceh, loathing of the military's brutal legacy extends from the humblest villager to the highest provincial official" (McBeth 1998).

The propinquity of the 1990–98 conflict also had a second, more concrete effect: It provided GAM with a pool of willing recruits, aspiring to take vengeance on the military.

## The Rise of GAM III

Between 1991 and 1998, there were few signs of GAM activity in Aceh and many locals came to believe that GAM no longer existed. After the government lifted the DOM in August 1998, there were reports of pro-independence neighborhood rallies, and displays of GAM banners and flags. Several Acehnese who had worked for the Indonesian Special Forces were killed or disappeared, although it was unclear who was behind these events. A journalist who visited Aceh in mid-November 1998 found no trace of GAM (McBeth 1998).

Yet in early 1999, GAM reappeared and began to grow more quickly than it ever had before. By July 1999, it reportedly had more than 800 men under arms, equipped with assault rifles and grenade launchers. By mid-2001, GAM had 2,000–3,000 regular fighters, and an additional 13,000–24,000 militia members; it was reportedly in control of 80 percent of Aceh's villages (ICG 2001a).

The sudden return of GAM cannot be explained by a change in funding. GAM appeared to have collected little revenue between 1991 and 1999, and it had lost Libya's sponsorship. The main causes for GAM's successful re-emergence may be the jump in popular support for Acehnese independence, resulting from the economic crisis that made independence and the retention of LNG revenues seem more attractive; the revelations of human rights abuses; and the government's low credibility. This shift in public opinion made it easier for GAM to recruit new members and, perhaps, to raise funds.[21]

At first GAM used force to conscript new members.[22] Over time, however, it began successfully to recruit the children of people who had been killed or tortured by security forces under the DOM, offering them the opportunity to avenge their parents. According to the Care Human Rights Forum, 16,375 children had been orphaned during the 1990–98 military crackdown (McBeth 1998). By mid-2000, these "children of the DOM victims" (*anak korban DOM*) constituted a significant corps of GAM fighters.[23] The *Jakarta Post* reported on July 30, 2000, that most of GAM's new recruits were children of the DOM victims.[24]

To fund itself, GAM used a combination of voluntary donations, taxes, extortion, kidnapping, and the sale of timber and cannabis. According to Indonesian intelligence sources interviewed by Schulze (2004), by 2003 GAM was collecting about 1.1 billion rupiah (approximately $130,000) a month through an extensive tax system levied on personal and business income and schools across the province; funds were also collected from Acehnese living in Malaysia, Thailand, and other parts of Sumatra, often under the threat of violence (Djalal 2000; ICG 2001a; Schulze 2003). These funding schemes were employed *after* GAM's reappearance. There are no indications that GAM has received assistance from Libya, or any other foreign government, since the late 1980s.

Members of GAM have also tried to raise money from the Lhokseumawe natural gas facility, through both direct and indirect forms of extortion. Between 1999 and March 2001, ExxonMobil reported a growing tally of violence and threats. Its company vans and pickups had been hijacked about 50 times; company airplanes were twice hit by ground fire when they tried to land; facilities were repeatedly attacked with gunfire and grenades; company buses were bombed, or stopped and burned, as they brought employees to work; four employees were killed while off-duty; and other employees were threatened (*Tempo* 2001a). From March to July 2001, the company was forced to shut down the LNG facility because of a lack of security.

Some of these security incidents may have been carried out by the army or by ordinary criminals. At least one, the kidnapping of eight employees, who were briefly held for ransom in May 2000, appeared to have been a freelance operation carried out by GAM members without the leadership's authorization. However, many of these incidents were part of efforts by GAM to extort money from ExxonMobil, to reduce the government's gas revenues, or both. By ransoming off a senior executive in early 2001, GAM allegedly raised about 5 billion rupiah (around $500,000) (Schulze 2004; *Tempo* 2001a). In March 2001, the GAM regional commander in the Lhokseumawe area, Muzakir Mualim, explained, "We expect them [ExxonMobil] to pay income tax to Aceh. We're only talking about a few percent of the enormous profit they have made from drilling under the earth of Aceh" (*Tempo* 2001a).[25] Previously, GAM had pledged that it would not attack foreign companies; the LNG facility attacks may represent a change in policy, or a split between the central GAM leadership and the regional GAM command.

As in 1977–79 and 1989–91, GAM has been hindered by a shortage of weapons. Although in 2001–2002 it had between 15,000 and 27,000 regular and irregular soldiers, they were thought to have only 1,000–2,500 modern firearms, one or two 60-mm mortars, a handful of grenade launchers, and some land mines. Most GAM fighters were armed with homemade or obsolete firearms, sharp or blunt instruments, or explosives (Davis 2001; ICG 2001a). Many of GAM's modern arms came from the Indonesian military, often purchased from corrupt officers (*Indonesian Observer* 2001; Lubis et al. 2000). GAM also purchased arms from Thailand and Cambodia, although the Indonesian navy has made it increasingly difficult for GAM to bring in weapons by boat (Davis 2001).

GAM's organization inside Aceh appears somewhat decentralized. GAM's military commanders—Abdullah Syafi'ie until his death in January 2002, and Mazukkir Manaf thereafter—have been appointed by the GAM leadership in Sweden and apparently remained loyal to it. There are frequent reports, however, that discipline inside GAM's armed forces is poor, and that its military structure is highly decentralized. The disjuncture between GAM's official policy of not attacking foreign companies and the many attacks on the LNG facility may imply that GAM units in the Lhokseumawe area are not fully under GAM's central control. Indeed, the GAM unit in this area has a reputation for being unusually violent, corrupt, and resistant to central control.[26]

GAM forces are divided into small groups of 10–20 men, who are at least formally under one of 17 local commanders. Even though GAM activity has been concentrated in the three districts where the movement has traditionally been the strongest—Pidie, East Aceh, and North Aceh—by 2000 GAM had a presence in every part of the province except Sabang, an island in the far north.[27]

Because of GAM's funding constraints, dearth of weapons, and limited manpower, it may never be able to defeat the Indonesian army and police on the battleground. Instead, it has developed a series of political tactics to build popular support and draw attention to the Acehnese cause. Since 1999, at least five strategies have been discernible.

The first has been a propaganda campaign that extols Aceh's glorious history, and denounces the "theft" of its mineral wealth by the Javanese. Speakers and pamphlets commonly suggest that if independent, Aceh would be as wealthy as Brunei, the oil-rich Islamic sultanate on nearby Borneo. This is an economic appeal, not a political one: Brunei is much wealthier, but less democratic than Indonesia. It is also misleading. If Aceh had been fiscally independent in 1998, its per capita GDP would have been $1,257; this would be about one-third higher than Indonesia's average GDP, but not close to Brunei's 1998 per capita income of $17,600.

The second strategy has been to mobilize public opinion against the Indonesian government by denouncing, and possibly provoking, military repression. Until the early 1990s, the central GAM messages were economic and historical. Since 1991, GAM has also focused on the military's human rights violations (Robinson 1998). In an interview with a British journalist, Ilias Pase, a GAM commander, suggested that GAM has at times provoked military reprisals in order to boost its support:

We know from experience how the security apparatus will respond [to our activities]. They will kill civilians and burn their homes. This makes the people more loyal to the GAM. And the people in Jakarta and outside can see that we are serious about our struggle. This is part of the guerrilla strategy. (Dillon 2001)

The Indonesian military is, unfortunately, all too eager to respond to provocations with brutality and, hence, fall into the trap set by GAM.[28]

The third strategy has been to disable the local government, and where possible, to replace it with GAM's own institutions. Hundreds of schools have been burned down and scores of teachers killed. Many local politicians and civil servants have also been killed, or recruited into GAM's parallel government structure (Schulze 2004). By 2001, as much as 80 percent of Aceh's villages were under GAM's control, and across most of the province, the Indonesian government had ceased to function.

The fourth strategy has been to drive Javanese settlers out of Aceh. In mid-1999, GAM forced at least 15,000 Javanese, some who had lived in Aceh since the 1970s, out of their homes (McBeth et al. 1999). This may reflect, in part, GAM's anti-Javanese ideology, the association of the Javanese with the military (who are loathed), and competition between the Acehnese and non-Acehnese over jobs. It also may have been caused by the fear that the army would organize non-Acehnese settlers into a militia to fight the separatists, as they did in East Timor. Indeed, by 2002 there were widespread reports that Javanese militias had formed, although it was unclear if they had been instigated by the military (ICG 2002; *Tempo* 2001b).

The final strategy has been to bring greater pressure on the Indonesian government by attracting international attention and sympathy. One tactic has been to cultivate the support of international human rights groups. Another approach, employed in mid-1999, was to empty dozens of villages, and move between 80,000 and 100,000 Acehnese into 61 refugee camps, provoking a refugee crisis (Cohen 1999). After drawing international media attention, villagers were allowed to return to their villages and these camps were largely closed down. A third tactic has been to use the promise of peace talks to draw in international actors as mediators and observers (Schulze 2004).

The army and police have responded to GAM with their own mix of strategies. These include attacking and killing GAM personnel, including its military leaders; detaining and torturing anyone believed to have information about GAM, or to be sympathetic to them; burning houses and buildings in villages where GAM may have a presence, or that are simply near recent GAM activities; and forcibly recruiting petty criminals and teenagers as informants. In 2001–02, the military and police had approximately 30,000 personnel in Aceh; by mid-2003, the number had grown to 50,000. They function in what the International Crisis Group calls "a virtual legal vacuum" and have committed a large number of atrocities (Human Rights Watch 2001; ICG 2001a).

The military's failure to contain the rebel movement could be attributed to ineptitude, corruption, and the profits generated by an ongoing conflict. Up and down the chain of command, soldiers profit from the war, and the war has given a political boost to the military as an institution (ICG 2001a). Efforts by both presidents

Habibie and Wahid to find peaceful solutions were subverted, perhaps deliberately, by the military.

The government and GAM have maintained a dialogue throughout much of the conflict, assisted by the Henry Dunant Centre, a private Swiss organization. Yet neither side seems willing to compromise on the core issue of Acehnese independence: GAM insists on it, and Jakarta rejects it. Still, the parties have twice agreed to cease-fires. In May 2000, they agreed to a "humanitarian pause," but this had little influence on the intensity of the conflict or the casualty rate, and was abandoned in 2001. In December 2002, they adopted a "Cessation of Hostilities Framework Agreement," which was hailed as the first step toward a settlement. Although it led to a sharp fall in the casualty rate, it was abandoned in May 2003 after being undermined by both GAM and the Indonesian military (Aspinall and Crouch 2003).

In retrospect, GAM may have agreed to the negotiations, and the cease-fires, for tactical reasons. Bargaining directly with the Indonesian government on foreign soil (Geneva) helped GAM attain a measure of international legitimacy as the representative of the Acehnese people. The December 2002 Framework Agreement also gave GAM a much-needed break from the fighting, allowing it to recruit new members and re-arm (Aspinall and Crouch 2003).

The government's strategy has been to combine military pressure on GAM with a political campaign to reduce GAM's popularity by granting Aceh greater autonomy from Jakarta. In August 2001, President Megawati signed a "Special Autonomy" law (Law No. 18 of 2001) that gave Aceh control of 70 percent of its oil and gas revenues for eight years, after which the arrangement would be subject to review. It would also partially implement Islamic law in Aceh, establish Islamic courts, introduce direct elections for the province's governor, and give the governor greater control over the Acehnese police. Yet by mid-2003, the Acehnese provincial assembly had made little progress in adopting the regulations needed to implement the new law, and in any case, the government's control of Aceh was too tenuous to implement the autonomy law's provisions. Moreover, as Aspinall and Crouch (2003) observe, the government has further hurt the credibility of the autonomy plan by placing heavy military pressure on the province, and by failing to prosecute the military's human rights abuses.

From 1998 to the beginning of 2003, the conflict killed over 4,300 people. Most of the victims were civilians (Human Rights Watch 2003; ICG 2001a).

## Conclusion

In general, the conflict in Aceh, Indonesia, fits the CH model of civil wars well. Aceh has many of the characteristics that Collier and Hoeffler identify as risk factors: It is relatively poor, is mountainous, lacks ethnic fragmentation, has a diaspora, suffered from conflict previously, and is highly dependent on the export of natural resources.

When GAM re-emerged in 1999, Indonesia was also only partly democratic; other scholars have suggested that partial democratization tends to raise the danger of conflict (DeNardo 1985; Fearon and Laitin 2003; Hegre et al. 2001). This chapter closely fits these arguments. Indonesia's move toward democracy in 1998–99 opened new political space for dissent, and allowed a free press to flourish. But the country's democratic institutions were still too weak to guide Acehnese dissent into non-violent channels. Elected officials had only partial control of the military, and the instability of the policy-making process made the government's promises of autonomy less credible.

Four additional factors can help provide a more complete explanation for the Aceh civil war. The first is the entrepreneurship of Hasan di Tiro, the founder of the separatist group GAM. The Aceh conflict was largely caused by the rise of GAM. It is the only organization in Aceh that has violently challenged the Indonesian state since 1963, and had it not formed, Aceh's recent history would be far different. The foundation and growth of GAM was largely the result of di Tiro's tireless efforts.

The second factor has been Acehnese grievances. If we look solely at the funding of GAM, we can partly explain why GAM failed to start a civil war in 1976–79 (due to lack of funds) and why it succeeded in 1989–91 (due to Libyan assistance); but we cannot explain why GAM re-emerged in 1999 and grew so quickly, when it had no apparent source of start-up funds. Alternatively, GAM's "failure" in 1976–79 and "success" in 1989–91 and since 1999 can be partly explained by fluctuations in Acehnese grievances, which were low in 1976 (when the LNG plant opened), higher in 1989 (when resentments had accrued against the LNG facility and migrants), and very high in 1999 (against the LNG facility, migrants, the economic crisis, and military repression). The rise in grievances lowered the costs of recruitment for GAM, and made it easier for GAM to gain local support and financing.

The third factor was the demonstration effect of the independence referendum allowed in East Timor. Almost immediately after the East Timor referendum was announced, a large and influential pro-referendum movement formed in Aceh. The demonstration effect was not confined to Aceh; it also boosted a virtually dormant independence movement in West Papua.

The fourth additional factor has been the credibility of the central government, which has undermined its efforts to reach a settlement. Government credibility appeared to fall sharply from 1987 to 2003; as a result, its offer of "special autonomy" for Aceh was widely scorned in the province, even though it appeared to satisfy local demands for greater resource revenues and better protection against human rights abuses. Although GAM has been unwilling to compromise on its demand for independence, a credible autonomy offer could have weakened GAM's popular support and made recruitment and fund raising more costly.

Finally, this chapter suggests that Aceh's natural gas facility has played a critical role in the conflict, albeit not through the mechanism that the CH model predicts. Collier and Hoeffler (2001) suggest primary commodities increase the likelihood of civil war by enabling nascent rebel groups to fund their "start-up" costs by looting and selling these commodities.

If Collier and Hoeffler are correct, we should have observed GAM raising money from resource predation before the civil war began—anytime before 1990, or between 1992 and 1998. While GAM attempted to extort money during these periods from Aceh's commodity sector (including the LNG complex and the agricultural sector), there is little evidence that they succeeded. Only after the civil war was under way (in 1990–91 and 1999–2002) did their extortion efforts pay off. I conclude that the looting of resources did not contribute to the *onset* of civil war in Aceh, though it may have contributed to the *duration* once it began.

There are three alternative ways, however, that Aceh's natural resource wealth appeared to influence the conflict. The first was by creating grievances over the distribution of resource revenues and jobs. The claim that non-Acehnese are stealing Aceh's resource wealth has been a central part of GAM's rhetoric since its birth in 1976, just months before the LNG natural gas plant began operations. This belief is now widespread among the Acehnese, and has given them a financial incentive to support independence, which they might see as a rational investment in their future. Although the economic attraction of independence may have meant little while the economy was growing quickly in 1976–79 and 1989–91, it heightened the conflict risk after the economic crisis of 1997–98.

Second, Aceh's natural gas wealth increased the risk of conflict by producing a larger military presence in the province and by inducing a more repressive response from the government to early signs of unrest. The government has placed its Military Operations Command (*Kolakops*) for Aceh directly in Lhokseumawe, home of the LNG facility. Lhokseumawe is also the base for one of Aceh's two Sub-Regional Military Commands, Korem 011 (*Komando Resor Militer*) (Robinson 1998).

The military has long had a central role in managing the LNG facility, in part out of fear that grievances over the distribution of its revenues would lead to security disturbances. According to Emmerson, the military had a major role in the LNG facility beginning in the 1970s, because the government believed that,

> once those facilities have begun to fill central coffers with foreign exchange, the claims of regionalists to the income from "their" resources must be prevented from undermining the unity of the nation—or, from a regionalist perspective, the hegemony of the center. (Emmerson 1983, 1233)

Officers assigned to protect the Lhokseumawe facility have periodically been involved in the abduction, torture, and execution of Acehnese in neighboring areas, whom they suspect are sympathetic to or associated with GAM (*Business Week* 1998; Solomon 2000; *Tempo* 2001a). The district of North Aceh (where the LNG complex is located) has suffered more violence than any of Aceh's 13 districts. Even *before* the complex was targeted by GAM for shakedowns in early 2001, North Aceh had the greatest number of people killed and injured, the largest number of offices burned, and the largest number of schools burned of any district in Aceh. The number of homes and businesses destroyed in North Aceh was more than double the number in East Aceh, which was the next most damaged district (BPS Aceh 2000). In 2002 GAM had far more men, and far more weapons, in North Aceh than in any other district (Schulze 2004).

Finally, Aceh's resource wealth may be making the civil war harder to resolve, by reducing the credibility of the government's commitments to regional autonomy. Even though the government adopted a "special autonomy" law for Aceh in August 2001, the measure was greeted in Aceh with widespread skepticism. The credibility of the government's promises was exceptionally low in Aceh, due in part to the military's human rights abuses, and the failure of national politicians to keep their promises. It may have been lowered even further because Aceh's resource wealth caused its people to doubt that the cash-strapped central government would adhere to the plan for fiscal autonomy once the war was over.

## Notes

I am indebted to Ed Aspinall, Nils Petter Gleditsch, Nicholas Sambanis, and Kirsten Schulze for their helpful suggestions on this chapter.

1. For clarity I always refer to the organization as GAM, even though it now formally calls itself the Aceh Sumatra National Liberation Front, and refers to its army as AGAM (*Angkatan Gerakan Aceh Merdeka*).
2. Civil wars are generally defined as conflicts between a government and a rebel group that generate at least 1,000 combat-related deaths. On the definition of civil war, see Sambanis (2001).
3. For example, the German invasion of Poland in 1938—a country that was, like East Timor, temporarily annexed by its conqueror—could hardly be classified as German civil war.
4. I develop and illustrate the claim that natural resources can influence civil wars in different ways in Ross (2002, 2003).
5. The resource export-to-GDP figures, and all other economic data, are derived from data in World Bank (2001) unless otherwise specified.
6. While ethnic dominance matters at the national level by creating grievances among minority groups, it is hard to see how it would increase the risk of civil war *within* a restive province, when the province itself is largely populated by an ethnic minority. Hence, I do not consider it here as a risk factor.
7. Economic figures for Aceh must be treated with care, because the boom in natural gas production—which began in 1977—produced quickly rising figures for the province's GDP, even though the vast majority of this revenue accrued to the central government and was spent in other provinces. For this reason, I prefer to use figures that subtract out the value of oil and gas production.
8. The Aceh rebellion declared itself part of the Darul Islam rebellion, which began in West Java in 1947, so it is sometimes referred to as the Darul Islam rebellion; I refer to it here as the Daud Beureueh rebellion to distinguish it from the Javanese movement.
9. GAM often prefers "Acheh" to the more common "Aceh," and appears to use the term "Acheh-Sumatra" to indicate that it seeks independence for all of the island of Sumatra, much or all of which it believes should come under Acehnese rule. See di Tiro (1984, entry for August 20, 1977) and Aspinall (2002).
10. According to Sjamsuddin (1984, 128), the central government believed that if GAM won Daud Beureueh's backing, GAM would also receive broad support from the

Acehnese people—and "transform the movement into a holy war that would be very difficult to quell."

11. The gas field proved to be about 50 percent larger than initially estimated, holding perhaps 20–21 trillion cubic feet of gas.

12. Interview with anonymous former Mobil employee, May 3, 2000.

13. GAM initially railed against Mobil Oil and foreign exploitation of Aceh's resources; by the late 1990s, GAM had dropped its stance against Mobil, but insisted they should pay taxes to GAM, not the Indonesian government.

14. Data on Aceh's GDP is from internal World Bank documents.

15. According to Kell (1995), between 10 and 20 GAM members survived the 1980s in Aceh, hiding out in the forests and producing cannabis to support themselves.

16. These early attacks may not have been carried out by GAM, but by defecting security officers who were fighting the antinarcotics initiative. GAM was only identified as an active party in June 1990. This adds credibility to Geoffrey Robinson's hypothesis that GAM capitalized on the defection of corrupt security officers, perhaps taking advantage of the opportunity to launch a new offensive (Robinson 1998).

17. On the meaning of the term "DOM," see Widjajanto and Kammen (1999).

18. Two key weaknesses were the inability of elected officials to control the military and the instability of the policy-making process, which made the government's commitments less credible.

19. On this point, see Hiorth (1986), Liddle (1986), and Robinson (1998).

20. This argument is drawn from Fearon (2001), who suggests that separatist conflicts are difficult to resolve, in part, because government promises of regional autonomy typically lack credibility. He also notes that when a region has lots of resource wealth—like Aceh— a government's promises of fiscal autonomy will be even less credible, since locals will anticipate that the central government's desire for resource revenues will eventually cause it to rescind its pledges of local autonomy.

21. It is also possible, however, that the end of authoritarian rule allowed Acehnese to express their previously guarded support for independence. I thank Ed Aspinall for emphasizing this point.

22. Author interview, Medan, June 2000.

23. Ibid.

24. It is possible that GAM's re-emergence was facilitated by the Indonesian military, although the evidence is sketchy. Several observers note that in late 1998 and early 1999 the military did little to stop GAM's reappearance, and that the military stood to gain both politically and financially from renewed conflict. Alternatively, GAM may have simply taken advantage of the military's temporary weakness to organize itself.

25. Some of GAM's attacks on the LNG facility have other motives. GAM has periodically attacked military units that happen to be based at the plant. In October 2000, 17,000 sticks of dynamite were stolen from one of the plant's warehouses, although GAM may not have been the perpetrator. There may also be an ideological component to some of GAM's activities around the LNG complex: GAM officials continue to denounce ExxonMobil for "exploiting Aceh's land for the benefit of the colonialist government in Jakarta" (*Jakarta Post* 2001).

26. Author interview, Jakarta, June 2000.
27. Author interview, Banda Aceh, June 2000.
28. This is a time-honored method for generating support for social movements; scholars of social movements sometimes call it "countermobilization."

# References

AI (Amnesty International). 1993. "Shock Therapy: Restoring Order in Aceh, 1989–1993." AI Index, ASA 07/21/93.

Aspinall, Edward. 2002. "Sovereignty, The Successor State, and Universal Human Rights: History and the International Structuring of Acehnese Nationalism." *Indonesia* 73 (April), 1–24.

Aspinall, Edward, and Harold Crouch. 2003. "The Peace Process in Aceh." Monograph, Washington, DC: East-West Center Washington.

BPS (Badan Pusat Statistik) Aceh. 1999. *Buku Saku Propinsi Daerah Istimewa Aceh 1998*. Banda Aceh, Indonesia: BPS Aceh.

———. 2000. "Ekspose Gubernur." Jakarta, June 7.

BPS (Badan Pusat Statistik) Jakarta. 1999. *Statistik Indonesia 1998*. Jakarta: BPS Jakarta.

*Business Week*. 1998. "Indonesia: What Did Mobil Know?" December 28.

Central Bureau of Statistics, Indonesia. 1971. "Population of Indonesia 1971." Jakarta.

Cohen, Margot. 1999. "Captives of the Cause." *Far Eastern Economic Review*, September 2: 16–18.

Collier, Paul, and Anke Hoeffler. 2001. "Greed and Grievance in Civil War." Policy Research Working Paper 2355, World Bank, Washington, DC.

Davis, Anthony. 2001. "Thailand Cracks Down on Arms for Aceh." *Jane's Intelligence Review*, 13 (6): June 1.

Dawood, Dayan, and Sjafrizal. 1989. "Aceh: The LNG Boom and Enclave Development." In *Unity and Diversity: Regional Economic Development in Indonesia Since 1970*, ed. Hal Hill, 107–123. Singapore: Oxford University Press.

DeNardo, James. 1985. *Power in Numbers*. Princeton, NJ: Princeton University Press.

Dillon, Paul. 2001. "Strategy of Provocation That Keeps Aceh's War in Public Eye." *The Scotsman Online*, May 17.

di Tiro, Hasan. [1958] 1999. *Democrasi untuk Indonesia*. Jakarta, Indonesia: Teplok Press.

———. 1984. *The Price of Freedom: The Unfinished Diary*. Markham, Ontario: Open Press Holdings.

Djalal, Dini. 2000. "A Bloody Truce." *Far Eastern Economic Review*, October 5.

Emmerson, Donald K. 1983. "Understanding the New Order: Bureaucratic Pluralism in Indonesia." *Asian Survey* XXIII, November 11: 1220–41.

Fearon, James D. 2001. "Why Do Some Civil Wars Last So Much Longer Than Others?" Paper presented at the World Bank-UC Irvine Conference, "Civil Wars and Post-Conflict Transition," Irvine, CA, May 18.

Fearon, James D., and David D. Laitin. 2003. "Ethnicity, Insurgency, and Civil War." *American Political Science Review* 97 (1): 91–106.

Hegre, Havard, Tanja Ellingsen, Scott Gates, and Nils Peter Gleditsch. 2001. "Toward a Democratic Civil Peace? Democracy, Political Change, and Civil War, 1816–1992." *American Political Science Review* 95 (1): 33–48.

Hill, Hal, and Anna Weidemann. 1989. "Regional Development in Indonesia: Patterns and Issues." In *Unity and Diversity: Regional Economic Development in Indonesia Since 1970,* ed. Hal Hill, 3–54. Singapore: Oxford University Press.

Hiorth, Finngeir. 1986. "Free Aceh: An Impossible Dream?" *Kabar Seberang* 17: 182–94.

Human Rights Watch. 2001. "Indonesia: The War in Aceh." Available from www.hrw.org/asia/indonesia.php.

———. 2003. "World Report 2003: Indonesia." Available from http://hrw.org/wr2k3/asia7.html.

ICG (International Crisis Group). 2001a. "Aceh: Why Military Force Won't Bring Lasting Peace." ICG Asia Report 17, Jakarta/Brussels.

———. 2001b. "Aceh: Can Autonomy Stem the Conflict?" ICG Asia Report 18, Jakarta/Brussels.

———. 2002. "Aceh: A Slim Chance for Peace." Indonesia Briefing, March, 27, Jakarta/Brussels.

*Indonesian Observer.* 2001. "Army Chief Denies GAM Obtains Guns from Pindad." April 12.

*Jakarta Post.* 2001. " ExxonMobil Monitors Situation After Threat." January 5.

Kell, Tim. 1995. *The Roots of Acehnese Rebellion, 1989–1992.* Ithaca, NY: Cornell Modern Indonesia Project.

King, Dwight Y., and M. Ryaas Rasjid. 1988. "The Golkar Landslide in the 1987 Indonesian Elections." *Asian Survey* 28 (September 9): 916–925.

Liddle, R. William. 1986. "Letter from Banda Aceh." *Far Eastern Economic Review,* December 4: 90.

———. 1988. "Indonesia in 1987: The New Order at the Height of Its Power." *Asian Survey* 28 (February 2): 180–191.

Lubis, Rayhan Anas, Hendra Meehan, and Lyndal Meehan. 2000. "Aceh Rebels Receive Military Assistance." *Detikworld,* August 20.

McBeth, John. 1998. "An Army in Retreat." *Far Eastern Economic Review,* November 19.

McBeth, John, Syamsul Indrapatra, Nate Thayer, and Bertil Lintner. 1999. "Worse to Come." *Far Eastern Economic Review,* July 29: 16–19.

Reid, Anthony. 2000. "Which Way Aceh?" *Far Eastern Economic Review,* March 16: 36.

Robinson, Geoffrey. 1998. "Rawan Is as Rawan Does: The Origins of Disorder in New Order Aceh." *Indonesia* 66 (October): 127–156.

Ross, Michael L. 2002. "Oil, Drugs and Diamonds: How Do Natural Resources Vary in Their Impact on Civil War?" In *Beyond Greed and Grievance: The Political Economy of Armed Conflict,* ed. Karen Ballentine and Jake Sherman, 47–72. Boulder, CO: Lynne Rienner.

———. 2004. "How Do Natural Resources Influence Civil War? Evidence from Thirteen Cases." *International Organization* 58 (Winter): 35–67.

Sambanis, Nicholas. 2001. "A Note on the Death Threshold in Coding Civil War Events." *The Conflict Processes Newsletter,* June.

Schulze, Kirsten E. 2004. "The Free Aceh Movement: Anatomy of a Separatist Organization." Monograph, Washington, DC: East-West Center Washington.

Sjamsuddin, Nazaruddin. 1984. "Issues and politics of Regionalism in Indonesia: Evaluating the Acehnese Experience." In *Armed Separatism in Southeast Asia,* ed. Joo-Jock Lim and S. Vani, 111–128. Singapore: Institute of Southeast Asian Studies.

Solomon, Jay. 2000. "Mobil Sees Gas Plant Become Rallying Point for Indonesian Rebels." *Wall Street Journal,* September 7: 1.

*Tempo.* 2001a. "Violence at Multinationals." March 20.

———. 2001b. "Deaths in Tanah Gayo." July 10.

van Klinken, Gerry. 1999. "What Is the Free Aceh Movement?" *Inside Indonesia* 89 (November 25).

Vatikiotis, Michael. 1990. "Ancient Enmities." *Far Eastern Economic Review,* June 28: 12–13.

———. 1991) "Troubled Province." *Far Eastern Economic Review,* January 24: 20–21.

Widjajanto, Bambang, and Douglas Kammen. 1999 "The Structure of Military Abuse." *Inside Indonesia 62* (April–June).

World Bank. 1992. *World Development Report 1992.* New York: Oxford University Press.

———. 2001. *World Development Indicators 2001.* CD-ROM. Washington, DC: World Bank.

# The Lebanese Civil War, 1975–90 | 3

SAMIR MAKDISI AND RICHARD SADAKA

The Lebanese civil war broke out in April 1975, 29 years after the withdrawal of foreign troops from Lebanon in 1946. The civil war was finally settled in October 1989, under an accord of national reconciliation negotiated by the Lebanese Parliament under Arab auspices in the town of Taif, Saudi Arabia. This agreement, known as the Taif Accord, was ratified the same month by the Lebanese Parliament. Actual fighting did not completely end, however, until a year later, in October 1990.

This chapter analyzes the Lebanese civil war using the Collier-Hoeffler (CH) model. After explaining the prewar conditions, we discuss the identities, interests, and organization of the multiple parties to the war and identify three phases of the war. We then evaluate the fit of the CH model to this case and consider alternative explanations.

We find that religious, rather than ethnic, fractionalization was a key factor in the Lebanese civil war. External intervention was also crucial. Because economic explanations of the causes of the Lebanese war are weak, the CH model, which gives great weight to economic factors, does a poor job in predicting the outbreak of the war. Factors identified by CH as potentially affecting civil war duration are, however, helpful in explaining the relatively long duration of Lebanon's civil war. Finally, we briefly examine the goals and actual results of the Taif Accord. We offer an assessment of the likely stability of this "sectarian" resolution to the conflict, taking into account that, until very recently, there was a continued Syrian military presence and strong political influence in the country. Under strong international pressure, Syrian troops were forced to withdraw from Lebanon in April 2005, and consequently Syrian influence greatly diminished.

## Prewar Conditions

### Rapid Economic Growth

The prewar Lebanese economy grew rapidly during the years 1946–75. The private sector, which was primarily trade- and services-oriented, with no significant

natural resource wealth, played the dominant role in economic development. Governmental policy was mostly noninterventionist and supportive of private sector initiatives. Domestically, a conservative fiscal policy was followed. Monetary policy
began to play a role only toward the end of the prewar period. Public sector management of economic enterprises was confined to a few public utilities. Externally,
a free foreign exchange system had been maintained since the early 1950s, permitting the private sector to interact freely with the outside world. In sharp contrast, neighboring countries (and indeed many other developing countries at the
time) maintained exchange controls and gave the public sector the leading role in
economic development.

The Lebanese private sector traditionally has been enterprising. Under these
favorable conditions for private sector initiatives, the national economy experienced
a broad-based expansion in the prewar period, while maintaining relative financial
stability. Lebanon attracted foreign capital and enterprises supplemented by emigrant
remittances from the Lebanese diaspora, especially from those living in the United
States and South America. The average annual rate of growth from 1950 to 1974 was
about 7 percent. The annual rate of inflation was estimated to be about 2–3 percent
until 1971; after that it increased, averaging about 8 percent in the three years prior
to the outbreak of the civil war. Per capita income increased significantly, standing in
1974 at about $1,200, one of the highest levels for a developing country at that time.[1]
Educational standards were also relatively advanced; for the same year, gross school
enrollment for the first and second levels stood at 74 percent. Again, this was a higher
level than found in neighboring Arab countries, as well in many other developing
countries.

Despite the robust economic growth, important socioeconomic disparities
existed. They were manifest in the strikingly uneven development among the various regions of the country and in the limited progress made in narrowing the gap
between rich and poor. A study conducted in the mid-1970s indicates that for
1973–74 about 54 percent of the population could still be classified as poor or relatively poor, 25 percent as middle class, and the remaining 21 percent as well-to-do
and very rich.[2] This was an improvement over the situation prevailing in the early
1950s. Compared to other developing countries, this inequality was also not overly
pronounced (Harik 1985). However, it must be considered in the context of
Lebanon's regional inequalities and their confessional dimensions. For example, the
position of the middle class was much more salient in Beirut (dominated by Sunni
Muslims and Christians) and the central mountain region (dominated by Christians)
than in regions like the south, the Beqa', the northeast, and Akkar in the north (dominated by Shi'a and Sunni Muslims), where large land holdings and class distinctions
were common.[3] This gave a clear confessional hew to the question of inequity
in income distribution, particularly in regard to the Shi'a community. As we
argue below, it is religious division—not ethnic division as argued by Collier and
Hoeffler—that has had an important bearing on postindependence political developments in Lebanon.

## Major Political and Military Tensions

What is striking about the prewar phase is that, robust economic growth and rising per capita income notwithstanding, the country faced major political tensions and confrontations. The underlying reasons are both domestic and regional. The domestic factor was directly related to the sectarian system for power sharing, principally among the three leading religious communities (the Maronites, the Sunnis, and the Shi'a). This system has been in place since independence in 1943, although it was modified under the Taif Accord (the system remained consociational).

While the constitution of the newly independent state guaranteed equal rights to all citizens, Article 95 specified that, for a temporary but unspecified period, religious communities would be equitably represented in public employment and cabinet posts. The principle of equitable representation was not defined. However, an unwritten national accord reached among political leaders on the eve of independence specified that the post of president of the republic was to be held by a Maronite Christian, that of the speaker of the house by a Shiite Muslim, and the premiership by a Sunni Muslim. This arrangement was later incorporated in the Taif Accord. In practice, a sectarian formula was also applied to cabinet posts that, more often than not, were apportioned among the six largest religious communities in the country (and the Armenians who are considered a separate community). Other officially recognized religious communities were often excluded from cabinet representation. An overall balance between Christians and Muslims has been maintained in the cabinet to this day. Appointments to most, if not all, public administration positions have been subject to time-honored sectarian considerations, particularly higher positions that were to be equally apportioned between the two communities. Similarly, parliamentary seats were distributed among the various religious communities in accordance with an agreed sectarian formula which, on the whole, favored the Christian community. The Christian sects combined were entitled to 55 percent of the total number of seats.

The office of president carried with it substantial executive powers. For example, the president chaired the council of ministers and appointed the prime minister and cabinet members, albeit after due consultation with major political actors whose views could not be ignored. With such presidential (and other governmental) prerogatives, the Maronite community emerged as the single most influential religious community in the pre-1975 period. This was reinforced by the electoral law that assigned a small majority of parliamentary seats to the combined Christian communities led by the Maronite community. In practice, the powers enjoyed by the president's office translated into a comparative advantage in appointments for higher administrative positions.

Despite the presidential prerogatives, the need to preserve the delicate sectarian balance, particularly between the three major religious groups, acted as a check on the powers of the presidency. When sharp disagreements arose between the president and the prime minister, there were serious cabinet crises with sectarian overtones. More significantly, the sectarian balance implied that no one single political, religious, or politicoreligious group (including the army) could impose its hegemony or ideology. This, as it turned out, had its positive aspect in that it tended to promote political liberalism, albeit in the context of the prevailing sectarian system. The prewar years were characterized by periodic parliamentary elections (no matter how imperfectly conducted), religious freedom, relatively free expression and association, the peaceful change of presidents and cabinets, and the growth of sectarian and nonsectarian political parties. Nonetheless, the dictum of delicate sectarian balance led to the emergence of a weak state and, as a consequence, the inability to implement substantive administrative reforms. The prevailing political system tended to foster corruption, nepotism, clientism, and laxity in upholding the public interest when it conflicted with private interests (Picard 1996a).

Although the Lebanese political system was functional, it was increasingly strained. Foremost were the constant domestic political calls by Muslim political leaders for a more equal power sharing between Christians and Muslims. Such calls carried with them a potential shift of economic benefits in favor of Muslims, arising from greater access to public sector employment as well as opportunities to participate in or control private economic enterprises that were largely in the hands of the Christian community. The Maronite establishment tended to ignore such calls, fearing the political implications of even a limited loss of constitutional power. Additional strains emanated from the uneven development among the various regions and wide disparities in income distribution that led to migration from rural to urban centers and to the unchecked and rapid growth of poor suburbs around the major cities (Beirut in particular). Indeed, in 1974 the religious leader of the Shi'a community, Imam Musa al Sadr, launched a political movement, "Amal," as a political and economic thrust intended to enhance the position of the Shi'a community in the Lebanese sectarian system, as well as to act as a countervailing force to the growing influence of Palestinian organizations in southern Lebanon. Amal presented itself as a "movement of the dispossessed," and its appeal was to a large extent based on the lagging socioeconomic conditions of the Shi'a community in comparison with other communities in Lebanon.[4] It was to develop, especially after 1982, into one of the major warring factions in the Lebanese civil war.

External factors also placed increasing strains on the Lebanese political system. Principal among these factors was the rising military power of resident Palestinian organizations, particularly after the 1967 Arab-Israeli war. While their activity was ostensibly directed at keeping the Palestinian cause alive and continuing the struggle to reclaim Palestine, these organizations' presence in Lebanon became intricately linked to Lebanese domestic political affairs. The domestic and regional political agendas could hardly be separated. The prevailing weaknesses of the political system were exploited by Palestinian organizations to enhance their political and military positions. For this purpose, they forged alliances with disenchanted Lebanese sectarian (Muslim) and nonsectarian political parties, as well as with groups that regarded such an alliance as a means to pressure the Maronite establishment to accept political reforms. The nature of the desired reforms differed from one Lebanese political group to another. Leftist and other nonestablishment groups wished to introduce fundamental changes to render the system less confessional. Traditional Muslim groups aimed at readjusting the sectarian formula to ensure a distribution of power more favorable to the Muslim community. For both groups, political reforms would have offered wider economic opportunities.

This combination of domestic and external factors eventually led to the outbreak of war on April 13, 1975. On that day, armed clashes broke out in a Beirut suburb between members of the Maronite-dominated Kataeb (Phalange) party and members of Palestinian organizations. The leader of the Kataeb was scheduled to participate in the dedication of a new church in the Beirut suburb of Ain al-Rammaneh. As a security measure, the area surrounding the church was closed to traffic. On the morning of that day, an unidentified car attempted to break through a security checkpoint. The resulting gun battle left four people dead, including two Kataeb party members. Armed men from the Kataeb and National Liberal (Maronite-dominated) parties took to the street. On the afternoon of that day, a bus carrying 30 passengers (some armed) belonging to various Palestinian organizations passed through Ain al-Rammaneh. Shooting broke out, leaving 27 of the passengers dead.

The clouds of an impending armed conflict between Christian parties and Palestinian organizations had been gathering for a number of years, particularly after the expulsion of the Palestinian Liberation Organization (PLO) from Jordan in 1970. With this expulsion, southern Lebanon became in practice the only sanctuary for PLO operations against Israel, no matter what measures the Lebanese state undertook to control Palestinian military activity. Fueled by mutual mistrust and opposing objectives, periodic armed clashes took place between the Palestinians and the Lebanese army and/or Christian parties.[5] All efforts, domestic and Arab, aimed at reconciling existing differences failed to produce more than a temporary reprieve. This was the prevailing atmosphere prior to the clash in the Beirut suburb that ignited the civil war (see el Khazen 2000; Salibi 1976, 54–98).

## Combatants and Phases of the Civil War

### Combatants

Although there were two main warring camps, the combatants in the civil war included both major and minor militias and parties. The main traditional Christian (Maronite) parties included the Kataeb and National Liberal parties. These parties were forcibly united in 1980 into one organization called the Lebanese Forces, whose combined fighting force was estimated to be 8,000–10,000 fighters. Minor militias included the Marada Brigade (mainly Maronite, located in the northern town of Zogharta with 700–800 fighters) and the Guardians of the Cedars. The latter militia was mainly Maronite, with 500 fighters; it merged in 1980 with the Lebanese Forces. This camp favored the existing political system.

The opposing camp was more heterogeneous. Apart from the PLO, it included several Lebanese political parties and groups, notably Amal (Shi'a) and the Progressive Socialist Party (Druze). The Palestinian armed groups numbered close to 8,000 fighters prior to the Israeli invasion of 1982. They constituted the main fighting force in the early years of the conflict. As the war unfolded, the Lebanese armed groups became stronger, especially after the bulk of Palestinian forces had to withdraw from the country following the Israeli invasion. The Amal Movement fighters were estimated at about 3,500 and the Progressive Socialist Party fighters at more than 5,000. The last few years of the war witnessed the growth of the Hizbullah Party (over 4,000 fighters), which focused primarily on resisting Israeli occupation and therefore operated mostly in southern Lebanon. Other members of this camp included the Syrian Nationalist Party (800–1,000 fighters, secular), the Communist Party (600–700 fighters, secular), and the Mourabitoon (at their peak 3,000, Sunni, mostly in West Beirut) (see table 3.1 for figures and references).

The large militias developed into elaborate organizations. To support their military activities, they set up public relations, social services, and other administrative offices. Their fighters were organized into ranks. On average, a soldier's salary was usually $75–$150 per month, which was higher than the prevailing minimum wage. Low-ranking officers were paid $170–$200 per month, while higher ranking officers

## Table 3.1 War Period Militias

| | Major militias | | |
|---|---|---|---|
| | | Strength | |
| Name | Dominant religious affiliation | Fighters | Total military and civilian personnel |
| Amal | Muslim Shi'a | 3,000–4,000 (1) | 10,000 (3) |
| Hizbullah | Muslim Shi'a | 4,000–4,500 (1) | 18,000 (3) |
| Lebanese Forces | Christian Maronite | 8,000–10,000 (1) | 20,000 (3) |
| Palestinian Militias | | 8,000 (2) | |
| Progressive Socialist Party | Druze | 5,000–6,000 (1) | 16,000 (3) |
| South Lebanon's Army | Christian and Muslim Shi'a | 2,000–2,500 (1) | |
| *Estimated Total* | | *30,000–34,000* | *64,000* |

| | Minor militias | |
|---|---|---|
| Name | Dominant religious affiliation | Strength (number of fighters) |
| The Marada Brigade | Christian Maronite | 700–800 (1) |
| Zghorta Liberation Army | Christian Maronite | 700 (2) |

*(Continued)*

## Table 3.1 War Period Militias (*Continued*)

| | Minor militias | |
|---|---|---|
| Name | Dominant religious affiliation | Strength (number of fighters) |
| The Guardians of the Cedars | Christian Maronite | 500 (4) |
| National Liberal Party | Christian Maronite | 2,000 (2) |
| National Bloc | Christian Maronite | 200 (2) |
| Baath Party | Muslim | 500 (1) |
| National Syrian PPS | Secular | 800–1,000 (1) |
| Saiqa | | 500 (2) |
| The Communist Action Organization | Secular | 100–150 (1) |
| Lebanese Communist Party | Secular | 600–700 (1) |
| Lebanese Arab Army (LAA) | | 2,000 (4) |
| The Najjadah | Muslim Sunni | 300 (4) |
| The Murabitun (The Sentinels) | Muslim Sunni | 3,000 (4) |
| Firqat an Nasr (Victory Divisions) | | 1,000 (4) |
| Waad Party | Christian | 600–700 (1) |
| Tanzim Sha'bi Saida | Muslim Sunni | 500 (1) |
| Arab Democratic Party | Muslim Alawi | 500 (1) |
| The Order of Maronite Monks | Christian Maronite | 200 (4) |
| *Estimated Total* | | *14,700–15,250* |

*Sources:* (1) Hamdan (1997); (2) O'Ballance (1998); (3) Richani (2001); (4) Library of the Congress (1987).

received between $250 and $400 a month (Atallah 2001). It was quite common for militias' military personnel to earn an amount exceeding their regular salary from side activities, most of which were illegal. High wartime unemployment acted as an incentive for young men to join the militias. In addition to paying their fighters, militias bore other costs associated with military conflict; these included the cost of equipment, ammunition, transportation, training, food, and medical supplies. It is estimated that total military costs constituted 60 percent of the large militias' budgets.

The remaining 40 percent of the militias' expenditures were divided among two main activities. First, all militias had an "information office." The parties communicated with the general public through press releases, press conferences, newspapers (which civilians were frequently forced to buy), radio stations, and, in some cases, TV stations. Some militias also had representation abroad. It is estimated that such public relations activities constituted 20 percent of the large militias' budgets. Second, militias became increasingly involved in providing social services, especially after the collapse of the Lebanese currency in the mid-1980s. They often provided scholarships for children's schooling, medical assistance (clinics and subsidized medicine), and food subsidies. These social services, which constituted about 20 percent of large militias' budgets, helped to lessen the militias' unpopularity among the population in their areas of operation.

The Lebanese, Syrian, and Israeli armies were also directly involved in the war. Syria initially supported the Christian/government camp with direct military intervention, but subsequently shifted its support to the opposing camp. Israel invaded Lebanon more than once (the largest invasion took place in June 1982). It backed the groups opposed to the PLO and created, after 1982, the so-called South Lebanon Army (2,000–3,000 fighters, Shi'a and Christians) that controlled a southern strip of the country until April 2000. Throughout the war, other forms of external intervention took place, mainly via financial support.

The combatants in the civil war thus comprised a multitude of parties that could be divided into two main camps: one in support of the state and one opposed to it. Within each camp there occurred frequent intramilitia fighting. The war was thus not one pitting the state against a well-defined rebel group. There was extensive military intervention by neighboring countries in support of one camp or the other.

## Phases of the War

The civil war period can be divided into three phases. The first phase was 1975–77, comprising two years of war followed by a year of relative peace. Fighting was mainly between Christian parties allied with the government and the PLO and its Lebanese allies. Beirut was a divided city. The PLO/Lebanese coalition had effective control of West Beirut. The Lebanese army and traditional Christian parties were in control of East Beirut. Fierce battles took place between the Kataeb party and Palestinian groups at the outskirts of Beirut in areas that included Palestinian refugee camps. This fighting ended with the Kataeb in control of the refugee camps in the northeast suburbs of Beirut and the forced eviction of their residents. Christian towns south of

Beirut, notably Damour, were ransacked by Palestinian and Lebanese militias. Atrocities were committed by both sides.

In April 1976, Syrian forces entered Lebanon in support of the government and its political allies and clashed with the opposing PLO/Lebanese coalition (the so-called National and Islamic Forces). The objective of this intervention was to contain the expanding military dominance—and, by extension, political power—of the PLO and their Lebanese allies.[6] This was followed by an Arab summit meeting held in Riyadh in October 1976 that called for a cease-fire that was to be supervised and enforced by an Arab Deterrent Force (ADF) consisting of troops from Syria, Sudan, Saudi Arabia, and Yemen. In practice, the Syrian forces that made up the bulk of the ADF were already in Lebanon.[7] The other Arab troops arrived in November and, with their arrival, Beirut was reunified.

The second phase of the conflict was 1978–82, which politically and militarily ended with the Israeli invasion of Lebanon in June 1982. This period witnessed an escalation in fighting between the main parties to the conflict in Beirut and elsewhere in the country. Both Israeli and Syrian troops became involved in factional fighting.[8] A significant development in July 1980 was the success of Bashir Gemeyal, leader of the Kataeb militia, in uniting by force all Christian militias into one organization named the Lebanese Forces. The country became effectively divided into regions that were militarily controlled by Syria, the Lebanese army and Lebanese forces, and the PLO and the Lebanese parties allied with it. Beirut was again divided into an eastern part, controlled by the Lebanese Forces and the Lebanese army, and a western part, controlled by the PLO/Lebanese coalition.

The third phase, from June 1982 to October 1990, was one of large-scale external intervention. This period began with the Israeli invasion of June 6, 1982 and concluded when the fighting ended a year after the acceptance of Taif Accord of October 1989. Shortly after moving into Lebanon, Israeli forces reached the outskirts of western Beirut and laid siege to it for almost two months.[9] Fighting took place between the PLO, Lebanese parties, and the Israeli army, and between the Syrian and Israeli armies in the Beqa' valley. Eventually, the United States brokered an agreement in the summer of 1982 by which the PLO forces were forced to withdraw from western Beirut and Lebanon, while Syrian troops withdrew from West Beirut.

Israel attempted to impose a friendly government with the election of Bashir Gemayel as president by the Lebanese parliament on September 14, 1982. However, Bashir was assassinated before taking office. Israeli troops then entered into West Beirut and briefly occupied it.[10] Following the assassination of Bashir Gemayel, parliament again met on September 22 and elected Amin Gemayel (the older brother of Bashir) for a six-year term as president. In the meantime, four Western powers (the United States, Britain, France, and Italy) agreed to send troops to Lebanon, ostensibly on a peacekeeping mission, which had as one of its goals the protection of the refugee camps in the greater Beirut area following the withdrawal of the PLO. These forces departed in early 1984; their mission ended without accomplishing its main objectives.[11]

The newly formed government of Amin Gemayel entered into negotiations with Israel for a peace treaty which, among other things, called for the withdrawal of Israeli troops from Lebanon. There was strong opposition to this treaty from Syria and its local allies on grounds that it would put Lebanon under Israeli control and undermine Syrian-Lebanese relations, weakening the Arab struggle for Palestinian rights. While the treaty was approved by parliament on May 17, 1983, it was not signed by the president and, hence, was never enforced.

This phase witnessed fierce fighting, particularly in the summer of 1983, between the Progressive Socialist Party (Druze dominated) and the Lebanese Forces in the Shouf Mountains east and southeast of Beirut. The end result was a mass exodus of Christian communities from the region, the destruction of many Druze and Christian towns, and the killing of hundreds of civilians. Similarly, until February 6, 1984, greater Beirut was under the control of the government. On that day, the Lebanese army was forced to withdraw from West Beirut, which again came under the control of militias and political organizations opposed to the government (primarily Amal and the Progressive Socialist Party). The civil strife between East and West Beirut was reignited, but it was not simply between the main Lebanese parties to the conflict. Intramilitia fighting frequently took place in both parts of the city, especially in the more heterogeneous West Beirut.[12] At the request of authorities in West Beirut, Syrian forces reentered this part of the city in February 1987 to maintain order and prevent intramilitia clashes.

The failure to elect a new president in September 1988 led to a unique two-government situation. When the six-year term of President Amin Gemayel was about to end in September 1988 without agreement on a successor, he unilaterally appointed the commander of the army, General Michel Aoun, as president of a council of ministers composed of the six members of the army command. The three Muslim members of the appointed council refused to serve. The existing government at the end of Gemayel's term refused to acknowledge the legitimacy of the council appointed by Gemayel and considered itself as the sole legitimate government of the country. Hence, two competing governments emerged.

The government of General Aoun refused to acknowledge the Taif Accord ratified by the Lebanese Parliament in October 1989. After a period of ferocious fighting, first between the army led by Aoun and Syrian army units, and then between pro-Taif Maronite forces (most notably the Lebanese Forces) and the army led by Aoun, the latter was forced by a joint Syrian-Lebanese military action to take refuge in the French Embassy. He was allowed to leave the country in October 1990, and his departure paved the way for the unification of the Lebanese government and public administration.[13]

Given the intensification of the war, it is not surprising that the 1982–90 period witnessed rapidly deteriorating economic and social conditions along with accelerating emigration. After 1984, the value of the Lebanese pound declined rapidly in nominal and real value. This was a period of increasing budgetary deficits and mounting inflation. The heavy human and economic toll mounted as the war raged.

To sum up, the forced eviction of Palestinian camps from the eastern districts of suburban Beirut in the pre-1982 phase of the war led to the creation of a central zone (including Beirut) that was effectively under the control of the Lebanese authorities.

In the wake of the Israeli invasion, there was a short-lived and costly attempt by the Maronite-dominated Lebanese Forces to expand to Druze strongholds in the mountain districts to the east of Beirut. Their failure led to an exodus of Christian communities toward regions controlled by the Lebanese government and Christian militias. Soon afterwards, the civil war settled into a relatively stable pattern of territorial control that largely corresponded to sectarian divisions. Throughout this phase, there were occasional intrafactional armed clashes, culminating in the 1988–90 war among parties who controlled East Beirut and the surrounding eastern and northern suburbs. The costs of the war were large. By some estimates, more than 144,000 died as a result of the war (5 percent of the population)[14] and tens of thousands were forced to leave their homes and villages and seek refuge elsewhere in the country (Ministry of the Displaced, 1992). The economy was damaged and indirect costs (forgone production) are estimated at anywhere between US$80 and $160 billion (at 1995 prices).[15]

# Causes and Duration of the Civil War

## Onset of the War

The CH model relates the incidence of civil war to a number of variables, including a social fractionalization index, an ethnic dominance dummy variable, income and economic growth, natural resource wealth, and population size (Collier 2000; Collier and Hoeffler 2001, 2004). How well does the CH model fit the Lebanese case?

Religious fractionalization in Lebanon can be regarded in two ways: (1) the composition of the population into various Christian and Muslim sects (currently there are 18 officially recognized religious communities, with the Maronite, Shi'a, and Sunni communities taken together dominating with an estimated 70–80 percent of the population)[16]; or (2) its broad division between the Christian and Muslim communities, which at the time of the outbreak of the civil war was estimated to be in the neighborhood of 45–55 percent respectively.[17] In the evolving pre-1975 political environment, calls for more equitable sectarian political power sharing centered on increasing the political power of the Muslim community as a whole vis-à-vis the Maronite community. Although the importance of increased participation of the Shi'a community in the formula for power sharing was recognized, this did not become explicit until the Taif Accord. For analytic purposes, it is more appropriate to consider that Lebanon's religious "map" is composed of two broad religious communities. This is primarily the way that Lebanon's religious fractionalization is treated by CH.

The Lebanese population is ethnically (linguistically) homogeneous, thus ethnic fractionalization does not play a role in the war. The small Armenian community (less than 7 percent of the population) is fully integrated into Lebanese political life while maintaining its cultural heritage. Because the social fractionalization index is a combination of the indices of religious fractionalization and ethnic fractionalization, and because the latter is low, Lebanon's social fractionalization index is low as well (see tables 3.2 and 3.3).

## Table 3.2 CH Model Coefficients for Core and Alternative Models

| Model | secm | lngdp | gy1 | sxp | sxp2 | frac | etdo | peace | lnpop | geogia | constant |
|---|---|---|---|---|---|---|---|---|---|---|---|
| Core | -0.0316 | | -0.1152 | 18.937 | -29.4432 | -0.0002 | 0.6704 | -0.0037 | 0.7677 | -2.487 | -13.0731 |
| Alternative | | -0.9504 | -0.098 | 16.7734 | -23.8005 | -0.0002 | 0.4801 | -0.0038 | 0.5105 | -0.9919 | -3.4375 |

*Note:* See note to table 3.3 for definition of abbreviations.

## Table 3.3 Data on Lebanon

| Year | secm | rgdpa | gy1 | sxp | frac | etdo | peace | pop | geogia | psecm | pgdpa |
|---|---|---|---|---|---|---|---|---|---|---|---|
| 1970 | 49 | 1,474.51 | 1.875 | 0.05 | 938 | 0 | 136 | 2,617,140 | 0.645 | 0.00720 | 0.02615 |
| 1995 | 77 | 626.65 | 6.750 | 0.044 | 938 | 0 | 50 | 4,005,000 | 0.644 | 0.00296 | 0.05590 |

*Note:* Variable names are as follows: secm, secondary school enrollment for males; lngdp, log of real per capita income; rgdpa, real per capita income; gy1, growth rate of real income; sxp, primary commodity exports as a percent of GDP; sxp2, square of sxp; frac, social fractionalization; etdo, ethnic dominance; peace, time at peace since last civil war; lnpop, log of population size; geogia, geographic fractionalization. psecm and pgdpa denote the probability estimates of civil war onset predicted by the core and alternative models, respectively.

According to the CH model, the risk of conflict rises with ethnic dominance. Ethnic dominance is defined as a case in which the largest single group comprises between 45 and 90 percent of the population. Lebanon is not characterized by ethnic dominance. However, we may postulate that Lebanon's religious divisions are akin to ethnic-linguistic divisions in other countries that witnessed civil wars. Thus, the fact that at least one of the two main religious communities in Lebanon made up more than 45 percent of the total was akin to ethnic dominance. If we reoperationalize the dominance variable in this way, the CH model comes closer to capturing the roots of the Lebanese civil war.

The CH model also relates the incidence of war to income, economic growth, and natural resource wealth. When the war started, Lebanon, with a small population of under 3 million, had one of the highest per capita income levels in the region (and a high income level relative to developing countries in general).[18] We noted earlier that the national economy had been expanding at a fast rate before 1975. Expanding employment opportunities should have lessened the risk of war by increasing the opportunity costs of the war. There was also little class conflict, given the limited role played by leftist parties or the workers' movement. Indeed, once the war started, it was the underprivileged on both sides of the sectarian/political divide that fought one another while various warlords (most of whom fought the war under "national" slogans) exploited sectarian feelings to prolong the conflict in order to achieve their private interests (see Makdisi 1977). Finally, Lebanon is not resource-rich, so its risk of civil war according to the CH model should have been low (for 1973–74 primary exports constituted less than 3 percent of GDP).

The CH model generates a low probability of war in Lebanon. For 1970, the probability was very small (2.6 percent), lower than the mean probability of civil war for the countries in the CH data set (around 6 percent).[19] The probability on the eve of the war in 1974 cannot be calculated because the model uses data organized at five-year intervals and excludes years of ongoing war.[20] But, because underlying conditions did not change significantly, the probability of war in 1974 should also have been low.[21] What kept rising, however, was the underlying political tension.

The prediction of a low probability of war by the CH model for Lebanon is not surprising. The ethnic dominance dummy variable takes a value of zero. Other variables that point to a low incidence of war for Lebanon (in comparison with the countries that experienced civil wars) include a higher growth rate than the mean for those countries, a very low ratio of natural resource wealth to GDP,[22] a relatively small population, and a higher geographic dispersion. However, the social fractionalization index for Lebanon was higher and the time distance from a past recorded conflict (1958) was shorter. But the last two variables are noneconomic. In other words, the main causes of the civil war in Lebanon are political rather than economic. Equally important, the CH model does not account for external intervention, which for Lebanon, as well as many other countries, was an important factor in the onset and duration of civil war.

Similarly, the calculation for 1995 also points to a relatively low probability of war breaking out (5.6 percent). The factors that account for the rise in this percentage in comparison with 1970 include a shorter time period from the end of last conflict (1990), a larger population, and lower real per capita GDP.[23] The effect of these variables more than compensated for the effect of per capita real GDP growth, which was higher in 1990–94 than it was in 1965–69.

All the above estimates emerge from the GDP (or "alternative") version of the CH model. By comparison, the secondary school enrollment (or "core") version produces a probability of war for 1970 of 0.72 percent and a probability of war for 1995 of 0.3 percent. These very low numbers reflect the strong traditional emphasis on education in Lebanese society. Because of this emphasis, it may be that secondary school enrollment is not a good proxy for economic opportunity. The probabilities emerging from the GDP version seem more reasonable. If we gave weight to the results of the secondary school enrollment version, we would end up with extremely low probabilities of war. This would lend further support to the contention that the causes of the war in Lebanon are not well represented in the CH framework.

The CH model finds little correlation between political repression or other grievance and the incidence of war. Variables such as land or income inequality or the level of democracy are statistically insignificant.

For Lebanon, economic variables such as income, economic growth, and natural resource wealth, tend, according to the CH model, to decrease the probability of civil conflict. Nevertheless, other socioeconomic factors helped to create a crisis situation. The pre-1975 uneven development among Lebanon's regions and the accompanying socio/sectarian divisions were factors which, given the appropriate circumstances, could be exploited to support violent political change via the unleashing of sectarian conflicts. In the early 1970s, rising inflationary pressures added to the "explosive" potential of these divisions.

The Lebanese confessional system did not lead to the oppression of one religious group by another, as may be the case in countries with major ethnolinguistic conflicts. Indeed, major attributes of liberal democracy, such as freedom of expression and openness to the outside, have been maintained. However, the sectarian formula for power sharing agreed to on the eve of independence came to be regarded by the Muslim community as unjust and a cause for political grievance. While not advocating the elimination of the confessional system, most of the Muslim leadership (allying itself in the early stages of the war with the PLO) pressed for a modified formula of power sharing that would give them a bigger role in running the affairs of the state. This implied a corresponding change in their involvement in public administration and their relative share of the public sector. Similarly, increasing political power meant increasing opportunities for the Muslim community to participate more widely in the national economy.[24] However, this picture should not obscure the fact that some of the actors involved in the conflict (individuals and political groups) genuinely embraced a secular viewpoint and were motivated by nonsectarian ideologies. To them, the conflict was a means to change the sectarian order toward a more secular and equitable system. This did not materialize in the postwar era. If anything, the sectarian nature of political behavior has become more pronounced.

Our above analysis suggests that, of the variables in the CH model, it is religious (as opposed to ethnolinguistic) fractionalization that was important as a determinant of the Lebanese war and that the other variables are not relevant. But, as noted earlier, it was the combination of internal and external factors that brought about the onset of the war. The key external factor was the political/military stance of the PLO and its conflict with the state, which invited more external interventions. These interventions also influenced the duration of the war, which we turn to next.

## Duration of the Conflict

Factors that affect the onset of war need not also explain its duration. In particular, the level of income affects duration to a lesser extent than it does onset and war duration has a nonmonotonic relationship with ethnolinguistic and religious fractionalization. Also, the odds of peace decline radically after the first year of conflict (Collier, Hoeffler, and Soderbom 2001). Other authors in examining the subject of duration, emphasize the emergence of war economies, which provide an economic incentive for wars to continue (Keen 2000; Richani 2001). Finally, external intervention plays a significant role. The average length of a civil war that had external interventions was nine years, whereas wars in which there was no external intervention had an average length of 1.5 years (Elbadawi and Sambanis 2000).

The Lebanese civil war lasted for a relatively long time (16 years). This was much longer than the average duration for the civil wars that have taken place since the end of the World War II, namely two years. The broad religious divisions within Lebanese society seem to fit the general pattern of fractionalization which helps to prolong conflicts. Two additional factors played a significant role: economic greed and external interventions.

Once the civil war broke out, economic gains accruing to the warring parties became a major factor that sustained the war. The militias sought to enhance their economic/financial position by various means: looting, confiscation of private property, imposing taxes in the regions under their control, cultivation and trading of drugs, trading in contraband, outright thievery (including in 1975–76 the pillaging of the port of Beirut and the downtown district), bank robberies, and fraudulent banking practices. Warring parties stood to gain a great deal financially from the ongoing war (see tables 3.4 and 3.5).

There are no reliable and systematic data on the financial resources accruing to the militias during the civil conflict. Scattered estimates, however, are available. By one estimate, the militias were able to amass $15 billion during the war in addition to funds received from outside sources (Corm 1994, 216–218). A comparable estimate of $14.5 billion (for the aggregate turnover of the so-called black or informal economy) was published in *Annahar* daily newspaper.[25] Added to the external financial assistance provided by intervening outside powers, the major militias had sufficient resources at their disposal to finance their costly military and civilian operations, permitting (or inducing) them to sustain the long-lasting and profitable armed conflict. Substantial personal wealth was accumulated by the various militia leadership and their henchmen.[26]

*Table 3.4*  **Estimates of Financial Resources Accruing to Militias During the Civil War**

| Militia | Amount | Description | Frequency and time frame |
|---|---|---|---|
| Lebanese Forces | US$75 million (1) | Annual budget of the Lebanese Forces | Annual |
| Lebanese Forces | US$40 million (1) | Share of the annual budget used to equip the Lebanese Forces militia troups and pay for their salaries (55 percent) | Annual |
| Lebanese Forces | US$25 million (2) | Israeli direct military help to the Lebanese Forces | Annual; 1976–1982 |
| Lebanese Forces | US$80,000 (3) | Earnings from controlling various ports incl. the fifth basin of Beirut port | Monthly |
| Lebanese Forces | US$100 million (1) | Total investment of the Lebanese Forces | |
| Lebanese Forces | US$60 million (1) | Total investment of the Lebanese Forces in real estate | |
| Lebanese Forces | US$5 million– US$6 million (4) | Total expenditures | Monthly; 1988 |
| Lebanese Forces | US$20 million (4) | Occasional sales of arms in foreign markets | |
| Lebanese Forces | US$5 million (4) | Sale of weapons and ammunition to the Lebanese Army | |
| Lebanese Forces | US$65 (9) | Monthly salary of the fighters | Monthly |
| Lebanese Forces | US$150 million– US$200 million (4) | Estimated gross annual income | Annual, 1982–1989 |
| PSP | US$60,000 (3) | Earnings from controlling the ports of Jiyeh and Khalde | Monthly |
| PSP | US$75 (4) | Monthly salary of the fighters | Monthly |
| PSP | US$70 million– US$100 million (4) | Estimated gross annual income | Annual, 1982–1989 |
| PSP | US$70 million– US$100 million (4) | Income from the ports of Khaldeh and Jyeh, importation of fuel, industrial projects in Shouf, taxation, and foreign aid. | Annually |
| PSP | US$100 million (4) | Grant from the PLO | 1987 |
| PSP | US$40 million (4) | Grant from the PLO, of which the first installment was received | 1987 |

*(Continued)*

## *Table 3.4* Estimates of Financial Resources (*Continued*)

| Militia | Amount | Description | Frequency and time frame |
|---------|--------|-------------|--------------------------|
| PSP | US$35 million (4) | Grant received from Libya | 1987 |
| Hizbullah | US$23 million (4) | Financial support from Iran | Monthly |
| Hizbullah | US$3 million (4) | Funding from Iran allocated for the recruitment of 25,000 fighters, who each will be paid US$100 per month | Monthly, 1987 |
| Hizbullah | US$100 (4) | Monthly salary of the fighters | Monthly |
| Hizbullah | US$36 million– US$60 million (4) | Estimated gross annual income | Annual, 1982–1989 |
| Amal | US$75 (4) | Monthly salary of the fighters | Monthly |

*Sources:* (1) Le Commerce 26.05.89; (2) Picard (1996b); (3) *Les Cahiers de l'Orient. Revue d'étude et de réflexion sur le Liban et le monde arabe*, deuxième trimestre (1988), no. 10, pp. 271–287; (4) Richani (2001).
*Note:* PSP, Progressive Socialist Party.

External interventions, particularly those by Lebanon's two regional neighbors, were critical in sustaining the war. Intervention included the provision of arms and substantial financing of the warring parties. One source holds that foreign financial assistance to the warring parties totaled twice the amount they raised locally, or about $30 billion, if not more.[27] There were also military interventions by Syria and Israel, and as well as a multinational peacekeeping mission. As Syria and Israel supported opposing groups, a *modus vivandi* was created that contributed to a prolonged war as Lebanese parties could not independently reach a negotiated settlement.

The role of Lebanese and Palestinian diasporas in sustaining the violence cannot be easily measured. The warring parties attempted to secure assistance from their respective communities abroad. This support took the form of political lobbying and/or propaganda, as well as financial assistance. No estimates of the inflow of these financial resources are available, but it is known, for example, that Palestinians working in Kuwait were subject to a tax on their earnings earmarked for the PLO. The impact of the Lebanese and Palestinian diasporas on the civil war was probably minor. Active support of the warring militias among the diaspora was in all likelihood confined to small groups.

The Lebanese case exhibits a perhaps atypical level of factionalism. There were multiple parties to the war that frequently broke down in intrafactional violence. Even the government(s) whose composition reflected sectarian divisions often included members who were sympathetic to the cause of the groups opposing the state. Governmental institutions kept functioning in various parts of the country controlled

*Table 3.5* **Estimates of Financial Resources Accruing to Militias During the Civil War**

|  | | | | Source I | | | | |
|---|---|---|---|---|---|---|---|---|
| Arms trade | Looting | Exploitation[a] | Smuggling | Bribes and extortion[b] | Ports | Drugs | Political money and military resources | Total |
| Average US$400 million Minimum US$100 million Maximum US$800 million Annually, 1975–1990 | Gross value of looted property US$2 billion of which US$500 million accrued to looters Annually, 1975–1990 | Profits US$50 million Annually, 1975–1990 | Illegal exports of fuel US$40 million Total, 1980–1989 | US$200 million Annually, 1975–1990 | Loss of tariff revenues of legal ports[c] Minimum US$15.5 million Maximum US$19.5 million Annually, 1975–1990 | Total exports[e] US$1.7 billion Total as of 1985 | US$10 billion 1975–1991 | Turnover of the Black Economy US$14.5 billion 1975–1990 US$900 million[f] Annually, 1975–1990 |
| Earnings from arms trade exceeded US$150 million Annually, 1975–1990 | | | Earnings from illegal exports of subsidized wheat US$20 million Total, 1987–1990 | | Average earnings from unloading, loading, and transport in illegal ports US$2 million Annually, 1980–1989 and US$8 million Annually, 1987–1989 Illegal earnings[d] US$2.1 billion Total 1975–1990 | | | |

Source II

| Pillaging[g] | Ransoms[h] | Embezzlement of banks[i] | Drugs and contraband | Confiscation of army arsenal | Total |
|---|---|---|---|---|---|
| Minimum US$5 billion Maximum US$7 billion Total, 1975–1990 | US$500 million Total, 1975–1990 | US$250 million 1982–1983[j] | Earnings from trade in drugs Minimum US$700 million Maximum US$1 billion Annually, 1975–1990 | Value Unknown[k] | Total earnings US$5 billion 1975–90 |

*Sources:* Source I: *Annahar,* October 15, 1990, p. 8; Source II: Corm (1994).

a. Exploitation includes imports and sale of expired medical supplies, imitation of products and selling them as originals, bank notes forgeries (esp. US dollars), etc.

b. Source I also reports that during 1975–90, illegal commissions on governmental projects and purchases totaled US$600 million and accrued to 200 government officials.

c. Due to the existence of illegal ports.

d. Earnings created by avoiding the payment of port charges and custom fees, both of which had generated abnormal profits for industrialists, merchants, and importers.

e. Another source, Couvrat and Pless (1993), estimates profits accruing from the drug business at US$2 billion for the period 1975–90.

f. Another source, Richani (2001), estimates the war economy's money circulated at US $900 million per year between 1978 and 1982, of which US $400 million was circulated by the PLO, US $300 million was donated by foreign sources to different militias, and US $200 million was acquired by militias from internal Lebanese sources through various means, including extortion, drug trafficking, and contraband.

g. Includes pillaging of the Beirut Port (1976), looting of the downtown district (1975/76), and confiscation of property.

h. Revenues from imposed tolls and taxes are not quantified.

i. In April 1976, the British Bank of the Middle East was subject to armed robbery. Estimates of stolen cash range from US$20 million to US$50 million. (*Source:* Fawaz 1993).

j. This figure pertains to the reserves embezzlement from the First Phoenician Bank and Capital Trust Bank.

k. Source II mentions that in the period 1982–83, the Lebanese army purchased about US$1 billion worth of arms from the United States, presumably as replacement for the confiscated arms and equipment.

by different sects/parties and paid the wages of their employees irrespective of their
political loyalties and the areas in which they served. Furthermore, external inter-
veners at times shifted their support from one side to another. For example, the
initial direct Syrian intervention in the early stages of the war was in support of traditional Maronite parties but later shifted to supporting groups opposing the
Maronites. Similarly, Israel, initially supported traditional Christian parties that fought
the Palestinians, but eventually created a surrogate army in the south that included
both Christians and Muslims.

## Resolving the Conflict: The Taif Accord and Beyond

The settlement under the Taif Accord was based on the reaffirmation of the principle of sectarian power sharing, albeit with a modified formula. The Accord drew on
earlier reform plans that, for various domestic and external reasons, could not be
implemented. The most significant of these was the Syrian-sponsored 1985 Tripartite
Agreement (between the Lebanese Forces, Amal, and the Progressive Socialist Party
militias), which proposed constitutional amendments, a number of which were similar to those subsequently adopted in the Taif Accord (Mailat 1992).

Although the Lebanese parties to the conflict might, after 16 years of war, have
become exhausted and ready to reach a settlement, it took external pressure to conclude the war. This was largely prompted by the Iraqi invasion of Kuwait in August
1990. This event encouraged outside powers (both Arab and Western) involved or
concerned with the Lebanese conflict to help settle it as a prelude to the launching
of the Allied campaign led by the United States to liberate Kuwait at the beginning
of 1991. Syria, a main actor in Lebanon's civil conflict, was one of the Arab countries
that supported this campaign. As noted earlier, the ratification of the Taif Accord did
not lead to the cessation of hostilities in Lebanon until the ouster of General Aoun
in October 1990 through direct Syrian military action undertaken with tacit U.S.
approval.[28]

The Accord created a more equitable sectarian formula for power sharing among
the two main religious communities by enhancing the position of the prime minister (Sunni Muslim), as well as that of the speaker of the house (Shi'a Muslim), and
curtailing some of the privileges that the president (Maronite) had enjoyed. For
example, the new Taif constitution stipulates that the appointment of the prime minister is to be determined by binding consultation with members of parliament, which
the president is required to conduct for this purpose. To that extent, the prime minister is no longer beholden to the president, as before, for his appointment. Also, the
council of ministers, which collectively was given wide executive powers, is chaired
by the prime minister unless the president chooses to attend its meetings, in which
case the president chairs. In practice, with some exceptions, the president has, so far,
chaired council meetings. As for the speaker of the house, his term of appointment
was extended from one to four years, which effectively freed him from the pressures
associated with one-year appointments. Furthermore, instead of the small advantage
previously enjoyed by the Christian community in parliament, the Accord specified

equal representation for the two communities. This same principle continued to apply to the council of ministers.

The essence of the political system, thus, remained unchanged. However, by read-justing the basis for sectarian power sharing, the Accord envisaged, in principle, a more collegial political governance among the major religious communities and, hence, a firmer basis for domestic political stability. One major manifestation of this anticipated collegiality is the enhanced power of the council of ministers, which is supposed to act as a collective governing body. In contrast with parliamentary acts that are taken by majority vote, the new constitution specifies that decisions of the council of ministers are to be arrived at by consensus and only failing that by major-ity vote. For "fundamental" questions facing the country, failing consensus, a major-ity of two-thirds is required, subject to parliamentary approval.[29] Significantly, the Taif Accord allowed for a temporary stay of Syrian troops in Lebanon to help the Lebanese authorities establish law and order; the eventual withdrawal of these forces was to be subject to the mutual agreement of the Syrian and Lebanese governments. As would be expected, until forced to withdraw in April 2005, Syria had exercised substantial political influence in postwar Lebanon.

A recent study on the successful settlement of civil wars argues that whatever rea-sons bring combatants to the negotiating table and their signing of power sharing pacts, the successful resolution of such wars would still require third-party security guarantees concerning the safety of the combatants and the enforceability of the agreed pacts.[30] The Taif Accord, which allowed for the presence of Syrian troops in Lebanon (albeit on a temporary basis), seems to support this conclusion. On the other hand, it is also important to understand the nature, extent, and duration of third-party (external) security intervention. The Lebanese case demonstrates that this interven-tion could go beyond its originally intended objectives. In as much as third-party security guarantees may be necessary to help postconflict governments enforce power-sharing pacts and maintain domestic peace, it is equally important to ensure that the third party entrusted with this task does not, for self-serving reasons, become perennially embroiled in domestic political processes and outcomes. This, of course, would depend on the nature of the agreed political compromises that paved the way for the resolution of civil conflicts and whether they are inherently stable in the long run—a matter that we cannot go into here.

In the case of Lebanon, the collegiate governance in the post-Taif period has not been successful so far. In particular, the council of ministers has not come to assume the enhanced role assigned to it in the constitution. Instead, the phenomenon of "troika rule" (the troika comprising the president of the republic, the speaker of the house, and the prime minister) emerged and has tended to dominate political life, particularly after 1992. Effectively, it undermined the privileges that the Taif Accord granted to the council of ministers as a collective governing body and diminished the role of individual cabinet members in decision making. Without going into the reasons that led to the troika rule, what is significant is that disagreements among council members were not necessarily settled within the council of ministers or parliament, but outside these institutions through reliance on the de facto "troika" system. Failing such a resolution, resort to Syrian mediation became necessary or mandatory in order to settle existing disputes. With Syria playing the role of the influential arbiter, domestic political flare-ups were not permitted to disrupt the political process.[31]

This, in turn, raises a fundamental question concerning the long-term workability of the Taif Accord in the absence of an outside steadying or arbitrating hand. Does it constitute the ultimate political framework that will ensure stability in the long run? While the diffusion of political power among the main religious communities was intended to contribute to sectarian stability, the post-Taif political experience reveals the persistence of potential sectarian elements of instability (though in the Lebanese case, as amply demonstrated, domestic stability cannot be isolated from regional influences). The question remains whether, in the absence of destabilizing external influences, the post-Taif political system is sufficiently viable to withstand internal shocks without outside assistance.

From the end of the civil war until April 2005, Syrian involvement was a major factor in determining political outcomes. Now that Syrian troops have withdrawn, the workability of the Lebanese system under the condition of greatly diminished Syrian influence is yet to be tested. Even if it is correct, as some argue, that the lack of firm stability in the post-Taif era, in large measure, was attributable to the dominating Syrian military and political presence, this would not negate the existence of elements of potential instability associated with the nature of the political system itself. For whatever its merits, the finely tuned sharing of political power among Lebanon's religious communities is inherently discriminatory. Conflicts among the various political and sectarian leaders have arisen, and can arise again in the future, over what they consider to be the rightful share of the religious community that each represents in managing the affairs of the state. Sectarianism has continued to act as the mainstay of political behavior. The Taif settlement notwithstanding, there is no guarantee that, as in the past, sectarianism will not be a destabilizing influence.

The question of how to move from a discriminatory sectarian system to a more stable nondiscriminatory political system or, alternatively, how to husband the present system to render it more stable, falls outside the purview of this chapter.[32] Nonetheless, we can postulate that the prewar circumstances that led to the civil war are not as relevant in the postwar period. Calls for more equitable power sharing among the major religious communities have been met. The Palestinian factor is no longer significant and the regional conflict is no longer as salient in Lebanese politics. In the absence of active destabilizing external influences, it is doubtful that the remaining potential elements of domestic instability mentioned above—most notably religious fractionalization—would, on their own, lead to a renewal of civil conflict. But this is a matter that requires further study before arriving at firm conclusions.

In addition, Lebanon's trade- and services-oriented economy, the traditionally dominant private sector, and the country's high educational attainment make a recurrence to war unlikely, because such a course would have high economic opportunity costs.

# Conclusions

The CH model is based on a simple portrayal of a war between the state and a single rebel group. This is, of course, oversimplification. The Lebanese case highlights the complicated dynamics that result from competition among several warring groups and their allies.

Religious fractionalization appears as an important cause of civil conflict in the Lebanese case, but it has not been fully examined in the CH model or in the literature more generally. It is not clear, for example, if religious fractionalization would have been as important a factor in Lebanon if the political system had been secular (nonsectarian). More cross-country research is needed to determine whether religious dominance plays the same role as ethnic dominance and under which conditions it can fuel civil war. Our study suggests that an interactive effect between educational attainment and religious dominance deserves further attention.

Repeated and competing external interventions played a major role in provoking, prolonging, and ending the civil war in Lebanon. Until its withdrawal in April 2005, Syrian military presence in the postwar period exerted significant influence over domestic politics. For Lebanon, the question that needs to be addressed is whether the post-Taif Accord political system is sufficiently viable to withstand internal shocks without some form of external involvement. If not, which political reforms are necessary to make the system viable?

More generally, this raises the related question of how to ensure that third-party security guarantees, which may be necessary to resolve civil conflicts and ensure the enforceability of power-sharing pacts in the immediate postconflict era, do not themselves permit or induce the guarantor to become embroiled in domestic political issues in pursuit of specific objectives, such as enduring political dominance. This may be especially relevant in cases where ethnolinguistic or religious factors had played an important role in the onset of such conflicts.

Economic motives for civil war were weak in this case. We can immediately discount the influence of natural resources. As the Lebanese economy was and remains heavily dependent on trade and services, the policy issue of diversification for the purpose of reducing the risk of potential conflict associated with natural resources does not arise. The rate of growth preceding the conflict pointed to lower, rather than a higher, risk of civil war. We, therefore, need to consider both the grievance (political agenda) and greed (economic agenda) elements in interaction. Once the civil war broke out, economic factors played an important role in prolonging its duration.

# Notes

1. For a review of the prewar economy, see Badre (1972) and Makdisi (1979).
2. See Schmeil (1976), quoted in Labaki and Rjeily (1993, 182).
3. On prevailing prewar conditions in the south, see Sâlih (1973).
4. However, the wide cultural and professional gap between Christians and Muslims at the beginning of independence was progressively reduced over the period under consideration. See, for example, Labaki and Rjeily (1993, 185).

5. Military confrontations took place between the Palestinian military organizations and the Lebanese Army in 1968 and 1969. The conflict was settled with Egyptian mediation in November 1969. While the PLO would nominally respect Lebanese sovereignty, the agreement allowed a measure of freedom for Palestinian groups taking action against Israel from Lebanese soil. Increased Palestinian activity brought them in armed conflict with Lebanese security forces and Christian parties.

6. A new president of the republic, Elias Sarkis, was elected by parliament in September 1976. He succeeded Sulieman Frangieh, whose six-year term had ended.

7. The ADF force consisted of 30,000 men, of whom 27,000 were Syrians.

8. For example, in March 1978, Israel invaded southern Lebanon. This military action resulted in 2,000 deaths and 250,000 displaced persons and ended with the deployment of UN troops on the Lebanese Israeli border. In 1980, Syria concentrated troops in the Beqa' valley and clashed with Kataeb militia entrenched in the city of Zahle near the Beirut-Damascus highway.

9. The invasion brought economic havoc in its wake. Estimates of damage to physical property alone exceeded $2 billion. See Council for Development and Reconstruction, *The Reconstruction Project,* April 1983, I.5.

10. The well-publicized massacres took place in the refugee camps Sabra and Chatila while the Israeli army was still in control of West Beirut.

11. U.S. and French army barracks were the target of suicidal attacks in October 1983 that resulted in high troop casualties. These incidents hastened their decision to withdraw. Prior to that, in April 1983, the U.S. Embassy located in West Beirut was blown up. It was later relocated to the eastern suburbs of Beirut.

12. After the Israeli invasion, Hizbollah, supported by Iranian funding, began to grow in the southern suburbs of Beirut and in Shi'a-dominated regions of the country. It frequently clashed with Amal in West Beirut for control of the Shi'a community. Clashes also occurred between the Progressive Socialist Party and Amal. During intramilitia warfare, the smaller Sunni militia, the Mourabitoon, was defeated. Intramilitia fighting occurred throughout the war not only in Beirut but also in other parts of the country.

13. As noted above, Syrian troops (which had originally entered Lebanon in 1976, the second year of the civil war) continued to be deployed in Lebanon until April 2005. Earlier, in May 2000, Israeli troops and their surrogate army had been forced to withdraw from the occupied areas in the southern part of the country under constant attacks from resistance groups, especially Hizbollah.

14. See report published in "Annahar," March 5, 1992. The figure excludes the death toll in Palestinian camps. The report cites a total of more than 184,000 injured, more than 17,000 who disappeared, and more than 13,000 who were maimed.

15. These are adjusted estimates based on available estimates for forgone production at 1974 prices. See Makdisi (2004, chapter 2).

16. Each of these communities probably constituted between 20 and 30 percent of the total population.

17. The last population census was conducted in 1932. Hence, no official estimates on the religious composition of the population have been available since that time.

18. For 1973–74, the two years preceding the outbreak of the civil war, estimates of real per capita gross domestic product (GDP) range from $1,000 to $1,300 (1974 prices).

19. Estimates obtained from Anke Hoeffler.

20. Calculating a probability of war for 1975 would be a misapplication of the CH model, which deals with the probability of a war starting in the subsequent five-year period beginning from a situation of peace. Lebanon was already at war in 1975.

21. Real per capita GDP was roughly 20 percent higher in 1974 than it was in 1970, while the average per capita real GDP growth in 1970–74 was approximately 45 percent higher than it was in 1965–69. The population increased by about 10 percent from 1970 to 1974.

22. According to the CH model, the incidence of civil war is likely to have a nonmonotonic relationship with the level of natural resources.

23. These variables are listed in order of increasing strength. In other words, the variable that played the greatest role in making the probability of war higher in 1995 than in 1970 was per capita GDP, followed by population, and so on.

24. In the private sector, Christian dominance of the economy declined over time as the Muslim communities grew in political and educational stature.

25. Issue of October 15, 1990, p. 8. One source reports that PLO investments in Lebanon—largely financed by Arab countries—were estimated at about $1.46 billion in the early 1980s (see Hamdan 1997).

26. Estimates of the direct costs of the war vary. Tarabulsi (1993) estimates the cost of a day's fighting at $150,000—$500,000. Picard (1996b) puts the cost of the war at $150 million to $1.5 billion a year. Assuming an annual average of $800 million, this implies a total loss of around $13 billion for the entire war.

27. See Corm (1994, 218). Some estimates put Libyan financial assistance to the PLO and their Lebanese allies at about $50 million a month, at least prior to 1982, which adds up to a total of $4.8 billion from 1975 to 1982. For the whole war period, *Annahar* (see note 25) estimates the total of political money and military resources at about $10 billion. Another source quotes an estimate of $300 million for the annual inflow of political money prior to 1982, for a total of $2.7 billion. See Nasr (1989).

28. After more than 14 years in forced exile, Aoun returned to Beirut on May 7, 2005 following the withdrawal of Syrian troops in the preceding months.

29. For a critical assessment of the Taif Accord, see Mailat (1992, 53–58).

30. See Walter (2002, 90–91 and 160–161).

31. Syria's substantial influence in Lebanon was publicly acknowledged and often referred to in the local press. On August 18, 1998, *An-Nahar,* daily, headlined its commentary on the local situation: "Syria is no longer embarrassed in declaring its choice of the new president." In Lebanese diplomatic jargon, Syria's accepted role as an arbiter and dispenser of advice to Lebanese politicians and officials was subsumed under close cooperation and coordination between the two countries, particularly when invoked in the context of Israeli plans to destabilize the Lebanese domestic situation.

32. Barbara Walter (2002, 167–168) notes that consociational power-sharing solutions are appealing to groups who fear political domination. But power-sharing pacts are not stable over time unless they evolve into liberal, open political institutions. For a relevant discussion and application to Lebanon, see Makdisi (2004, chapter 5).

# References

Atallah,Tony. 2001. "The Organization of the Internal War: A Modern Conflict Strategy in a Diverse Society (The Lebanese Case, 1975–1990)." Doctoral dissertation. Lebanese University, Beirut.

Badre, Albert. 1972. "Economic Development of Lebanon." In *Economic Development and Population Growth in the Middle East,* ed. C. A. Cooper and S. A. Alexander. New York: Elsevier.

Collier, Paul. 2000. "Economic Causes of Civil Conflict and Their Implication for Policy." In *Managing Global Chaos,* ed. C. Crocker, F. Hampson, and P. Aall, 143–82. Washington, DC: U.S. Institute of Peace.

Collier, Paul, and Anke Hoeffler. 2001. "Greed and Grievance in Civil War." Policy Research Working Paper 2355, World Bank, Washington, DC.

———. 2004. "Greed and Grievance in Civil War." *Oxford Economic Papers* 56 (4): 563–95.

Collier, Paul, Anke Hoeffler, and Måns Soderbom. 2001. "On the Duration of Civil War." Working Paper, World Bank, Washington, DC.

Corm, G. 1994. "The War System: Militia Hegemony and the Re-establishment of the State." In *Peace for Lebanon? From War to Reconstruction,* ed. D. Collings, 215–230. Boulder, CO: Lynne Reinner Publishers.

De Soysa, I. 2000. "The Resource Curse: Are Civil Wars Driven by Rapacity or Paucity." In *Greed and Grievance: Economic Agendas in Civil Wars,* ed. M. Berdal and D. M. Malone, 113–36. Boulder, CO: Lynne Reinner Publishers.

Elbadawi, I., and N. Sambanis. 2000. "External Intervention and the Duration of Civil Wars." Paper presented at the World Bank Conference on the "Economics and Politics of Civil Conflicts," Princeton University, Princeton, NJ, March 18–19.

el Khazen, Farid. 2000. *The Breakdown of the State in Lebanon, 1975–1976.* London: I. B. Taurus.

Fawaz, N. 1993. "Traboulsi: De la violence. Fonctions et rituels." In *Stratégie II, Peuples Méditerranéens,* 57–86. Paris: Editions Anthropos.

Gleditsch, N. P., H. Strand, M. Eriksson, M. Sollenberg, and P. Wallensteen. 2000. "Armed Conflict 1946–99: A New Dataset." Paper presented at the World Bank Conference on "Identifying Wars: Systematic Conflicts Research and Its Utility in Conflict Resolution and Prevention," Uppsala University, June 8–9.

Hamdan, Kamal. 1997. *Le conflit Libanais: Communautes religieuses, classes sociales, et identite nationale.* France: Garnet Editions.

Harik, Iliya. 1985. "The Economic and Social Factors in the Lebanese Crisis." In *Arab Society, Social Science Perspectives,* ed. S. Ibrahim and N. Hopkins, 412–31. Cairo: The American University in Cairo Press.

Keen, David. 2000. "Incentives and Disincentives for Violence." In *Greed and Grievance: Economic Agendas in Civil Wars,* ed. M. Berdal and D. M. Malone, 19–41. Boulder, CO: Lynne Reinner Publishers.

Labaki, B., and K. Abou Rjeily. 1993. *Bilan des Guerres du Liban, 1975–1990.* Paris: Editions L'Harmattan.

Library of the Congress. 1987. "Country Report: Lebanon." Available online at: www.memory.loc.gov/frd/cs/lebanon/lb_appnb.html.

Mailat, Joseph. 1992. *The Document of National Understanding, a Commentary.* Beirut: Center for Lebanese Policy Studies.

Makdisi, Samir. 1977. "Economic Aspects of the Lebanese Crisis." In *The Lebanese Crisis.* Cairo: Arab Organization for Education, Culture and Science. (in Arabic)

———. 1997. *Financial Policy and Economic Growth, the Lebanese Experience.* New York: Columbia University Press.

———. 2004. *The Lessons of Lebanon: The Economics of War and Development.* London: I. B. Tauris.

Ministry of the Displaced. 1992. "The Movements and Regions of the Displaced." In *The Issue of Displacement in Lebanon, 1975–1990.* Beirut, Lebanon: Ministry of the Displaced.

Nasr, Salim. 1989. " The Political Economy of the Lebanese Conflict." In *Politics and The Economy in Lebanon,* ed. N. Shehadi and B. Harny. Oxford: Center for Lebanese Policy Studies.

O'Ballance, E. 1998. *Civil War in Lebanon, 1975–92.* Houndmills Basingstoke Hampshire: Macmillan.

Picard, Elizabeth. 1996a. *Lebanon, A Shattered Country.* New York: Holmes and Meier.

———. 1996b. "Liban: La matrice historique." In *Economie des guerres civiles,* ed. Jean Ruffin, 62–103. Paris: Hachette.

Reynal-Querol, M. 2002. "Ethnicity, Political Systems and Civil Wars." *Journal of Conflict Resolution* 46 (1): 29–54.

Richani, Nazih. 2001. "The Political Economies of the War Systems in Lebanon and Colombia." Paper presented at the World Bank Conference on the "Economics of Civil Wars," Oslo, June 11–13.

Salibi, Kamal. 1976. *Cross Roads to Civil War, Lebanon 1958–1976.* Beirut: Caravan Books.

Sâlih, Farhân. 1973. *Lubnân al- Junûbî, wâqi'uha wa qadâyâhû [Southern Lebanon, Its Reality and the Issues It Faces].* Beirut: Dar Al Talia.

Schmeil, Yves. 1976. *Sociologie due system politique Libanais.* Grenoble: Universitaire de Grenoble.

Tarabulsi, F. 1993. *Identites et solidarites croisées dans les conflits du Liban contemporain.* Doctoral dissertation, University of Paris VIII.

Walter, Barbara. 2002. *Committing to Peace: The Successful Settlement of Civil Wars.* Princeton, NJ: Princeton University Press.

# Crime, Violence, and Political Conflict in Russia

4

YURI ANDRIENKO
AND LOUISE SHELLEY

Russia's historically high levels of violent crime and political violence had been suppressed by Soviet authorities, but reemerged with the liberalizations of the late 1980s and 1990s. In the wake of the dissolution of the Soviet Union, Russia has the fourth highest level of homicides in the world, in part as a consequence of the ongoing conflict over Chechen independence (WHO 2002). The Chechen war has increased political violence and crime in the rest of Russia.

This chapter uses traditional indicators of violence as well as a new measure of conflict to analyze the high levels of violence in the transitional period in Russia. The transition period that we analyze extends from 1992 to 2000. The new measure of conflict that we use incorporates sociopolitical indicators and experts' assessments and it is measured at the level of Russian regions (see annex for a description). We compare certain hypotheses from the economic literature on crime to the "greed and grievance" model developed by Collier and Hoeffler (2001). According to Collier and Hoeffler, conflict is generated by poor economic conditions, availability of easily appropriated resources, and grievance against rich (ethnic) groups. These conditions result in violence. Whereas the Collier-Hoeffler (CH) model seeks to establish the causes of civil war, our analysis explores more broadly the relationship between conflict and violence in Russian society, and we explain the dynamics of crime.

The CH model focuses on civil war. Russia has a civil war in Chechnya, but conflict in other parts of Russia does not rise to the level of civil war. But Russia, based on our measure of conflict, has several regions with substantial conflict in addition to Chechnya. We argue that the Chechen war has provoked a strong countrywide authoritarian reaction in an effort to prevent the breakdown of order.

The Chechen conflict is based on deep historical rifts between Chechens and the Russian central state. The violence there is multifaceted and differs from that in other regions of Russia. It includes the violence committed by the Chechens, the Russian military, and the MVD (Ministry of Interior) troops that transcends the norms of military actions. Violence includes kidnapping, hostage taking, and rape, which are criminal acts, used there for political purposes. When such acts are committed within a civil conflict such as the one in Chechnya, we consider them as acts of political violence. Outside Chechnya, for example, in adjoining regions of southern Russia, incidents of such violence (e.g., homicide and rape) are considered criminal acts.

The data used in this study include traditional indicators of violence, such as those for homicide, rape, and assault. We also examined the violence that results from the war in Chechnya. In spite of the common belief that much of the violence was linked to the growth of organized crime, only a small portion of the recorded violence is associated with organized crime. Much of the violence is linked to the societal transition after the collapse of the Soviet Union. We argue that this period of intense property redistribution contributed to the rise in intrapersonal violence. We focus on the interplay between political violence and crime and on the contagion effects of the Chechen conflict. The case of Chechnya provides support for the CH model because of the availability of war-related capital, external financial support for the rebellion, and the limited economic opportunities for the domestic population. The rest of our analysis of crime and violence in Russia is also broadly consistent with the CH model.

This chapter is organized into two parts. In the first part, we describe the historical development of common and political crime and violence in Soviet Russia and then in the Russian Federation. We focus on the relationship between conflict and crime in Russia and on the war in Chechnya. In the second part, we describe our data and econometric methods and discuss our empirical findings.

## Historical Overview and Analysis

Violent revolutions in 1905 and 1917, World War I from 1914 to 1918, a civil war from 1917 to 1921, and years of resistance to Bolshevik rule caused enormous loss of life in Russia. Massive state repression followed in the late 1920s as Stalin initiated the purges that would last throughout his rule into the early 1950s. World War II resulted in huge casualties as the Soviet Union was invaded. Millions of combatants and civilians lost their lives in the war and many died in the forced deportations of the war years.

### Crime and Violence in Soviet Russia

The Russian revolution in 1917 and the subsequent civil war had a major impact on the patterns of both violent and political crime. Crime became one of the major urban problems in the two largest cities of Moscow and Leningrad (Gernet 1924, 1927). At this time, a significant amount of violent and property crime was committed by youths, urban migrants, and those displaced by the revolution.

The civil war (1917–21) was extremely violent. Violence ended in the western Russian Federative Republic in the early 1920s, but raged on in other parts of the country, particularly Central Asia, throughout the decade. Although political resistance to the revolution had been largely suppressed in the major cities, it continued in more remote parts of the country throughout the decade. The militia, the army, and the security police (the Cheka) suppressed the White opposition that had withdrawn to Siberia after being routed by the Red Army in the western parts of the country (Shelley 1996).

The 1920s continued as a period of great instability in the criminal and political arena. Female criminality rose significantly and women's crime became more violent. In Moscow and Leningrad, murders were often premeditated and some professional criminals committed multiple contract murders (Shelley 1982).[1]

Very different patterns of violence occurred in other parts of the country. Banditry was rampant in the eastern parts and violent clashes between the militia and the criminals resulted in many fatalities on both sides (Nikolaev 1959, 42–49; 1967, 228–53). The bandits, armed by opponents of the Soviet regime, added an important political dimension to the ordinary crime. The use of the regular police to address social conflict had important long-term consequences for the maintenance of social and political order.

With Stalin's ascension to power in the late 1920s, political crime became the focus of his law enforcement policies. During this period, the high level of violence was state sponsored, as the state began a mass campaign to collectivize agriculture and purge enemies of the state. Widespread resistance to collectivization by the peasantry resulted from Stalin's decision to order the end of all privately owned farms and to force the agricultural population into collective farms. The ignominious role of the army, the Cheka (security police), and the regular police in subjugating the peasantry and eliminating the *kulaks* in the 1930s has been extensively documented (Conquest 1986).

The intense repression of the Stalinist years resulted in both political conformity and low crime rates. Professional criminals were rounded up and sent to labor camps for lengthy sentences, which did not eliminate them but contributed to the low incidence of crime. Millions were sent to these camps, often for petty crimes, which led to a criminalization of the population with long-term implications for post-Stalinist society.

Stalin fought wars against both external and internal enemies. Not only were individual "enemies of the state" singled out for repression, but whole nationalities were viewed as suspicious. During the war, whole nations, particularly those from the Caucasus, were deported to Siberia and Central Asia (Conquest 1961). As shown later, the deportation of the Chechens and their difficult return to their homeland after Stalin's death has had an impact on their contemporary levels of criminality.

Crime rates in the former Soviet Union were lower than in other industrialized countries. Crime rates were low due to a combination of high rates of incarceration, highly repressive law enforcement, limitations on internal travel, and closed frontiers.

A different geography of criminality than in western countries existed in the USSR. In most industrialized countries, there is a direct correlation between the level of urbanization and the level of criminality. In the USSR, because urban centers were favored and could exile serious offenders and limit the settlement of youthful males, this relationship between crime and urbanization did not exist. An internal passport system regulated domestic travel and prevented internal migration without militia permission. Residence in large cities was prohibited to serious offenders released from labor camps. Former offenders were forced to settle in secondary cities and rural areas, which had very high rates of crime. Therefore, crime was greater in the secondary cities of the Soviet Union and lower in the major urban centers (Shelley 1980). The legacy of this unique geography of crime continues as the highest rates of crime are still recorded in many regions that are not major urban centers (see figure 4.1).

Since former convicts were prohibited from settling in almost any city of significant size, many former offenders settled near the labor camps from which they were released (Shelley 1981a). Therefore, the Urals and Siberia and parts of the Russian Far East absorbed very large numbers of hardened criminals who continued to commit very serious crime, often in association with their fellow ex-convicts. This explains the higher rates of crime near labor camps—something that we also find in our analysis.

Violence was always high in the former Soviet Union relative to other forms of criminality (Shelley 1981b, 1987). Even though there were strict controls on weapons, crimes were committed by such means as knives and axes. Often these crimes were precipitated by alcohol abuse, and the long cold winters in small apartments aggravated interpersonal relations. These same conditions continue to explain crime in our analysis.

Gorbachev's policies of *perestroika and glasnost* (openness) had a major impact on crime. Crime increased and became more violent. According to official statistics,

*Figure 4.1* **Map of Russia Showing Number of Homicides per 100,000 Population in Year 2000**

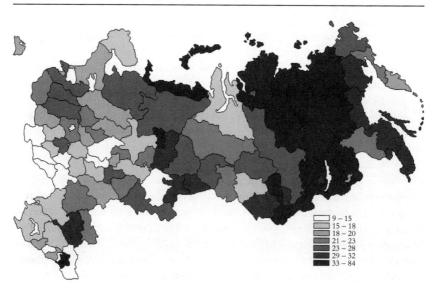

the overall crime rate and homicide rate doubled from 1987 to 1991. Organized crime also grew, merging the shadow economy with the criminal underworld and corrupt state.

Steps taken to make the justice system more accountable and humane inadvertently contributed to the rise of crime. Large numbers of inmates were released into a society that no longer guaranteed employment and in which no social safety net of unemployment insurance or social services existed. The hundreds of thousands of released ex-offenders could not be monitored because militia resources were diverted to more pressing problems of ethnic conflict and mass political demonstrations.

The growth in crime and the increasing severity of criminality were perhaps unavoidable in the transitional period, but many policies undertaken during *perestroika* contributed to the rise in crime. For example, the introduction of prohibition in 1985, the month Gorbachev assumed power, contributed to the rise of organized crime as it had in the United States in the 1920s. In the USSR, the impact of prohibition was more acute, because this massive transfer of resources to organized crime and corrupt bureaucrats coincided with the reintroduction of private business and the initial phases of privatization of state property. Consequently, from its inception, private capital was commonly acquired with the proceeds of criminal activity.

Campaigns to reduce corruption in law enforcement may have improved the administration of justice, but they did not reduce crime. Dismissed law enforcement personnel were often recruited by the rapidly growing organized crime networks. Replacements could not be found because militia work was underpaid and dangerous and citizens no longer felt compelled to serve the state.

Ethnic conflict in the final years of the Soviet period facilitated further violence. Following attacks on symbols of Soviet authority, the militia and the army, many weapons were acquired by citizens. Police stations and army posts were razed and demobilized military personnel sold weapons to supplement their meager incomes and buy drugs. National groups, particularly those in the Caucasus, imported weapons to further their causes.

Some had predicted that the USSR would collapse in mass political violence. Instead, high rates of intrapersonal violence and organized crime became the legacy of the USSR in successor states. The problems of intrapersonal violence and nationalist violence were particularly pronounced in the southern border regions of the Caucasus.

## Crime During the Transition

Despite significant regional differences in crime rates, there are certain important common trends over the last decade in the diverse regions of Russia. Crime rates fell during the first year of Gorbachev's rule when prohibition was introduced. They then grew during the final four years of the Soviet period. Crime grew particularly fast after three shocks: the large amnesty from labor camps at the end of the Soviet period, price liberalization in 1992, and the economic crisis of 1998.

In the transitional period of the 1990s, violent crime rates rose dramatically; this was a consequence of rising organized crime, increasing poverty and income disparity, a high level of alcohol consumption, and rising mortality. Homicide rates tripled during the years from 1988 to 1994. The most noted increase in criminality was in the crimes linked to the new market economy where the growth rate was more than double that for other categories of criminality (Luneev 1997).

Adult crime rates, unlike those of juveniles, did not level off in the second half of the 1990s. Instead, crime rates for violent acts committed by adults grew dramatically both in the domestic and the public sphere. The killings associated with organized crime and banditry were notable. In certain large cities with significant organized crime groups, such as Moscow, St. Petersburg, and Ekaterinburg, there were many killings associated with the division of territory (Saviuk 1999).

Violent crime not associated with organized crime also increased. Part of this is explained by the availability of weapons, which were tightly controlled during the Soviet period (Shelley 1987). The availability of arms, facilitated by the small weapons trade of Russian organized crime and former military personnel, made many ordinary acts of crime more violent than in the past. Consequently, Russia had 22 mortalities from homicides and assaults per 100,000 population, which is the fourth highest rate in the world after Colombia, El Salvador, and Brazil, according to the *World Report on Violence and Health*. It is triple the rate of the United States and approximately 10 times that of Western Europe. In the years before the transitional period (1965–90), both the United States and Soviet Russia had similarly high levels of violence (Pridemore 2001). Both countries also incarcerated about 0.7% of their populations, because of their reliance on imprisonment as a sanction and the imposition of lengthy sentences.

Examining the data from the city of Moscow obtained from the International Crime Victim Survey (ICVS) revealed that the risk of victimization from violence is comparable to that of the capitals of higher income countries and other transitional countries, but lower than that of the capitals of Latin America included in the survey (UNDP 2001; Van Kesteren, Mayhew, and Nieuwbeerta 2000). National data from crime victimization surveys in Belgium, France, the Netherlands, Poland, and the United States revealed that 1 percent of the population had been victims of assault in 1999. Similar ICVS data from different cities revealed a 1 percent victimization rate in Moscow, Budapest, Tbilisi, and Vilnius, about 3 percent in Bogotá and Buenos Aires, and 5 percent in Johannesburg.

According to the ICVS, there was a very low rate of reporting of crime by Moscow residents, indicating little public faith in the police.[2] Only a quarter of serious crimes against persons and private property are reported to the police, a much lower rate than in Western European cities where half of all crimes are reported (del Frate and Van Kesteren, 2004). Moreover, not all reported crimes are registered by the police. For example, the ICVS shows that in Moscow for the 11 categories of crime in which victims were surveyed, there were 80 crimes per 100 inhabitants in 1995, whereas the Moscow police registered one crime per 100 inhabitants in that year.[3]

## Ethnic Conflict, Crime, and Political Violence

Ethnic conflict in the late 1980s had an impact on politically motivated violence and on criminal violence. In fact, the unusually high rates of violence in Russia in the contemporary period suggest that there is a strong spillover effect from areas of violent civil conflict partly through the exposure of military personnel to violence and civil war.

Until the dissolution of the Soviet Union, there was no serious violent ethnic conflict in the country. But, according to one Russian demographer (Moukomel 1998, 1),

> In the late 1980s civil wars broke out in six out of fifteen Soviet Republics, four of the six were in the Caucasus, including one war on Russian territory. Deaths totaled about 100 thousand in the nine largest conflicts in the period 1988–1996. . . . These conflicts among ethnic, confessional, or tribal groups affected more that 10 million people, or about 3% of the population of the former USSR.

Many politicians underestimated the risk of such violence, believing that good relations existed among the diverse ethnic groups of the former Soviet Union.

The Russian Federation includes more than 100 ethnic groups. Russians dominate, accounting for 80 percent of the population. There are 21 national republics with either a distinct ethnic majority or large titular group. Many of these autonomous republics are sites of ongoing or potential violence.

The ethnic conflict in the Caucasus has affected crime rates and crime patterns, particularly in the south of the country. Russia includes the highly unstable North Caucasus region and borders the unstable South Caucasus. Russian military personnel trade in arms, and many of the local personnel on the southern Russian border and in the neighboring Caucasian states have engaged in significant smuggling across the borders. Arms and drug trafficking and kidnapping are particularly pronounced in this region, and local business people are pressured to launder money for the Chechen crime groups. The instability in Georgia prior to the Rose revolution exacerbated the criminal situation in the region because criminals found safe haven there.

## Conflict in Chechnya

The war in Chechnya has occurred in two periods: 1994–96 and 1999 to the present. Much greater military force has been used by the Russians in the second period. A significant difference between the two periods is the provision of funding by supporters of terrorism in the second period. In the first period, there was a strong link between political violence and organized crime and the war was sustained with profits from organized criminal activity. The second period of war has been partly supported by international funding by Islamic terrorist networks.

The average monthly fatalities in the Chechen conflict are estimated from the official reports to be 178 (and 813 wounded) in the first stage, 1994–96, and 117 (399 wounded) in the second stage, since 1999. The first military assault began with Chechnya's efforts to obtain autonomy (Lieven 1998). The Russians justified their attack, in part, as an attempt to root out organized crime (Lieven 1998; Seely 2001). Chechen organized crime in the 1990s was only one part (not the controlling part) of Russian organized crime.

The Chechens, exiled from their homeland by Stalin for more than two decades, had an extensive diaspora that existed in many regions of the former Soviet Union and abroad. Experienced traders, they helped run lucrative farmers' markets and were active participants in the shadow economy in the Soviet period as were many other Caucasian groups. Chechens were identified by the Soviet era militia as an important organized crime group. They occupied second- and third-tier hotels in Moscow as their bases of operations. Their activities included running auto-theft rings, extorting sellers in markets, and trading in arms and drugs.

Chechnya, before the bombing campaigns that destroyed its infrastructure, was relatively wealthy with significant petrochemical factories and oil reserves, the richest in the Caucasus after the reserves near Baku, Azerbaijan (Lieven 1998).

The Russian military in the first stage of the war encountered much more resistance than it had anticipated. Chechen war efforts were funded by a diversity of sources, including the domestic and foreign Chechen diaspora community, revenues from the diversion of oil and its sale, organized crime activity including the narcotics trade, and the Islamic community abroad through charitable foundations and also through Islamic mosques (i.e., collections in London mosques provide approximately £50,000 a week).

The war seemed to end in 1996 with the Russians failing to secure a clear victory. There were many forces that would work to ensure that the peace was not permanent. Among these were Russian military and political officials who could not accept the failure of Russia to secure its dominance over the Chechens, an ethnic group long in conflict with the Russians. There was much political and financial interest that ensured the absence of a permanent peace. Furthermore, there has been a "spiral and cycle of violence that makes the conflict impossible to resolve" (Jersild 2004, 368). Civil society, generally weak in Russian society, could not provide a counterbalance to the strong military and political interests pushing for renewed conflict. There was almost no civil society in Chechnya, and Russian human rights groups, according to a leading activist, once the cease-fire was declared, failed to stay adequately engaged.[4]

The resumption of the fighting in 1999 provides some illustration for the greed-versus-grievance hypothesis. There were enormous financial incentives to keep the war going. The Russian high military command has made millions for itself by siphoning off and diverting some of the Chechen oil production. Young Russian combatants have secured valuables for themselves by raiding Chechen households. Some of their pay and loot has been bartered with Chechens for drugs (Gentleman 2001).

Funding for Chechnya was diversified in the second war and the nexus between external Islamic funding, terrorism, and the Chechen conflict has become evident.

Arabs and Pakistanis, possibly associated with al-Qaeda, have collected funds in Mosques in London, whereas in the 1990s the Chechens did much of their own collection of funds.[5]

The Russian government has accused the al-Qaeda network of funneling millions of dollars to the Chechen cause. Moscow's charges seem to be affirmed by the appearance of Omar Khattab, an Arab, connected to the al-Qaeda network, who provided another source of funding (RFE/RL 2002). Through him, equipment, supplies, food, and training were provided to the Chechens. Some suggest that the amount funneled through Khattab may be exaggerated to conflate the Chechen drive for autonomy with the al-Qaeda terrorist network. But American analyses of money flows suggest that support from Islamic charities flowed from Muslims in the Arab world to Muslims in the Balkans and in the Caucasus (USIP 2002).

## Empirical Analysis

Next, we empirically test the link described previously between the rise in common (criminal) violence and a rise in the level of political violence and civil conflict. Civil conflict is intensified by violence and is rooted in a poor economic situation and ethnic polarization. We test this hypothesis as well as others. We test whether violence increases as the quality of life declines; or as a result of fundamental changes in wealth and property distribution; or as the deterrence effect of law enforcement declines; or as the economy weakens and income inequality increases. Grievances generated by ethnic polarization should lead to higher rates of criminal violence. A positive correlation should exist between the level of urbanization and violence because urban areas have more wealth, greater anonymity, and often lower rates of crime detection. These hypotheses are drawn partly from the CH model and partly from the economics literature on crime.

### Data and Empirical Model

Our study of Russian crime utilizes the CH model (2001; see also Collier and Hoeffler 1998). According to this model, the risk of initiation of conflict depends on gains minus costs:

$$p(T) \quad T - \text{Costs}\big[Y, C(\text{ELF})\big],$$

where $p$ is the probability of rebel victory, $T$ is per capita taxable base of the economy, $Y$ is the per capita income, and $C$ is coordination cost, which is the function of ethnolinguistic fractionalization (ELF). Similarly, our economic model of criminal behavior says that an offender commits a crime taking into account the similar expression:

$$p \quad Y - \text{Costs}(Y, p, F),$$

where $p$ is the probability of not being caught and $F$ is the size of the fine in case of punishment. Since income $Y$ is both a benefit and a cost, its total effect is ambiguous.

In the CH model, civil war risk is a function of opportunities and grievances (Collier, 2000; Collier and Hoeffler, 2001). Both opportunities and grievances also explain common crime. The low costs of committing an offense and the presence of crime-specific capital are measures of opportunities for offenders. Our empirical analysis examines reported crime as a function of crime clearance rates, life expectancy, per capita income, income growth, past crime rate, and the contagion measure of the Chechen conflict. Measures of grievances include ethnic hatreds, sociopolitical conflict, and economic inequality. These are represented in our analysis by ethnic polarization, sociopolitical conflict indicators, and the Gini index.

Crime statistics were classified from the Stalinist period until Gorbachev's *glasnost* policy (Luneev 1997). With the collapse of the Soviet Union, Russia inherited the statistical data reporting and recording methods of the USSR. This provided continuity, albeit with the weaknesses of the Soviet data collection system. Economic and socioeconomic statistics, conforming to international reporting methods, are now available for Russia since the first half of 1990s. Therefore, there are now national and regional data available in most areas for a 10-year period.

Russia is divided into 89 regions and of these only 77 can be included in this study because the Chechen and Ingush Republics have weak statistical collection capacity. Another 10 regions, autonomous *okrugs* (independent subregions) are excluded because their statistics are included in those of a larger region.

In our econometric analysis, we used crime rates for violent and property offenses as well as violent property crimes. We explored the relations among socioeconomic, demographic, and other variables and crime. Table 4.1 contains the definition, statistical descriptions, and sources of all variables. The data consist of 691 observation points for 77 Russian regions covering the nine years of the transition period 1992–2000. To test the hypotheses, we used a wide variety of panel data, which consist of short time series across a large number of regions. Most panel series have nine years of observation points, but the income inequality measure, the Gini index, is constructed for seven years, whereas education, ethnic polarization, deterrence, and reform indicators have only one point in time and are thus assumed to be stable over time.

Social and demographic data come from the Russian State Statistical Administration (*Goskomstat*), including quality-of-life indicators and economic and demographic variables. Quality-of-life indicators include life expectancy at birth and level of education of the population. Together with per capita income, these two indicators constitute the Human Development Index (HDI) constructed by the United Nations Development Programme (UNDP). Socioeconomic indicators include average real income, unemployment rate, and income inequality. Demographic indicators include the degree of urbanization, population mobility, and ethnic diversity, as measured by the level of ethnolinguistic fractionalization[6] and ethnic polarization as introduced by Esterban and Ray (1994), as calculated from census data. To examine deterrence, we analyze such factors as the strength of the police force and prison capacity. To examine general sociopolitical conflict in Russian regions, an index was constructed by specialists of the Center for the Study and Resolution of Conflicts.

*Table 4.1* **Descriptive Statistics and Variable Definitions**

| Name | Definition | Obs | Mean | SD | Min | Max | Source |
|---|---|---|---|---|---|---|---|
| Homicide mortality rate | Number of mortalities from homicide and assault, per 100,000 population | 691 | 28.6 | 16.2 | 3.6 | 144.5 | Ministry of Health |
| Homicide mortality rate, males | Number of mortalities from homicide and assault, males per 100,000 males | 691 | 45.9 | 26.8 | 5.3 | 244.3 | Ministry of Health |
| Homicide mortality rate, females | Number of mortalities from homicide and assault, females per 100,000 females | 691 | 12.9 | 6.5 | 1.1 | 48.1 | Ministry of Health |
| Registered homicide rate | Number of registered by police homicides and attempted homicides, per 100,000 population | 691 | 20.6 | 9.0 | 3.7 | 81.0 | Ministry of Interior |
| Total registered crime rate | Number of registered crimes, per 100,000 population | 460 | 1,891 | 566 | 614 | 3,855 | Ministry of Interior |
| Registered assault rate | Number of registered by police assaults, per 100,000 population | 691 | 40.1 | 26.6 | 6.0 | 292.5 | Ministry of Interior |
| Registered rape rate | Number of registered by police rapes, per 100,000 population | 691 | 8.3 | 4.3 | 1.8 | 47.1 | Ministry of Interior |
| Registered open stealing rate | Number of registered by police open stealing, per 100,000 population | 691 | 89.4 | 46.9 | 12.0 | 291.0 | Ministry of Interior |
| Registered assault with intent to rob rate | Number of registered by police assault with intent to rob, per 100,000 population | 460 | 24.0 | 10.0 | 6.2 | 56.6 | Ministry of Interior |
| Cleared homicides | Share of cleared homicides during the period, percent | 691 | 80.7 | 9.9 | 22.2 | 100.0 | Ministry of Interior |
| Real cleared homicides | Share of cleared homicides during the period in the total number of mortalities from homicide and assault, percent | 691 | 63.3 | 22.4 | 23.1 | 229.3 | Authors' calculations based on Ministry of Interior and Ministry of Health statistics |

*(Continued)*

**Table 4.1 Descriptive Statistics and Variable Definitions (*Continued*)**

| Name | Definition | Obs | Mean | SD | Min | Max | Source |
|---|---|---|---|---|---|---|---|
| Cleared crimes | Share of cleared crimes during the period, percent | 460 | 72.0 | 7.0 | 52.8 | 92.1 | Ministry of Interior |
| Cleared assaults | Share of cleared assaults during the period, percent | 691 | 77.0 | 9.9 | 36.5 | 98.1 | Ministry of Interior |
| Cleared rapes | Share of cleared rapes during the period, percent | 691 | 86.3 | 7.9 | 48.9 | 100.0 | Ministry of Interior |
| Cleared open stealing | Share of cleared open stealing the period, percent | 691 | 54.4 | 13.2 | 14.4 | 89 | Ministry of Interior |
| Cleared assault with intent to rob | Share of cleared assault with intent to rob during the period, percent | 460 | 69.0 | 12.0 | 33.0 | 96.6 | Ministry of Interior |
| Quality of life | Life expectancy from birth, years | 691 | 65.6 | 2.4 | 55.3 | 72.3 | Goskomstat of Russia |
| Industrial output | Industrial output at constant 1990 billion rubles per 100,000 population | 691 | 0.19 | 0.09 | 0.02 | 0.50 | Recalculated from Goskomstat statistics |
| Real income | Real income per capita in 25-good-busket | 691 | 3.5 | 1.6 | 1.3 | 17.2 | Calculations based on Goskomstat statistics |
| Unemployment | Share of unemployed people in labor force, percent (ILO methodology) | 691 | 10.7 | 5.0 | 2.8 | 32.0 | Goskomstat of Russia |
| Alcohol abuse | Number of people hospitalized in stationary medical facilities with diagnosis of alcohol psychosis, per 100,000 population | 691 | 79.1 | 42.0 | 0.0 | 220.7 | Ministry of Health |
| Net migration | Number of arrivals less departures, per 10,000 population | 691 | 7 | 105 | −1104 | 200 | Goskomstat of Russia |
| Conflict | General sociopolitical conflict indicator | 691 | 9.2 | 6.8 | 0.2 | 61.4 | Institute of ethnology and anthropology, Moscow |

| Variable | Description | | | | | | Source |
|---|---|---|---|---|---|---|---|
| Contagion of Chechen conflict | Sociopolitical conflict in Chechnya divided by distance from the region to Chechnya | 691 | 0.06 | 0.10 | 0.00 | 0.68 | Calculations based on the previous variable |
| Ethnic polarization | Esteban and Ray measure of ethnic polarization, alpha=1.6 | 691 | 0.09 | 0.04 | 0.02 | 0.15 | Calculations based on Goskomstat Census of population 1989 |
| ELF | Ethnolinguistic fractionalization | 691 | 0.29 | 0.19 | 0.05 | 0.85 | Calculations based on Goskomstat Census of population 1989 |
| Educational attainment | Average years of education of population above 15 years of age | 691 | 9.4 | 0.5 | 8.7 | 11.1 | Calculations based on Goskomstat Microcensus 1994 |
| Small privatization | Share of privatized business in trade, catering, and household services as of 1996, percent | 691 | 82 | 32 | 20 | 306 | "Rossiyskie regiony posle viborov—96", ed. Lavrov A. M., Yuriditcheskaya literatura, Moscow, 1997 |
| Prison capacity | Number of beds in correctional institutions, per 100,000 population | 691 | 327 | 143 | 77 | 913 | Moscow Center for Prison Reform www.prison.org |
| Urban population | Share of urban population, percent | 691 | 69.3 | 12.7 | 23.5 | 100.0 | Goskomstat of Russia |
| Winter temperature | Average temperature in January, °C | 691 | −11.3 | 7.5 | −43.9 | 3.2 | Goskomstat of Russia |
| Summer temperature | Average temperature in July, °C | 691 | 18.6 | 2.7 | 10 | 27.1 | Goskomstat of Russia |

*(Continued)*

*Table 4.1* Descriptive Statistics and Variable Definitions (*Continued*)

| Name | Definition | Obs | Mean | SD | Min | Max | Source |
|---|---|---|---|---|---|---|---|
| Gini index | Measure of inequality in income distribution | 460 | 0.34 | 0.06 | 0.22 | 0.62 | Authors' calculations based on Goskomstat statistics |
| Drug users | Number of registered drug users, per 100,000 population | 691 | 69.8 | 80.7 | 2.1 | 515.6 | Ministry of Health |
| Industrial output growth | Growth of industrial output at constant 1990 billion rubles per 100,000 population | 691 | −0.06 | 0.15 | −0.54 | 0.69 | Calculations based on Goskomstat statistics |
| Real income growth | Growth of average real income per capita in 25-good-busket | 691 | −0.03 | 0.29 | −0.72 | 1.17 | Calculations based on Goskomstat statistics |

*Note:* Obs, number of observation points.

Detailed description of the index construction is provided in the annex. We have also constructed a measure of contagion from the Chechen conflict for every region. This index is the ratio of sociopolitical conflict in Chechnya and the distance of a region from the Chechen Republic.

The crime statistics used here are the rates of officially registered crimes and their clearance rates for all major offenses as collected by the Russian Federation Ministry of the Interior. The crimes for which there are registered statistics include the following: homicide,[7] assault, rape, *grabezh* (open stealing, or robbery), *razboi* (assault with intent to rob), larceny-theft, and hooliganism (intentional acts violating public order).[8] We have also used as an alternative source the mortality statistics from the Ministry of Health (i.e., total mortality from homicides and assaults for males and females also divided by sex).

The base model is a dynamic panel data model with the crime rate as the dependent variable and lagged crime rate and a set of other indicators as independent variables, taking the form:

$$y_{it} = \alpha \; Y_{it-1} + \beta \; X_{it} + \gamma \; Z_i + \delta_t + \varepsilon_{it}$$

The model includes time-varying and invariant independent variables and time-specific effect.

Estimation is based on the General Method of Moments (GMM) for a system of equations in levels and first differences using some relevant moment conditions. The use of the system GMM estimator not only greatly improves the precision, but also greatly reduces the finite sample bias (Blundell, Bond, and Windmeijer 2000). Instead of the usual assumption of strictly exogenous explanatory variables, this approach allows us to assume that some explanatory variables could be endogenous (Arellano and Bond 1991, 1998). This means that they could be affected by past and present realizations of a dependent variable but not by its future values.

## Variables in the Empirical Analysis

In the core model, in addition to the predetermined lagged dependent variable, only three explanatory variables are assumed to be endogenous: life expectancy, clearance rate, and conflict. The first two are endogenous because their calculation reflects criminal statistics. Conflict is also potentially endogenous, because its increase is an expected response to violence. Other variables in the regression are assumed to be exogenous. Lagged first differences of endogenous independent variables and a lagged dependent variable are used as instruments for the equation in levels, and second lags of dependent and endogenous variables are instruments for the equation in first differences.[9] A special block matrix of instruments is constructed in this case. All exogenous variables are also used as instrumental variables.

In addition to the clearance rate (the number of reported crimes solved by the police), prison capacity was examined as a potential measure of deterrence. Using capacity as an independent variable, as opposed to the total prison population, we avoid a causality problem in the analysis. Most of Russia's detention facilities were built in the Tsarist and Stalinist periods. They are located in the coldest regions and their location was not determined by a high level of criminalization in a region. In economic terms, every additional sentenced criminal does not lead to the construction of an additional prison place, because it may be very expensive to build in a particular locale. Regional crime data may be affected by post-labor camp release policies which leave many released offenders close to their places of confinement.

The system dynamic panel data model was estimated by GMM for 11 types of crime. Core regression results are shown in table 4.2. In four regressions for total crime, larceny-theft, assault with intent to rob, and hooliganism, a second-order serial correlation test is rejected indicating that the model is not correctly specified (not reported). In addition we estimated core regression with the Gini index (not reported). In this case, regressions are done on the reduced sample of observation points, but we observe a similarity of results with the previous table. Conflict and ethnic polarization, persistence over time (dynamic process), the strength of the police force, and the quality of life are found to be the strongest determinants of violence.

Table 4.3 shows the results of the regression analysis for a wide set of independent variables. All the basic conclusions still hold, but conflict is significantly positive only for homicide and rapes in this case. Similar to the findings in Fajnzylber, Lederman, and Loayza (2000), the results for all seven types of crime are persistent over time. The long-run effects seem to be increasing with less serious forms of crime. Therefore, a thief is more likely to commit similar crimes in the following year than a person who committed assault or murder. This is a general finding in criminology concerning homicide data and indicates that Russia conforms to general patterns of recidivism. In the following sections, we discuss the major findings in relation to the hypotheses.

## Relationship of Conflict to Violence

Econometric analysis confirms our main hypothesis that conflict leads to more violence and that the Chechen conflict has contagion effects. We find that contagion for the Chechen conflict is significantly positive for rape and homicides of males. Also, both the degree of sociopolitical conflict and ethnic polarization significantly affect the levels of all violent crimes studied. As table 4.4 indicates, violent crimes that are most sensitive to conflict and ethnic polarization are: rapes, homicide (including attempted), homicide mortality, and assaults, in descending order. Nonviolent crimes are not found to be sensitive to conflict and grievance arising from ethnic confrontation.

The recorded rape rate has declined by 54 percent in Russia during the transitional period. This may be the result of an increasing unwillingness to report such crimes given low expectations of apprehending the offenders. We did find, however, a positive link between rapes and regions of conflict, which conforms to the previously established relationships between rape and wartime violence

## Table 4.2 GMM Core Regression Results

| Variable | Homicide | Homicide mortality | Homicide mortality, males | Homicide mortality, females | Assault | Rape | Robbery |
|---|---|---|---|---|---|---|---|
| Crime, lag | 0.376*** | 0.661*** | 0.742*** | 0.328*** | 0.788*** | 0.384*** | 0.868*** |
| Conflict | 0.190*** | 0.128*** | 0.231*** | -0.0006 | 0.104*** | 0.126*** | -0.230*** |
| Clearance rate | -0.065*** | -0.059*** | -0.076*** | -0.032*** | -0.056*** | 0.044*** | -0.421*** |
| Life expectancy | -2.10*** | -2.62*** | -3.33*** | -1.67*** | -1.90*** | -0.712*** | -1.36*** |
| Ethnic polarization | 27.4*** | 26.2*** | 27.9*** | 12.7*** | 16.3*** | 14.8*** | -12.1** |
| Contagion of Chechen conflict | 0.871 | 5.67*** | 7.93*** | -0.395 | -2.22 | 2.18*** | 5.11*** |
| Constant | 154*** | 190*** | 244*** | 122*** | 147*** | 47.3*** | 125*** |
| No. observation points | 691 | 691 | 691 | 691 | 691 | 691 | 691 |
| No. years | 9 | 9 | 9 | 9 | 9 | 9 | 9 |
| No. regions | 77 | 77 | 77 | 77 | 77 | 77 | 77 |
| Sargan test, p value | .359 | .283 | .173 | .560 | .234 | .369 | .170 |
| FO serial correlation test, p value | .000 | .001 | .000 | .000 | .000 | .000 | .000 |
| SO serial correlation test, p value | .273 | .721 | .371 | .935 | .360 | .662 | .968 |

*Note:* The matrix of instruments is constructed from second lags of crime, conflict, clearance, and life expectancy for the equation in first differences, while first lags of differenced crime, conflict, clearance, and life expectancy are instruments for the equation in levels. Ethnic polarization and contagion are assumed to be an exogenous variable. They are included in the list of instruments.

The asterisks in this and following tables denote statistical significance of coefficients: *significant at 10%; **significant at 5%; ***significant at 1%.

## Table 4.3 GMM Extended Regression Results

| Variable | Homicide | Homicide mortality | Homicide mortality, males | Homicide mortality, females | Assault | Rape | Open stealing |
|---|---|---|---|---|---|---|---|
| Crime, lag | 0.3*** | 0.639*** | 0.685*** | 0.386*** | 0.609*** | 0.247*** | 0.762*** |
| Conflict | 0.143*** | 0.022 | 0.044 | -0.02 | -0.246*** | 0.107*** | -0.266** |
| Clearance rate | -0.141*** | -0.105*** | -0.161*** | -0.041*** | -0.701*** | -0.082*** | -0.968*** |
| Life expectancy | -1.76*** | -1.59*** | -2.26*** | -1.13*** | -2.96*** | -0.54*** | -0.666*** |
| Unemployment | 0.009 | 0.025 | -0.004 | 0.02 | -0.082** | -0.075*** | 0.325*** |
| Net migration | 0.005*** | -0.001 | -0.004** | 0.004*** | -0.0001 | 0.003*** | -0.01*** |
| Alcohol abuse | -0.007** | -0.002 | 0.004 | -0.003 | -0.011 | -0.001 | -0.039*** |
| Drug users | 0.005*** | 0.004*** | 0.005 | 0.003*** | 0.013*** | -0.002 | -0.006 |
| Industrial output | 2.17 | -3.9** | -7.54*** | -0.697 | -0.673 | 0.029 | 22.9*** |
| Real income | -0.032 | -0.031 | -0.14 | 0.013 | -0.103 | 0.112** | -1.39*** |
| Industrial output growth | 0.013 | 2.87*** | 6.01*** | -0.69 | 0.195 | -0.282 | -12.6*** |
| Real income growth | -0.7** | -1.27*** | -1.1** | -0.862*** | -2.83*** | -0.524*** | -0.301 |
| Prison capacity | 0.001 | 0.0003 | 0.0004 | -0.0001 | 0.005** | 0.003*** | 0.016*** |

| | | | | | | |
|---|---|---|---|---|---|---|
| Reform | 0.015*** | 0.015*** | 0.018*** | 0.015*** | 0.002 | 0.038*** |
| Urban population | −0.011 | −0.02 | −0.058** | 0.029*** | −0.17*** | −0.079*** |
| Education | −1.33*** | −0.769 | −0.52 | −1.68*** | −5.28*** | −0.87*** |
| Ethnic polarization | 27.9*** | 27.6*** | 36.6*** | 21.6*** | 6.67 | 22.1*** |
| Winter temperature | −0.203*** | −0.147*** | −0.209*** | −0.096*** | −0.432*** | −0.023 |
| Summer temperature | −0.14*** | 0.026 | 0.117** | −0.042** | −0.349*** | −0.121*** |
| Constant | 150*** | 131*** | 186*** | 96.3*** | 329*** | 62*** |
| No. observation points | 691 | 691 | 691 | 691 | 691 | 691 |
| No. years | 7 | 7 | 7 | 7 | 7 | 7 |
| No. regions | 77 | 77 | 77 | 77 | 77 | 77 |
| Sargan test, $p$ value | .931 | .147 | .135 | .397 | .046 | .335 |
| FO serial correlation test, $p$ value | .000 | .000 | .000 | .000 | .000 | .001 |
| SO serial correlation test, $p$ value | .196 | .632 | .344 | .946 | .411 | .675 |

*Note:* The matrix of instruments is constructed from second lags of crime, conflict, and clearance for the equation in first differences, while first lags of differenced lagged crime, conflict, and clearance are instruments for the equation in levels. Other regressors are used as instruments.

## Table 4.4 Impact on Crimes from Additional Variance of Independent Variable (Percent)

| Variable | Homicide | Homicide mortality | Homicide mortality, males | Homicide mortality, females | Assault | Rape | Open stealing |
|---|---|---|---|---|---|---|---|
| Conflict | 7 | 2 | 3 | 0 | 2 | 10 | −1 |
| Ethnic polarization | 5 | 3 | 2 | 3 | 1 | 7 | 0 |
| Clearance | −3 | −5 | −4 | −5 | −1 | 4 | −6 |
| Life expectancy | −24 | −21 | −17 | −32 | −12 | −19 | −3 |
| Education | −3 | −1 | −1 | −6 | −6 | −5 | −1 |

*Note:* Calculations of impact are based on regression results and discriptive statistics in tables 4.1 and 4.2, and in addition on table 4.3 for education.

(Brownmiller 1993). Rape is a tool of aggression in conflict regions. Women in conflict regions may be more willing to report these crimes because they see this as a reflection of political aggression against them and are not as concerned that the police will not find the perpetrators.

The rise in homicide in conflict areas is consistent with previous research in other regions of the world, which suggests that violent crime is higher in regions with serious and sustained conflicts (Archer and Gartner 1976). More recently, this relationship between high rates of violence in conflict areas has also been found in Latin America (Fajnzylber et al. 1998). The results we obtained support the CH model on grievance and higher levels of criminal violence.

Our hypothesis that ethnic fractionalization generates grievances, leading to higher rates of crime is confirmed by our data. We find that there will be more grievances in the future because of the changing ethnic structure of the population and rising fractionalization. The very low birth rate among Russians, the continued high level of mortality, and the exodus of Russians, particularly women of child-bearing age, will result in a diminished Russian population. The growing Islamic populations in Russia[10] that may not identify with Russia (this does not apply to all such groups) and the growth of Chinese and other Asian immigrants in Siberia and the Far East may lead to higher ethnic polarization and, therefore, to more conflicts and violence.

### Relationship between Quality of Life and Violence

Life expectancy, one of the components of the HDI even after controlling for its endogeneity, is significantly negative for any type of crime analyzed. The correlation is very high especially for violence: One additional year of life expectancy in Russia "saves" lives for about two females and three males per 100,000 persons of the respective sex annually or, in nominal figures, for 1,400 women and 2,200 men.

We investigated the dynamics of life expectancy in Russia during the 20th century.[11] The life expectancy of a 30-year-old male today is exactly the life expectancy of similar males 100 years ago (Institut narodnogo khozyaistva RAN 2001). Our calculations show that a drop from 70 to 64 years in life expectancy of a 30-year-old male since 1965 could contribute to an additional 20 deaths from homicides and assaults per 100,000 males annually. This decline in life expectancy explains over half of the growth in homicides between 1965 and 2000, which was from 10 to 45 per 100,000 males.

Another component of HDI, the average level of educational attainment, is significantly negative for violent crimes. The human development effect in terms of education and life expectancy has a strong impact on crime. Every additional year of education reduces rates of violence by 6–13 percent for different types of crime. An additional standard deviation in life expectancy, equivalent to 2.4 years, has a very large and negative effect on violence. Thus, it reduces the number of assaults by 12 percent and the homicide mortality rate for females by 32 percent as shown in table 4.5.

As in most countries in the world, violent crime rates in Russia are found to be higher where people are less educated. The possible explanation of this phenom-

## *Table 4.5* Conflict Regression Results

| Variable | Coefficient |
| --- | --- |
| Conflict, lag | 0.771*** |
| Homicide mortality | −0.011** |
| Life expectancy | −0.096*** |
| Real income | −0.113*** |
| Unemployment | 0.024*** |
| Ethnolinguistic fractionalization | 0.881*** |
| Education | 1.21*** |
| Urban population | −0.042*** |
| Winter temperature | −0.028*** |
| Summer temperature | 0.047*** |
| Constant | −0.728 |
| No. observation points | 691 |
| No. years | 9 |
| No. regions | 77 |
| Sargan test, *p* value | .191 |
| FO serial correlation test, *p* value | 0 |
| SO serial correlation test, *p* value | .769 |

*Note:* The matrix of instruments is constructed from second lags of homicide and life expectancy and second, third, and fourth lags of conflict for the equation in first differences, while first lags of differenced conflict, homicide, and life expectancy are instruments for the equation in levels. Other regressors are used as instruments.

enon is that well-educated people seem not only to live healthier and longer lives (Deev and Shkolnikov 2000), but also have less aggression against other people and within their families. More educated people can also better understand the long-term consequences of causing serious harm to their victims. They have more security and more to lose through their violence. Although in the case of organized crime, there may be the opposite story connecting crime and education. Crime groups and contract killers have appeared in places where qualified workers, large businesses, money flows, and shadow economy were concentrated, especially in Moscow, the Urals, and Siberia. As a result, during the transition period, some highly publicized contract assassinations occurred in Moscow and some industrial centers, where several popular journalists, members of parliament, bankers, heads of enterprises, mayors, and governors were victims of contract killers. Most of these several hundred assassinations have not been solved.

## Impact of Deterrence on Violence

One of our robust results is that the effectiveness of police, approximated by the clearance rate, is significantly negative in all cases: Police have a deterrent effect on crime such as Eide has found (Eide, Aasness, and Skjerpen 1994). In contrast, the prison system may actually contribute to the growth of crime. There is a positive correlation of about 0.3 between prison capacity and crime. Our analysis shows that regions with higher prison capacity have more assault, rape, and robbery. Russia's high rate of incarceration may generate crime because youthful offenders learn from more experienced fellow convicts. Released offenders are forced to settle near their former labor camps, where they have no roots and limited opportunities for legitimate employment. Released offenders often rapidly commit new crimes and return to the labor camps. This may explain why the coldest regions close to the labor camps have the highest rate of violence (see figure 4.1).

## Impact of Income and Growth on Violence

We use two measures of income—real industrial production per capita and real income per capita—and two measures of growth. We find that only growth reduces crime. Thus, crime is countercyclical because economic growth provides more opportunities for employment in the legal economy. This is consistent with the logic of the CH model (with reference to civil war). But we cannot confirm that lack of economic development contributes to a rise in crime. Neither the volume of industrial production nor average income is significant in determining crime rates.

A process of inequitable economic development is, however, costly to the social order of society. Crime sharply increased after the initiation of reform and then stabilized. The measure of income inequality, the Gini index, is found to have a positive effect on all crimes (significantly positive in half of the cases). Analysis of the Russian experience confirms the findings in the empirical literature that higher inequality in income distribution generates more violence (Soares 2001).

## Impact of Economic Reforms on Violence

The process of privatization contributed significantly to criminal violence. Thus, we found that there was a higher level of violence in regions in which the massive first wave of privatization occurred in the small business sector. Small-scale business privatization is shown to have a positive effect on crime, which was significant in five out of seven regressions, and this was true, in particular, for all four homicide regressions.

Although some Russian economists used small business privatization as an economic reform indicator, in Russia this may not be an accurate indicator of reform because of the intrusion of organized crime into this sector (*Rossiyskie regiony posle viborov—96* 1997; Volkov 2002). This may also explain why privatization is so positively correlated with homicide. In a turbulent Russia, economic reform may serve as a measure of potential gains in criminal industry and not as a source of legitimate economic opportunities.

## Impact of Alcohol and Drug Addiction on Violence

Despite the previously found relationship between alcohol abuse and crime, we did not find this relationship in our data (Andrienko 2001). We did not find that the proxy for alcohol consumption, the number of people hospitalized in stationary medical facilities with diagnosis of alcohol psychosis, has any significant impact on crime. This may have occurred because we did not use a very precise measure of alcohol abuse (the number of individuals suffering from alcohol psychosis is underestimated especially in rural areas, where medical assistance is not so easy obtained). The number of drug users, registered by the Ministry of Health, is positively linked to homicide and assault.

## Impact of Climate on Violence

The severe Russian climate increases significantly the rate of violent crime. Russia has the greatest number of people living in intense cold, the greatest concentration being in Siberia. The harsh climate affects people's behavior as they have to spend more time indoors, tend to consume strong alcoholic drinks, and have less opportunity for recreational activity. For every 10°C that the Russian winter and summer is colder than in Europe, our calculation reveals that the level of violence is increased by approximately 10 percent. Thus, there is a large negative correlation between winter climate and violence, about −0.6 for homicides and assaults.

## Relationship between Migration and Violence

The official statistics provide data on official migration, much of which consists of well-educated migrants from former Soviet states (Zaionchkovskaia 1994). Illegal migrants who are more marginalized and with greater likelihood of committing acts of violence are not reflected in official statistics. Therefore, our data only provide partial confirmation for the positive impact of population mobility on violent crime. A positive correlation between migration and homicides and rapes is observed for women but is not observed for homicide mortality in males. From the existing data, we cannot determine whether hostility toward some migrants results in higher rates of victimization. Russians returning from other countries of the former Soviet Union are often better educated and more qualified workers. However, their return contributes to tightness in the local labor market and this may cause conflict (Zaionchkovskaia 1994).

## Relationship between Urbanization and Violence

Crime rates are generally higher in urban areas, although in many societies violence is higher in rural areas. The results obtained in our study are ambiguous. More urbanized areas have higher rates of homicide among females and less rape among females and homicide among males. This contradicts the general findings of the ICVS that show that crime grows dramatically with the level of urbanization (Andrienko 2002; Van Kesteren et al. 2000).

This may reflect a legacy of the Soviet period when there was not a positive correlation between the level of urbanization and crime because youthful males were prohibited from moving to large cities and serious offenders were permanently exiled from large cities to rural communities and smaller towns. Therefore, the Soviet Union represented an anomaly in which there was not a positive correlation between the level of urbanization and crime (Shelley 1980).

## How Violence Affects Conflict

To analyze the impact of violence on conflict, we used a dynamic panel data regression (see table 4.5). A specification search was conducted to determine significant determinants. Conflict is found to be persistent over time and increases significantly with ELF[12] and the unemployment rate, but decreases with higher life expectancy, real income, and urbanization. This finding is consistent with the CH model (except for the result on fractionalization, which is the opposite from what Collier and Hoeffler found). But note that "conflict" here is not equivalent to civil war, as in Chechnya, but reflects other forms of conflict within Russian society.

Two unexpected results were identified. First, conflict is higher in regions with higher educational levels. This might suggest that the negative sociopolitical developments of the transition were clearer to those with better education, who were more frustrated by this, consistent with relative deprivation theories (e.g., Gurr 1970).

Second, conflict falls with higher levels of violence (homicides), but this is not a robust result. The impact of violence on conflict appears to be inverse U-shaped. Conflict rises with violence until a certain threshold level of violence is reached. At the maximum of this conflict, there may be so many people eliminated on each side that conflict starts to fall. This conclusion is based on adding the square of homicides to the model. Results indicate that both the linear and quadratic terms are significant with a positive and negative sign, respectively.

These results suggest that the subjugation of Chechen rebels by the Russian army and the persistent blood feuds among the Caucasians are examples of the likelihood of violence being diminished by the large number of casualties. Obviously, if members of rival rebel groups kill each other, this reduces the risk of large-scale conflict. The same applies to contract killings in organized crime. The more crime bosses are killed, the lower is the likelihood of *razborki* (large-scale criminal group conflicts) leading to large internecine group conflict (Kriminologicheskaya Assotsiatsiya 1998).

## Conclusion

This chapter established a relationship between crime, violence, civil war, and latent conflict in Russian society. Russia, throughout much of the transitional period, has been characterized by a high level of violence. The rate of violence is associated with the political transition and the long-lasting war in Chechnya. Ordinary crime—in particular violent crime—across the Russian Federation is significantly affected by the level of sociopolitical conflict in Chechnya. Chechnya has had a strong spillover effect on crime in the North Caucasus regions that are closest to Chechnya, but it has also had an impact on crime rates throughout Russia.

Recorded levels of violence are generally higher in developing and transitional countries. Russia, despite its high levels of education and international standing, has patterns of violence that are commonly found in the developing world and in countries with significant conflicts within their borders. High rates of violence are present throughout Russian society and the problem has become worse with the transition. Violence increases as one moves east in Russia. Part of this pattern is explained by the severe climate and the Soviet legacy of settlement of released convicts near labor camps. The traditional patterns of violence in these regions were exacerbated by the transition. Our empirical results show that violence resulted from inequitable distribution of wealth, rapid privatization, a fall in real income, and increased drug addiction. Compounding the problem was the decline in the social safety net and the rise of organized crime. The dramatic drop in life expectancy also contributed to the rise in levels of violence.

We found that several measures of both opportunity and grievances used in the CH model are very important in explaining ordinary crime rates in Russia. The location of homicides provides some confirmation of the CH hypothesis that violence will be more likely if there is conflict over the division of natural resources.

Russia's homicide rate is one-third that of Colombia, a country that has been engaged in civil war for decades. Russia's homicide rate places it halfway between the homicide rate of countries with civil war and countries at peace. Although the war in Chechnya is confined to a relatively small region of the country, the recruitment of combatants nationwide and their return to their home communities after their period of service facilitates spillover effects across Russia. This may explain why Russia's rate of homicide is almost double that of Ukraine, which has had a more peaceful transition.

Our research shows that the effects of the Chechen war on crime are most pronounced in regions near Chechnya. The constructed sociopolitical conflict index reveals that conflict is highest in Chechnya, Ingushetia, Karachaevo-Cherkessia, Dagestan, Krasnodar, Tyva, and Severnaya Osetia. All but one of these regions is in the North Caucasus. There is also an especially strong positive correlation between conflict and some socioeconomic indicators (in descending order: unemployment, ethnolinguistic fractionalization, drug use, size of rural population, and ethnic polarization) and a small significant positive correlation with violence (see table 4.6).

We also discussed that the Chechen conflict has changed over time as a function of external sources of funding. Furthermore, the presence of valuable natural resources, the existence of a significant diaspora, and the availability of foreign mercenaries, are all factors that have prolonged the civil conflict. These findings are consistent with the CH model.

An important new result is that, despite the common perception that violent crime and property crime are very different, we obtain very similar results in all regressions. We do find that conflict and ethnic polarization have a significant posi-

*Table 4.6* Correlation of Socioeconomic Indicators with General Conflict Indicator

| Variable | Correlation |
| --- | --- |
| Unemployment | 0.46 |
| ELF | 0.42 |
| Drug users | 0.31 |
| Birth rate | 0.24 |
| Infant mortality | 0.21 |
| Ethnic polarization | 0.21 |
| Homicide | 0.19 |
| Summer temperature | 0.17 |
| Industrial output growth | 0.14 |
| Homicide mortality | 0.12 |
| Real income | −0.13 |
| Hooliganism | −0.13 |
| Larceny-theft | −0.19 |
| Net migration | −0.19 |
| Industrial output | −0.26 |
| Urban population | −0.30 |
| Alcohol abuse | −0.34 |
| Death rate | −0.35 |

*Note:* Based on 691 observations.

tive impact on violent crimes, whereas income disparity has a positive impact on all crimes registered by the police but rape. The stability of violence rates over time, the strength of the police force, and the quality of life are the strongest determinants of violence.

Finally, we return to our main finding on the link between the level of societal violence and conflict. Violent crime in Russia is at a level usually found in countries at civil war. Russia's civil war in Chechnya has a broad impact on crime in the entire country. But Chechnya does not explain everything. Our conjecture is that high rates of violent crime in Russia are an indicator of more generalized conflict underlying Russian society.

# Annex: Sociopolitical Conflict Indicator

The Center for the Study and Resolution of Conflicts at the Institute of Ethnology and Anthropology in Moscow, in cooperation with the Network for Ethnic Monitoring and Early Warning of Conflict, has assessed sociopolitical conflict in some Russian regions and former Soviet states. Qualitative assessment is based on regional expert views of 46 conflict indicators developed by Professor Tishkov. Indicators are subdivided along seven broad categories: (1) environment and natural resources; (2) demography and migration; (3) power, state, and policy; (4) economy and social sphere; (5) culture, education, and communication; (6) contacts and stereotypes; and (7) external conditions. Every indicator is rated in two scales, A and B. Scale A has a range of $\{-2, -1, 0, 1, 2\}$ and shows the influence of an ethnopolitical indicator for the overall conflict situation in a region, with $-2$ showing a negative situation. Scale B has a range of $\{0, 1, 2\}$ and measures the significance of the indicator for societal conflict: 2 means strong impact and 0 means no impact. The consolidated conflict index for the given indicator j is nonzero only for negative values on scale A and defined as:

$$CI_j = \begin{cases} -\dfrac{A\,B}{4} \text{ for } A < 0 \\ 0 \text{ otherwise} \end{cases}$$

The general sociopolitical conflict indicator is calculated as the sum of consolidated indices of conflict:

$$\text{Conflict} = \sum_{j=1}^{46} CI_j$$

The index is available for 1996–2001 for regions included in the Network for monitoring. For other years and regions, they applied a similar methodological approach and based all expert estimation on ethnographical publications and statistical information.

# Notes

1. The same phenomenon exists today as major urban centers have more violence connected to professional crime, whereas in most of the country, violent crime is connected to the circumstances of daily life.
2. See also the recent sociological surveys on the legal culture of the population and the political resources of reforms held by the Russian Academy of Civil Service in Moscow: http://www.rags.ru/s_center/opros/polit_res_reform/index.htm.
3. Reporting rates for homicide are apparently higher because it is a more dangerous crime for society and there is less possibility for the police to hide such crimes. In order to ensure that such latent crime does not change the results of our analysis, we also used alternative data sources, particularly for homicides.
4. Interview with Liudmila Alexeeva, Moscow Helsinki Group, July 2001.
5. Interview with individual who accompanied the Chechens to the mosques, March 2002.
6. ELF is calculated as the probability that two people who meet randomly do not belong to the same ethnic group.
7. The homicide data of most countries in the world include deaths that result from homicide, but in Russia the total homicide rate also includes attempted homicides that do not result in death, whereas assaults that subsequently result in death are not recorded as homicides.
8. See Berman (1972) for definitions and translations of these crimes.
9. The set of instruments is supplied by the relevant moment conditions:

$$E\left[Y_{it-2}, \Delta\varepsilon_{it}\right] = 0,$$

$$E\left[X_{it-2}, \Delta\varepsilon_{it}\right] = 0,$$

$$E\left[\Delta Y_{it-1}, \varepsilon_{it}\right] = 0,$$

$$E\left[\Delta X_{it-1}, \varepsilon_{it}\right] = 0,$$

which emerge from assumed endogeneity and stationary property of the model.
10. Thus, ratio of Islamic to Orthodox traditionally confessing population in Russia has increased from 1/16 in 1926 to 1/10 in 1999 according to Bogoyavlenski (1999).
11. Currently, life expectancy at birth is 58 for males and 72 for females.
12. When ethnic polarization is used instead of ELF, it is not statistically significant.

# References

Andrienko, Yuri. 2001. "V poiskakh ob'yasneniya rosta prestupnosti v Rossii v perekhodni period: kriminometritcheski podkhod." *Economitcheski zhurnal Vishei Shkoli Economiki* 5 (2): 194–220.

———. 2002. "Crime, Wealth and Inequality: Evidence from International Crime Victim Surveys" [online]. E-prints 01-214E, Economic Education and Research Consortium, Moscow. http://www.eerc.ru/details/download.aspx?file_id=3861.

Archer, Dane, and Rosemary Gartner. 1976. "Violent Acts and Violent Times: A Comparative Approach to Postwar Homicide Rates." *American Sociological Review* 41: 937–63.

Arellano M., and S. Bond. 1991. "Some Tests of Specification for Panel Data: Monte Carlo Evidence and an Application to Employment Equations." *Review of Economic Studies* 58: 277–97.

———. 1998. "Dynamic Panel Data Estimation Using DPD98 for Gauss: a Guide for Users." Mimeo.

Berman, Harold J. 1972. *Soviet Criminal Law and Procedure: The RSFSR Codes,* 2nd ed. Cambridge, MA: Harvard University Press.

Blundell, Richard, Stephen Bond, and Frank Windmeijer. 2000. "Estimation in Dynamic Panel Data Models: Improving on the Performance of the Standard GMM Estimation" [online]. London, UK: The Institute for Fiscal Studies, 2000 WP #00/12. http://ideas.repec.org/p/ifs/ifsewp/00-12.html.

Bogoyavlenski, D. 1999. "Etnitcheskiy sostav naseleniya Rossii." *Naselenie i Obschestvo* 41 (November): 1–4.

Brownmiller, Susan. 1993. *Against Our Will: Men, Women and Rape.* New York: Ballantine Books.

Collier, Paul. 2000. "Doing Well out of War: An Economic Perspective." In *Greed and Grievance Economic Agendas in Civil Wars,* ed. Mats Berdal and David M. Malone. Boulder, CO: Lynne Rienner Publishers.

Collier, P., and A. Hoeffler. 1998. "On Economic Causes of Civil War." *Oxford Economic Papers* 50: 563–73.

———. 2001. "Greed and Grievance in Civil War." Policy Research Working Paper 2355, World Bank, Washington, DC.

Conquest, Robert. 1961. *Power and Policy in the U.S.S.R.* New York: St. Martin's Press.

———. 1986. *The Harvest of Sorrow.* New York: Oxford University Press.

Deev, A., and V. Shkolnikov. 2000. "Neodnorodnost' smertnosti: analiz individualnyikh dannyikh." In *Neravenstvo i smertnost' v Rossii,* ed. V. Shkolnikov, E. Andreeva, and T. Maleva. Moscow: Carnegie Center February.

del Frate, Alvazzi, and John Van Kesteren. 2004. "Criminal Victimization in Urban Europe: Key Findings from the 2000 International Crime Victims Survey" [online]. Turin: UNICRI. http://www.unicri.it/wwd/analysis/icvs/publications.php.

Eide, Erling, Jorgen Aasness, and Terie Skjerpen. 1994. "Economics of Crime: Deterrence and the Rational Offender." In *Economic Analysis,* 227. Oxford: North-Holland.

Esterban, J., and D. Ray. 1994. "On the Measurement of Polarization." *Econometrica* 63 (4): 819–51.

Fajnzylber, Pablo, Daniel Lederman, and Norman Loayza. 1998. "Determinants of Crime Rates in Latin America and the World: An Empirical Assessment." [online]. World Bank, Washington, DC. http://www.worldbank.org/research/conflict/papers/fajnzy.htm.

———. 2000. "Crime and Victimization: An Economic Perspective." *Economia* Fall: 219–302.

Gentleman, Amelia. 2001. "Rebels Have Nothing to Lose." http://www.calguard.ca.gov/ia/Chechnya/Chechnya%20-%20Rebels%20Have%20Nothing%20to%20Lose.htm. Accessed December 4, 2004.

Gernet, M. N. 1924. *Prestupnyi mir Moskvy.* Moscow: Pravo i zhizn.

———. 1927. *Prestupnost' i samoubiistvo vo vremiia voiny i posle nee.* Moscow: Tsentral'noe sta-tisticheskoe upravlenie SSSR.

Gurr, Ted Robert. 1970. *Why Men Rebel.* Princeton, NJ: Princeton University Press.

Institut narodnogo khozyaistva RAN—Tsentr demographii i ecologii cheloveka. 2001. *Vosmoi ezhegodniy demographicheskiy doklad "Naselenie Rossii 2000."* Moscow: Institut nar-odnogo khozyaistva.

Jersild, Austin. 2004. "The Chechen Wars in Historical Perspective: New Work on Contemporary Russian-Chechen Relations." *Slavic Review* 63: 2.

Kriminologicheskaya assotsiatsiya. 1998. *Organizovannaia Prestupnost',* Vol. 4, ed. Azalia Dolgova. Moscow: Kriminologicheskaya assotsiatsiya.

Lieven, Anatol. 1998. *Chechnya: Tombstone of Russian Power.* New Haven, CT: Yale University Press.

Luneev, V. V. 1997. *Prestupnost' XX veka.* Moscow: Norma.

Moukomel, V. 1998. "Demographicheskie posledstviya etnicheskikh I regionalnikh konfli-tov v SNG." *Naselenie i Obschestvo* 27 (April): 1–4.

Mukhin, Vladimir. 2005. "Krovavaya ariphmetika voin: Ot men'shego k bol'shemu" [online]. *Nezavisimoe Voennoe Obozrenie* 18 (427). May 20. http://nvo.ng.ru/notes/2004-10-29/8_arithmetics.html.

Nikolaev, P. F. 1959. *Omskaia militsiia v pervye gody sovetskoi vlasti (1917–1923).* Omsk: Arkhivnyi otdel UVD ispolkoma Omskogo oblastnogo soveta deputatov trudiaskchikhsiia.

———. 1967. *Sovetskaia militsiia Sibiri (1917–1922).* Omsk: Zapadno-sibirskoe knizhnoe izdatel'stvo.

Pridemore, W. 2001. "Using Newly Available Homicide Data to Debug Two Myths about Violence in an International Context." *Homicide Studies* 5 (August): 266–74.

RFE/RL (Radio Free Europe/Radio Liberty). 2002. "Crime, Corruption and Terrorism Watch." 2 (4), January 31. http://www.rferl.org/corruptionwatch/2002/01/4-310102.asp.

*Rossiyskie regiony posle viborov—96.* 1997. ed. A. M. Lavrov. Moscow: Yuriditcheskaya literatura.

Saviuk, L. K. 1999. *Pravovaia Statistika: Uchebnik.* Moscow: Iurist.

Seely, Robert. 2001. *Russo-Chechen Conflict, 1800–2000: A Deadly Embrace.* London: Frank Cass.

Shelley, Louise I. 1980. "The Geography of Soviet Criminality." *American Sociological Review* 45 (February): 111–22.

———. 1981a. "Internal Migration and Crime in the Soviet Union." *Canadian Slavonic Papers* 23 (March): 77–87.

———. 1981b. *Crime and Modernization: The Impact of Industrialization and Urbanization on Crime.* Carbondale, IL: Southern Illinois University Press.

———. 1982. "*Historical Trends in Moscow and Leningrad Crime.*" *Soviet Union* 1: 43–45.

———. 1987. "Interpersonal Violence in the Soviet Union." *Violence, Aggression and Terrorism* 1 (2): 41–67.

———. 1996. *Policing Soviet Society: The Evolution of State Control.* New York: Routledge.

Soares R. R. 2001. "Development, Crime, and Punishment: Accounting for the Interna-tional Differences in Crime Rates." Chicago, IL: Department of Economics, University of Chicago. Mimeo.

UNDP (United Nations Development Programme). 2001. *Human Development Report 2001* [online]. New York: UNDP. http://hdr.undp.org/reports/global/2001/en.

USIP (United States Institute of Peace). 2002. "Lawless Rule versus Rule of Law in the Balkans" [online]. December, No. 97. www.usip.org/pubs/specialreports/sr97.html.

Van Kesteren, John, Pat Mayhew, and Paul Nieuwbeerta. 2000. "Criminal Victimization in Seventeen Industrialized Countries: Key Findings from the 2000 International Crime Victims Survey" [online]. The Haague: Research and Documentation Center of the Ministry of Justice. http://www.unicri.it/wwd/analysis/icvs/publications.php.

Volkov, Vadim. 2002. *Violent Entrepreneuers: The Use of Force in the Making of Russian Capitalism.* Ithaca: Cornell University Press.

WHO (World Health Organization). 2002. *World Report on Violence and Health 2002* [online]. Geneva: WHO. http://www.who.int/violence_injury_prevention/violence/world_report/en/.

Zaionchkovskaia, Zhanna A. 1994. *Migratia naselenia i rinok truda v Rossii.* Moscow: Institute for Economic Forecasting.

# Conflict, Violence, and Crime in Colombia

5

FABIO SÁNCHEZ, ANDRÉS SOLIMANO,
AND MICHEL FORMISANO

This chapter analyzes the relationship between armed conflict and multiple forms of violence and criminal activity in Colombia. Colombia's civil war is one of the longest running civil wars in the world. We explain the war's intractability as a result of complex linkages across political conflict, violence, and criminal activity.

The main focus on this chapter is on the dynamics of armed conflict. We find evidence of a spiral of violence—measured by the homicide rate—and other forms of criminal activity, particularly linked to the insurgents' efforts to finance the civil war through kidnapping, extortion, and cultivation of illicit crops. We agree with the main hypothesis of the Collier-Hoeffler (CH) model, as we argue that the Colombian civil war has produced an explosion of illegal activities, violence, and crime that in turn allows the continuation and expansion of the civil war. However, we go beyond this model as we examine how an initial shock of violence and crime prompted by a rebel group in a particular region propagates through contagion or imitation to neighboring regions. Thus, our approach contributes to the understanding of the dynamics of violence and crime that accompany domestic conflicts and civil wars.

This chapter is divided into six sections. The first section overviews the history of domestic conflict and civil war in Colombia since the 19th century, focusing on the period of *La Violencia* (1946–62). The second section discusses the origins and consolidation of the Revolutionary Armed Forces of Colombia: People's Army (FARC-EP) and the National Liberation Army (ELN) guerrillas and illegal self-defense groups. The third section describes the evolution of the violence and criminal activity indicators, in particular, homicide, kidnapping, and drug trafficking. The fourth section analyzes the dynamics of the relationship between political conflict and violent crime from a theoretical and empirical point of view. We use spatial analysis techniques to examine clusters and diffusion dynamics of criminal activity. In the fifth section, we use spatial econometric analysis to explain determinants of the different types of crimes at the municipal and departmental level. We conclude with an overview of the argument and a discussion of the fit of the CH model to this case.

# Conflict in Colombia

Colombian history is often seen as a long series of civil wars and violence dating to 1839. The first civil war—the war of the Supremes (*Guerra de los Supremos*)—began only a few years after Colombia was liberated from Spain in 1819. It was fought between supporters of Simon Bolivar (*El Libertador*), who attempted a coup d'état against the *santanderistas* (supporters of Francisco de Paula Santander, one of the leaders of Colombian independence). The war ended in 1841 and led to the founding of the Liberal and Conservative parties that have dominated Colombian politics. In 1851, Colombia was again at civil war. Historians (e.g., Alape 1985; Fischer 1991; Jaramillo 2001) have counted 54 civil wars in the 20 years between 1851 and 1871.

The period from 1902 to 1948 was one of relative calm, though one with growing social conflict. A slow process of industrial and financial modernization was accompanied with agrarian movements in the 1920s and 1930s. Land tenants demanded better working conditions and the right to cultivate coffee, whereas native Indians demanded the restitution of their communal land. Meanwhile, thousands of peasants in the frontier regions invaded the newly formed landed properties (*haciendas*), reclaiming the public land that they had lost (LeGrand 1986). The Liberal party, which promoted agrarian reform during the 1930s, lost power in 1946 and the assassination of liberal leader Jorge Eliécer Gaitán in April 1948 marked the beginning of the period known as *La Violencia*.

Accusing the Conservative government of the murder, Liberals and Communists took to the mountains. In November 1949, the Communist party began to organize self-defense groups for the peasants. Popular discontent was on the rise as violence also rose and the government of Ospina Perez (1946–50) imposed a state of siege in November 1949. The Liberal party abstained from the elections. Armed resistance spread among small guerrilla groups in the Eastern Plains, Antioquia's southwest, the south of Córdoba, and Tolima. Laureano Gómez won the 1950 uncontested election, continuing the repression against the Liberals (Henderson 1984; Molina 1973).

In June 1953, General Rojas Pinilla staged a military coup and the violence escalated, leading to the fall of the military regime and the birth of the *Frente Nacional* in 1958. The new political regime was grounded on a alternating power scheme between Liberals and Conservatives (Hartlyn 1993). The *Frente Nacional* agreement ended *La Violencia* but did not eradicate guerrilla groups and excluded the Communists and other leftist parties from government.

There are several competing hypotheses on the origin of *La Violencia*. Guerrero (1991) argues that it was rooted in earlier conflicts between Colombian states. Others focus on the social and agrarian movements of the 1920s and 1930s, or on hatreds, party interests, land despoilment, and religious persecutions dating to the 19th century (Alape 1985; Jaramillo 1991). Ramsey (1981) locates the roots of *La Violencia* in the repression of the social movements of the 1920s, and Guzmán, Fals, and Umaña (1962) and others point to persecutions of Conservatives by Liberals in the 1930s to explain the Conservatives' desire for revenge, fed by the Catholic Church.

Others disagree. Deas (1991) claims that *La Violencia* is not rooted deeply in Colombian history and he identifies major differences between the 19th-century conflicts and the political oppression of the 1930s. An important difference is that in the 19th century wars the army was a party from the outset in contrast to *La Violencia*, where most of the fighting involved paramilitary groups. Earlier civil wars in Colombia were also of shorter duration and lower intensity and were not accompanied by rising crime.

Tovar (1999) points to state weakness as the main explanation of the violence while LeGrand (1986) argues that land disputes between agricultural entrepreneurs and settlers led to violence. According to LeGrand (1986) entrepreneurs offered the settlers the option of expulsion or tenant labor. A small agrarian resistance coalesced, leading to the first demonstrations of rural protest. As urban populations were mobilized, the violence spread widely (Pécaut 1985, 1987).

These studies offer several plausible hypotheses about the origins of *La Violencia*, but they do not analyze the *dynamics* of violence. In 1946, before *La Violencia* began, the homicide rate was low and it increased dramatically during 1950s and across all regions according to homicide data collected by the Ministry of Justice (Ministerio de Justicia 1961) shown in table 5.1.

However, table 5.1 shows that there were important differences in the homicide rate between departments during *La Violencia*. In fact, there were regional differences in conflict dynamics over time and in the spatial diffusion of violence during *La Violencia*. Although it is important to understand such patterns to explain the depth and duration of violence in Colombia, they have not been examined extensively. A recent study (Chacón and Sanchez, forthcoming) showed that regional differences in the intensity of civil conflict during *La Violencia* were mostly explained by the degree of local political polarization between Liberals and Conservatives and less by historical land conflict or rural poverty.

# Rise and Consolidation of Illegal Armed Groups

In this section we present a short historical account of the rise of illegal armed groups. This will help us to understand the conflict's recent dynamics and to grasp more accurately the relationship between conflict and crime.

## Rise and Evolution of the FARC

Following *La Violencia* and after the establishment of the *Frente Nacional,* the number of violent confrontations and deaths decreased drastically, although they never reached the prewar levels. Guerrilla and peasant self-defense groups emerged in regions such as Marquetalia (in the south of Tolima), Aríari in the Eastern Plains, and Sumapaz. These regions began to be called "independent republics" and were strongly attacked by the army and air force in 1963, particularly in Marquetalia. After the retreat of the military, the peasant resistance groups reorganized under

Table 5.1 Departmental Homicide Rate per 100,000 Inhabitants, 1946–60

| Departments | 1946 | 1947 | 1948 | 1949 | 1950 | 1951 | 1952 | 1953 | 1954 | 1955 | 1956 | 1957 | 1958 | 1959 | 1960 |
|---|---|---|---|---|---|---|---|---|---|---|---|---|---|---|---|
| Antioquia | 8.7 | 6.2 | 8.8 | 14.5 | 25.8 | 25.0 | 45.6 | 33.9 | 21.3 | 23.5 | 29.4 | 24.2 | 38.4 | 38.3 | 41.6 |
| Atlántico | 3.1 | 3.0 | 9.2 | 9.2 | 12.1 | 9.7 | 6.2 | 7.6 | 7.6 | 6.6 | 7.5 | 4.7 | 6.0 | 6.6 | 6.3 |
| Bolívar | 3.0 | 1.5 | 2.4 | 5.2 | 4.3 | 6.0 | 5.5 | 6.4 | 6.1 | 6.1 | 4.6 | 7.6 | 5.2 | 5.0 | 11.8 |
| Boyaca | 12.8 | 17.8 | 32.1 | 50.6 | 33.5 | 35.9 | 38.2 | 25.3 | 20.1 | 17.0 | 19.2 | 19.7 | 26.6 | 22.3 | 27.9 |
| Caldas | 6.6 | 7.9 | 14.1 | 29.0 | 30.1 | 34.7 | 37.0 | 41.8 | 42.2 | 51.8 | 59.5 | 91.0 | 117.0 | 81.1 | 43.5 |
| Cauca | 9.3 | 7.0 | 11.9 | 12.6 | 11.7 | 15.5 | 14.8 | 15.9 | 19.9 | 26.1 | 27.6 | 32.1 | 44.8 | 27.1 | 25.9 |
| Córdoba | 1.4 | 1.4 | 1.4 | 1.4 | 1.4 | 1.4 | 1.4 | 2.9 | 9.3 | 5.1 | 9.5 | 8.5 | 8.1 | 6.4 | 4.7 |
| Cundinamarca | 11.9 | 9.3 | 11.5 | 17.5 | 23.6 | 31.2 | 35.0 | 22.4 | 17.5 | 22.3 | 18.0 | 18.9 | 24.7 | 22.9 | 23.7 |
| Chocó | 1.8 | 1.8 | 1.8 | 3.6 | 9.8 | 13.3 | 18.6 | 5.9 | 8.1 | 3.6 | 14.3 | 12.1 | 14.7 | 10.4 | 11.0 |
| Huila | 6.0 | 3.8 | 8.5 | 12.2 | 10.0 | 23.2 | 18.4 | 59.0 | 50.9 | 47.6 | 99.9 | 47.3 | 68.3 | 21.8 | 31.9 |
| Magdalena | 5.3 | 6.3 | 12.1 | 17.9 | 17.2 | 14.9 | 9.5 | 17.9 | 15.1 | 12.2 | 11.5 | 14.1 | 14.2 | 12.5 | 11.8 |
| Narino | 9.6 | 11.4 | 8.6 | 9.2 | 5.9 | 8.9 | 6.9 | 6.4 | 9.1 | 11.0 | 5.6 | 8.5 | 9.0 | 10.3 | 8.0 |
| Norte de Santander | 48.0 | 77.1 | 46.0 | 79.5 | 53.5 | 43.5 | 52.0 | 51.0 | 46.3 | 47.7 | 51.5 | 49.6 | 62.7 | 66.4 | 56.8 |
| Santander | 16.1 | 30.0 | 40.3 | 86.5 | 37.4 | 43.5 | 57.0 | 46.9 | 36.1 | 40.2 | 41.9 | 36.2 | 59.0 | 50.6 | 56.0 |
| Tolima | 8.5 | 7.2 | 11.4 | 13.9 | 31.2 | 47.6 | 86.7 | 63.4 | 47.9 | 98.1 | 164.1 | 115.6 | 133.7 | 100.7 | 62.8 |
| Valle | 19.4 | 16.7 | 21.6 | 69.3 | 76.2 | 68.1 | 83.5 | 44.9 | 33.1 | 57.0 | 54.6 | 87.5 | 97.3 | 62.4 | 51.2 |
| Intendencias | 14.5 | 5.7 | 15.2 | 27.1 | 35.3 | 45.7 | 60.9 | 40.3 | 20.4 | 24.4 | 21.2 | 28.8 | 27.4 | 29.6 | 27.9 |

Source: Ministerio de Justicia (1961).

the name Southern Block (*Bloque Sur*) with the support of the Communist party. A year later, they established themselves as the FARC.Thus, the peasant self-defense groups of southern Tolima, with support from the Communist party, called the First Guerrilla Conference in 1965. In this conference, they set as their main objectives the subsistence of the movement and the transformation of their forces into mobile guerrillas.

The rise of the FARC peasant guerrilla groups in the 1960s has remote origins in the so-called peasant leagues. Guerrilla movements rose first in those regions where the agrarian movement was stronger (Pizarro 1991) and where frustration over the failure of agrarian reform was more intense. Conflict between political parties also determined the formation of guerilla groups (Gilodhés 1985; Pizarro 1991). No short-term economic conditions, such as high inflation or poor economic performance, could explain the emergence of those groups. In contrast, structural causes, such as the crisis of *minifundio* (small property of land) or unequal land distribution, are more plausible explanations of the rise of the guerrilla groups.The FARC rose as an organization that "gathered the tradition of Colombian agrarian struggle that started in the 1920s."[1]

The Second Guerrilla Conference was held in April 1966 in the region of the Duda River. In this meeting, the FARC pledged to expand guerilla activities nationwide. During this period, the guerrillas expanded slowly.The FARC did not have a national presence in the 1970s; they instead concentrated in a few regions, including Tolima, Cauca, Meta, Huila, Caquetá, Cundinamarca, the Urabá region, and the Mid-Magdalena River (*Magdalena Medio*). By 1978, the FARC had enrolled 1,000 men.

The 1980s marked a drastic turn in the growth and consolidation of the FARC. In May 1982, after the Seventh Guerrilla Conference, the group added "EP" to its acronym (which stood for "People's Army," see www.farc-ep.org), revising their *modus operandi* and objectives.Thus, they decided to bring the war to the urban centers and use kidnapping and intimidation to obtain financing, which allowed them to grow (Bottía 2002; Gómez Buendia 1991).The FARC expanded their influence to the east and established the Central Mountain Range as their strategic axis of expansion to the west.The success of their financing plan allowed them to grow from 1,000 men fighting on seven fronts in 1978, to more than 16,000 men fighting on 66 fronts in 2000.

## Emergence and Evolution of the ELN

The National Liberation Army (ELN) was created under the influence of the Cuban revolution.The initial core was formed by 16 men who started to operate in 1962. In 1965, the ELN launched its first attack against the police post in the town of Simacota.Their strategic objectives were the assumption of power by the poor and the defeat of the national oligarchy, the armed forces, and North America's imperialist economic, political, and military interests (Medina 2001).Their commitment to armed confrontation granted this group a large amount of publicity in idealistic circles, such as university students. By the end of 1965, 30 men were enrolled in the group.[2]

Between 1966 and 1973, the ELN gained momentum. By 1973, it had 270 men, though the retaliation for the attack on the police post of Anorí (in Antioquia) almost led it to its extinction. Between 1974 and 1978, the ELN underwent a slow recovery, changing leaders constantly and revising its objectives. Since the 1980s, this guerrilla group grew significantly and became active in other regions of Colombia. By 2000, the ELN had enrolled 4,500 men, distributed across 41 fronts throughout much of the country.[3]

The recovery and expansion of the ELN are partly the result of a change in strategy as the ELN began imitating the FARC's strategies. The ELN also benefited from extortions done by the Domingo Laín front in the oil region of Sarare, against the foreign companies in charge of the construction of the Caño Limón–Coveñas pipeline (Offstein 2002). Today, the ELN is the second largest guerrilla group in Colombia and is financed by extortion, alliances with drug trafficking cartels, and kidnapping. It is half as big as the FARC, but it causes as much damage and violence.

## Illegal Self-Defense Groups (Paramilitary Organizations)

Self-defense groups came into being in the 1980s under the government of Belisario Betancur. They were sponsored and financed by land owners and initially made an army of not more than 1,000 men. They quickly adopted an offensive strategy, performing certain functions of the state, fighting against the guerrillas, and murdering leftist leaders and so-called "friends of the guerrilla" (Cubides 1999). They were consolidated in a counterinsurgency organization known as the United Self-Defense of Colombia (AUC). They entered areas traditionally dominated by guerrillas, such as Urabá in Antioquia, Cordoba, and Meta and Putumayo (Presidencia de la República 2002).

In the 1990s, these groups grew exponentially and they now have more than 10,000 men scattered throughout the country. They have perpetrated murders and massacres to intimidate or displace the population, thus cutting into the guerrillas' local support networks. Most people attribute most of the massacres to this group. The AUC finances its activities with contributions from landowners, cattle dealers, and even urban business people whom they protect. Just like guerrilla groups, they receive financing from drug traffickers (selling protection for illicit crops) and there is some evidence that they use kidnapping to raise ransom.

## Violent Crime and Drug Trafficking in Colombia

Below we present the trends and patterns of crime in Colombia from the 1950s for homicide and from the 1980s for kidnapping and property crime. We analyze the change in crime in the recent past. Many variables affect the crime rate, but drug trafficking and armed conflict seem to be the cause of the recent sharp increase in the crime rate in Colombia.

## Homicide

As expected, there is a high correlation between political conflict (war) and the homicide rate in Colombia. The first period of intensification of homicide violence took place between 1950 and the beginning of the 1960s, which corresponds with *La Violencia* (see figure 5.1). The military coup in 1953 reduced the number of violent deaths only temporarily. The homicide rate increased again, reaching a record level of 50 homicides per 100,000 inhabitants (hphti) in 1957. Soon after the *Frente Nacional* political agreement, the homicide rate began to decrease, reaching approximately 20 hphti by the end of the 1960s.

The second cycle of rise in homicides began in the 1980s and persists to this day. At first, this increase corresponded with the strong growth of the cocaine trade and the consolidation of the drug cartels. Later, it also corresponded to strengthening of the guerrilla groups. The homicide rate escalated, reaching its highest level of 81 hphti in 1992; from then on, the homicide rate decreased slightly, although the trend was reversed in recent years coinciding with the intensification of armed conflict and the fortification of the guerrilla and paramilitary groups.

Colombia has had a high homicide rate for long periods of time, but there has been a clear increase over time (see figure 5.1). The 1990s had the highest homicide rate in the last 50 years. There are important regional differences (see table 5.1), but in all regions the general trends have been the same over time.

Deaths due directly to the guerilla and paramilitary war are included in the homicide rate and may count for around 15 percent of total reported homicides.[4] These numbers can be misleading for several reasons. First, some homicides attributable to those groups are not counted in official figures. Second, as we will show later, these

## *Figure 5.1* Colombia's Homicide Rate (1945–2000)

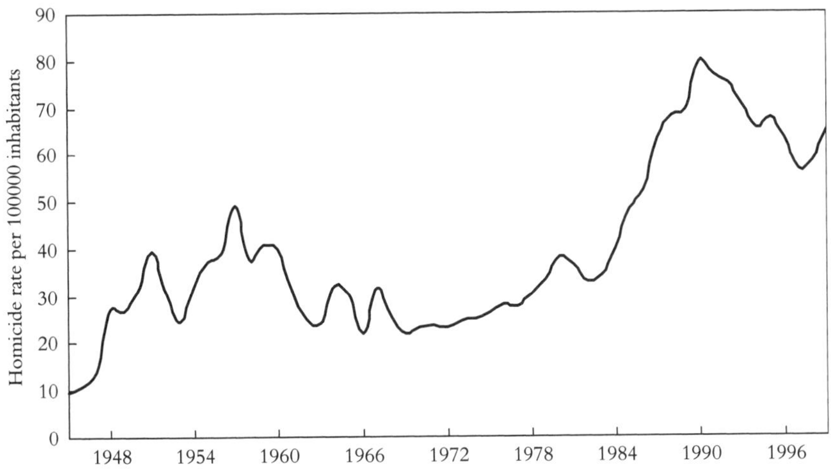

*Source:* National Department of Statistics and National Police.

numbers obfuscate some of the connections between deaths related to the war and the overall homicide rate that is also the result of criminal violence. We argue that the separation of political and criminal violence is misleading.

## Kidnapping

In addition to homicides, kidnapping is the main criminal activity related to the Colombian conflict. At the end of the 1980s, this type of crime increased dramatically along with the strength of the guerrilla organizations and paramilitaries. In the early 1960s, there were very few cases of kidnapping. During the 1980s and 1990s, kidnapping grew from 258 cases in 1985 to 3,706 cases in 2000 (see figure 5.2).

Kidnappings also expanded spatially over time. In 1985, only the least-inhabited departments had no kidnappings and there were no departments (states) with more than 35 kidnappings a year. In 1990, there were kidnappings in most of the country and there were some departments in which kidnappings exceeded 100 per year. Data from *Pais Libre* for 1999–2000 indicate that between 1999 and 2000, 50 percent of the kidnappings can be attributed to the FARC and the ELN guerrillas, showing an average of 1,430 kidnappings per year for these two groups. For the same period, 6 percent of the cases were attributed to the paramilitary groups, and 10 percent to groups of common criminals.

## Drug Trafficking

One of the factors that is most closely related to the persistence and intensification of the Colombian conflict is drug trafficking, yet the importance of drug trafficking for the war changed over time. In the 1980s, Colombia became the largest cocaine exporter in the world, supporting the growth of the Medellín, Cali, and Caribbean Coast cartels. Because drug trafficking was so profitable, and given their financial

**Figure 5.2 Kidnappings and Guerrilla Attacks, 1984–99**

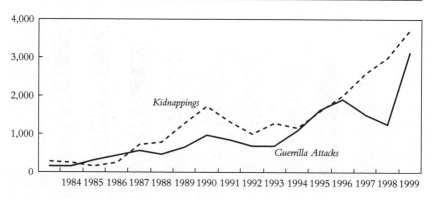

Source: National Department of Security and National Police.

needs, Colombian guerrillas began to charge taxes on illicit crops, on cocaine laboratories located in the jungle, and on intermediaries. These taxes were in exchange for protection from governmental actions against this business, and were intended to limit competition in the market (Molano 1990; Thoumi 2002). During the 1980s, the cocaine business decreased steadily from around 9 percent of gross domestic product (GDP) in 1985 to just under 2 percent in 2000 (Rocha 2000; Steiner 1997). However, on average the income derived from illegal drug trade has been around US$2 billion per year (Rocha 2000; Steiner 1997). The profits generated by this business resulted in violent fights within the different cartels, between the cartels and the guerrillas, and between the cartels and the government, causing a significant increase in the number of homicides during the 1980s. Drug trafficking also affected government institutions, leading to intimidation, corruption, and a weakening of the judicial system, which further emboldened crime (Gaviria 2000; Sanchez and Nuñez 2000).

Following the eradication of illegal crops in Peru and Bolivia at the beginning of the 1990s, cocaine crops moved to Colombia. More precisely, they moved to the regions of the frontier in southern Colombia, mainly appearing in the territories controlled by the FARC. From then on, the number of hectares cultivated with cocaine grew from 20,000 in 1990 to 160,000 in 2000, while the number of laboratories that produced cocaine paste scattered in the jungle increased. The dismantling of the Medellín and Cali cartels in the first half of the 1990s, along with the boom of the Mexican cartels, allowed the FARC and the AUC to increase their importance in the business of drug trafficking. Figure 5.3 shows the correlation between the increase in the number of hectares cultivated with cocaine and the number of FARC men. Because of their increase in participation in the drug business,

## *Figure 5.3* FARC Men and Size of the Cocaine Crops

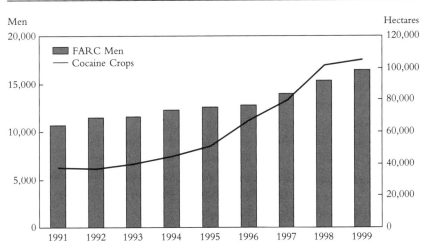

Source: National Direction of Drug Affairs and National Department of Security.

guerrillas were able to take over additional resources that allowed them to expand their military capacity, and therefore to intensify the Colombian conflict (Cubides 1999; Echandía 1999; Rangel 1999). Both the guerrillas and the AUC today finance a great part of their activities with resources provided by the drug business, and at the same time exchange drugs for armaments in the black market.

## Property Crimes and Road Piracy

Property crime has averaged around 250 instances per 100,000 inhabitants (phti) (see figure 5.4). This pattern is quite different from the one for homicides and kidnapping, which grew during the period under analysis. The department with the highest rate is Bogotá, with an average of over 600 crimes phti from 1985 to 2000, although the rate decreased in later years. Geographically isolated departments have the lowest crime rate (Putumayo, Vichada, or Vaupés).[5]

Road piracy has increased significantly: from 206 cases in 1985 to 1,557 in 1993, and 3,260 cases in 2000. Therefore, the rate per 100,000 inhabitants increased from 0.64 in 1985 to nearly 8 in 2000. The worst regions are in Antioquia, Bogotá, and Santander. There is not a very precise explanation of the causes of the increase in road piracy, although this crime is associated with guerrilla activities, mainly by the ELN, and with groups of common criminals.

In the next section, we discuss in more detail the link between common crime and crime and violence related to the political conflict.

# Relationship between Conflict and Violence

The dynamics of violence in the Colombian conflict have been understudied. The data presented previously suggest a dynamic relationship between the activities of

*Figure 5.4* **Property Crime Rate and Road Piracy Rate**

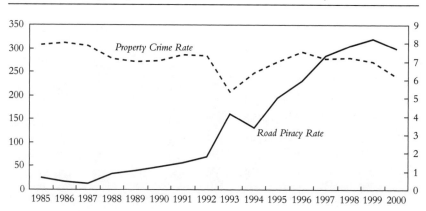

*Source*: National Police.

guerillas and paramilitaries, as well as drug cartels in their effort to establish their territorial control and extract resources. All of these groups aimed to control the population, and violence or the threat of violence was a strategy to achieve that objective (Salazar and Castillo 2001). Control of the population, in turn, is useful because it allows the guerillas to enrich themselves through drug trafficking and other crime. Over time, political and criminal violence in Colombia became indistinguishable.

Other analysts have pointed out the geographical relationship between homicide rates, the influence of armed groups, and drug trafficking activities (Echandía 1999, 2001; Rubio 1999; Sanchez and Nuñez 2000). According to Rubio (1999), in 1995, in 9 of the 10 regions with higher homicide rates there was an active presence of guerrilla groups, compared to a national presence of 54 percent. In 7 of these 10 regions drug trafficking activities had been detected, compared to a national level of 23 percent; in the same manner, paramilitary presence exceeds the national average. The effect of the conflict on homicide violence is so large that almost all homicides in Colombia in 1995 (93 percent) occurred in municipalities in which the presence of at least one of the three illegal armed groups had been detected. The municipalities without the presence of illegal actors account for 36 percent of the country's municipalities, comprising only 14.9 percent of the population, and their homicide rate (39 phti) was much lower than the national average, although it was still high by international standards.

The transmission mechanisms underlying this relationship are terror and intimidation. The absence of the state creates a space for the development of parastatal organizations that establish their authority through violence. The data show that there is a geographic correspondence between the presence of illegal armed groups, high homicide rates, and the existence of illegal crops (Thoumi 2002). The eastern departments that had the highest rates of violence in 1985 with homicide rates of more than 65 phti became the second most violent in the 1990s, having a homicide rate less than 35 phti in 2000. In contrast, the departments of the Andean region register the highest homicide rates today. In fact, violence in departments (states) such as Antioquia has risen considerably as a result of the expansion of the conflict in particular in the rural areas of the department. Antioquia had extremely high rates of homicide, mostly concentrated in metropolitan Medellin where drug trafficking was a very significant activity. The expansion of conflict from 1985 to 2000 changed the patterns of violence in the country. Violence, measured by the homicide rate, rose in the regions where political conflict became more intense.

## Diffusion of Conflict to Violent Crime

Spatial econometric methods can be used to explain the patterns of diffusion of criminal activities and of illegal armed groups. Higher violence or greater presence of illegal groups in certain spatial units (regions, municipalities) spreads to neighboring units, creating an expansion of violence. Through contagion, a spatial unit can spread violence to neighboring units even if the latter may not have factors that create violence. In the case of homicides, contagious diffusion involves criminal organizations that perpetrate crimes leading to more homicides. For example, an illegal organization competing for the control of a certain territory can trigger attacks and retaliations from other organizations fighting for the same territory. The attacks and retaliations can involve nonparticipant individuals or towns, causing a generalized increase of violence.

The patterns of contagious diffusion of violence and crime can be divided in two forms. The first is *relocation,* which occurs when violence moves from one region to another because of either an increase in law enforcement presence or the exhaustion of illegal profits in a given region. The second is *diffusion,* which occurs when violence and criminal activities spread out from the center toward neighboring spatial units, but the center continues having high crime rates. Another mechanism is *hierarchical diffusion,* which consists of criminal activity dissemination that does not require spatial contact and takes place through imitation or innovation (Cohen and Tita 1999). For example, groups of criminals learn and imitate the guerrillas' or paramilitaries' techniques (homicide, kidnapping, extortion, etc.), leading to an increase in the crime rate of other regions.

## Spatial Indicators of Conflict and Violence

A number of indicators can be used to show the relationship between conflict— measured by an index of the presence of illegal armed groups—and violence and crime. Figures 5.5–5.8 show the relationship between the standardized local homicide rate[6] and homicide rates in neighboring municipalities, and between illegal armed group presence in neighboring municipalities and local and neighboring homicide rates. The correlation between local and neighboring indicators shows the different patterns of space association between municipalities.

In figure 5.5, we examine the relationship between the local homicide rate and the average homicide rate of neighboring municipalities.[7] Each point is located on the Euclidian space local homicide rate–neighbor homicide rate. Each point in the space is either low (*L*) or high (*H*) relative to the other local or neighbor observations. Consequently, the space is formed by four quadrants with points where both local and neighbor homicide rates are high (quadrant *H, H*), one of them is high and the other one low (*H, L*), low and high (*L, H*), or low and low (*L, L*). We can see that the spatial relationship for homicide rates between local and neighboring municipalities is positive with a correlation coefficient of 0.5. In addition, the points located in the (*H, H*) quadrant, outside the circle denoting a distance of two standard deviations from the point estimate, are groups of municipalities with very high homicide rates. These are groups or clusters of municipalities that we call "hot spots."

Figures 5.6–5.8 show the relationship between groups of neighboring municipalities with illegal armed actor presence, and homicide rates in neighboring municipalities. They all show that a grouping pattern between these two variables exists. Thus, groups of municipalities with low homicide rates coincide spatially with groups of municipalities with a low presence of illegal armed actors, whereas groups

*Figure 5.5* Local and Neighbor Homicide Rate
(1995–2000 mean)

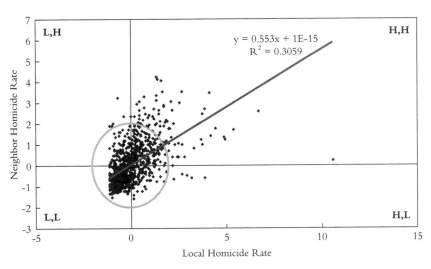

*Source*: Calculations of the authors.

*Figure 5.6* Neighbor FARC vs. Neighbor Homicide Rate
(1995–2000 mean)

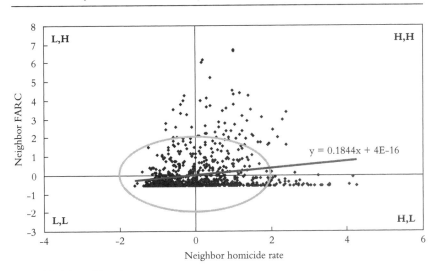

*Source*: Calculations of the authors.

*Figure 5.7* **Neighbor ELN vs. Neighbor Homicide Rate (1995–2000 mean)**

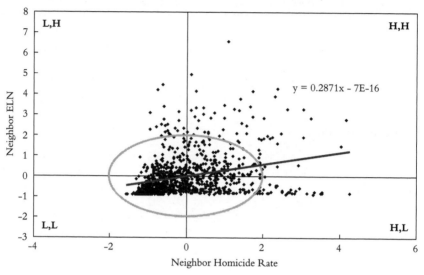

Source: Calculations of the authors.

*Figure 5.8* **Neighbor Common Criminals vs. Neighbor Homicide Rate (1995–2000 mean)**

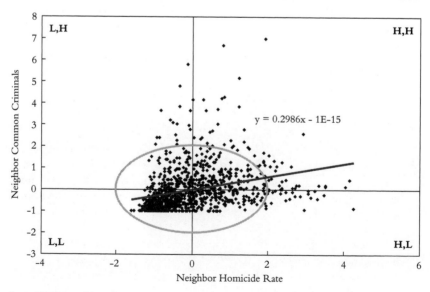

Source: Calculations of the authors.

with high homicide rates coincide with a high presence of illegal groups. The correlation is positive and significant for the FARC (0.18), the ELN (0.29), and the groups of common criminals (0.30) (this includes the paramilitaries). In addition, in all cases we detect groups of municipalities that are "hot spots," that is a high presence of illegal armed groups with groups of municipalities with high homicide rates. Thus, the relationship between the presence of illegal armed groups in neighboring municipalities and the homicide rate in the local municipality is positive. This means that regional presence of illegal armed groups is associated with local violence, even if there are no factors that generate violence in the local municipality.

## Spatial Dynamics of Conflict and Violent Crime

In order to determine the diffusion *dynamics* of violence and crime we must analyze how the local-neighbor combinations of violent crime, conflict, and violence change over time. The dissemination can take place between neighboring municipalities or between municipalities that are not close geographically to one another.

There are several possible patterns and changes over time. For example, the share of local municipalities with high homicide rates could increase. This can happen simultaneously both with an increase or a decrease of the neighbors' homicide rate. The same occurs with the relationship between the changes in local or neighbor homicide rates and changes in the presence of illegal armed groups in the neighbors. There are two types of contagious diffusion (figure 5.9). First, there could be an expansion between neighbors, when the violence rate is low in the local municipality and high in the neighbor, and changes to high in the local municipality and to high in the neighbor, that is, a group of municipalities changes from quadrant $(L, H)$ to quadrant $(H, H)$. The opposite case can also occur, where a group of municipalities can change from quadrant $(H, L)$ to quadrant $(L, L)$. Second, there could be relocation between neighbors, when the violence rate changes from low in the local municipality and high in the neighbor, to high in the local municipality and low in the neighbors, that is, a group of municipalities changes from quadrant $(L, H)$ to quadrant $(H, L)$. The opposite case is also possible, in which a group of municipalities changes from quadrant $(H, L)$ to quadrant $(L, H)$.

The dynamics of hierarchical expansion can be classified in the following way (figure 5.10):

1. Isolated increase or decrease, which is present when the violence rate in the local municipality increases (decreases) without the neighbor's rate being high (low) or decreases (increases) without the neighbor's rate being low (high). Local municipalities move from quadrant $(L, L)$ to quadrant $(H, L)$ in the case of an increase, and from quadrant $(H, H)$ to quadrant $(L, H)$ in the case of a decrease.
2. Global increase or decrease, which takes place when both the local municipality and its neighbor move together from low violence rates to high ones, or from high ones to low ones. In the first case of a global increase, they move from quadrant $(L, L)$ to quadrant $(H, H)$ and in the case of the global decrease they change from quadrant $(H, H)$ to $(L, L)$.

## *Figure 5.9* Contagious Diffusion Patterns

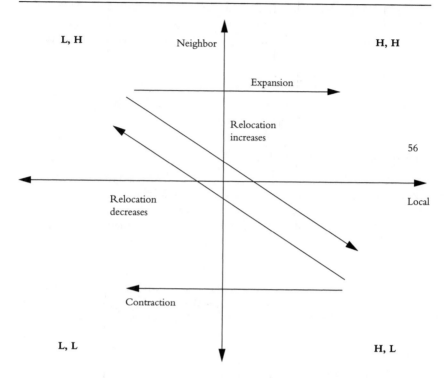

In figures 5.11–5.14, we show evidence of contagious and hierarchical expansion between 1995–97 and 1998–2000 as a result of the following combinations: (a) local homicide–neighbor homicide; (b) neighbor homicide–neighbor FARC; (c) neighbor homicide–neighbor ELN; and (d) neighbor homicide–neighbor paramilitary. The combination of local homicide–neighbor homicide (figure 5.11) shows that 56 municipalities presented contagious diffusion of expansion and relocation of violence, and 46 of them presented contagious diffusion of contraction and relocation of violence. On the other hand, 55 municipalities had increasing hierarchical diffusion, both isolated and global, whereas decreasing hierarchical diffusion, both isolated and global, appeared only in 26 municipalities.

Figure 5.12 shows the results for combinations of neighbor homicide–neighbor FARC, which illustrates how regional FARC expansion is translated into regional increases of violence. For the 1995–97/1998–2000 period, the results show that 94 groups of neighboring municipalities experienced contagious diffusion of expansion or relocation, whereas 56 groups experienced contagious diffusion of contraction or relocation. On the other hand, 55 groups of municipalities had increasing hierarchical diffusion, whereas 26 groups of municipalities experienced decreasing hierarchical diffusion. This means that regional increases in the homicide rates were

## *Figure 5.10* Hierarchical Diffusion

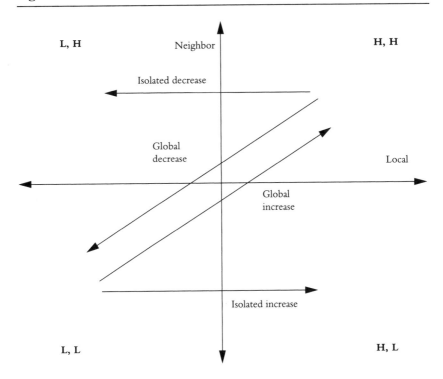

preceded by high previous regional presence of FARC in 75 percent of the cases. The other 25 percent are caused by increasing hierarchical diffusion. In addition, the number of groups of neighboring municipalities that had increases in violence rates (either of contagious or hierarchical diffusion) was greater than the number of groups with decreases.

The combinations of neighbor homicides–neighbor ELN are shown in figure 5.13. Here, 59 groups of neighboring municipalities presented increasing contagious diffusion or relocation in their violence rates, whereas 28 groups of neighbors experienced decreasing contagious diffusion or relocation. On the other hand, 20 groups of neighboring municipalities had decreasing hierarchical contagious diffusion, whereas 32 had decreasing hierarchical diffusion. Again, 75 percent of the groups of neighboring municipalities (within the neighbor homicides–neighbor ELN combinations) that had increases in their standardized violence rates had a high previous presence of ELN.

Figure 5.14 shows the same diagram for neighbor homicide rates–neighbor paramilitary. We can see that 103 municipalities experienced increasing contagious diffusion or relocation, and 32 had increasing hierarchical diffusion. Additionally, 75 municipalities experienced decreasing contagious diffusion, and 75 had decreas-

# Figure 5.11 Local and Neighbor Homicide Rate (number of municipalities that experienced change between 1995–98 and 1998–2000)

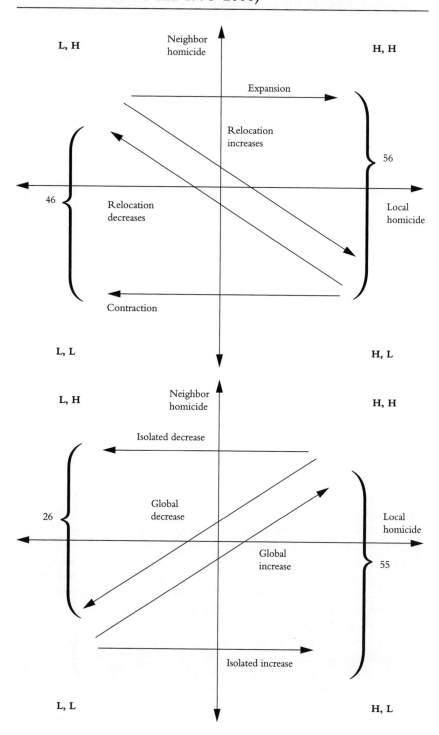

# *Figure 5.12* Neighbor Homicide Rate vs. Neighbor FARC (number of groups that experienced change between 1995–98 and 1998–2000)

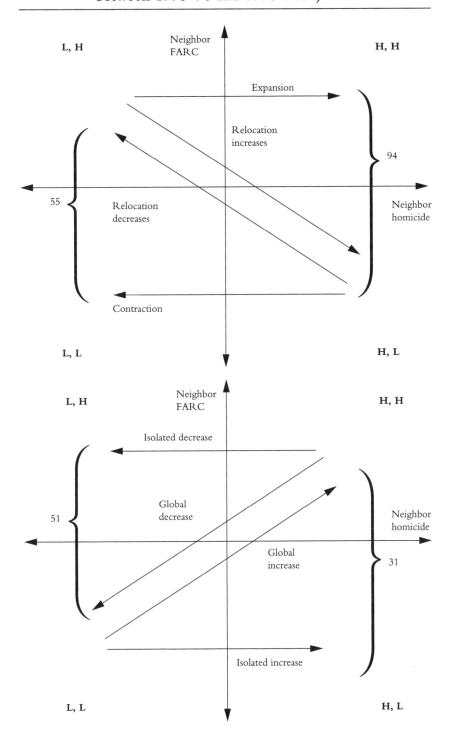

## Figure 5.13 Neighbor Homicide Rate vs. Neighbor ELN (number of groups that experienced change between 1995–98 and 1998–2000)

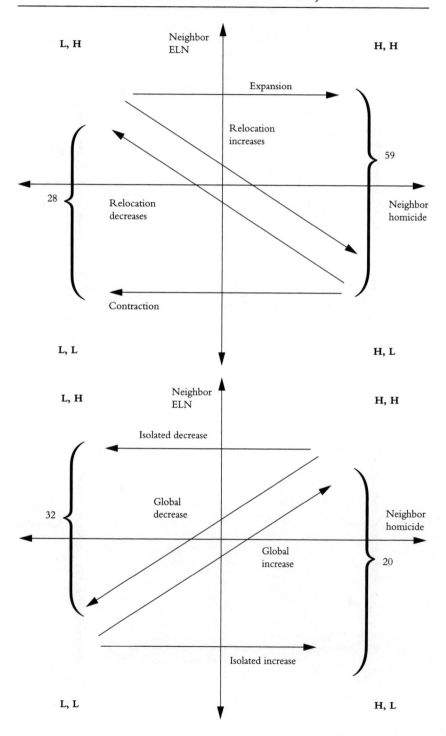

**Figure 5.14** Neighbor Homicide Rate vs. Neighbor Common Criminals (number of groups that experienced change between 1995–98 and 1998–2000)

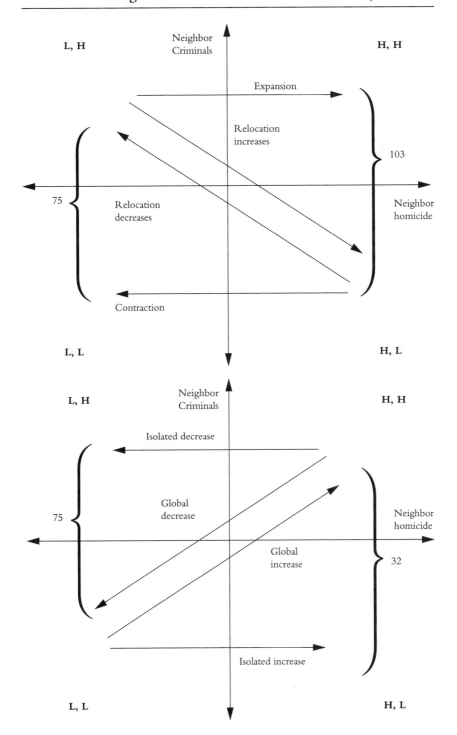

ing hierarchical diffusion. Therefore, during the period analyzed, Colombia experienced the largest increase of illegal self-defense groups, which led to an increase of violence. Accordingly, in 78 percent of the groups of neighboring municipalities where standardized homicide rates increased, there was a large presence index of illegal self-defense groups.

Finally, we analyzed other combinations of (a) local homicides–local FARC presence; (b) local homicides–neighbor FARC presence; (c) neighbor homicides–local FARC presence; and (d) local homicides–local ELN presence. All these analyses show that most of the diffusion of violence is caused by contagion or relocation, which is always preceded by high presence of illegal armed groups.[8]

## Econometric Evidence

The preceding discussion leads us to formulate several hypotheses about the relationship between conflict, violence, and crime in Colombia. Some researchers have argued that Colombia is a violent country, because of cultural or other historical reasons. Only 10–15 percent of all homicides are associated with the war or drug trafficking (Comision de Estudios Sobre la Violencia 1987). Thus, other homicides are often explained as an outcome of "intolerance" or the "violent nature" of Colombian society. A central hypothesis of this chapter is that Colombia has experienced cycles of violence associated with political conflict during the 1950s and with drug trafficking and conflict since the latter half of the 1980s, with specific patterns of diffusion in time and space. This means that the studies attributing "only" 15 percent of homicides to conflict or drug trafficking and the rest of them to "street" violence or "intolerance" are misleading as they do not take into account the effects of diffusion and persistence of violence caused by a initial shock of violence originated in conflict, drug trafficking, or political violence.

Violence (homicide) is one of the means of gaining territorial control by illegal armed groups and not an end in itself. We argue that there is a correlation between the spatial presence of these groups and violent crime, especially crime against civilians. The violence is self-sustaining: The initial shock of violent crime persists through time and is diffused across space, leading to a permanent increase in the homicide rate in the local geographic unit and in the neighboring units.

Related to the above, we hypothesize that the increase in kidnapping is clearly related to the growth of the financing needs of illegal armed groups. Although some of the kidnappings have "political" objectives, most of them are aimed at obtaining ransom. In addition, kidnapping generates innovation and imitation patterns by other criminal organizations, which perpetuates it as a crime. According to Restrepo, Sánchez, and Martínez (2004), more than 75 percent of the kidnapping victims pay ransom, nearly 20 percent are rescued by the authorities, and 5 percent die in captivity.

Drug trafficking is another crime related to the expansion of illegal armed groups. In particular, the growth of illicit crops is the result of the geographic expansion of these organizations, insofar as it generates sources of finance (Collier and Hoeffler

2001). The drug cartels, mainly in the 1980s, shattered and debilitated the judicial system, creating favorable conditions for other types of crimes.

The existence of illegal armed groups, which debilitates state presence through intimidation, annihilation, or expulsion, facilitates the rise of groups of common criminals and the increase of other types of crimes, particularly property crimes.

Social conditions such as inequality, poverty, and the lack of social services could be causes of both violent crime and property crime (Fajnzylber, Lederman, and Loayza 1998), and they may facilitate the organization and growth of rebel groups, consistent with the CH model. However, the *conflict triggers by means of diffusion and persistence, particular dynamics both of violent and common crime. Although violence and crime as conflict may be related with objective socioeconomic variables, those variables cannot explain violence dynamics. The contagion, diffusion, and persistence of violence do not depend on those socioeconomic conditions.* In other words, the dynamics are more important that original causes in explaining the magnitude and duration of the violence.

## Data

To test these hypotheses, we use spatial econometric techniques. The dependent variables are the municipal homicide rates between 1990 and 2000, departmental kidnapping rates, and rates of road piracy and property crimes between 1985 and 2000. We also estimate a model of kidnappings at the municipal level for the 1995–2000 period.

The explanatory variables in our model are departmental and municipal guerrilla attack rates, both for the local spatial unit and the neighbors, departmental per capita drug trafficking income, and justice inefficiency measured as the number of homicide arrests divided by the number of homicides in each department. In addition, we include socioeconomic variables such as poverty, measured using the unsatisfied basic needs (UBN) index (measuring, for example, lack of running water, domiciles with dirt floor, overcrowding), inequality in the distribution of rural property measured by the Gini index, and departmental and municipal school enrollment rates (data from the Ministry of Education, several years).

## Methodology

Given the fact that we analyze our variables across connected geographical spaces, there may be spatial correlation between the dependent variable(s) across units (e.g., in the levels of violence in the local unit and in the neighboring departments or municipalities). For example, homicide rates in a geographical unit can be correlated with the homicide rate of neighboring geographical units, with the social condition of the neighbors, or with factors that generate violence in the neighbors. This was shown in the previous section, when we presented indicators of the local concentration of violence.[9]

Our econometric techniques control for such spatial correlation. Spatial autocorrelation is very similar to the temporal autocorrelation in time series. However, in time series this problem is exclusively unidirectional (i.e., the past explains the present), and this can be corrected with a lag operator. In contrast, space dependency is multidirectional because all regions can affect one another. This does not allow the use of a time series lag operator and requires that we use a contiguity spatial (or spatial lag) matrix[10] to obtain correct estimates. Maximum likelihood estimation can address the problem of spatial autocorrelation and allows us to capture the spatial diffusion and spillover effects that we discussed earlier. We can also analyze spillovers from one municipality to another as well as estimate the influence of independent variables from one neighboring spatial unit on the dependent variable in the local unit.

## Estimation Results

Tables 5.2 and 5.3 display the results of the estimations for homicide and kidnapping. With respect to homicide, the results confirm both Becker's (1968) and Fajnzylber et al.'s (1998) model of criminal behavior and our own hypotheses (see above) on the dynamic and spatial effects of political conflict on crime. Two models were estimated for the homicide rate: one for 1990–2000 and another one for 1995–2000. In table 5.2 (first two columns of the results), we have data on our variables for common crime and paramilitaries for the 1995–2000 period.

TEMPORAL AND SPATIAL DYNAMICS. The results show that the lagged homicide rate of the local municipality has a positive and significant effect on the homicide rate in the local municipality. This means that a shock on the homicide rate increases the homicide rate over time. The homicide rate of the neighbor has a positive effect on the local homicide rate, supporting our hypothesis about contagious diffusion. Accounting for temporal and spatial effects, we find that a single homicide generates approximately four homicides in the long run.[11] There is also a small but significant effect of the lagged homicide rate of the neighbor on the local municipality's homicide rate. Table 5.2 also includes the results from a probit model, estimating the probability of occurrence or nonoccurrence of a kidnapping in a local municipality. The results show that kidnapping generates important spatial and time persistence and spillover/diffusion.

Table 5.3 presents a probit model for the periods 1946–50 and 1958–63 at a municipal level.[12] These periods correspond to the initial and final stages of *La Violencia*. It can be observed that, for the periods of early violence (1946–50) and late violence (1958–63), the lagged spatial variables are significant. Spatial effects are positive and significant in both periods, which supports the diffusion hypothesis. In addition, the political variables included in the models[13] show that the most violent municipalities were the ones with political polarization in the 1946 elections. However in the 1958–63 period, the political variables lost all their significance, which indicates an important change in the patterns of violence.

The results from department-level homicide and kidnapping rate estimations for 1986–2000 are also included in table 5.3 and they confirm once again the diffusion

**Table 5.2** Estimations of Homicides and Kidnappings, Municipal Level

| | Dependent variable | | | |
| | Homicide rate | | Kidnapping rate | |
| Variable | 1990–2000 | 1995–2000 | 1995–2000 | 1998–2000 |
|---|---|---|---|---|
| Constant | 20.61*** | 16.81*** | −1.32*** | −1.01*** |
| *Spatial and Temporal Dynamic* | | | | |
| Neighbor homicide rate | 0.21*** | 0.12*** | | |
| One-year lagged homicide rate | 0.68*** | 0.56*** | | |
| Neighbor one-year lagged homicide rate | −0.03* | 0.05** | | |
| Neighbor kidnapping rate | | | 0.21*** | 0.29*** |
| One-year lagged kidnapping rate | | | 1.01*** | 0.92*** |
| Neighbor one-year lagged kidnapping rate | | | −0.09 | −0.07 |
| *Armed Actors* | | | | |
| ELN presence | 2.06*** | 2.64*** | 0.01** | −0.09** |
| Neighbor ELN presence | 0.05*** | 0.54 | −0.01* | −0.28*** |
| FARC presence | 1.63*** | 4.13*** | 0.1*** | 0.16 |
| Neighbor FARC presence | 2.65 | 3.15*** | 0.1 | −0.19 |
| Delinquency presence | | 10.70*** | 0.01* | 0.01 |
| Neighbor delinquency presence | | 4.64 | 0.05*** | 0.08 |
| ELN and delinquency interaction | | −1.21* | | |
| FARC and ELN interaction | | 0.04 | | |
| FARC and delinquency interaction | | −0.07*** | | |

*(Continued)*

Table 5.2 Estimations of Homicides and Kidnappings, Municipal Level (*Continued*)

| | Dependent variable | | | |
|---|---|---|---|---|
| | Homicide rate | | Kidnapping rate | |
| *Variable* | *1990–2000* | *1995–2000* | *1995–2000* | *1998–2000* |
| *Justice and Drug Trafficking* | | | | |
| Justice efficiency | −14.35*** | −15.56*** | | |
| Drug trafficking incomes | 2.19*** | 4.29*** | 0.07 | 0.11 |
| Neighbor drug trafficking incomes | | | 0.12** | 0.08 |
| *Social* | | | | |
| Poverty rate | −0.11*** | −0.15*** | 0.00** | 0.00 |
| Neighbor poverty rate | | | 0.01*** | 0.01*** |
| Education coverage | −0.08 | −0.08 | 0.02* | 0.01 |
| Neighbor education coverage | | | −0.01 | −0.02 |
| GINI of property value | 1.50 | 5.09 | 0.27 | 0.00 |
| Neighbors GINI of property value | −12.13** | −6.96 | −0.43* | −0.50 |
| **Estimation Method** | Autoregressive Maximum Likelihood (pooled) | Autoregressive Likelihood | Autoregressive Probit (pooled) | Autoregressive Probit (pooled) |
| $R^2$ | 0.6017 | 0.4617 | | |
| No. of observations | 9,850 | 5,910 | 5,910 | 2,955 |
| Log-likelihood | −89,494.918 | −52,437.39 | | |
| Sigma$^2$ | | | 1.067 | 1.0787 |
| No. of 0 | | | 4125 | 2153 |
| No. of 1 | | | 1785 | 802 |

*Note:* ***significant at 99%; **significant at 95%; *significant at 90%.

Table 5.3  Estimations of Homicides and Kidnappings, Department Level

| | Dependent variable | | | | |
| | Early violence | Late violence | Homicide rate | Kidnapping rate | |
| Variable | 1946–1950 | 1958–1963 | 1986–2000 | 1986–2000 | 1990–2000 |
|---|---|---|---|---|---|
| Constant | −1.51*** | −1.61*** | 33.37*** | −1.28 | −4.58 |
| *Spatial and Temporal Dynamic* | | | | | |
| Neighbor violence | 0.18*** | 0.18*** | | | |
| Dep. homicide rate 1946 | 0.01* | | | | |
| Early violence | | 0.42*** | | | |
| Neighbor homicide rate | | | 0.27*** | | |
| One-year lagged homicide rate | | | 0.68*** | | |
| Neighbor one-year lagged homicide rate | | | −0.31*** | | |
| Neighbor kidnapping rate | | | | 0.20 | 0.11 |
| One-year lagged kidnapping rate | | | | 0.61 | 0.57 |
| Neighbor one-year lagged kidnapping rate | | | | 0.02 | 0.01 |
| *Illegal Armed Groups* | | | | | |
| Guerrilla presence | | 1.37*** | | | |
| Neighbor guerrilla presence | | 1.95*** | | | |
| ELN presence | | | −1.92 | 1.53 | 1.84 |
| Neighbor ELN presence | | | 12.71* | 1.05 | 2.79 |
| FARC presence | | | 0.48 | 0.12 | 0.34 |
| Neighbor FARC presence | | | 11.80*** | 1.79 | 2.04 |
| *Justice and Drug Trafficking* | | | | | |
| Justice efficiency | | | −40.06*** | −1.83 | −1.79 |
| Drug trafficking incomes | | | 6.98*** | −0.08 | −0.29 |

(Continued)

Table 5.3 Estimations of Homicides and Kidnappings, Department Level (*Continued*)

| | Dependent variable | | | | |
|---|---|---|---|---|---|
| | Early violence | Late violence | Homicide rate | Kidnapping rate | |
| Variable | 1946–1950 | 1958–1963 | 1986–2000 | 1986–2000 | 1990–2000 |
| *Economic and Social* | | | | | |
| Departmental agricultural and livestock GDP | | | 27.53*** | 5.7 | 7.5 |
| Poverty rate | | | 0.04 | −0.01 | 0.00 |
| Education coverage | | | −43.50*** | −0.22 | −0.28 |
| GINI inequality index of area | | | 0.000002* | 1.20 | 2.71 |
| Neighbor GINI inequality index of area | | | 0.000004** | | 3.54 |
| *The period of "La Violencia"* | | | | | |
| Land conflicts | 0.02 | 0.04 | | | |
| Granted hectares | 0.34* | 1.03*** | | | |
| Peripheral | | | | | |
| Political variables | | | | | |
| Liberal supremacy | 0.59*** | −0.07 | | | |
| Liberal control | 0.85*** | 0.23 | | | |
| Conservative control | 0.72*** | 0.19 | | | |
| Electoral competition | 0.95*** | 0.21 | | | |
| **Estimation Method** | Probit Spatial Autoregressive | Probit Spatial Autoregressive | Spatial Autoregressive | Spatial Autoregressive | Spatial Autoregressive |
| Interaction | NO | NO | YES | NO | NO |
| $R^2$ | | | 0.7916 | 0.6179 | 0.6135 |
| No. of observations | 755 | 755 | 480 | 480 | 320 |
| Log-likelihood | | | −3149.57 | −2338.36 | −1521.01 |

*Note:* ***significant at 99%; **significant at 95%; *significant at 90%.
Calculations taken from Chacón and Sánchez (forthcoming).

hypothesis. The lagged homicide rate in the neighboring department is negative and significant (with a coefficient of −0.35). This shows the possible existence of a spatial-temporal relocation mechanism of violent crime, because increases in the neighboring department's homicide rate in the previous year predict decreases in the local department's homicide rate in the current year. Similarly, the departmental kidnapping rates show persistence (with a 0.6 coefficient) of spatial diffusion (with a 0.2 coefficient). But the relocation effects are not statistically significant (see table 5.3).

ILLEGAL ARMED GROUPS. The results confirm our hypothesis that there is a positive and significant relationship between political conflict and homicide. The local presence of illegal armed actors has a positive and significant effect for all the groups. This means that these groups are not only a very important factor in the generation of violence, but also that the fulfillment of their strategic objectives of territorial control is accompanied by the use of violence. The presence of illegal armed groups in neighboring municipalities is only positive and significant in the case of the FARC. This implies that this group has "influence areas" that go beyond municipal borders. The interaction between paramilitary groups and guerrillas is negative although small, which would suggest that mutual dissuasion exists at a municipal level. The presence of illegal armed actors, in particular the FARC, increases the probability of kidnapping. A similar result is obtained with the presence of groups of common criminals in the local and the neighboring municipalities.

In the department-level estimations, neither local ELN nor FARC had significant coefficients. However, the neighboring variables of both the FARC and ELN have the expected positive sign and are statistically different from zero (table 5.3).[14] The presence of illegal armed groups has a positive and significant effect on the departmental kidnapping rates, especially local ELN, neighboring ELN, and neighboring FARC. This means that the presence or activity of armed groups is highly correlated with high levels of violence.

JUSTICE AND DRUG TRAFFICKING. As was expected, the effect of justice efficiency has a significant negative effect with respect to the municipal homicide rate. A greater action of justice dissuades and incapacitates criminals. However, departmental drug trafficking income is positive and significant in explaining violent crime. Because of the nature and size of illegal profits generated by this activity, a positive effect on the homicide rate is expected. The justice variables were not significant in explaining municipal kidnappings.

As obtained for municipalities, at a departmental level, justice efficiency negatively affects the homicide rate, while drug trafficking affects it positively and significantly (see table 5.3); thus, the less justice efficiency, the more violence, and the more drug trafficking, the more violence. In the case of the departmental kidnapping rate, justice efficiency has the expected negative sign.

SOCIAL CONDITIONS. Among the social variables, only poverty is significant and negatively associated with the homicide rate. The Gini coefficient has the expected sign, but it is not significant. With respect to kidnapping, also, local poverty has a negative (as expected) and significant coefficient. In contrast, poverty in the neighboring unit is positive and significant.

In the case of the department-level homicides for the 1986–2000 period, the coefficient of poverty, measured by the UBN index, was not significant. Both the local and the neighbor property Gini are significant and positive in the explanation of violence, although the magnitude of the coefficient is quite small. For the period of *La Violencia,* the existence of previous land ownership conflicts positively affected the violence probability, but the effect was not significant. In addition, the percentage of the distributed hectares as the total municipality surface was related to a higher violence probability (table 5.3). On the other hand, none of the departmental social variables has a significant effect on the kidnapping rate.

## Property Crimes and Road Piracy

The econometric results on department-level property crimes and road piracy[15] are shown in table 5.4.

TEMPORAL AND SPACE DYNAMICS. The estimations show that the departmental property crime rate has high temporal persistence (0.89) and experiences a diffusion effect from neighboring departments (0.3). There are also relocation effects, because an increase in the rate in the neighboring departments predicts a decrease in the rate in the local department. Road piracy persistence is very high (0.94) with diffusion effects from neighboring departments (0.1).

ILLEGAL ARMED GROUPS. The variables of local illegal armed actors do not have statistically significant effects on property crimes or on road piracy. Only neighboring ELN presence affects road piracy.

JUSTICE AND DRUG TRAFFICKING. The variable of justice efficiency has negative effects on property crimes at a departmental level. The effect of this variable on road piracy, although negative, is not significant. Drug trafficking income does not affect the behavior of property crimes or road piracy, because the coefficient that resulted from the estimation is not statistically different from zero.

SOCIAL CONDITIONS. Social conditions affect property crimes as suggested by crime theory. While poverty has a negative impact on these crimes by decreasing expected loots, wealth concentration (measured as property concentration) increases them. On the other hand, neighbor poverty increases property crimes in the local department; this shows that a relocation effect exists. Finally, none of the social variables are significantly associated with property crimes.

Overall, we find that conflict or war measured by the activity or presence of illegal armed groups both locally and regionally affects positively both violence and crime. Social conditions such as poverty or inequality are only weakly linked to them.

## Table 5.4  Departmental Estimations of Property Crimes and Road Piracy

| | Dependent variable | | | |
|---|---|---|---|---|
| | *Property Crimes Rate* | | *Road Piracy* | |
| | *1986–2000* | | *1986–2000* | |
| Constant | 2.55 | 2.70 | 0.004 | 0.03 |
| *Temporal Dynamics* | | | | |
| One year lagged property crimes rate | 0.88*** | 0.88*** | 0.942*** | 0.96*** |
| *Armed Actors* | | | | |
| ELN presence | 0.04 | 0.04 | 0.033 | 0.02 |
| FARC presence | −0.03** | −0.04** | 0.006 | 0.02 |
| *Justice and Drug Trafficking* | | | | |
| Justice efficiency | −2.84** | −3.58*** | −0.030 | −0.02 |
| Drug trafficking incomes | 0.25 | 0.36 | 0.004 | −0.002 |
| *Economic and Social* | | | | |
| Poverty rate | −0.02 | −0.03 | 0.000 | −0.001 |
| GINI inequality index of area | 6.11 | 6.18 | 0.073 | 0.22 |
| *Spatial Dynamics* | | | | |
| Neighbor property crimes | 0.03* | 0.30*** | 0.106*** | 0.31*** |
| Neighbor one year lagged property crimes rate | | −0.30*** | | −0.32*** |
| Neighbor ELN presence | | −0.06 | | 0.03 |
| Neighbor FARC presence | | 0.04 | | 0.06 |
| Neighbor justice efficiency | | 1.74 | | −0.11 |
| Neighbor drug trafficking incomes | | −1.82* | | 0.02 |
| Neighbor poverty rate | | 0.04 | | 0.00 |
| Neighbor GINI inequality index of area | | 0.00 | | 0.08 |
| Estimation Method | Spatial Autoregressive | Spatial Autoregressive | Spatial Autoregressive | Spatial Autoregressive |
| $R^2$ | 0.8372 | 0.8507 | 0.7821 | 0.796 |
| No. of observations | 448 | 448 | 448 | 448 |
| Log-likelihood | −2480.5899 | −2465.24 | −900.59 | −889.81 |

*Note:* ***significant at 99%; **significant at 95%; *significant at 90%.

149

## Decompositions

In order to quantify the contribution of the different explanatory variables in the homicide and kidnapping rate dispersion between the different geographic units, several decomposition exercises were undertaken using the coefficients from our estimations. This decomposition explains the municipal homicide rates for the periods 1990–2000 and 1995–2000 and the departmental kidnapping rate for 1990–2000.

The methodology used to carry out the decomposition begins with the complete data sample (dependent and independent variables) and orders it according to values of the dependent variables (homicide and kidnapping rates). Next, the sample is divided in five parts (quintiles) and the average value of all the variables in each one of these quintiles is obtained. We calculated the differences between quintiles based on the following identity:

$$TH_{t,i} - TH_{t,j} = \sum \beta_k \times \text{MET} \times \left( X_{t,i} - X_{t,j} \right),$$

where $TH_{t,i} - TH_{t,j}$ is the difference of the estimated average rate between the $i$ and $j$ quintiles, the expression $(X_{t,i} - X_{t,j})$ is the difference in the average value of the explanatory variables between the $i$ and $j$ quintiles, $\beta_j$ is the coefficient of the $k$ variable, whereas MET is the temporary spatial multiplier, which allows us to calculate the long-term persistence and contagious effects.

$$\text{MET} = \frac{1}{\left(1 - \alpha\right)} + \frac{1}{\left(1 - \rho\right)^2} + \frac{1}{\left(1 - \delta\right)^2},$$

where $\alpha$ is the temporary coefficient (the one that accompanies the lagged dependent variable), $\rho$ is the spatial coefficient (the one that accompanies the neighbor dependent variable), and $\delta$ is the relocation coefficient (the one that accompanies the lagged neighbor dependent variable).[16]

The descriptive statistics by quintile of the municipal homicide rate for the periods 1990–2000 and 1995–2000 and the departmental kidnapping rate for 1990–2000 show that these variables present a high variance. Thus, the homicide rate of the less violent municipalities for the period 1990–2000 was on average 3.1 hphti and 2.56 hphti for the 1995–2000 period, whereas the same variable in the 20 percent more violent municipalities was 167.97 hphti and 156.10 hphti for the first and second periods, respectively. This pattern of high oscillation is similar in the lagged, neighbor, and lagged neighbor homicide rates, corroborating the persistence, contagious or spillover effects, and relocation hypotheses. The behavior of the armed actors' activity is similar to one of the dependent variables, with high differences between quintiles. Thus, the conflict activity indicator for the FARC is 0.92 for the most violent quintile (compared with 0.33 for the less violent quintile), and 0.42 for the ELN group (compared with 0.15 for the less violent quintile) in the period 1990–2000. For 1995–2000 this indicator took a value of 1.23 for the FARC for the most violent quintile (0.43 for the less violent), and 0.55 for the ELN (0.19 for the less violent).

The delinquency activity indicator[17] was 0.29 in the higher quintile (0.06 for the less violent) for the 1995–2000 period, with the differences between quintiles for the FARC activities being much more considerable.[18]

The justice and drug trafficking variables are associated inversely with violence. The efficiency of justice is considerably higher in the lower homicide rates quintile, whereas drug trafficking income has a greater magnitude in the most violent quintile. The social variables used to explain the homicides were the UBN index as a measure of poverty, school enrollment rates, the Gini index, and the neighbor Gini index. The statistics show that the UBN index (poverty) in the less violent municipalities is greater than the same index in the most violent ones. The rest of the social variables do not exhibit any type of pattern; they rather show similar numbers across all quintiles.

On the other hand, the descriptive statistics of the departmental kidnappings for the 1990–2000 period show that the average kidnapping rate in Colombia is about 5.46 kidnappings per 100,000 inhabitants (kphti) oscillating between 0.46 kphti in the quintile with smaller kidnappings rates and 14.82 kphti in the greater rate quintile. The lagged, neighbor, and lagged neighbor kidnapping rates behave the same way as the dependent variable. The variables of illegal armed actors' activity FARC, ELN, neighbor FARC, and neighbor ELN is higher in the departments with greater kidnappings rates. The quintile with the greater kidnappings rates has equally greater activity of the illegal armed actors. The justice efficiency demonstrates special importance; the quintile with greater kidnapping rates has indicators of justice efficiency considerably smaller and the opposite is true for the quintile with smaller rates. For this exercise, not only were social variables included but also an economic variable was included, the agricultural output as a percentage of the departmental total output. This variable gathers the rural effect over the region. The social variables behave in a very similar way in all the quintiles without showing any type of special tendency and, as in the case of the homicides, the poverty is greater in the quintile with a smaller kidnapping rate. The agricultural output, on the other hand, behaves the same as the dependent variable; there is greater agricultural output in quintiles with greater rates of kidnapping, and the opposite in those with smaller rates.

The decomposition analyses (tables 5.5 and 5.6) show that the percentage of the difference between the homicide and kidnapping rates between the first quintile (lower quintile) and all the other quintiles and the average is explained by each one of the independent variables (including the persistence and contagious effects). Thus, the differences in the homicide rates between quintiles of municipalities for the 1990–2000 period are explained by the justice and drug trafficking variables. These explain more than 50 percent of the difference between a low and high quintile of homicides, followed by the armed conflict variables, which contribute 31 percent to the explanation and where the FARC activities are those that have a greater effect. Finally, the social variables like poverty, educative cover, neighbor Gini, and Gini have a contribution of 17 percent, with poverty being the only one that contributes in a significant way to the explanation of the difference between quintiles of both extremes.

## Table 5.5  Municipal Homicide Rate Decomposition, 1995–2000

| Variable | Percent of long-term difference between most violent and least violent quintile | | | | |
| --- | --- | --- | --- | --- | --- |
| | Q5-1 | Q4-1 | Q3-1 | Q2-1 | Mean-1 |
| Long-term difference Qi-Q1  i = 2,3,4,5,mean | 41.33% | 27.98% | 11.88% | 1.96% | 16.63% |
| *Illegal Armed Groups* | *52.65%* | *43.62%* | *30.64%* | *−56.65%* | *43.89%* |
| FARC activity | 26.1% | 12.7% | 1.2% | −54.5% | 16.1% |
| ELN activity | 7.6% | 5.3% | 0.1% | −12.1% | 5.3% |
| Delinquency activity | 19.5% | 19.6% | 17.2% | 38.3% | 19.6% |
| Neighbors FARC activity | 5.8% | 3.8% | 1.2% | -73.7% | 2.6% |
| Neighbors ELN activity | 0.7% | 0.8% | 0.4% | 1.2% | 0.7% |
| Neighbors delinquency activity | 3.2% | 4.8% | 5.9% | 11.7% | 4.3% |
| ELN and delinquency neighbors | -2.1% | -2.7% | 0.0% | -1.4% | -2.0% |
| ELN and FARC neighbors | 0.8% | 0.1% | -0.1% | 0.5% | 0.4% |
| FARC and delinquency neighbors | -8.8% | -0.9% | 4.8% | 33.3% | -3.2% |
| *Justice and Drug Trafficking* | *35.6%* | *41.1%* | *37.0%* | *48.3%* | *37.9%* |
| Justice efficiency | 13.1% | 16.3% | 20.9% | 41.2% | 16.0% |
| Drug trafficking incomes | 22.4% | 24.8% | 16.1% | 7.1% | 22.0% |
| *Social Variables* | *11.80%* | *15.8%* | *32.4%* | *108.40%* | *18.2%* |
| Poverty rate | 11.8% | 15.1% | 31.8% | 106.5% | 18.0% |
| Education coverage | 0.1% | 0.2% | 0.5% | 0.8% | 0.2% |
| Gini of property value | 1.4% | 2.0% | 4.8% | 14.5% | 2.4% |
| Neighbors Gini of property value | -1.5% | -2.0% | -4.7% | -13.4% | -2.4% |

*Note:* Temporary spatial multiplier = 3.25.

This same analysis for 1995–2000 shows that the illegal armed groups explain 53 percent of the difference between the low and high quintiles of homicide rates. The FARC group continues being the armed group with greater effects, followed by the delinquency groups (paramilitaries) and the ELN. The justice and drug trafficking variables take second place in contribution, explaining 36 percent of the difference. The effect of the social variables is explained almost in its totality by poverty; as in the previous case, the social factors continue to be those with a smaller explanatory percentage.

## Table 5.6 Departmental Kidnapping Decomposition, 1990–2000

| Variable | Q5-Q1 | Q4-Q1 | Q3-Q1 | Q2-Q1 | Mean-Q1 |
|---|---|---|---|---|---|
| | | | *Percent of long-term difference between most violent and least violent quintile* | | |
| Long-term difference | 8.42% | 5.06% | 4.34% | 2.83% | 4.16% |
| Qi-Q1 i = 2,3,4,5,mean | | | | | |
| *Illegal Armed Groups* | *54.82%* | *31.51%* | *15.87%* | *–3.82%* | *33.02%* |
| FARC activity | 2.3% | 1.0% | -0.5% | -4.0% | 0.5% |
| ELN activity | 29.7% | 12.1% | 9.0% | 4.8% | 17.7% |
| Neighbors FARC activity | 3.6% | 4.2% | -7.3% | -20.7% | -1.9% |
| Neighbors ELN activity | 19.3% | 14.2% | 14.7% | 16.0% | 16.7% |
| *Justice and Drug Trafficking* | *19.6%* | *28.2%* | *29.9%* | *31.0%* | *25.4%* |
| Justice Efficiency | 13.6% | 21.4% | 24.2% | 30.1% | 20.0% |
| Drug trafficking incomes | 6.0% | 6.8% | 5.6% | 0.9% | 5.4% |
| *Social* | *25.6%* | *40.3%* | *54.3%* | *72.8%* | *41.6%* |
| Agro GDP | *16.8%* | *25.2%* | *28.5%* | *29.4%* | *23.0%* |
| Poverty rate | 0.8% | 1.2% | 1.9% | 5.8% | 1.8% |
| Education coverage | 9.7% | 15.4% | 17.7% | 28.4% | 15.3% |
| Gini of property value | -2.0% | -3.2% | 1.3% | 1.9% | -1.1% |
| Neighbors Gini of property value | 0.3% | 1.6% | 5.0% | 7.3% | 2.5% |

*Note:* Temporary spatial multiplier = 3.

The last analysis was of the departmental kidnapping rate for 1995–2000. Armed conflict explains a considerable 55 percent of the long-term difference between quintiles, the ELN for the case of kidnappings being the most influential variable. In second place, we found the social and economic variables, where the departmental agricultural output stands out. This variable measures the rural effect (that is, a proxy of the geographic difficulties of the region) and the educative cover. Finally, the justice and drug trafficking variables contribute 20 percent of the explanation of the differences.

In conclusion, we find that the differences in violence and crime rates between municipalities are mostly explained by conflict (presence or activity of illegal groups), drug trafficking, and justice efficiency. Social conditions explained only a small proportion of such differences.

## Conclusion

Since the 19th century, Colombia has experienced civil wars and other conflicts that have resulted in high rates of violent and other crime. Persistence and contagion mechanisms account for much of that violence, both in recent years and during *La Violencia* (1946–62).The increase in the homicide rate was uneven throughout time and space because the propagation mechanisms were different. The traditional hypotheses state that the causes of *La Violencia* were political polarization and peasant struggle for land.Although these factors could have motivated the war, they have a small role in explaining the variation in the levels of violence throughout time and space. The regional differences in the intensity and duration of violence are explained by the activities of the liberal guerrillas, bandits, and other irregular groups.Those groups rose mainly in the Andean region in the center of the country and were supported by the civil population. Their local and regional strength and the response capacity of the conservative forces explain the differences in the intensity of the conflict.The confrontations caused murders, massacres, and general destruction in certain places. Most of the victims were peasants. Henderson (1984) calculates that out of the 525 deaths caused by *La Violencia* in the town of Líbano (Tolima), 86 percent were peasants, 5 percent soldiers, and 3 percent bandits. In this town the most bloodthirsty killers—nicknamed, among others, Tarzan, *Sangrenegra* (Blackblood), and *Desquite* (Revenge)—moved around at will (Sánchez and Meertens 1983).

The second cycle of violence in the second half of the 20th century began in the mid-1980s, more in urban than in rural areas, and related to the activity of cocaine traffic.At that time, although the guerrillas had begun an expansion and consolidation process, the effects on violence only began to be felt at the beginning of the 1990s. Our analysis shows that (a) there is a strong spatial correlation between the conflict and all violence indicators and (b) changes in levels of local or neighboring municipal violence indicators are preceded by previous activities of illegal armed groups.Therefore, violence is caused neither by inequality or poverty nor by intolerance.

The econometric results show that violence persists over time and that there is spatial diffusion in all types of crimes.The efficiency of justice, drug trafficking, and, to a great extent, the activity of illegal armed groups are among the significant determinants of violence. In addition, kidnapping is mostly explained by the presence of such groups.

Property crimes, in addition to the factors that influence persistence and diffusion, are lower as the efficiency of justice gets better, higher with higher inequality, and lower with higher poverty rates—results consistent with economic theories of crime.An important result is that property crimes are not directly affected by the presence of illegal armed groups.There are several factors that discourage guerrilla and paramilitary groups from perpetrating property crimes.Among them, the existence of common criminal bands that specialize in property crimes and the difficulties of trading stolen objects when there is not a support criminal network. Finally, the only illegal group that had an effect on road piracy was the ELN.

What is the significance of these results for the CH model? Collier and Hoeffler examine the relationship between predation and conflict, but conflict is much more than armed clashes between rebels or illegal groups (financed by predation) and government forces. Conflict bears the logical and rational use of homicidal violence (Kalyvas 2000) by the rebels (and sometimes by the government forces). Conflict weakens the judicial system and erodes the social capital, facilitating the contagion of violent behavior to the rest of the population and thereby making it easier for the rebels to spread the conflict.

The relationship between conflict, violence, and criminal activity is complex. However, the results of our research strongly show that the dynamics of conflict not only determine the deaths directly caused by conflict, but also the dynamics of *global* violence in the country. This happens because the diffusion mechanisms of criminal activity, which begin with an initial shock on the homicide rate, are transmitted through space and time, increasing the homicide rate of both the local and the neighboring spatial unit. This is an important finding since it questions the false separation between conflict homicides and "common" homicides, and bases the explanation of violence on a unique cause. This misleading separation (which has also been questioned by other authors [see Llorente et al. 2001]) has led to erroneously explaining Colombia's high rates of violent crime as motivated by a "culture of violence" or an "intolerant" society.

# Notes

We thank Ana Maria Diaz, who helped with the spatial analysis, and Mario Chacón and Silvia Espinosa, who did a great job editing the final text. The comments of the participants in the Yale seminar were very helpful, particularly those of Norman Loayza.

1. "FARC-EP: 30 Years of Struggle for Peace, Democracy and Sovereignty," available at: www.farc-ep.org.
2. Among its members was the priest Camilo Torres, who perished during his first combat. Unexpectedly, his death would make him and his group very famous among leftist European circles. With this recognition, ELN started attacking towns, robbed the local bank (*Caja Agraria*) in order to finance its actions, and defined its area of operations in Santander, Antioquia, and southern Cesar.
3. In 1983, the ELN only had a presence on three fronts in Antioquia, Santander, the Mid-Magdalena River (*Magdalena Medio*), southern Cesar, and the Sarare region. In the late 1980s, it grew gradually from northern Cesar to the country's southwest and started attacking urban areas.
4. For the period 1995–2000, on average, 26 percent of deaths were attributed to the FARC-EP, 13 percent to the ELN, and 52 percent to urban militias and illegal self-defense groups (Administrative Department of Security, DAS).
5. These departments, however, may have some underreporting problems, especially with respect to property crime.
6. Standardized means $(X_i - X_{mean})/SD$, where $X_i$ is the value of observation $i$ of variable $X$, $X_{mean}$ is the mean value, and $SD$ is the standard deviation.
7. The average neighbor homicide rate is constructed as the sum of the other municipalities' homicide rate, weighed by the inverse of the distance between the local municipality and the other municipalities.

8. These results are available from the authors upon request.

9. Spatial autocorrelation in the dependent variable violates some of the assumptions of OLS estimation (as a result of lack of independence of observations). OLS estimation with spatially correlated data would generate correlated residuals and lead to an overvaluation of the variance of the estimator's vector. It also biases the variance of the residuals, invalidating statistical inferences based on the standard $t$ test and leading to an $R^2$ value that is higher than it should be.

10. A contiguity matrix for $N$ geographic units is symmetrical $(N \times N)$, with values of zeros in the diagonal (because there is no vicinity of each geographical unit with itself) and in the other elements of this matrix the vicinity criteria of the other spatial units $N_i$ and $N_j$ are included (for $i \neq j$). These values differ according to the vicinity criterion that is used. If the matrix that is used is 1/Distance, elements $i$ and $j$ of the matrix, for $i$ different from $j$, are filled with the inverse of the distance between municipalities $i$ and $j$, so that geographical units that are farther away from one another have smaller values. If the matrix that is used is binary 1 km, only those elements of the matrix where the distance between the spatial units is smaller than 1 km are filled with ones, and the rest of the matrix is filled with zeros. The diagonal is filled with zeros, and then all the matrices are standardized horizontally, so that the horizontal sum of the elements of the matrix equals 1 (Moreno and Vayas 2001).

11. The 0.6 coefficient in the lagged variable implies that one additional homicide generates 2.5 homicides in the long term. Similarly, one homicide causes a spatial increase (in all municipalities) of 1.6 homicides. Taking space and time into account, one homicide generates four homicides in the long run. The spatial effect increases by more than 60 percent the purely temporal effect of a homicide.

12. The spatial autoregressive probit models predict the probability of violent deaths for the periods 1946–50 and 1958–63. The models include, beside the spatial variables, political, geographical and land conflicts variables. These models were taken from Chacón and Sanchez (forthcoming).

13. The political variables were constructed using the 1946 municipal elections. The municipalities were classified according to the percentage of votes in favor of a political party (municipalities with 80 percent or more votes for a party were classified under supremacy of that party, between 60 and 79 percent under control, and between 40 and 60 percent for any of the parties under electoral competition). All these political variables were included as dummy variables. For the 1958–63 period, we also controlled for the presence of local and neighbor guerrillas.

14. The aggregation of variables from small regional units (municipalities) to large units (departments) decreases the variance of the aggregated variables and, therefore, its statistical importance. In the regressions for departmental homicides, we controlled for the spatial interaction of illegal armed groups and drug trafficking income, among other variables.

15. Unfortunately, data for municipal property crimes do not exist.

16. The temporary spatial multiplier of the municipal homicide rate for the period 1990–95 is 4.72 and for the period 1995–2000 it is 3, whereas for the kidnapping rate for 1990–2000 it is 3.

17. The delinquency variable is included only in the regression that explains the munici-pal homicide rate for the period 1995–2000; there is not any information for previous periods.
18. The neighbor illegal armed actors variables do not maintain in a strict way the patterns of greater activity in quintiles with high homicide rates and minor activity in those with low rates, the same as the interaction variables ELN and Delinquency, ELN and FARC, and FARC and Delinquency, included only in the 1995–2000 period.

# References

Alape, Arturo. 1985. *La paz, la violencia: testigos de excepción*. Bogotá: Editorial Planeta.
———. 1989. *Las vidas de Pedro Antonio Marín, Manuel Marulanda Vélez, Tirofijo*. Bogotá: Editorial Planeta Colombiana.
Becker, Gary. 1968. "Crime and Punishment: An Economic Approach." *Journal of Political Economy* 76 (2): 169–217.
Bottía, Martha. 2002. "La presencia municipal de las FARC: es estrategia y contagio, mas que ausencia del estado." Mimeo, Universidad de los Andes.
Chacón, Mario, and Fabio Sanchez. Forthcoming. "Political Polarization and Violence dur-ing 'La Violencia,' 1946–1963."
Cohen, Jacqueline, and George Tita. 1999. "Diffusion in Homicide Exploring a General Method for Detecting Spatial Diffusion Processes." *Journal of Quantitative Criminology* 15 (4): 451–494.
Collier, Paul, and Anke Hoeffler. 2001. "Greed and Grievance in Civil War." Policy Research Working Paper 2355, World Bank, Washington, DC.
Comision de Estudios Sobre la Violencia. 1987. *Colombia: violencia y democracia*. Bogotá, Colciencias: Universidad Nacional de Colombia.
Cubides, Fernando. 1999. "Los paramilitares y su estrategias." In *Reconocer la guerra para con-struir la paz*. Bogota: CEREC.
Deas, Malcom. 1991. "Algunos interrogantes sobre la relación entre guerras civiles y vio-lencia." In *Pasado y presente de la violencia en Colombia*, ed. Ricardo Peñaranda and Gonzalo Sánchez. Bogotá: Fondo Editorial CEREC.
Echandía, Camilo. 1999. "Expansión territorial de las guerrillas Colombianas: geografía, economía y violencia." In *Reconocer la guerra para construir la paz*. Bogotá: CEREC.
———. 2001. "La violencia en medio de conflicto armado en los años noventa." La Facultad de Finanzas, Gobierno y Relaciones Internacionales de la Universidad Externado de Colombia.
Fajnzylber, Pablo, Daniel Lederman, and Norman Loayza. 1998. "¿Qué causa el crimen vio-lento." In *Corrupción, crimen y justicia: una perspectiva económica*, ed. Mauricio Cárdenas and Roberto Steiner, 53–95. Bogotá: Tercer Mundo Editores—LACEA.
Fischer, Thomas. 1991. "Desarrollo hacia afuera y revoluciones en Colombia, 1850–1910." In *Pasado y presente de la violencia en Colombia*, ed. Ricardo Peñaranda and Gonzalo Sánchez. Bogotá: Fondo Editorial CEREC.
Fuerzas Armadas Revolucionarias de Colombia. Available at: www.farc-ep.org.
Gaviria, Alejandro. 2000. "Rendimientos crecientes y la evolución del crimen violento: el caso Colombiano." In *Economía, crimen y conflicto*. Bogotá: Universidad Nacional de Colombia.

158 Understanding Civil War

Gilodhés, Pierre. 1985. "La violencia en Colombia, bandolerismo y guerra social." In *Once ensayos sobre la violencia,* ed. Marta Cárdenas. Bogotá: Fondo Editorial CEREC.

Ramsey, Russell. 1981. *Guerrilleros y soldados.* Bogotá: Tercer Mundo Editores.

Rangel, Alfredo. 1999. "Las FARC-EP: una mirada actual." In *Reconocer la guerra para construir la paz.* Bogotá: CEREC.

Restrepo, E., F. Sánchez, and M. Martínez. 2004. "Impunidad o Castigo. Análisis emplicaciones de la investigación penal en secuestro, terrorismos y peculado." Documento CEDE 2004–09, Facultad de Economía, Universidad de los Andes, Bogotá.

Rocha, Ricardo. 2000. *La economía Colombiana tras 25 años de narcotráfico.* Bogotá: Siglo de Hombre Editores, UNDCP.

Rubio, Mauricio. 1999. *Crimen e impunidad: precisiones sobre la violencia.* Bogotá: Tercer Mundo Editores.

Salazar, Boris, and Maria del Pilar Castillo. 2001. *La hora de los dinosaurios. Conflicto y deprecación en Colombia.* Bogotá: Fondo Editorial CEREC.

Sanchez, Fabio, and Jairo Nuñez. 2000. "Determinantes del crimen violento en un país altamente violento: el caso de Colombia." In *Economía, crimen y conflicto.* Bogotá: Universidad Nacional de Colombia.

Sánchez, Gonzalo, and Mario Aguilera. 1991. "Memorias de un país en guerra. Los mil días 1899–1902." In *Pasado y presente de la violencia en Colombia,* ed. Ricardo Peñaranda and Gonzalo Sánchez. Bogotá: Fondo Editorial CEREC.

Sanchez, Gonzalo, and Donny Meertens. 1983. *Bandoleros, gamonales y campesinos: el caso de la violencia en Colombia.* Bogotá: Ancora Editores.

Steiner, Roberto. 1997. *Los dólares del narcotráfico,* Cuadernos de Fedesarrollo 2, Bogotá.

Thoumi, Francisco E. 2002. *El imperio de la droga—narcotráfico, economía y sociedad en los andes.* Bogotá: Editorial Planeta.

Tovar, Hermes. 1999 *Colombia: Droga, economía, guerra y paz.* Bogotá: Editorial Planeta.

# The "Troubles" of Northern Ireland

## Civil Conflict in an Economically Well-Developed State

6

DOUGLAS WOODWELL

Located on the northwest periphery of the European continent, far from the center of European affairs, Northern Ireland was, and would likely have remained, distant from the thoughts of most scholars had it not been for the outbreak of the "Troubles." During the period from 1969 until 1994,[1] Northern Ireland became the scene of the worst political violence in Western Europe. The conflict yielded a death toll of 3,281 deaths (through 1998)[2] and tens of thousands were injured (Hayes and McAllister 2001; Smith 1999). In a region with a population of slightly over 1.5 million residents, few were left untouched by the violence, instability, and social polarization that characterized the era.

Although the casualty figures are large in the aggregate, the conflict took place over the span of a quarter-century, meaning the average death toll per year was only slightly more than 100. Whereas violence escalated quickly after the onset of the conflict, peaking at almost 500 deaths in 1972, there were only two years after 1978 in which more than 100 total deaths attributable to the conflict occurred within the region.[3] Thus, the conflict in Northern Ireland represented a long, but for the most part not particularly intense, conflict relative to most of the civil wars considered by Collier and Hoeffler (2001).

Even though the violence did not rise to the level of most civil wars, it still represents an anomaly in that it occurred within a highly developed society. This chapter starts out by discussing if the Collier-Hoeffler (CH) "greed and grievance" model fits the case of Northern Ireland. Of the variables in the CH model, ethnic dominance is the only one that appears to be directly related to the outbreak of violence. Otherwise, the CH model would predict a low risk of civil war in Northern Ireland, because the region had relatively high per capita income and a growing economy, high secondary school enrollment, not particularly unfavorable geography and demographics, no relevant primary commodities, and a long history without political violence.

After discussing the onset of the violence, I also analyze the conflict's long duration, drawing on the relevant theoretical and empirical literature for insights on the determinants of war duration and conflict resolution. Factors that I argue contributed to the conflict's long duration include: the strategic-tactical choices pursued by the Irish Republican Army (IRA); the presence of strong, but normatively restrained, state; the ability of the IRA to sustain financing through a network of illegal activities; and the presence of a demographically mixed and polarized population, which aided both militant recruitment and concealment. Efforts to resolve the conflict emerged largely from the cooperative efforts of governments in London and Dublin—efforts that eventually proved successful in marginalizing the influence of the more radical elements in Northern Irish political life.

## Roots of the Troubles in Northern Ireland

For almost 50 years following the partition of Ireland in 1920, intercommunal and state-societal relations in Ireland were characterized by an atmosphere of fragile stability. Despite the political and economic marginalization of minority Catholics and the dominance of majority Protestants over the levers of industry and state, expressions of violent discontent were generally disorganized and isolated until the 1960s. During the 1960s, however, the dominant social order and accompanying stability that characterized the postpartition era began to erode, and, by the early 1970s, had unraveled completely. This chapter begins by exploring underlying conditions, such as ethnic domination, as well as structural factors, such as the availability of financing for militant groups, that transformed the political scene in Northern Ireland from stability to protest to violence.

### Developing Ethnic Dominance: Northern Ireland before the 1960s

The recurring element that stands out in the history of Northern Ireland before the outbreak of violence is the politically, socially, and economically dominant role of Protestants in the region vis-à-vis Catholics. Collier and Hoeffler define an ethnically dominant majority as an ethnic group that comprises 45–90 percent of a state's population. They find that the existence of an ethnically dominant group moderately increases conflict propensity across all states. As I explain below, it is the specific nature of ethnic dominance in Northern Ireland that provided particularly fertile ground for violence in 1969.

In order to understand the issues at stake in 1969, it is necessary to provide a brief historical overview. The modern-day Protestant community of Northern Ireland descends primarily from Scottish settlers who began arriving in significant numbers in the 17th century after Britain assumed control of Ulster, which was the last unconquered province in Ireland. After mass settlement began, Protestants received preferential political and economic treatment in comparison to the treatment of the native Catholic population. Land was redistributed to Protestants to such a degree that at the beginning of the 18th century, Catholics owned only 14 percent of available farmland in Ireland (Kelley 1988, 7). Legislation, known simply as the "Penal Laws," was enacted, which made the right of first-born sons of Catholics to inherit land contingent on their conversion to Protestantism, further dispossessing remaining

Catholic land owners.[4] At the end of the century, a joint Catholic-Protestant rebellion against British rule, led by the United Irishmen of Protestant Wolfe Tone, was defeated in 1798. Subsequently, the Parliament that had existed in Dublin was dismantled, and Ireland became an integral part of the United Kingdom.

The cooperation that had existed between sections of the Catholic and Protestant populations was short-lived. A movement by Daniel O'Connell in the 1820s and 1830s led to expanded civil rights for Catholics, but O'Connell's calls for Catholic ascendancy severely alienated the Protestant population. At the same time, the industrial revolution was arriving in Belfast, buoyed by the burgeoning linen and shipbuilding industries. Working-class Protestants and Catholics competed heavily for jobs and Belfast began to develop the patterns of sectarian residential segregation that characterize the city today. The pressures of the industrial revolution and inward migration to the city fostered major sectarian rioting that occurred in 1835, 1843, 1857, 1864, and 1872 (Kelley 1988, 18).

The political entity of Northern Ireland came into existence with the Government of Ireland Act of 1920,[5] by which Great Britain granted Ireland a large degree of independence as the Free State of Ireland, while retaining six counties in the North[6] that were to compose the more closely politically and economically integrated territory of Northern Ireland. The Government of Ireland Act granted Northern Ireland a separate Parliament from the Free State, while allowing continued participation at Westminster.

Within their newly created regional Parliament at Stormont, Protestant leaders in Northern Ireland acted rapidly to maximize the power of the majority Protestant community. Protestant leaders sought political primacy through the gerrymandering of local electoral districts and the abolition of proportional representation in favor of a first-past-the-post (single-member district plurality) system. Furthermore, only rate-payers, those owning or renting "rate-able" property and their spouses,[7] were allowed to vote. This disenfranchised proportionally larger amounts of the poorer Catholic minority. In the wake of changes by Protestants in electoral laws, Nationalist[8] parties lost in more than half the electoral districts in which they had previously held majorities. Because elections were essentially determined by a gerrymandered religious head count, unopposed elections became the norm and political change in government was almost nonexistent.

Meanwhile, the economic stratification that had arisen during the colonial era continued under the new regime. Partly because of discrimination and partly because of the reluctance of many within the Catholic minority to swear loyalty oaths that were required of public servants, Protestants comprised approximately 90 percent of the state work force, including the Royal Ulster Constabulary (RUC) (Alcock 1994, 42–44). Many private sector work places, however, had similar patterns of employment, with few Catholics to be found in major industries such as shipbuilding and heavy engineering. Throughout the entire period from 1921 until 1969, Catholic unemployment was generally over twice that of Protestant unemployment, with Protestants holding higher positions in most industries (McKittrick and McVea 2000, 12).

The RUC was given free reign to deal with subversives. The Stormont Parliament passed the Special Powers Act, which allowed for arrests and searches without warrants, internment without trial, and bans on meetings and publications. Together with the auxiliary Ulster Special Constabulary, also known as the "B Specials," the RUC became the Protestant armed wing of the Protestant political establishment.

In the decades following partition, however, the peace was kept and the political situation stabilized. Despite the secessionist desires of most Catholics and the irredentist goals of the South,[9] the declaration of an independent Irish Republic in 1948, and the continued presence of small numbers of IRA radicals,[10] no major ethnonational or sectarian violence took place for almost 50 years.

The onset of the Troubles is linked to the historical conditions that bred political and economic inequality between the two religious communities in Northern Ireland, creating a ranked (Horowitz 2000, 22–29) society, in which group differences were reinforced by social class. According to Horowitz, ranked systems may exhibit periods of great stability, but "when the cement cracks . . . the edifice usually collapses." The Troubles are consistent with Horowitz's hypothesis.

## Outbreak of Violence

Many countries fit the criteria of having an ethnic group consisting of 45–90 percent of the population, the standard for "ethnic dominance" in the CH model. Almost all developed countries have that distinction. However, most of these countries only have a single ethnic group larger than 10 percent of the population. Thus, political grievances from subordinate groups are only likely to present a serious threat to the state on a regional or subregional level if the group is ethnically concentrated. Northern Ireland was different. It included a dominant group of Protestants, comprising 59 percent of the population (in the 1971 census), and a subordinate group of Catholics, comprising 32 percent of the population.

In the CH data set, only five countries with a gross domestic product (GDP) per capita more than $5,000 in 1970—Oman, Israel, Switzerland, Belgium, and the United States—had a dominant ethnic group and a subordinate ethnic group consisting of over 10 percent of the population.[11] Unlike Northern Ireland, representative institutions in Switzerland and Belgium were (and still are) specifically structured with the goal of ensuring minority rights and power sharing.

The United States, although it has not developed ethnic consociationalism,[12] promoted minority rights in the late 1960s as a result of the civil rights movement. The political gains made by black Americans during this period provided the single greatest source of inspiration for the civil rights movement in Northern Ireland, and it is no coincidence that the song most associated with both movements was "We Shall Overcome." In highly literate, politically liberal countries where citizens have widespread media access, "demonstration" effects can be extremely powerful.[13] This is especially the case when the country providing the demonstration is as influential as the United States. Nobel Peace Prize winner John Hume even went so far as to state that, "The American civil rights movement gave birth to ours" (quoted in Dooley 1998, 117).

Terrence O'Neill, who became prime minister of the Stormont Parliament in 1963, sought to alleviate Catholic alienation within Northern Irish society through a series of political gestures. With unemployment at 11.2 percent and rising at the beginning of his term (Kelley 1988, 80), O'Neill's political rhetoric was intended to facilitate the softening of sectarian cleavages as part of an overall program of political and economic modernization. In the most important symbolic gesture of his term, O'Neill hosted Irish Taoiseach (prime minister) Sean Lemass in 1965, the first such visit since partition.

O'Neill's new approach to politics in Northern Ireland, however, drew criticism from both sides. Especially after the Lemass visit, sections of the Unionist community appeared to be "in open revolt" against O'Neill (McKittrick and McVea 2000, 36). At the same time, many Catholics became disenchanted with what was perceived as a lack of serious political action. O'Neill's economic modernization program yielded little for depressed Catholic areas, with new investment mainly ending up in Protestant areas with Protestant work forces.

Catholics who sought to hasten the pace of political reform formed several small organizations in the mid-1960s. Emerging in 1967, the Northern Ireland Civil Rights Association (NICRA) became the umbrella organization that coordinated the activities of civil rights groups throughout the region. The earliest rallying point for NICRA supporters had been "one-man-one-vote," indicating the importance placed by civil rights activists on achieving a more equitable political system with fairer electoral districting and an end to the rate-payer voting qualification. At the same time, the civil rights movement also protested the more general cultural inequality perceived by the Irish-Catholic community. Ruane (1999, 157) notes that, in Northern Ireland, "cultural inequality is embedded in the landscape, place names, public buildings and official culture." Perceptions of cultural and political subordination, more than strict material deprivation, accounted for the affiliation of the majority of civil rights protestors with nationalist movements and ideology. In 1969, the average Northern Irish Catholic was in fact wealthier than the average Catholic in the Republic of Ireland (Dingley 2001, 455).

*Relative* material inequality vis-à-vis Protestants, however, was an important political grievance of civil rights protestors, who sought the removal of perceived structural barriers that limited opportunities for Catholics. Thus, the fact that the conflict emerged during a time of overall economic prosperity (McGarry and O'Leary 1995, 851) remains secondary to the fact that, shortly after the conflict began,[14] the differential rates in employment were such that 6.6 percent of Protestant men were jobless compared with 17.3 percent of Catholic men. Equally important, Protestants were disproportionately represented in higher paid job sectors, such as engineering and finance, while Catholics were disproportionately employed in lower paid jobs, such as construction and clothing manufacturing. One poll taken in Northern Ireland in 1968 revealed that 74 percent of Catholics agreed that Catholics were treated unfairly in some parts of the region and 55 percent approved (versus 27 percent disapproved) of the idea of Catholics "protesting strongly" against religious discrimination (Smith and Chambers 1991, 56).

The seminal event in the civil rights movement occurred on October 5, 1968 in Derry/Londonderry.[15] Although banned by the minister of home affairs, a civil rights march that included three Westminster MPs took place within the city. RUC forces assailed the protestors at the Burntollet Bridge in what was widely perceived as an excessive display of force. In response to the global public embarrassment that the march represented, as well as increasing pressure from pro-reform Prime Minister Harold Wilson in London, O'Neill offered a reform package that responded to some of NICRA's demands. Henceforth, housing was to be apportioned on a need-based points system, an ombudsman was appointed to hear citizen grievances, the voting system would be partially reformed, the Special Powers Act would be reviewed, and a special development commission would be established in Derry/Londonderry. Although initially welcomed by much of the Catholic community, frustration grew as reforms were only partially instituted and, then, only in a diluted form as a result of concessions made by O'Neill's faction in order to preserve a tenuous hold on Unionist leadership.

Within the context of continued instability and frequent small-scale rioting, opposition to O'Neill's reforms mounted in late 1968 and early 1969. In mid-February 1969, 12 hard-line Unionist Stormont MPs met to demand O'Neill's resignation. At the end of the month, the pro-O'Neill faction of the Unionist party scraped by with a narrow victory in Stormont, but the reformists were seriously weakened. Public pressure intensified even more after a series of bombings took place against public utilities.[16] The growing sense of public instability led to O'Neill's resignation in April 1969.

The legal reforms pursued by O'Neill arrived too late to mitigate the "Sorcerer's Apprentice"[17] effect that he had brought about during his term in office. The liberal wing of the Unionist camp was, ultimately, unable to overcome the resistance of mainstream Unionists, who feared that major concessions would eventually deliver Northern Ireland into the hands of Dublin. O'Neill's calls for reform heightened Catholic expectations, without delivering the far-reaching structural changes for which many had hoped. Rather than stabilizing the situation, limited reforms, which had come about as a reaction to civil rights protests, only encouraged broader protest by civil rights leaders. At the same time, escalating protests and rioting fed Unionist fears that a mass uprising among Catholics was imminent; this led to counterprotests and mob violence. As John Hume wrote in retrospect: "Whereas in the United States the structures of democracy were resilient enough to encompass the challenge of civil rights . . . our struggle was perceived as a threat to the very survival of the society itself" (1996, 45).

The Northern Ireland case points to the importance of examining not just the role of democratization in civil conflict, but also the dangers inherent in attempting to reform democratic structures. Efforts to bring about more equitable social and political conditions for Catholics created a situation reminiscent of the type of transitional democracy associated with civil conflict (Hegre et al. 2001), rather than a strong, stable, deep-rooted system of free and fair representation. Socially mobilized Catholics were neither harshly repressed nor provided any significant political outlet for articulating community grievances. The attempted repression of civil rights activists by the RUC that did occur fanned the flames of violence by creating a new central grievance. This grievance of protestors against the behavior of the region's heavily Protestant police forces thus rose endogenously out of the growing instability (O'Dochartaigh 1997, 310). Grievances concerning the nature of state politics were reinforced, and perhaps surpassed, by grievances concerning the nature of state violence.

Regional instability and sectarian violence escalated even further by midyear. The so-called "Battle of the Bogside," which began on August 12, 1969, is considered by many to mark the beginning of the 24-year conflict. A Loyalist association, known as the Apprentice Boys, conducted their annual march in Derry/Londonderry commemorating the triumph of Protestants over Catholic James II in 1690. Events spiraled out of control when Catholics clashed with the marchers, and rioting began throughout the predominantly Catholic Bogside neighborhood. Rioting soon spread to other cities in Northern Ireland, most notably Belfast.

The violence ended only after London sent in military troops. The troops were greeted warmly by most within the Catholic community, which tended to view the British military as a welcome alternative to the RUC and B Special forces. Although the British presence, at first, seemed to have reestablished a semblance of order, extremists in both communities were quietly arming themselves and preparing for the more organized violence that was to ensue.

Arising out of the turmoil, one development above all else ensured that the violence wracking Northern Ireland would continue well into the future: the creation of the Provisional IRA. After the failure of the low-intensity Border Campaign of 1956–62, the IRA had increasingly shifted away from militarism in favor of a more gradualist approach to encouraging political change. By the end of 1969, a majority of the IRA leadership favored abandoning the long-standing policy of abstentionism, which entailed the refusal of the organization's political wing, Sinn Fein, to recognize or take part in the activities of the Stormont, Westminster, or even Dublin Parliaments. In January 1970, the abstentionism debate provoked the resignation of the most radical members of the organization, who decided to form the "Provisional" IRA.[18] It was the new leadership of the Provisional IRA that took advantage of the lingering romantic symbolism associated with militant republicanism in order to attract and organize the increasing population of radicalized Catholic youths in Northern Ireland.

What started as civil rights-related rioting was able to develop into a much larger conflict because of the fundamental political difference regarding the legitimacy of the Ireland-Northern Ireland border. Whereas communal socioeconomic grievance drove the civil rights movement, the rise of the IRA framed Catholic-Protestant divisions in terms of the nature of ethnoreligious self-determination. In the view of IRA radicals, the complete realization of civil rights for Catholics could only be actualized with the transfer of rule in Northern Ireland to Dublin. The fact that Republicans and Nationalists viewed themselves as a foreign Irish diaspora in British Northern Ireland provided the opportunity for the civil rights movement to morph into a violent campaign for secession. The ascendance of the IRA fits a larger international pattern within which large ethnic diasporas are more prone to engage in campaigns of civil violence than other minorities.[19] This is more likely when a neighboring country claims the region in which they live.

By the mid-1970s, the IRA was increasingly prepared to broaden its initial campaign of scattered bombings, and membership had reached approximately 1,000 (Kelley 1988, 137). The underground legitimacy of the Provisional IRA was established when, on June 26–27, 1970, rioting that broke out in the Falls community of Belfast resulted in a gun battle between IRA members defending the Catholic St. Matthew's church and a disorganized group of militant Protestants. However, the events of the day also marked the end, for the most part, of the largely unorganized, less lethal, sectarian violence that had been characteristic of the Troubles up until that point.

## Economic Factors Affecting the Onset of Conflict

Although one can debate whether the Troubles of Northern Ireland constitute a civil war per se, the level of violence that ensued was unusual for a highly developed region. Table 6.1 shows predicted conflict probabilities in both Northern Ireland and the United Kingdom based on variables utilized by Collier and Hoeffler.

Regardless of whether one uses data estimates for the entire United Kingdom or more regional estimates for Northern Ireland, the CH model estimates less than a 2 percent probability of civil war in 1970, the year in which the Provisional IRA first began launching organized attacks. This low estimate reflects the many constraints faced by Republican militants in Northern Ireland.

First, Northern Ireland was, at the time of the outbreak of violence, economically well developed by worldwide, if not European, standards. High levels of education[20] and the fact that IRA members were generally not paid meant that militancy did not provide an alternate route of employment for young men. Reinforcing these factors was the fact that Northern Ireland was in a period of economic growth when the conflict began and continued to be for several years after its onset, although, as mentioned earlier, unemployment among Catholic men stood at 17.3 percent in 1970.

Furthermore, as an economically well-developed state, the United Kingdom possessed formidable state security forces with capabilities far beyond those available in less-developed countries. Throughout most of the period of the Troubles, London stationed approximately 19,000 soldiers (Sinn Fein Web site) in the region, including hundreds of SAS Special Forces, and developed a deep intelligence network with a web of informants. At the same time, British security efforts were conducted in tandem with the RUC, which numbered 13,500, including reservists, by the end of the Troubles (Police Service of Northern Ireland Web site). Economic wealth, when viewed as a proxy for local capacity and the ability of a state to maintain a monopoly of violence within its territorial boundaries (Fearon and Laitin 2001), was higher in the United Kingdom than in any other country that encountered significant political violence during this period.

## Table 6.1 Northern Ireland and United Kingdom, 1970

| Country | Male sec. ed. (%) | GDP growth rate | Primary exports/ GDP | (Primary exports/ GDP)$^2$ | Social fraction | Ethnic domin | Peace duration | Log, popul. | Geographic dispersion | Prob (war) |
|---|---|---|---|---|---|---|---|---|---|---|
| Northern Ireland | 74 | 3.5[a] | 0.09[b] | 0.0081 | 3,192[c] | 1 | 286 | 14.2 | 0.7 (UK) | 0.004 |
| United Kingdom | 74 | 2.4 | 0.03 | 0.0009 | 1,318 | 1 | 286 | 17.8 | 0.7 | 0.019 |

a. 10-year growth rate; 5-year growth rate was slightly higher.

b. Figures for Northern Ireland exports are not available for this period. However, the structure and size of the Northern Irish economy, as well as the level of urbanization in the region, suggests a primary export/GDP percentage that likely lies about halfway between Ireland (0.15) and the United Kingdom as a whole (0.03). This figure assumes that Great Britain also represents an "export" market for Northern Ireland.

c. Uses population composition of: one-third Catholics, two-thirds Protestant; one-third Irish, two-thirds British.

As a large country (with the 11th largest population in 1970), the United Kingdom would have a higher risk of war than a small state (see CH model). The most likely place for a war in large states is in border areas, because larger states are more likely to be home to "peripheral" minorities due to historical imperial expansion of the metropole. The situation of Catholics, as a peripheral minority group seeking independence, in this sense, parallels an important geographic factor for conflict in other states.

However, despite residing in the periphery, geography did not favor Republican militants. Insurgency in peripheral areas is favored when the insurgents'"territorial base [is] . . . separated from the territorial base of the center by water or distance" (Fearon and Laitin 2001, 14), which was not the case in Ireland.[21] Within the context of a developed society, the IRA also could not take advantage of"rough terrain, poorly served by roads, at a distance from . . . state power" (p. 11) in a manner similar to insurgencies in developing countries. Republican militants in Northern Ireland instead blended into sympathetic urban settings—well within reach, yet also hidden from, the security forces of the British state.

The leadership of the Provisional IRA launched the group into a violent campaign because they perceived that rebellion was a viable proposition, even though the group suffered originally from a dearth of men and *matériel*. Many of the "greed" opportunities that influence the onset of war in the CH model do so not because of the ready availability of such resources at the present, but rather because radical groups are willing to gamble that, once war starts, they will be able to garner the necessary finances, weaponry, and manpower in the course of the conflict.

As opposed to the well-funded local and British security forces, the IRA began as a poorly funded organization of"volunteers."[22] How did IRA leadership expect to support a militant campaign? Clearly not through primary exports, as Collier and Hoeffler suggest many Third World rebel movements have financed themselves. Primary export commodities have comprised a relatively modest part of the Northern Irish economy during the latter half of the 20th century.[23]

The IRA did fund itself, however, through networks of criminal and semilegal activities that Collier and Hoeffler argue are central to many rebel movements. First, regular bank robberies supplied periodic influxes of cash to the organization. Although admitting that the amount obtained from IRA robberies is difficult to estimate, Horgan and Taylor (1999, 13) suggest that robberies may have been the "main 'outwardly' source of funding" for the group. Organized crime and racketeering also financed the IRA (Silke 1998, 345), although the amount garnered from such activities is uncertain. These activities included major crimes such as extortion and kidnapping, as well as widespread smaller crimes such as welfare fraud and the establishment of illegal drinking clubs. There may have been involvement by the IRA in the drug trade as well, but this is a somewhat uncertain and controversial subject. "Legitimate" businesses that the IRA conducted and profited from included "construction firms, shops, restaurants, courier services, guest houses, cars and machinery, [and] pubs" (Horgan and Taylor 1999, 8).

A further source of funding for the IRA derived from supporters abroad, particularly in the United States. The largest organization representing the IRA in the

United States was Northern Aid (NORAID), an organization set up ostensibly to collect money for the families of dead and imprisoned IRA militants. However, in 1981, a U.S. district court judge ruled that NORAID actively funded military operations in the North. Estimated to have sent at total of $3.6 million to Ireland from 1970 to 1991, NORAID's contributions represented a small, but not insignificant, part of the IRA's income, which is estimated to have amounted to approximately $10 million a year.[24]

The IRA's fund raising enabled the purchase of small arms and major arms shipments were also contributed by sources within the United States and from the Libyan government. The first large influx of weapons came from shipments of smuggled Armalite hunting rifles, which were obtained by radical Republican operatives in the United States throughout the 1970s (Bell 2001, 481). Although the true scale of arms shipments originating from the United States and ending up in Northern Ireland is unknown, a shipment seized in September 1984 aboard an Irish fishing trawler yielded seven tons of weaponry (Guelke 1996, 523).

Secret shipments from the United States are thought to have largely ended by the mid-1980s (Bell 2001, 481), but were replaced by a much larger and more significant influx of modern weapons supplied by the Libyan government. Although the size of shipments that were delivered by the Libyan government is unknown, the 150-ton shipment seized upon the *Eksund* by the French navy in 1987 revealed a scope of direct arms shipments unprecedented in the IRA's history (and undoubtedly much larger than anything coming from the United States or elsewhere).

One last important source of firepower for the IRA was homemade weaponry. IRA sympathizers and militants manufactured significant numbers of bombs and mortars, in particular, throughout the period of the "Troubles" (Horgan and Taylor 1999, 4–5). Although the arms produced by the IRA were not inherently complex, and were composed largely of legally obtainable components, the production of large amounts of homemade arms was facilitated greatly by the economically developed environment within which the IRA operated.

The IRA remained a cohesive guerrilla organization in large part because of its sophisticated funding and supply efforts. The financial context for the IRA was decidedly different from that of antigovernment rebels in the Third World, but the ability to raise funds, even if not from "primary exports," was equally important.

## Conflict Duration and the Long March to Resolution

Whether one marks the end date of the conflict in Northern Ireland as 1994 (IRA cease-fire), 1995 (Framework Documents), or 1998 (Belfast/Good Friday Agreements), it is clear that the Troubles represent one of the longest running conflicts in the world since the Second World War. Northern Ireland's conflict dragged on for the same two reasons why any conflict lasts over a significant period of time: The parties could not defeat each other in the battlefield, but they were also unwilling, or unable, to reach a mutually acceptable settlement. Why was this so?

## Sustaining the Conflict

While financial and material income is important for militant groups, so too is a ready supply of recruits. There is disagreement in civil war literature on whether demographic patterns facilitating ethnic-based recruitment are most associated with conflict onset or duration. Elbadawi and Sambanis (2000) suggest a parabolic relationship between ethnic fractionalization and civil war, with midlevels of ethnic fractionalization most associated with conflict onset. While Collier and Hoeffler do not find the same relationship with respect to war onset, Collier, Hoeffler, and Söderbom (2001) find that longer conflict duration is associated with countries with a few large ethnic groups.

It is unclear whether the demographic balance in Northern Ireland facilitated war onset, but it is clear that the IRA, with a coherent (if not simplistic) ideology and clearly defined ethnic base from which to recruit, achieved the internal unity and cohesion needed to maintain its operations after the violence had started. The IRA represented, or claimed to represent, a single social group and it was from the predominantly working class Catholic community that it recruited its members.

Because religion and ethnicity[25] clearly reinforce one another in Northern Ireland, it is difficult to relate the ethnoreligious divide to Collier and Hoeffler's social fractionalization index. More appropriate for analysis in Northern Ireland is the ethnic fractionalization index utilized in Collier, Hoeffler, and Söderbom (2001). If we assume, for simplicity's sake, that one community comprises one-third of the population (Catholics) and the other comprises two-thirds (Protestant), Northern Ireland's ethnic fractionalization (56) is slightly higher than the population average (42).

Although the demographic conditions for ethnic polarization in Northern Ireland provided the seeds of communal violence, endogenous interactions within the context of the growing crisis provided fertile ground for the explosion of violence that developed in the early 1970s. The death toll that had slowly been escalating in late 1970 and early 1971 multiplied after Stormont Prime Minister William Faulkner introduced a policy of internment in August 1971. Faulkner introduced these measures, which entailed imprisonment without trial for suspected militants, in the hope that the IRA would be squelched as it had been at the end of the Border Campaign.[26] Unlike the scattered militants of the Border Campaign, however, the IRA had developed into a large, well-organized force by 1971, and was beyond the point of being easily stamped out. As figure 6.1 shows, interment actually marked a large escalation of violence. Utilized exclusively against Catholics for the first one and one-half years, internment served further to inflame Republican militant sentiment (O'Leary and McGarry 1993, 197) and the ethnic polarization upon which it fed.

As violence and instability grew, so too did the number of recruits for the IRA. O'Duffy (1995, 750) labels the period 1972 through early 1974 as a high point for the IRA, when the organization was "rich in both manpower and *matériel*." Rather than ending the conflict, the introduction of internment triggered a strong escalation

*Figure 6.1* Deaths by Month in the Northern Ireland Conflict

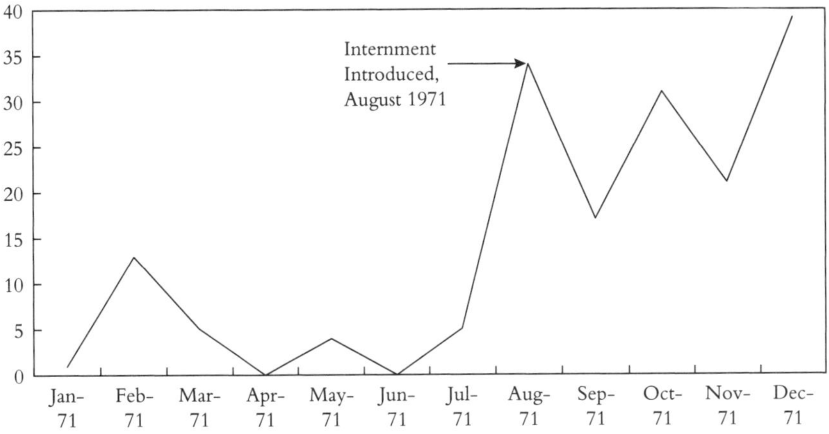

Source: Index of Deaths.

that ultimately allowed Republican militants to deal more easily with the resource constraints that they faced. A ready pool of ethnic/religious recruits, accompanied by a web of financial and material procurement efforts, allowed Republican militants to continue their violent attacks for decades, albeit never at the level of the early years.

After the intense initial years of the conflict, generalized war weariness had taken hold in the Catholic community by the end of 1974, and support for Republican movements began to ebb. Negative publicity, as well as internment and other security policies were beginning to take its toll on the IRA; it had witnessed hundreds of its members killed or imprisoned (Kelley 1988, 110). At the same time, secret contacts with British representatives bred a perception within IRA leadership that Britain was ready to compromise, and perhaps even send its soldiers home. The IRA declared a cease-fire at the end of 1974, which was to last until the end of 1975.[27]

The British government responded to the cease-fire both politically and militarily. Politically, internment and military operations were severely curtailed, and "incident centers" were established in Catholic areas in order to handle reports of abuses by security forces. Militarily, however, the British government used the cease-fire to enhance its intelligence presence in, and surveillance of, the Republican movement. When the cease-fire ended in November 1975, British intelligence networks had laid the groundwork for a massive and successful crackdown on the IRA in the subsequent years.

In response to the growing successes of the security forces, important internal changes were instituted in the IRA. A cell structure was instituted, making the organization more difficult to penetrate because of the creation of smaller operational units and a looser hierarchical structure. IRA leadership also decided to apply violence more carefully and focus on achieving specific political goals (O'Duffy

1995, 755). Despite these changes, however, the IRA, which had had perhaps over 1,000 militants five years earlier, reportedly had fewer than 250 by the end of 1977 (Kelley 1988, 285).

Recognizing that outright military victory was unachievable, IRA leadership placed renewed emphasis on guerrilla-style tactics[28] in a conscious effort to adopt a "long-war" strategy, one which Republican militants hoped would eventually lead to British withdrawal due to war weariness. According to Stam (1996), the choice of combatant tactics has a major influence on war duration, with guerrilla wars tending to be the longest of all. This is because "soldiers must spend a great deal of their energy simply surviving away from a large military supply organization and hiding from those who would eliminate them" (p. 120). Guerrilla warfare, however, can only sap an adversary's will to fight, not decisively defeat an opponent.

Generally, groups choose guerrilla-style tactics because they are forced to do so. The IRA was too constrained to fight conventionally,[29] but too strong to be defeated militarily. The constraints were due to many of the factors suggested by Collier and Hoeffler, including unfavorable geography and a strong (British) central government supported by a strong tax base and able to field a formidable security force.[30]

Collier et al. (2001) suggest that forest cover is associated with longer conflicts. Guerrilla movements, in particular, may utilize forest cover to evade state security forces, thus protracting the average conflict in more heavily forested states. However, with relatively little mountainous or wilderness area in Northern Ireland,[31] there was little choice but for IRA militants to hide within urban settings and residential areas. Much of the violence in Northern Ireland took place in urban areas, with 55 percent of fatalities occurring either in Belfast or Derry/Londonderry alone (see Index of Deaths).

Thus, Northern Ireland became home to "urban guerrilla" warfare, with the rural areas playing only a marginal role in the violence. Although it is the least-urbanized region in the United Kingdom, Northern Ireland is still urbanized compared to most countries.[32] The ability of scattered Republican militants to hide among Catholic civilians greatly hindered the ability of the British to bring force to bear, despite their formidable military and intelligence capabilities. Major security efforts in Catholic neighborhoods increased public alienation and led to higher levels of recruitment by radicals.[33] Furthermore, working within the bounds of a liberal democratic United Kingdom, potential civilian abuses resulting from higher levels of force were politically difficult for any government in London to justify. Mutual constraints faced both by British security forces, operating within urban environments in a democratic state, and by those of the IRA and other groups, who faced a strong state security apparatus within a highly developed state, ultimately led to the long, low-level conflict that transpired.

## Ending the Conflict

Some rare peace accords bring about lasting and comprehensive political settlements seemingly overnight. Most conflicts, however, end after a long process of fits and starts surrounded by alternating periods of optimism and dashed hopes. Just as conflicts are sustained by a lack of military progress, the unwillingness or inability of parties to seek a negotiated settlement similarly prolongs conflict. IRA ideology was based on the idea that compromise was impossible, and its traditional goal has focused on driving the British out of Northern Ireland militarily.[34] Similarly, Britain regarded the IRA as a criminal enterprise, and made only limited political gestures to the organization before the 1990s. London's contempt for the IRA, however, was exceeded by the contempt expressed by the Unionist community of Northern Ireland, which was, as a whole, as unwilling to make concessions to Republican militants as Republican militants were to abandon their campaign of violence.

The irredentist dimension of the conflict rendered it such that London and Dublin first needed to come to terms with one another on issues involving Northern Ireland, before it could be hoped that local parties could similarly engage in meaningful dialogue. As the United Kingdom and the Republic of Ireland increasingly came to view the conflict in the North as a common problem, and as the two countries increasingly cooperated in the creation of new institutions intended to facilitate peace, the main challenge became overcoming the intransigence of local parties opposed to compromise. Peace was finally achieved through a series of deliberate policies set in motion by London and Dublin that successfully nudged community and elite opinion toward moderation, making compromise a viable option.

The British government discovered as early as the mid-1970s just how difficult it would be to impose peace in Northern Ireland. The introduction of internment led the Social Democratic and Labour party (SDLP), the main voice for the moderate "constitutional" nationalists, to withdraw from the Stormont Parliament in protest. The massive instability rocking Northern Ireland, as well as the lack of any Catholic representation after the SDLP walkout, led the British government permanently to suspend the Stormont Parliament in February 1972.[35]

After disbanding the Stormont Parliament, the British government began planning the creation of a new regional governing body that would guarantee Nationalist representation while offering the Republic of Ireland a limited advisory role in Northern Irish affairs. London oversaw a new governing assembly, constructed so as to provide power sharing between Unionists and Nationalists, at Sunningdale in January 1974. The assembly was a short-lived and dismal failure. Unionist sentiment, which had always opposed the assembly, grew even more resolute after its creation. On May 15, a little-known trade association, named the Ulster Workers Council (UWC), coordinated a general strike against the agreement. The UWC strike was a complete success, leading to the resignation of Faulkner at the end of May and the dissolution of Sunningdale. Over two decades would pass before another attempt was made to reconstruct representative local government.

With no political settlement in sight, the IRA persevered and continued operations through the 1970s into the 1980s. A prison hunger strike led by Bobby Sands in March 1981 brought the IRA its greatest propaganda victory to date, leading London to increasingly reassess its role in the region. The March 1981 hunger strike, the second in four months, was initiated to protest treatment of Republican militants as criminal, rather than political, prisoners. The attention gained by the hunger strikers was magnified when Sands, representing Sinn Fein, was elected in a by-election to the British Parliament six weeks into the strike. The IRA and INLA[36] hunger strikers never saw their demands met, but the subsequent death of Bobby Sands and nine others brought international attention to the Republican cause in a way that terror tactics never had. After the hunger strikes of 1980–81, Sinn Fein became an increasingly significant force at the polls in Northern Ireland, despite the standing refusal of its candidates to assume office.

First steps toward a lasting peace were taken in the period leading up to the 1985 Anglo-Irish accord. Prime Minister Margaret Thatcher, a hard-liner vis-à-vis the Republican hunger strikers and known for her commitment to British sovereignty, seemed unlikely to compromise on Northern Ireland. Nevertheless, Thatcher built a relationship of trust with Taoiseach Garrett Fitzgerald that led to the first major breakthrough.

The recent political successes of Sinn Fein troubled both Thatcher and Fitzgerald, who feared the eclipse of the constitutional Nationalists of the SDLP (McKittrick and McVea 2000, 159). Thatcher looked to the Republic of Ireland both as a source of diplomatic burden sharing for issues related to the troubled North and as a partner on security issues. Thirty-six meetings of negotiators from both sides produced the Anglo-Irish (or Hillsborough) Agreement, which granted the Republic new consultative roles in the governance of Northern Ireland. At the core of the agreement was the creation of the Intergovernmental Conference, at which Irish ministers could express their views on issues related to the North. Significantly, the agreement also began with a joint statement that the status of Northern Ireland could only be changed through the consent of the populations of both the North and South; this was the first such declaration by an Irish government.

The SDLP expressed pleasure at the new linkages with Ireland, while Sinn Fein expressed disdain that the consent principle was being applied to the North, and decried the "copper-fastening of partition." Representatives of the Unionist UUP and DUP were dismayed by the agreement, because it was viewed as weakening London's authority and providing a beachhead for Irish involvement in the North. Loyalists, who had mentioned the potential of "civil war" on several occasions since the rise of Sinn Fein (Guelke 1988, 75), once again began warning of the possibility of a full-scale outbreak of hostilities. Despite the protests, however, no organized action similar to the UWC strike of 1974 ever occurred. Imposed from above, the Anglo-Irish Agreement represented a new era of cooperation between the United Kingdom and Ireland; Northern Ireland was no longer viewed as a point of contention as much as it was a common problem for the two governments.

Accompanying the public contacts that had arisen between British and Irish officials after the Anglo-Irish Agreement was a growing network of secret diplomatic channels established between Northern Irish Republicans and Nationalists, as well as both governments and Republican leaders.[37] Meanwhile, John Hume, leader of the SDLP, hammered out a declaration intended to provide a common framework for peace in the years ahead. While doing so, he conferred with Taoiseach Charles Haughley and his successor, Albert Reynolds. More importantly, Hume had maintained secret contacts, since 1988, with Sinn Fein leader Gerry Adams (Cochrane 1997, 185).

In the context of growing political success, a consensus developed in the mid- and late 1980s among the Sinn Fein leadership that violence was limiting support for the party, and preventing it from potentially constituting a mass movement (Alonso 2001). The nonviolent hunger strikes had propelled Sinn Fein onto the political scene in a manner that armed militancy never had, while attacks, such as the notorious 1987 bombing at Enniskillen,[38] were propaganda disasters that sapped strength from the party. Unable to advance their cause through violence, it became increasingly clear to leaders like Adams that the best possible avenue for the advancement of the Republican cause lay in the political arena.

Violent Republican militancy was somewhat effective in bringing about changes desired by the Catholic community in Northern Ireland, but not because the IRA achieved its goal of "driving the Brits out." Rather, quite the opposite effect was achieved. Despite the fact that a majority of British citizens favored withdrawal[39] (Guelke 1988, 100), Republican violence pressured London into adopting a larger governing role for Britain while forcing a smaller one for Ulster Unionists; this trend stretched from the collapse of Stormont right on through much of the peace process. However, while the primary goal of Ulster Unionists was to remain firmly entrenched in the United Kingdom, the primary goal of the United Kingdom was to end the violence and return stability to the region.

The seemingly zero-sum questions regarding the British military presence and whether or not Northern Ireland was to exist as a political entity were replaced by a situation in which both Unionists and Republicans could reap concrete benefits from a cessation of violence. However, a willingness to reach a peaceful solution does not necessarily mean that both sides have the ability to do so. The only way a sustainable political settlement could be reached would be for each side successfully to suppress its more radical and militant elements.

The network of negotiations produced the Joint Declaration for Peace, also known as the "Downing Street Declaration" of December 15, 1993. The agreement was essentially a statement of principles, intended to placate Nationalists without infuriating Unionists. In the agreement, the Irish government was declared responsible for supporting "proposals for change in the Irish Constitution which would fully reflect the principle of consent in Northern Ireland." In other words, they pledged to move toward the revocation of Articles 2 and 3 laying claim to Northern Ireland. The most important symbolic recognition of respect, however, was the craftily written statement that reaffirmed the principle of consent, while allowing for eventual reunification:

> The British Government agree that it is for the people of Ireland alone, by agreement between the two parts respectively, to exercise their right of self-determination on the basis of consent, freely and concurrently given, North

and South, to bring about a united Ireland, if that is their wish. (Cochrane 1997, Appendix II).

The lengthy negotiations needed to create the mutually acceptable institutions necessary to meet the goals laid out in the declaration were to last for more than four years.

Violence continued in Northern Ireland well into 1994, with little change in its intensity or frequency. Nevertheless, Gerry Adams was permitted to travel to the United States in February 1994. This was a gesture by the Americans that infuriated the British government (McKittrick and McVea 2000, 197). Following the Downing Street Declaration and Adams's trip, months of internal deliberation within Sinn Fein and the IRA finally resulted in the IRA cease-fire of August 1994. The IRA cease-fire was accompanied soon thereafter by Loyalist paramilitary cease-fires, largely ending the violence in the region. As figure 6.2 shows, the relatively stable annual death toll that characterized the conflict since the late 1970s was decisively reduced after 1994 (with the exception of the massive Omagh bombing of 1998 by "Real IRA" militants).

In February 1995, the Irish and British governments jointly published a series of proposals known as the "Framework Documents." Drafted without input from local parties in Northern Ireland, the Framework Documents were intended to form the basis of negotiations among all parties over the coming years. The documents represent the culmination of the era of British-Irish intergovernmental cooperation, which began with the Anglo-Irish Accord.

## *Figure 6.2* Total Deaths per Year, 1969–99

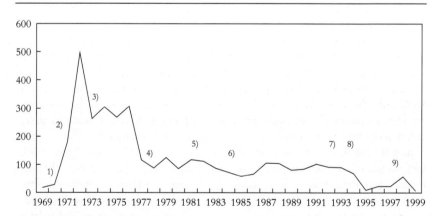

*Source*: McKittrick and McVea 2000, 325.
1) Provisional IRA formed, Jan. 1970; 2) Internment introduced, Aug. 1971;
3) IRA cease-fire, 1973; 4) IRA adopts "long war" strategy, 1977;
5) Hunger strikes, 1981; 6) Anglo-Irish Accord, Nov. 1985;
7) Downing Street Declaration, Dec. 1993; 8) IRA cease-fire, Aug. 1994;
9) Good Friday Agreement, April 1998

The documents offered suggestions for future internal governance in Northern Ireland, and broadly outlined future North-South (Northern Ireland–Republic of Ireland) and East-West (United Kingdom–Republic of Ireland) institutions. Representing a clear departure from strict majoritarian principles favored by Unionists, these documents proposed a collective presidency and a new assembly, governed by rules requiring "weighted majorities." The documents also contained an implicit threat by the British to Unionists in Northern Ireland declaring that if internal governing arrangements failed, the British government would nevertheless pursue its commitments to "promote co-operation at all levels" across the island.

With Unionists preferring the status quo to compromise, and the British and Irish governments able to offer little to change this attitude, the British simply eliminated the status quo as an option altogether. By presenting the Unionists with a stark choice—either take part in the process or watch the process take place without you—Unionists were forced either to accept the practicality of compromise or reject compromise solely on an ideological basis. British policy redefined the political options for Unionists and, in doing so, provided David Trimble with a thin majority of Unionist support.

The May 1997 general elections brought Tony Blair to power, and signaled a new round of negotiations between parties. Despite intense pressure arising from the roughly half of the Unionist community that rejected the peace talks—pressure that was intensified by the refusal of the IRA to reveal and turn over its weaponry—Trimble's UUP remained part of the negotiations.

The negotiations yielded the Belfast (Good Friday) Agreement, which was announced on April 10, 1998. The agreement represented a more refined version of the Framework Agreements. Once again, the document addressed the main issues of internal governance, North-South institutions, and East-West institutions. In addition, the document detailed measures concerning constitutional changes, decommissioning, security and policing, and paramilitary prisoners.

The finalized agreement provided for an assembly elected by proportional representation with a single transferable vote. The executive was to be headed by a first minister and a deputy first minister with identical powers, who were to be elected by "parallel consent," ensuring that a moderate Unionist and moderate Nationalist would hold the posts (Ruane and Todd 1999, 14). The joint leaders of the executive would oversee 10 executive departments, which would be headed by party leaders allocated proportionally to party strength in the assembly.

A new North-South body was formed, as envisioned in the Framework Agreements. The North-South Ministerial Council was to "develop consultation, co-operation and action within the island of Ireland" within 12 functional areas (Alcock 2001, 175).[40] In addition to the Intergovernmental Conference established in 1985, East-West relations would be overseen by a newly established British-Irish Council, composed of representatives from the Northern Irish, Welsh, and Scottish Assemblies, as well as the British and Irish governments. The Council's duties were somewhat vague, with the ability to set up modes of cooperation parallel to the North-South Council, but no legal requirement to do so (Ruane and Todd 1999, 15).

The Intergovernmental Conference would retain duties not devolved to the Northern Ireland Assembly, including, most importantly, security and policing issues.

Furthermore, the agreement mandated changes to Articles 2 and 3 of the Irish constitution that had long been sought by Unionists. Article 2 was reformulated to replace the definition the Irish national territory with a definition of the Irish nation, and Article 3 was similarly reworked to include the principle of Northern consent into Irish aspirations for Irish unity.

The agreement was subsequently approved on both parts of the island. In the Republic of Ireland, the agreement received an overwhelming 94 percent "yes" vote, with a turnout of 56 percent. In Northern Ireland, 71 percent of voters approved the agreement, with a turnout of 81 percent (Dunn 1999, 725). The vote in the North also revealed continued division among Unionist voters, whose vote was split down the middle.

The avenues of negotiation leading to the Belfast Agreements had largely been defined by the Framework Documents—which had been drafted entirely by British and Irish officials—with very little local input. London and Dublin succeeded in promoting peace by undercutting, or at least redefining, the preferences of the more intransigent members of the two communities in the North. Leaders in the Republic of Ireland, who had never viewed the IRA fondly, dealt a political blow to the Republican cause when they, in the 1985 Anglo-Irish Agreement, agreed to respect the principle of Unionist consent in the North. By agreeing that any future change in the status of the North would occur only if enough of the Unionist community agreed to it, the Irish government essentially signaled to the IRA that, even if it managed to drive the British out, that unification of the North with the Republic would not be the end result. The portion of the Unionist community that rejected the Anglo-Irish treaty curiously ignored this momentous change of position by the Irish government.

The web of secret contacts that developed in the early 1990s were key to bringing about an IRA cease-fire, which was the first necessary condition if the process were to move forward, and a key condition that had not been actualized before the Sunningdale assembly had convened. The secret nature of the talks allowed leaders to bypass the necessity of maintaining political cohesion within the ranks of each side. In the past, leaders such as O'Neill and Faulkner had failed in their efforts to reach compromises because of splits in the Unionist camp, and more recent Unionist and Sinn Fein representatives have faced similar issues of maintaining legitimacy while making concessions. After the talks became public, the internal cohesion issue continued to plague the leaders involved, but the process was, by that point, well underway and better able to survive the backlash of hard-liners within each camp.

## Conclusion

While many of the key variables utilized by Collier and Hoeffler fail to capture the situation in Northern Ireland, many of the causal mechanisms that underlie their model are generally relevant. For instance, while primary export commodities such as diamonds and oil played no role in the outbreak of violence in Northern Ireland, the creation of an underground network of criminal financing was essential to the viability of armed militancy. Thus, although the focus of the CH model on the importance of securing financial and material funding for rebellion is certainly relevant to the Northern Ireland case, this case also shows that resources for insurgency may be creatively extorted from numerous sources and rebels are not only limited to natural resource exploitation or diaspora-based funding.

The aggregate level of violence that occurred in Northern Ireland was uniquely high within the developed world. However, during most years, the fighting was not on the scale that one would normally associate with "civil war." The conflict lasted many years at low intensity. This suggests the need to consider the issue of conflict intensity in conjunction with the question of the financial underpinning of insurgency. Unlike many of the insurgent groups analyzed by Collier and Hoeffler, the IRA did not rely on fixed point resources that required high levels of violence to secure and protect. As a result, the IRA was able to initiate its campaign at a low cost and limited violence near the minimal level that it needed to survive while keeping the insurgency ongoing. A direct linkage exists between the intensity of civil violence and both the nature and amount of resources necessary to fund a sustained campaign of insurgency.

This chapter further suggests that ethnic dominance, the primary grievance factor in the CH model, played a major role in the instability that lent itself to insurgency. The nature of ethnic dominance in Northern Ireland was so profoundly important because of the "ranked" structure of society: two large groups with one clearly dominant politically and economically over the other. Grievances resulting from the groups' income and employment differences reinforced feelings of ethnic dominance among Catholics.

Ethnoreligious polarization helped sustain the conflict for decades. As Collier et al. (2001) suggest, the demographic nature of Northern Ireland, with a small number of large ethnic groups, fostered both recruitment efforts and helped maintain the internal cohesion of Republican and Loyalist paramilitaries. Geographic factors, however, played no role in extending the conflict in Northern Ireland. Stripped of geographic features that would have aided in evading capture, the IRA pursued a course of urban guerrilla warfare—a strategy that lent itself to a long struggle. With neither the British government nor the IRA able decisively to defeat the other, a search for alternative solutions began in earnest in the mid-1980s.

The peace process was engineered mainly through British-Irish cooperation, with each government creatively applying pressure in order to redefine the preferences of local parties in Northern Ireland. The importance of "outside" intervention in the affairs of Northern Ireland cannot be overemphasized. The fact that there were only two major ethnic players at the negotiating table made compromise harder, as one would expect to be typically the case even when the larger group makes concessions to respect the group rights of the smaller group (Elster 1995, 124). By providing inducements and punishments, the British and Irish governments were able to redefine the interests of the parties by placing them in a larger, more regional context, so they helped the peace talks.

In the aftermath of the agreement, problems have continued to arise. Political deadlock, particularly concerning issues surrounding the continuing existence of the IRA and its refusal to fully disarm, led to the collapse of the regional Stormont government and the renewed imposition of direct rule by Great Britain in 2002. The IRA has traditionally viewed itself as the defense force of the Catholic community in Northern Ireland (O'Doherty 1998), and relinquishment of its weapons implies leaving the Catholic community at the mercy of the British and Ulster Protestant majority.[41] Current reform of the Police Service of Northern Ireland (the renamed RUC), including a sustained effort to hire more Catholics into the organization, should enable local security forces to play a more neutral role in society and alleviate this security dilemma to some degree.

Another reason IRA militants have refused to fully disarm, however, has little to do with political goals or the interests of the Catholic community. IRA militants, like their Protestant paramilitary counterparts, have continued to perpetuate their organization's existence through organized crime and vigilantism—tactics which depend upon maintaining a certain level of militarization. However, ties between Sinn Fein and its increasingly discredited "armed wing" have had important ramifications for ongoing political negotiations, especially in the wake of the IRA-attributed Northern Bank robbery in December 2004 and the murder of Robert McCartney in January 2005. Given the growing political toll that IRA actions have inflicted upon Sinn Fein, it is likely that republican political leadership will become increasingly amenable to calls for the final disbandment of the remaining militants.

Northern Ireland does not suffer from the obstacles present in many developing countries that are associated with a lack of access to the material and financial resources needed to sustain peace efforts. As a region with abundant local capacities for peace (Doyle and Sambanis 2000), Northern Ireland needs more political will than economic support to make progress toward conflict resolution. Although conflicts involving deeply held identities are intrinsically difficult to solve, we have seen important compromises on issues once thought of as intractable.

In terms of economic and political opportunity, many concrete grievances of Catholics have been resolved through measures promoting fairer employment practices and the creation of more inclusive governance structures. The "border question" has not been permanently resolved, but it likely has been for the immediate future. The Catholic population, which now stands at approximately 43 percent of the total population after decades of faster growth than the Protestants, will become the majority in Northern Ireland in less than three decades (O'Leary 1995, 710). When that time comes, it might bring renewed social chaos to Northern Ireland. However, with the growth of transnational organizations such as the EU and the accompanying erosion of European state sovereignty, in several decades it is possible that the question of which group comprises the majority in the North, or on the island as a whole, will no longer be as salient an issue.

# Notes

1. Although an IRA cease-fire in August 1994 greatly reduced the level of violence, a comprehensive settlement was not reached until April 1998.
2. Between the 1994 IRA cease-fire and the April 1998 Belfast (Good Friday) Accords, 67 additional people lost their lives (Malcolm Sutton: an Index of Deaths—CAIN Web Service). In addition, this figure reflects deaths in Northern Ireland, and not in Great Britain (125), the Republic of Ireland (107), or other countries (18).
3. Those years are 1979 (113 killed) and 1981 (101 killed). (CAIN Web Service). These statistics only reflect deaths within Northern Ireland. Deaths in other regions (Great Britain, mainly) push the death tolls in 1982, 1987, 1988, and 1991 above 100.
4. Most of its provisions were revoked at the end of the 18th century.
5. The act was negotiated in its final form, voted upon, and enacted in 1921.
6. Although many Unionists refer to Northern Ireland as "Ulster," the entity that was created in 1921 was comprised of only six of the nine counties that made up the historical province of Ulster.
7. A maximum of two voters were allowed per household, so subtenants, servants, and adult family members within the same domicile were not allowed to vote.
8. Since its creation, the major political cleavage that has existed in Northern Ireland has been between pro-British "Unionists" and pro-Irish "Nationalists." Although not all Unionists are Protestants, and not all Nationalists are Catholics, religion and political affiliation in Northern Ireland have been largely complementary. The more radical, and often militant, strands of unionism and nationalism that became prominent in the later Troubles were known as "loyalism" and "republicanism," respectively.
9. The desirability of eventual reunification with the North was enshrined in articles 2 and 3 of the Irish constitution, which was enacted during the 1930s.
10. The IRA was organized in 1918 as a guerrilla movement to force British acquiescence to Irish independence. By the 1930s, its goal was to reunify Northern Ireland with the South. Small in number, the IRA carried out infrequent and sporadic assassinations during the 1930s, 1940s, and early 1950s. During the period 1956–62, IRA militants launched a series of attacks known as the "Border Campaign." Resulting in 19 deaths, the campaign was crushed after internment (imprisonment without trial) policies were introduced. Several hundred militants were arrested with the cooperation of the Republic of Ireland, which subsequently banned the IRA (Alcock 1994, 54).
11. Rerunning the CH model and substituting the ethnic dominance variable with an interacted dummy variable indicating both the presence of ethnic dominance and presence of an ethnic minority comprising more than 10 percent of a state's population results in a higher propensity of conflict outbreak (coefficient = 0.83, $p < .03$). Altering the interacted variable so that it denotes states characterized by ethnic dominance and *one* minority group over 10 percent yields even stronger results (coefficient = 1.24, $p < .01$).
12. Arguments among scholars concerning the effectiveness of consociational arrangements as a whole, and in Northern Ireland in particular as a result of such arrangements within the Good Friday Agreements, still continue. Although such a discussion is beyond the purview of this study, it is clear that consociationalist structures are more

appropriate in some states than others, and not necessarily the only viable solution for maintaining ethnic harmony.

13. An empirical investigation of diffusion, focusing on the effect of the civil rights movement in the United States on other developed countries, is discussed by Hill et al. (1998). Their results suggest that a combination of factors, particularly exposure to television within more highly ethnically fractionalized societies during periods of mass protest in the United States, had a positive and significant effect on protest. The variables most associated with a high propensity of diffusion apply to the situation in Northern Ireland in the 1960s. For a comprehensive account of interactions between Catholic activists of the 1960s and the American civil rights movement, see Dooley (1998).

14. The employment information is from 1971 Census Data. Little information exists before 1971 concerning the differential economic status of the two communities (Smith and Chambers 1991, 17).

15. To this day the name of the town, known as Derry to Nationalists and Londonderry to Unionists, remains a point of contention. From this point I will simply refer to the town by both names.

16. The bombing campaign was originally attributed by the RUC to IRA militants. However, it was later discovered that members of the Protestant Ulster Volunteer Force (UVF) were the true perpetrators. The UVF, a Loyalist group banned in 1966, sought the downfall of O'Neill because of his perceived concessions to Nationalists (McKittrick and McVea 2000, 49).

17. The "Sorcerer's Apprentice" analogy is utilized in a variety of fields to denote the unleashing of forces that yield consequences that spiral beyond one's control. The term originates from Goethe's 1797 poem "der Zauberlehrling," but is perhaps best known as the centerpiece of the 1940 Disney film *Fantasia*.

18. While the remaining members of the "Official" IRA conducted scattered attacks over the next two years, the group ended its militant campaign in May 1972. By the late 1970s, the Official IRA had distanced itself from militancy altogether and had evolved into the Workers' party. Henceforth, all references to the IRA will pertain to the Provisional IRA.

19. I empirically tested this proposition with a database that I constructed for other purposes. The data codes all disapora that: (1) represent over 3 percent of the "foreign" country, and (2) live in countries adjacent to their "homeland" (for example, Jews in Russia would not be included). To have engaged in civil violence, the group must meet the definitions set out by the Upsalla data set (25 deaths). I find that 27 percent of states with diaspora witnessed civil violence *attributable to militants representing the diaspora* (1951–91; $n = 1,148$), whereas only 21 percent of states without a diaspora witnessed *any civil violence by any militant group* (1951–91; $n = 8,789$).

20. At 74 percent, the United Kingdom ranked 13th in the world in secondary school attendance in 1970. Ireland was significantly poorer than the United Kingdom, but still maintained very similar attendance levels at 71 percent.

21. Fearon and Laitin suggest that noncontiguous regions are prone to insurgency because of the weakness of state capacity in these areas. Although lessened state capacity might be a contributing factor, it is just as likely that the increased propensity for rebellion reflects the status of many of these territories as colonies. This provides a powerful moti-

vation, rather than mere opportunity, for violence. The "anticolonial" motivation of militant Republicans stood at the center of their political grievances.

22. Members and leaders of both Loyalist and Republican paramilitaries sometimes referred to their members simply as "volunteers" as a way of reinforcing the fact that members fought out of ideological conviction without monetary compensation (or physical coercion). Sambanis (2001) suggests that the potential of a "rebel who might otherwise require the promise of loot to fight a war to offer his or her rebel labor for free" is a distinctive trait of ethnic conflicts versus nonethnic conflicts.

23. Modern estimates of Northern Irish exports by industry (including those to Great Britain) are difficult to obtain, and estimates from 1970 are largely impossible to obtain. However, Collier and Hoeffler have data for the United Kingdom as a whole (2.9 percent) and the Republic of Ireland (15.2 percent). With a level of industrialization and rural settlement in Northern Ireland roughly halfway between the United Kingdom and Ireland at the time, it is likely that the percentage of primary commodities exported was probably an average of the two countries. Data from 2000–2001 show that exports from the "Food, Drink, and Tobacco" sector combined with "Wood and Wood Products" came to 14 percent of Northern Ireland's GDP, suggesting an export structure closer to Ireland than the United Kingdom (Department of Enterprise, Trade, and Investment (UK)–Statistical Research Branch, Web site).

24. Horgan and Taylor (1999) present 12 estimates derived from secondary sources that approximate the IRA's annual income. Recent estimates vary from $6 million to over $15 million, but cluster around $10 million.

25. Ethnicity is a slipperier concept than religious affiliation in Northern Ireland. Although there is a well-known Irish-British dimension to ethnic identity, some also argue for a separate Ulster identity for some Protestants (Gallagher 1995) and/or a separate "Northern Irish" identity, with which 25 percent of Catholics identify (White 1998).

26. See note 10.

27. The cease-fire was a tenuous one, however. Deaths inflicted against the security forces were halved, but 33 members of the police and military were still killed. Civilian deaths actually increased markedly in this year as a result of sectarian violence directed against innocents (committed by the IRA as well as the Protestant UDA and UVF paramilitaries) and internecine violence among Republicans.

28. No common standard exists differentiating guerrilla-style warfare from terrorist acts, although the distinction between attacking military and civilian targets certainly affects most people's reaction toward actions taken by militant groups. Nevertheless, whether a group is a terrorist or guerrilla movement, the nature of these groups' tactics make it necessarily more difficult to stamp them out than a conventional army.

29. Adams wrote in *Free Ireland: Towards a Lasting Peace* that there had not *yet* been a "classic development from guerrilla action to mass military action registering territorial gains," indicating that a long-term goal of the IRA had indeed taken into account the possibility of a future conventional campaign (quoted in O'Doherty 1998, 100).

30. Many of the variables that sustained conflict in Northern Ireland are unique to the region, and are appropriately analyzed separately from the overall characteristics of the entire United Kingdom. Other variables make more sense to look at on the state level. When

examining each casual factor, it will be noted whether the data utilized are regional or state level.

31. The Forestry Service owns approximately 5 percent of the land in Northern Ireland, providing a rough estimate of the extent of wilderness area in the region. Most of the interior of Northern Ireland consists of rolling hills, with mountain chains rising to 2,796 feet (860 m) along the northeast, northwest, and southeast peripheries of the region (CAIN Web site).

32. Currently 88 percent of United Kingdom citizens live in urban areas, as opposed to 77 percent in Northern Ireland. "Urban" population for Northern Ireland includes all portions of the population living in towns, regardless of the size of the town. In addition to 377,400 residents living in "open countryside," 312,800 citizens reside in small towns with populations under 10,000 (Department for Regional Development, United Kingdom, Web site).

33. This was particularly true in the early years of the conflict, when events now infamous to Catholics, such as the "Rape of the Falls" area of Belfast, which entailed widespread house-to-house searches by security forces, led to increasing tension and polarization.

34. Alonso (2001, 136) relates a quotation from a speech given by Gerry Adams in 1983, in which he declared "armed struggle is a necessary form of resistance . . . [that] becomes unnecessary only when the British presence has been removed . . . if at any time Sinn Fein decide to disown the armed struggle they won't have me as a member."

35. The final straw for London was the refusal of William Faulkner to accede to Prime Minister Edward Heath's demands that internment be gradually phased out, security force oversight transferred completely to London, and Catholics provided guaranteed representation in government.

36. Although significantly smaller than the IRA, the Irish National Liberation Army (INLA), formed in 1976, was the second largest Republican paramilitary group since the late 1970s. The group specialized mostly in assassinations against high-profile targets. INLA militants were responsible for 117 deaths during the conflict, while other smaller Republican paramilitaries inflicted a combined total of 218 deaths (Hayes and McAllister 2001, 903).

37. Secret negotiations began between British and Sinn Fein representatives in 1990, although they did not become frequent until the beginning of 1993 (McKittrick and McVea 2000, 189).

38. The bombing of a parade for war veterans at Enniskillen killed 11 Protestants. The negative publicity received by the IRA was intensified by the presence of cameras at the parade that documented the bombing's aftermath.

39. Guelke reports Gallup poll results from 1969, 1971, 1974, and 1981, all of which reveal widespread support in Britain for the idea of Irish unification and British withdrawal. In 1981, for instance, 63 percent of respondents said they would vote against Northern Ireland remaining in the United Kingdom if a referendum were held.

40. Those areas included: agriculture, education, transport, environment, inland waterways, social security, tourism, inland fisheries, aquaculture, health, urban and rural development, and EU programs.

41. As Walter (2002) argues, one of the greatest challenges in resolving civil conflicts across the globe involves overcoming the security dilemma faced when one group is required to disarm unilaterally. Clearly, the situation surrounding peace negotiations in Northern Ireland has been no exception.

# References

Alcock, Antony. 1994. *Understanding Ulster.* Armagh, UK: Ulster Society Publications Ltd.
———. 2001. "Lessons from Europe." In *Northern Ireland and the Divided World,* ed. John McGarry. Oxford: Oxford University Press.
Alonso, Rogelio. 2001. "The Modernization in Irish Republican Thinking Toward the Utility of Violence." *Studies in Conflict and Terrorism* 24: 131–44.
Bell, J. Bowyer. 2001. "The Irish War." *Studies in Conflict & Terrorism* 24: 475–84.
Cochrane, Feargal. 1997. *Unionist Politics and the Politics of Unionism since the Anglo-Irish Agreement.* Cork, Ireland: Cork University Press.
Collier, Paul, and Anke Hoeffler. 2001. "Greed and Grievance in Civil War." Policy Research Working Paper 2355, World Bank, Washington, DC.
Collier, Paul, Anke Hoeffler, and Måns Söderbom. 2001. "On the Duration of Civil War." Presented at the World Bank-UC Irvine Conference on "Civil War Duration and Post-Conflict Peacebuilding," Irvine, CA, May 18–20.
Dingley, James. 2001. "The Bombing of Omagh, 15 August 1998: The Bombers, Their Tactics, Strategy, and Purpose Behind the Incident." *Studies in Conflict and Terrorism* 24: 451–65.
Dooley, Brian. 1998. *Black and Green: The Fight for Civil Rights in Northern Ireland and Black America.* London: Pluto Press.
Doyle, Michael, and Nicholas Sambanis. 2000. "International Peacebuilding: A Theoretical and Quantitative Analysis." *American Political Science Review* 94: 779–802.
Dunn, Seamus. 1999. "Northern Ireland: A Promising or Partisan Peace?" *Journal of International Affairs* 52 (2): 719–34.
Elbadawi, Ibrahim, and Nicholas Sambanis. 2000. "External Interventions and the Duration of Civil War." Paper presented at the World Bank's Development Economic Research Group (DECRG), Princeton, NJ, March 18–19.
Elster, John. 1995. "Transition, Constitution-Making and Separation in Czechoslovakia." *European Journal of Sociology* 36: 105–34.
Fearon, James, and David Laitin. 2001. "Ethnicity, Insurgency and Civil War." Paper presented at the American Political Science Association, San Diego, CA, August 30–September 2.
Gallagher, Michael. 1995. "How Many Nations Are There in Ireland?" *Ethnic and Racial Studies* 18 (4): 715–39.
Guelke, Adrian. 1988. *Northern Ireland: The International Perspective.* Dublin: Gill and Macmillan.
———. 1996. "The United States, Irish Americans, and the Northern Ireland Peace Process." *International Affairs* 72 (3): 521–36.
Hayes, Bernadette, and Ian McAllister. 2001. "Sowing Dragon's Teeth: Public Support for Political Violence and Paramilitarism in Northern Ireland." *Political Studies* 49: 901–22.

188 *Understanding Civil War*

Hill, Stuart, et al. 1998. "Tactical Information and the Diffusion of Peaceful Protests." In *The International Spread of Ethnic Conflict,* ed. David Lake and Donald Rothchild. Princeton, NJ: Princeton University Press.

Hegre, Håvard, et al. 2001. "Toward a Democratic Civil Peace? Democracy, Political Change and Civil War, 1816–1992." *American Political Science Review* 95 (1): 33–48.

Horgan, John, and Max Taylor. 1999. "Playing the 'Green Card'—Financing the Provisional IRA: Part 1." *Terrorism and Political Violence* 11 (2): 1–38.

Horowitz, Donald. 2000. *Ethnic Groups in Conflict.* Berkeley: University of California Press.

Hume, John. 1996. *A New Ireland: Politics, Peace, and Reconciliation.* Boulder, CO: Roberts Rinehart.

Kelley, Kevin. 1988. *The Longest War: Northern Ireland and the I.R.A.* London: Zed Books Ltd.

McGarry, John, and Brendan O'Leary. 1995. "Five Fallacies: Northern Ireland and the Liabilities of Liberalism." *Ethnic and Racial Studies* 18 (4): 837–61.

McKittrick, David, and David McVea. 2000. *Making Sense of the Troubles.* Belfast: Blackstaff Press.

O'Dochartaigh, Nial. 1997. *From Civil Rights to Armalites: Derry and the Birth of the Irish Troubles.* Cork, Ireland: Cork University Press.

O'Doherty, Malachi. 1998. *The Trouble with Guns: Republican Strategy and the Provisional IRA.* Belfast: Blackstaff Press.

O'Duffy, Brendan. 1995. "Violence in Northern Ireland 1969–1994: Sectarian or Ethno-national?" *Ethnic and Racial Studies* 18 (4): 740–72.

O'Leary, Brendan. 1995. "Introduction: Reflections on a Cold Peace." *Ethnic and Racial Studies* 18 (4): 695–714.

O'Leary, Brenden, and John McGarry. 1993. *The Politics of Antagonism: Understanding Northern Ireland.* London: Athlone Press.

Ruane, Joseph. 1999. "The End of (Irish) History? Three Readings of the Current Conjuncture." In *After the Good Friday Agreement: Analyzing Political Change in Ireland.* Dublin: University College Dublin Press.

Ruane, Joseph, and Jennifer Todd. 1999. "The Belfast Agreement: Context, Content, Consequences." In *After the Good Friday Agreements,* ed. Joseph Ruane and Jennifer Todd. Dublin: University College Dublin Press.

Sambanis, Nicholas. 2001. "Do Ethnic and Nonethnic Civil Wars Have the Same Causes? A Theoretical and Empirical Inquiry (Part 1)." *Journal of Conflict Resolution* 45 (3): 259–383.

Silke, Andrew. 1998. "In Defense of the Realm: Financing Loyalist Terrorism in Northern Ireland—Part One: Extortion and Blackmail." *Studies in Conflict and Terrorism* 21 (4): 331–62.

Smith, David, and Gerald Chambers. 1991. *Inequality in Northern Ireland.* Oxford: Clarendon Press.

Smith, M. L. R. 1999. "The Intellectual Internment of a Conflict: The Forgotten War in Northern Ireland." *International Affairs* 75 (1): 77–98.

Stam, Allan. 1996. *Win, Lose, or Draw: Domestic Politics and the Crucible of War.* Ann Arbor: University of Michigan Press.

Walter, Barbara. 2002. *Committing to Peace: The Successful Settlement of Civil Wars.* Princeton, NJ: Princeton University Press.

White, Robert. 1998. "Don't Confuse Me with the Facts: More on the Irish Republican Army and Sectarianism." *Terrorism and Political Violence* 10 (4): 164–89.

# Web Sites

CAIN Web Service. http://cain.ulst.ac.uk/ni/geog.htm.

Department for Regional Development, United Kingdom. http://www.drdni.gov.uk. See "Shaping Our Future" Publication, Chapter 8.

Department of Enterprise, Trade, and Investment (UK)—Statistical Research Branch. http://hrpd.fco.gov.uk/downloads/intvoc.annex1.pdf.

Police Service of Northern Ireland. http://www.psni.police.uk/museum/text/ruc.htm.

Sinn Fein. http://sinnfein.ie/bmgii/barmy.html.

# Bosnia's Civil War

## Origins and Violence Dynamics

7

STATHIS N. KALYVAS AND NICHOLAS SAMBANIS

The civil war in Bosnia has received heavy coverage in the popular press and in scholarly writings. The fact that the war took place in Europe, the extent of ethnic cleansing and killing, the investigations of the ICTY (the International Criminal Tribunal for the Former Yugoslavia), the deployment of several large United Nations (UN) peace operations, and the use of an assortment of humanitarian assistance projects by nongovernmental organizations (NGOs) have all attracted attention to this civil war and have resulted in the accumulation of a large descriptive corpus on the war. Despite this wealth of information, we still do not know which theories of civil war best explain this war and what lessons might be drawn from Bosnia that could inform existing theories of civil war.

There are many rival explanations of the onset of civil war in Bosnia. Most explanations cannot fit neatly in a theoretical framework that tries to explain more than just Bosnia. Reading case studies or reports on the war, it is hard to know what we might learn from Bosnia that we can generalize to other wars. We make an effort to integrate an analysis of the Bosnian war with broadly applicable theories by considering the fit of the Collier-Hoeffler (CH) model to this case (Collier and Hoeffler 2001). In doing so, we consider alternative explanations and weigh them against the predictions of the CH model.

We also analyze the patterns of violence in the Bosnian war and try to sort out the various competing explanations for the violence. The majority of works about the patterns of violence were written from authors whose main experience was limited to Sarajevo. This city, a journalist points out (Loyd 2001, 179), "had an inordinate media prestige as the Bosnian capital, which distracted journalists from much of what was happening elsewhere." However, the war was mainly conducted in the countryside. Much information collected by NGOs has two possible problems. First, because it seeks human rights violations, it focuses on sites of mass violence rather than sites of nonviolence, thus generating truncated data. There is an abundance of studies on Sarajevo, Prijedor, Kozarac, and Srebrenica during the war, but very little on the rest of the country. Second, it tends to privilege acts of violence rather than nonviolent acts that precede and follow violent ones and may be essential in understanding the occurrence of violence. This is a more general problem of reporting and can eventually be addressed only through extensive fieldwork. We do not have exhaustive data on patterns of violence during the Bosnian war, but we have systematized existing data collected by the UN, the U.S. State Department, and Human Rights Watch. We use these data along with first-hand accounts of the violence as a first step toward a more comprehensive mapping.

This chapter is organized in five sections. In the first section, we provide a brief historical background to the Bosnian war. Next, we discuss the application of the CH model to explain war onset and we link it to the other Yugoslav wars, given the patterns of contagion and diffusion between them. In the third section, we analyze the patterns of violence. In the last section, we conclude with an overview of the CH model's fit to this case and suggestions for modifications of the CH model on the basis of our analysis of Bosnia.

## Background to the Conflict

It is hard to know when to start in summarizing events that may be relevant to the Bosnian civil war. We start in 1980, when President Tito died, and power began to be held by an unstable collective presidency that rotated among leaders selected by the assemblies of Yugoslavia's six republics and two autonomous regions. Tito had suppressed the voicing of ethnic sentiments in politics and the new regime was marked by a rise in nationalist sentiment. In 1985, the Serbian Academy of Sciences drafted a memo that condemned Tito and the Party state for three decades of anti-Serb policies. The Academy blamed these policies for regional disparities in income and accused the Albanian majority in Kosovo of "genocidal" anti-Serb policies. Nationalist sentiment intensified when Slobodan Milosevic, heading the Serbian Communist party, made a powerful speech in Kosovo that rallied enough popular support to allow him to crack down on his opposition and purge the party of reformist rivals.

Milosevic, as president of Serbia, spearheaded the decision to curtail Kosovo's autonomy. In 1990, Serbia dissolved the Kosovo assembly and the province was ruled directly from Belgrade. In response, ethnic Albanian legislators in the province declared Kosovo a Republic. In January, the League of Communists split along ethnic lines. This was a mark of growing nationalist intolerance in the country, foreshadowing the oncoming conflict.

Federal elections that Ante Markovic, then the federal prime minister, wanted were never held, because Slovenia and Serbia boycotted the idea. The message to political elites was that they did not need to make broad appeals; it was enough for them to win locally (in their own republic). In April 1990, elections in Slovenia led to a dramatic victory by a Center-Right coalition, which immediately began drafting a new constitution that would allow Slovenia to secede. In Croatia, nationalist leader Franjo Tudjman and the Croatian Democratic Union won a majority. In response to these developments, the Krajina Serbs, a long-established Serbian minority on Croatian territory, started campaigning for autonomy in August, arguing that if Croatia could secede from Yugoslavia, they should also be allowed to secede from Croatia. Local Serb militias mobilized and set up roadblocks to stop official Croatian interference in a referendum. Milosevic announced that if Yugoslavia disintegrated, some border changes would be required to keep all Serbs under a single nation. Amidst intensifying conflict, in March 1991, Serbs in the Croatian Krajina region declared themselves autonomous and were recognized by Serbia. The power-sharing arrangement at the Center collapsed when Serbs refused to accept a Croat as president, violating the terms of Yugoslavia's rotating presidency.

In June 1991, both Croatia and Slovenia proclaimed their independence from Yugoslavia. The Jugoslav National Army (JNA) did not put up much resistance and withdrew from Slovenia's territory, but its reaction vis-à-vis Croatia's secession was very different. In August 1991, war broke out in Croatia between Croatian militias and local Serbs and the JNA, which attempted to take control of the strategically important cities of Vukovar and Dubrovnik.

By September 1991, the UN had authorized a 14,000-man peacekeeping force for the region and imposed an economic embargo on Serbia and Montenegro (under Security Council Resolution 713). The Secretary General launched a mediation effort, headed by former U.S. Secretary of State Cyrus Vance, leading to a cease-fire agreement in Croatia in early 1992 and the deployment of the first UN peacekeepers during the winter of 1992. The main task for the peacekeepers was to help extract JNA units from Croatian territory and temporarily establish UN Protected Areas (UNPAs).

In January 1992, preempted by Germany's support for Croatian independence, the European Community decided to recognize Croatia and Slovenia, but deferred action on Bosnia, where nationalist conflict was also brewing, pending the results of a referendum on independence. In March, a Muslim majority, with a significant Serb majority dissenting, voted for independence. As soon as the votes were counted, Serbs set up roadblocks around major cities, cutting them off from the mostly Serbian countryside. The Serb-controlled JNA assisted Bosnian Serbs, who begun leaving the cities. A Bosnian Serb parliament was set up. In April, the Europeans recognized Bosnia, as did the United States. In response to continued Serb aggression, the UN Security Council imposed economic sanctions against Yugoslavia (Serbia and Montenegro) at the end of May. During the summer of 1992, a growing humanitarian crisis in Bosnia led to the deployment of UN peacekeepers to facilitate the delivery of humanitarian relief. The UN imposed a "no-fly zone" over Bosnia in October 1992 and UN peacekeepers were preventively deployed to the Former Yugoslav Republic of Macedonia (FYROM) in 1993. In May 1993, the UN declared Sarajevo and five other Muslim enclaves "safe areas" under UN protection. NATO agreed in June to use air power to protect UN forces if attacked. In August, NATO declared its readiness to respond with air strikes, in coordination with the UN, in the event that UN safe areas, including Sarajevo, came under siege. This decision temporarily ended the strangulation of Sarajevo. The UN peacekeeping mission was transformed into an enforcement mission, under chapter VII of the UN Charter. But that was not the end of the violence.

In February 1994, in response to a Bosnian Serb attack that killed 68 civilians in a Sarajevo marketplace, NATO issued an ultimatum that if Bosnian Serb heavy weapons were not withdrawn from UN-monitored exclusion zones around the capital, Bosnian Serb forces would be subject to air strikes. In early 1994, with UN-EU diplomatic efforts stalled over territorial issues, the United States began more active efforts to encourage a settlement. In March 1994, U.S. mediation produced an agreement between the Bosnian government, Bosnian Croats, and the government of Croatia to establish a federation between Muslims and Croats in Bosnia. Fighting between the two sides ceased. In April, NATO employed its first air strikes against Bosnian Serb forces to halt a Serb attack on the eastern enclave and UN safe area of Gorazde. In the spring of 1994, the United States, Russia, Britain, France, and Germany established a five-nation Contact Group, with the goal of brokering a settlement between the federation and Bosnian Serbs. On May 6, the UN, under Security Council Resolution 824, declared Serajevo, Tuzla, Zepa, Gorezde, Bihac, Srebrenica, and their surroundings as safe areas to deter armed attacks by the Bosnian Serb forces. Later in the year, new fighting erupted between the Bosnian government, antigovernment Muslims in Bihac (supported by Krajina Serbs), and Bosnian Serbs. NATO responded by expanding the range for air strikes into Serb-controlled Croatia. In December, with the help of former U.S. President Jimmy Carter, the sides agreed to a four-month cessation of hostilities. When the period expired, fighting resumed, and in May, the Bosnian Serb forces renewed attacks on Sarajevo and began threatening Srebrenica.

In the spring of 1995, Bosnian Serb attacks on the safe areas led to a massacre of Bosnian Muslims in Srebrenica and prompted U.S. President Clinton to insist that NATO and the UN make good on their commitment to protect the remaining safe areas. The Allies threatened broad-based air strikes if the safe areas were attacked again. When the Bosnian Serbs tested this ultimatum, NATO undertook an intensive month-long bombing campaign. United States-led mediation produced an agreement by the parties to basic principles of a settlement as well as a cease-fire, which went into effect in October. Proximity peace talks toward settlement began in Dayton, Ohio on November 1. The parties agreed to the Dayton settlement on November 21 and the terms of the treaty were signed in Paris on December 14, 1995. That was the end of the Bosnian war and the start of a long period of UN peacekeeping and peacebuilding.

## The CH Model and the Outbreak of Civil War

The CH model of civil war onset stands in sharp contrast to political theories of civil war, such as theories that emphasize the role of relative deprivation (Gurr 1970), political grievance (Gurr 2000; Hegre et al. 2001), or nationalist ideology as the key causes of secessionist violence.

Economic models (such as CH) focus on how violence is organized and consider first and foremost the economic opportunity cost of violence and the availability of external financing. Ethnic diasporas and lootable natural resources make rebellion feasible in these models, which also explore the links between geography and population concentration on the one hand and the likelihood of violence on the other hand.

Do these models apply to Bosnia? Did poverty and lack of economic opportunity motivate the violence? Some authors (e.g., Sudetic 1998) have observed a connection between patterns of mobilization and job losses in bankrupt public enterprises. What was the role of natural resources and diaspora assistance financing the war? For instance, it was often reported that fighting was concentrated in areas in which mining activities were important (e.g., the village of Hambarine in Northwestern Bosnia, where fighting broke out early on, lay in a geographical position connecting the town of Prijedor with the Ljubija mine). We try to establish patterns of diaspora support for the rebels (Bax 2000) and we conduct a brief survey of the Yugoslav economy to identify key characteristics of that economy—rates of growth, dependence on primary exports, unemployment rates, regional disparities in growth and income distribution—to determine any links between such characteristics and the outbreak of violence.

We consider how these economic explanations compare to models focusing on political determinants of the outbreak of violence. An alternative explanation to the CH model is that political grievances during the transition from Communism provided the spark for the violence and motivated the masses to participate in the war. We focus on the stability and legitimacy of state institutions and the role of political elites in mobilizing mass support for violence.

Both economic and political models consider the impact of ethnic divisions and nationalist scripts of violence, though the impact of such divisions is usually significant only in political models. To what extent did religious or ethnic divisions cause or fuel the war (once war started)? How could we distinguish, in the case of Bosnia, between the political and economic explanations for violence and the consequences of ethnic divisions? We explore these questions as well as the extent to which the gradual partition of Yugoslavia fueled secessionist conflict in the remaining Republics and provinces informational spillovers or contagion effects.

## Bosnian Data and CH Predictions

The Bosnian war is unfortunately excluded from the CH analysis. The CH data set is missing data for most key variables in the model for both five-year periods during which Bosnia was an independent country (1990–94, 1995–99).[1] We collected these missing data using a number of resources, including the Yugoslav census and reports from the Yugoslav statistical service as well as secondary sources. When information on Bosnia was not available, we used data for Yugoslavia for 1990 to fill in missing values in the CH data set.[2] We describe the data for Bosnia in the following text, focusing on key variables in the CH model. We then use these data to obtain the CH model's predictions for Bosnia.

At first glance, the CH model's emphasis on income seems to fit the case well, because Bosnia was poorer than most Yugoslav republics (see table 7.1). We used

*Table 7.1* Income per Capita and Inequality by Region, 1988 and 1990

| Country | 1988 income per capita (pa) | 1990 income per capita (current US$) | Population in 1990 | Relative income 1988 | Relative income 1990 | Gini (1988 income) |
|---|---|---|---|---|---|---|
| Bosnia | 2,124,319 | 2,365 | 4,516 | 76.2 | 67.8 | 24.4 |
| Montenegro | 2,062,042 | 2,484 | 644 | 73.9 | 71.1 | 25.6 |
| Croatia | 3,234,631 | 4,468 | 4,685 | 116.0 | 127.8 | 22.1 |
| Macedonia | 1,790,902 | 2,282 | 2,131 | 64.2 | 65.3 | 30.9 |
| Slovenia | 5,529,722 | 7,610 | 1,953 | 198.3 | 217.7 | 19.3 |
| Derbia | 2,523,329 | 3,379 | 5,849 | 90.5 | 96.7 | 25.0 |
| Kosovo | 1,062,039 | 854 | 1,983 | 38.1 | 24.4 | 27.7 |
| Vojvodina | 3,166,398 | 4,320 | 2,048 | 113.6 | 123.6 | 26.5 |
| Yugoslavia | 2,788,443 | 3,496 | 23,809 | 100.0 | 100.0 | 24.5 |

*Source:* Sambanis and Milanovic (2004).

income and inequality figures from Sambanis and Milanovic (2004), who collected their data from household surveys to compute the relative income and Gini coefficients for all Yugoslav republics. They do not have real income data (adjusted for purchasing power parity, PPP) for Yugoslavia, but rather use 1990 constant dollars. Thus, we converted our data to PPP-adjusted income to match the CH data and did so by dividing the CH real income data for Yugoslavia in 1990 (4,548) with our own current dollar figures for the same year (3,496), yielding a factor of 1.30, which we then multiplied with the Bosnian mean 1990 income of 2,365 current dollars, yielding a real income figure of 3,098. Income (interpersonal) inequality (*ygini*) for Yugoslavia for 1990–94 is equal to 31.88 in the CH model. The Sambanis and Milanovic (2004) data give a slightly different figure at 29.3. The Gini for 1988 for Bosnia is 24.4, equal to the mean for Yugoslavia (24.5 in 1988), as shown in table 7.1.

The value for regime type is also missing in the CH data set (also in the Polity database, which serves as the source for CH). We coded an anocracy, given that instability emerged immediately after the Muslim referendum for independence. This case makes clear the endogeneity of regime type to many of the same conditions that could lead to the outbreak of violence.[3]

Collier and Hoeffler use a variable measuring *peacetime* (i.e., time since the last civil war). The longer lasting the peace, the less likely is a new war, according to the CH model. *Peacetime* should be 0, because Bosnia was created out of the violent dissolution of Yugoslavia, so a variable measuring previous war should be coded 1 to account for the Croatian war of secession in 1991.

Population size is significant in the CH model. The population of Bosnia in the CH model (4,450,000) is different from the values given in Fearon and Laitin

(3,837,707) for 1992. Our data are closer to those of Collier and Hoeffler, counting 4,510,000 people in Bosnia in 1990.

We computed ethnic and religious fractionalization for Bosnia from scratch. Yugoslavia was relatively less religiously fractionalized (*rf* = 58) than Bosnia (*rf* = 71). We code the CH variable *ethnic dominance* equal to 0, since the largest group in Bosnia, the Muslims, were 43.7 percent of the population in 1991 and the second largest group, the Serbs, made up 31.4 percent. The third largest group, the Croats, made up 17.3 percent of the population, and 5.5 percent were self-classified as "Yugoslavs" in the census, so we cannot assign them to any of the other categories. The ethnolinguistic fractionalization score for Yugoslavia (75) is closer to that in Bosnia (67). We computed the ethnolinguistic fractionalization (ELF) index using data from the Yugoslav census of 1991, which identifies four main ethnic groups: Muslims, Serbs, Croats, and others.[4] The fractionalization (*frac*) score for Yugoslavia (4,350)[5] is lower than in Bosnia (4,899), which suggests that the probability of war in Bosnia should have been lower, according to the CH model.

Mountain cover—which is thought to increase the risk of war by making the conduct of insurgency easier for rebels—is equal to 60.5, which is two standard deviations higher than the average. Forest coverage is equal to 39.22, which is somewhat higher than the average.[6] Thus, both of these "technologies" of insurgency were conducive to civil war in Bosnia, consistent with the CH model.

We can now compute the probability of civil war in Bosnia in two ways: first as an out-of-sample prediction based on the CH data without Bosnia and then as a within-sample prediction. A comparison of the two estimates can help identify the impact of Bosnia on the model.

By plugging in the values for the variables in the CH model and using the coefficient estimates obtained from the model without the Bosnia observations, we can obtain out-of-sample probability estimates for war onset in Bosnia.[7] The probability of civil war onset in 1990–94 in Bosnia is 0.05. This is lower than the average for all country-years (0.07). By filling in missing values for Bosnia and reestimating, we computed the within-sample probability estimate for Bosnia, which is equal to 0.08—higher than the out-of-sample estimate and the average for all country-years.

It is striking how influential Bosnia is in the model. Adding this observation results in the coefficient for real income (*rgdpa*) dropping by 13 percent. Additionally, the square of primary commodity exports (*sxp2*) and the fractionalization variable (*frac*) are now completely nonsignificant (see table 7.2). Thus, while Bosnia seems inconsistent with the CH prediction that higher social fractionalization should decrease civil war risk, social fractionalization ceases to be significant when we add Bosnia to the analysis.

We find that Bosnia is an influential observation in the model.[8] Bosnia is not an outlier except if we do not correct the CH coding of *peacetime,* in which case Bosnia would be an influential outlier. Bosnia and the first Croatian war are among the most influential observations, along with Congo-Brazzaville in 1997, Iran in 1970 and 1975, Turkey in 1990, and Cyprus in 1970. These are all civil war countries with higher than average income per capita (except Congo, which has lower than average income).[9]

*Table 7.2* CH Model of Civil War Onset (1960–99), with and without Bosnia (Coefficients and Standard Errors [in parentheses] Reported)

| Variable | Bosnia dropped | Bosnia added |
|---|---|---|
| Per capita real income | −0.0003 | −0.00026 |
| | (0.0001)*** | (0.0001)** |
| Growth rate of income | −0.119 | −0.122 |
| | (0.04)*** | (0.04)*** |
| Primary commodity exports/GDP | 10.83 | 9.22 |
| | (4.53)** | (4.38)** |
| Primary commodity exports squared | −15.38 | −13.04 |
| | (8.65)* | (8.33) |
| Social fractionalization | −0.00014 | −0.000117 |
| | (0.00007)* | (0.000077) |
| Democracy level | −0.034 | −0.041 |
| | (0.05) | (0.051) |
| Months at peace since 1960 | −0.0033 | −0.0036 |
| | (0.0009)*** | (0.00097)*** |
| Log of population size | 0.374 | 0.336 |
| | (0.116)*** | (0.113)*** |
| Constant | −7.47 | −6.72 |
| | (2.11)*** | (2.05)*** |
| Observations | 753 | 754 |
| Pseudo-$R^2$ | 0.198 | 0.195 |
| Log-likelihood | −153.7 | −156.41 |

*Note:* *** significant at .01; ** significant at .05; * significant at .10.

In the CH model, much of the work is done by the *"peacetime"* variable, because other variables do not change much over time (nothing changes in Bosnia, because we only have one observation). If Bosnia had been an independent state with no prior civil war since 1960, then its estimated risk of war would have been 5.4 times lower than the within-sample estimate, which is computed by setting Bosnia's *peacetime* equal to 0.[10] *Peacetime* is intended to measure, indirectly, the availability of war-specific capital. Such a measure should not be limited to measuring spillovers from a previous civil war in the same country, but rather should capture all sources of war-specific capital. In the context of Bosnia (as well as other wars in former Yugoslavia), the presence of the JNA in each region was crucial. The JNA should have deterred conflict escalation, but the fact that it was Serb-dominated meant that it became available to Bosnian Serbs and Croatian Serbs in their conflict against regional governments. More to the point, war capital is not confined to tangible goods. Memories of past conflict, which can fuel nationalist sentiment, are also forms of conflict capital. Most case histories (e.g., Glenny 1999) emphasize the impact of memory from the intra-Yugoslav violence during World War II. Despite the more than 50 years that intervened between the Croat violence against the Serbs under German rule, the historical legacy of the Ustashe looms large in the fears of Serb minorities in Croatia and can help explain the Krajina Serbs' movement for secession immediately after Croatia's independence. Let us now see how each component of the CH model applies to the Bosnian case.

## Ethnic Fragmentation

Much of the popular discourse about Yugoslavia has centered on so-called "ancient hatreds" between Serbs, Croats, Bosnian Muslims, and Albanians. We should therefore start by considering whether ethnic dominance or ethnic fragmentation could explain Bosnia's war.

A cursory look at the data on Yugoslavia's ethnic makeup suggests a poor fit of this case to the CH ethnic dominance thesis. The largest ethnic group in the Yugoslav federation was the Serbs whose relative share of the population dropped from 42 percent in 1961 to 36.2 percent in 1991. The Serbs do not make the 40–45 percent cut used by the CH model to establish ethnic dominance.

However, accounts of Yugoslavia's politics suggest a polarized environment. An informal way to consider how the country's ethnic makeup might capture this polarization would be to measure the ELF index in the way that ethnic difference might be *perceived* by each group if relations between each group and all the others are hostile. From the perspective of the Serbs, a politically meaningful ELF index in Bosnia would combine all non-Serbs in a single group and would be computed as: ELF: $100*\{1 - [(0.315*0.315) + (0.685*0.685)]\} = 43.155$ From the perspective of the Muslims, the ELF index that captures the Muslim/non-Muslim divide would be: ELF: $100*\{1 - [(0.437*0.437) + (0.563*0.563)]\} = 49.206$. This exercise shows how viable coalitions among groups change the degree of effective, politically relevant ethnic differentiation in a country. The picture that emerges from these new ELF indices is one of a much less fragmented society and one much closer to what we would consider a polarized society. Ethnic and religious polarization has been shown to increase the risk of civil war, so this would make Bosnia more consistent with theory and large-$N$ empirical results.

An interesting argument, raised by those who consider Yugoslavia's ethnic diversity as inconsequential with respect to the war, is that there was substantial exogamy (intermarriage) in Yugoslavia. Exogamy was, according to several accounts, widespread and this suggests to many analysts that a Yugoslav national identity was prevalent and there was not a substantial basis for ethnic hatred.[11] But in a careful quantitative study of exogamy in Yugoslavia, Botev (1994) argues that there is no clear upward trend in the rate of exogamy in Yugoslavia and there were also important regional variations in exogamy rates. Moreover, no clear pattern emerges between the rate of intermarriage and demand for secession in different regions. Croatia and Slovenia both seceded and both had a rising intermarriage rate from 1962 to 1989.[12]

By contrast, Kosovo and Macedonia both wanted to secede and had rapidly declining intermarriage rates.[13] Montenegro had a declining exogamy rate and Serbia and Bosnia had stable rates (at 12.9 and 11.9, respectively, for 1989). It is interesting that endogamy rates (i.e., no intermarriage) for both Serbs and Croats were lower in Bosnia than in other Republics. All three major groups had remained relatively closed in Bosnia (Botev 1994, 474–5). By contrast, the proportion of mixed marriages is highest in the region with the lowest level of ethnic conflict, Vojvodina. But Botev (1994) shows that this is more due to the fact that Vojvodina includes several small groups and less to a marked attitudinal difference among major groups in that region (though he notes that Serbs are slightly less endogamous there).

Yugoslavia censuses offer us a rare (for quantitative studies) view into the fluidity of ethnic identification. The Yugoslav census provides data on individuals' self-declared ethnic identification and there is evidence of identity switch that corresponds to the timing of intensifying nationalist sentiment in the country (see table 7.3, with data on ethnic composition by republic). The category of "Yugoslav" in the census was meant to capture those who did not want to emphasize their ethnic affiliation and, according to some scholars, this category captured Yugoslav communalism. The rise from 1.4 percent to 5.5 percent in the share of the population who identified themselves as Yugoslavs in the 1970s was a sign of a growing "sense of community" and political integration.[14] By contrast, in the late 1980s and early 1990s, this trend was reversed in the states with most intense conflict. In Bosnia, many self-identified Yugoslavs seemed to have shifted to the "Muslim" category both in the 1971 census and the 1991 census.[15] In Croatia, the Yugoslav category had been increasing through the 1961, 1971, and 1981 censuses, but the percentage of Yugoslavs dropped from 8.2 to 2.2 in the 1991 census.[16] Some of them seem to have moved to the "Croat" category, whereas others may have moved out of Croatia because of the war. In Serbia, the number of Yugoslavs seems to have dropped almost by half in the 1991 census (the number of Serbs increased proportionately), whereas in Kosovo, the Muslim and Albanian categories seem to have been merged in 1991 and there is a steady decline in the share of Serbs in the population from around 25 percent in 1961 to 10 percent in 1991. This decline is not explained only by population growth rates, but rather indicates the steady out-migration of Kosovo Serbs and growing domination of Albanians (90 percent in 1991).

By all accounts, these ethnic differences in Yugoslavia mattered because of a pattern of ethnic discrimination. Top positions in the bureaucracy were distributed "equally" among the six republics and two provinces (according to the parity principle, or *kljuc* in Serbo-Croatian). Thus, relative to their population size, Serbs and, particularly, Montenegrins were overrepresented and Croatians and Slovenes were underrepresented (most members of the League were Serbs and Montenegrins). The Serbs dominated the Army's officer corps. Yugoslavia was stable as a de facto confederal state with each republic having its own autonomous Communist party, but its stability rested on the principle of "weak Serbia, strong Yugoslavia."

We might propose a modification of the CH ethnic dominance variable that might help capture the impact of ethnic difference in federal or decentralized states.

## *Table 7.3* National Composition of Yugoslavia, 1961–91, by Republics and Provinces (Percent of Total Population)

| Republic | 1961 | 1971 | 1981 | 1991 |
|---|---|---|---|---|
| **Bosnia-Herzegovina** | 100 | 100 | 100 | 100 |
| Serbs | 42.8 | 37.3 | 32.2 | 31.4 |
| Muslims | 25.6 | 39.6 | 39.5 | 43.7 |
| Croats | 21.7 | 20.6 | 18.4 | 17.3 |
| Yugoslavs | 8.4 | 1.2 | 7.9 | 5.5 |
| Montenegrins | 0.4 | 0.3 | 0.3 | |
| Albanians | 0.1 | 0.1 | 0.1 | |
| Slovenes | 0.1 | 0.1 | 0.1 | |
| Macedonians | 0 | 0 | 0 | 0 |
| Other | 0.9 | 0.8 | 1.5 | 2.1 |
| **Croatia** | 100 | 100 | 100 | 100 |
| Serbs | 15 | 14.2 | 11.6 | 12.2 |
| Muslims | 0.1 | 0.4 | 0.5 | 0.9 |
| Croats | 80.2 | 79.4 | 75.1 | 78.1 |
| Yugoslavs | 0.4 | 1.9 | 8.2 | 2.2 |
| Montenegrins | 0.2 | 0.2 | 0.2 | 0.2 |
| Albanians | 0 | 0.1 | 0.1 | 0.3 |
| Slovenes | 0.9 | 0.7 | 0.5 | 0.5 |
| Macedonians | 0.1 | 0.1 | 0.1 | 0.1 |
| Other | 3.1 | 3 | 3.7 | 5.5 |
| **Macedonia** | 100 | 100 | 100 | 100 |
| Serbs | 3 | 2.8 | 2.4 | 2.2 |
| Muslims | 0.2 | 0.1 | 2.1 | |
| Croats | 0.3 | 0.2 | 0.2 | |
| Yugoslavs | 0.1 | 0.2 | 0.8 | |
| Montenegrins | 0.2 | 0.2 | 0.2 | |
| Albanians | 13 | 17 | 19.7 | 21 |
| Slovenes | 0.1 | 0.1 | 0.1 | |
| Macedonians | 71.1 | 69.3 | 67 | 64.6 |
| Other | 12 | 10.1 | 7.5 | 12.2 |
| **Montenegro** | 100 | 100 | 100 | 100 |
| Serbs | 3 | 7.5 | 3.3 | 9.3 |
| Muslims | 6.5 | 13.3 | 13.4 | 14.6 |
| Croats | 2.2 | 1.7 | 1.2 | |
| Yugoslavs | 0.3 | 2.1 | 5.4 | 4 |
| Montenegrins | 81.3 | 67.2 | 68.5 | 61.8 |
| Albanians | 5.5 | 6.7 | 6.5 | 6.6 |
| Slovenes | 0.2 | 0.1 | 0.2 | |

*(Continued)*

*Table 7.3* National Composition of Yugoslavia (*Continued*)

| Republic | 1961 | 1971 | 1981 | 1991 |
|---|---|---|---|---|
| Macedonians | 0.1 | 0.1 | 0.2 | |
| Other | 0.9 | 1.3 | 1.3 | 3.7 |
| **Serbia** | 100 | 100 | 100 | 100 |
| Serbs | 74.6 | 71.2 | 66.4 | 65.8 |
| Muslims | 1.2 | 1.8 | 2.3 | 2.4 |
| Croats | 2.6 | 2.2 | 1.6 | 1.1 |
| Yugoslavs | 0.3 | 1.5 | 4.8 | 3.2 |
| Montenegrins | 1.4 | 1.5 | 1.6 | 1.4 |
| Albanians | 9.2 | 11.7 | 14 | 17.2 |
| Slovenes | 0.3 | 0.2 | 0.1 | 0.1 |
| Macedonians | 0.5 | 0.5 | 0.5 | 0.4 |
| Other | 9.9 | 9.4 | 8.7 | 8.4 |
| **Serbia "proper"** | 100 | 100 | 100 | 100 |
| Serbs | 92.4 | 89.5 | 85.4 | 87.3 |
| Muslims | 1.7 | 2.4 | 2.7 | |
| Croats | 0.9 | 0.7 | 0.6 | |
| Yugoslavs | 0.2 | 1.4 | 4.3 | 2.5 |
| Montenegrins | 0.7 | 1.1 | 1.4 | |
| Albanians | 1.1 | 1.2 | 1.3 | |
| Slovenes | 0.3 | 0.2 | 0.1 | |
| Macedonians | 0.4 | 1.1 | 0.5 | |
| Other | 2.3 | 2.4 | 3.7 | 10.2 |
| **Vojvodina** | 100 | 100 | 100 | 100 |
| Serbs | 54.9 | 55.8 | 54.4 | 57.2 |
| Muslims | 0.1 | 0.2 | 0.2 | 0 |
| Croats | 7.8 | 7.1 | 5.4 | 4.8 |
| Yugoslavs | 0.2 | 2.4 | 8.3 | 8.4 |
| Montenegrins | 1.8 | 1.9 | 2.1 | 2.2 |
| Albanians | 0.3 | 0.2 | 0.1 | 0 |
| Slovenes | 0.8 | 0.8 | 0.9 | 0.8 |
| Macedonians | | | | |
| Other | 10.2 | 9.7 | 9.1 | 9.7 |
| **Kosovo** | 100 | 100 | 100 | 100 |
| Serbs | 23.5 | 18.4 | 13.3 | 10 |
| Muslims | 0.8 | 2.1 | 3.7 | |
| Croats | 0.7 | 0.7 | 0.6 | |
| Yugoslavs | 0.5 | 0.1 | 0.2 | 0.2 |
| Montenegrins | 3.9 | 2.5 | 1.7 | |

(*Continued*)

## Table 7.3 National Composition of Yugoslavia (*Continued*)

| Republic | 1961 | 1971 | 1981 | 1991 |
|---|---|---|---|---|
| Albanians | 67 | 73.7 | 77.5 | 90 |
| Slovenes | 0 | 0 | 0 | |
| Macedonians | 0.1 | 0.1 | 0.1 | |
| Other | 3.5 | 2.4 | 2.9 | |
| **Slovenia** | 100 | 100 | 100 | 100 |
| Serbs | 0.8 | 1.2 | 2.2 | 2.4 |
| Muslims | 0 | 0.2 | 0.7 | 1.4 |
| Croats | 2 | 2.5 | 3 | 2.7 |
| Yugoslavs | 0.2 | 0.4 | 1.5 | 0.6 |
| Montenegrins | 0.1 | 0.1 | 0.2 | 0.2 |
| Albanians | 0 | 0.1 | 0.1 | 0.2 |
| Slovenes | 95.6 | 94 | 90.5 | 87.6 |
| Macedonians | 0.1 | 0.1 | 0.2 | 0.2 |
| Other | 1.2 | 1.4 | 1.6 | 4.7 |

*Source:* Woodward (1995) and Yugoslav census (Savezni Zavod za Statistiku 1992).

Rather than coding if the country as a whole is dominated by a single ethnic group, we can look at each region (the republics in former Yugoslavia) and measure the ethnic or cultural difference between that region and the center. That difference would be maximized if the region was dominated by a national minority (as in the case of Slovenia, Croatia, and Kosovo) *and* if most of the members of the regional majority lived in that region and were not dispersed throughout the country.[17] Such a measure, applied to Yugoslavia, would help explain the demand for self-determination in Slovenia, Croatia, and Kosovo and the lack of such demand in Vojvodina, Montenegro, and Serbia. Serbia was, of course, the core state (Serbs made up 87 percent of Serbia "proper"), and it was poorer than some of the regions, so it did not have the incentive to secede. There was ethnic dominance in Vojvodina, but it was the Serbs—not a national minority—that dominated the region (57 percent of the population), which helps explain the lack of a significant movement for independence and the absence of war.

Montenegro seems on the surface to pose a problem for this theory, as it is dominated by Montenegrins (62 percent) but it did not have a significant demand for self-determination and there was no civil war. But, Montenegrins were net beneficiaries in Yugoslavia and were culturally similar to the Serbs (both were Christian Orthodox and more than 30 percent of them think they *are* Serbs). The fact that Montenegro's second largest minority is Muslim (14.6 percent) and that the region borders Bosnia to the north and Albania to the south might suggest an explanation for the majority's reluctance to secede: The Christian Orthodox Serb majority had to be weary of a possible Muslim independence movement, supported by its Muslim neighbors if Montenegro decided to secede from Serbia. Montenegro is also poor (see table 7.1; in 1990, its average household income was a third lower than the Yugoslav average), so increased sovereignty for it would come at a significant economic cost, because it would have to provide for defense and other public goods and services now covered mostly by Serbia.[18]

Thus, the theory does seem to fit, and despite this economic constraint there was a substantial constituency for independence in Montenegro. This was evident in the 2001 Republican Parliamentary elections, where nationalists in favor of independence won more than 40 percent of the vote (see table 7.4). The Liberal Alliance of Montenegro (LSCG) was founded on January 26, 1990 with Slavko Perovic as its first president. The party's key objective is Montenegrin independence and membership in the United Nations and the party has wide electoral support.

Moreover, during the time of Croatia's secession, the Serb-controlled JNA, together with the Territorial Defence Force and Montenegrin police special units, launched a joint attack on Dubrovnik using heavy artillery, navy, and air force on October 1, 1991. The Montenegrin leadership justified this as a "war for peace" to counter the "Croat fascist authorities" which could stage an attack on Montenegro from Dubrovnik. That attack might have been interpreted as a signal of the Center's likely reaction to a Montenegrin attempt at secession; it certainly demonstrated that

*Table 7.4* **Montenegro Republic Parliamentary Elections, April 22, 2001**

| | Votes | | Deputies | |
|---|---|---|---|---|
| List | Number | Percent | Number | Percent |
| The Victory is Montenegro's (DPS + SDP) | 153,946 | 42.36 | 36 | 46.8 |
| Liberal Alliance of Montenegro (LSCG) | 28,746 | 7.91 | 6 | 7.8 |
| Together for Yugoslavia (SNP + NS + SNS) | 148,513 | 40.87 | 33 | 42.9 |
| People's Socialist Party (NSS) | 10,702 | 2.94 | 0 | — |
| Srpska Radikalna Stranka (SRS)–Vojislav Seselj | 4,275 | 1.18 | 0 | — |
| Demokratska Unija Albanaca | 4,232 | 1.16 | 1 | 1.3 |
| Bosnjacko-muslimanska demokratska partija | 4,046 | 1.11 | 0 | — |
| Demokratski Savez Crne Gore | 3,570 | 0.98 | 1 | 1.3 |

Source: Various Montenegrin news sources; see www.izbori.org.yu/e-rezultati.html [accessed 10/22/2001].

Note: Electorate: 447,673; turnout: 366,152 (81.79 percent); irregular ballots: 2,748 (0.75 percent); regular ballots: 363,404.

Montenegrin elites, which had long since been dominated by the Serb Communist party, would not facilitate a secession.

Elite loyalty to Serbia was apparent in the agreement to support the Zabljak Constitution. A high-level agreement between the Socialist party of Serbia and the Socialist Democratic party of Montenegro decided to form a new state, the Federal Republic of Yugoslavia. The so-called Zabljak Constitution was named after the location of the meeting where the constitution was signed by Ratko Markovic, representing Serbia, and Zoran Zizic, representing Montenegro. Only the ruling parties of the future federation took part in the meeting and neither the Serbian National Assembly nor the Serbian citizens opted for the Constitution and new federation. The Montenegrin government called a referendum on March 1, 1992 when about 63 percent of citizens of Montenegro supported a new federation. The Constitution was adopted on April 27, 1992 by the Parliament of the Federal Republic of Yugoslavia. The Constitution allowed for bicameral Federal Assembly, consisting of the Chamber of Citizens with 138 seats, 30 of which belonged to Montenegro, and the Chamber of Republics, for which the two federation members delegated 20 parliament representatives each. In practice, leaders opposed to Milosevic were quickly ousted from office.

To sum up, the CH ethnic dominance argument may be relevant as a partial explanation of Yugoslavia's civil wars, but dominance must be political, not simply numerical, so the CH measure for this variable is only tangentially relevant. With reference to secessionist wars in particular, ethnic difference between the regions and the center may be more important than ethnic dominance at the national level.

How does our narrative suggest that ethnic dominance might have increased the risk of civil war in Yugoslavia and Bosnia? We can identify three mechanisms: (a) ethnic dominance translated into a pattern of political hegemony of the majority over the minority; (b) ethnic dominance by the Serb majority led to a perception of economic inequity, as small yet rich republics dominated by ethnic minorities subsidized large, poor republics dominated by the majority[19]; and (c) as the country became less fractionalized and more polarized, the minorities' fear of domination increased (so this suggests that we should focus on changes to the level of ethnic fractionalization, not the level itself). As the regions (Croatia and Bosnia) became ethnically dominated by an ethnic minority (which was also a regional titular majority), the expectation would have been one of greater political dominance and hegemony over the residual minorities, which would increase those minorities' fears and push them toward the use of violence. Serb populations in Croatia and Bosnia rationally expected their rights to be reduced, as they witnessed a shift toward greater and more direct control by a perceived hostile group. This gave rise to Serbian unification nationalism in Croatia and Bosnia, supported by irridentist nationalism in mainland Serbia.[20]

## Economic Growth

The rate of growth of the Yugoslav economy dramatically declined from 1989 to 1991 from a rate of approximately 1–2 percent to −15 percent, whereas the decade previous to that was relatively stable with rates between 0 and 5 percent (Woodward 1995, 55). This trend seems consistent with the CH model's expectations.

Yet, growth *must* be negatively affected by civil war and by lower-level violence, so simply looking at Bosnia's negative growth rate in 1991–92 will lead us to miss the spillover effects from the Croatian war. Civil war reduced investment, output, and access to markets in all Yugoslav republics. In Croatia in early 1991, 90 percent of the state budget was allocated to the war, more than 200,000 men were drafted, and taxes were imposed to raise money to fund the war.[21] This creates an endogeneity problem that is not necessarily a problem for the CH analysis, but it might be a problem for other studies (e.g., Fearon and Laitin 2003), which do not drop observations of ongoing war in analyzing the risk of new war onset.

Moreover, in countries that are integrated in regional markets, war in one country will reduce growth in all neighboring countries.[22] The effect is undoubtedly stronger in countries emerging from collapsed federations, as in the former Yugoslav and Soviet republics. Thus, the war in Croatia helped cause negative growth in Bosnia; and the rate of growth in Macedonia dropped to −18 percent in January 1992, undoubtedly as a result of losing access to Yugoslav markets (as well as a trade embargo from Greece, which was indirectly related to the war and Greece's ensuing fears of Macedonian irridentist designs on the Greek part of Macedonia). This example suggests the difficulty in justifying the independence assumption between neighboring states in large-$N$ studies and suggests the need for a much more complicated estimation strategy that would take into account such spillover effects.

## Economic Inequality

Income inequality is nonsignificant in the CH model (as in several other econometric studies of civil war). This result might seem counterintuitive, because earlier theories (e.g., Gurr 1970) emphasized the impact of relative deprivation in motivating violence. One explanation for this counterintuitive result is that Collier and Hoeffler and other analysts are using the wrong measure of inequality. Econometric studies have typically looked for direct linear effects between the Gini index, which measures interpersonal (or vertical) inequality, and civil war onset. Different measures of inequality may be more relevant in explaining war outbreak in Bosnia and Yugoslavia. Yugoslav society was a deeply unequal society, if we measure inequality by the differences in mean incomes in the different constituent republics (see table 7.1). The ratio of the top to bottom regional income—an index of inequality—was high at 5.2 for 1988 and getting higher, reaching 8.9 in 1990. (Contrast this to the much lower ratio of 2.17 in the USSR in 1988.) These figures are consistent with Sambanis and Milanovic's (2004) theory that higher levels of interregional inequality will increase the risk of violent demands for self-determination and suggest that interregional inequality might be a variable worth considering in expanding the CH model, at least when the CH model is used to explain secessionist conflicts.

The fact that rich yet small (in terms of population) regions provided the bulk of fiscal transfers to the poorer, larger regions generated an incentive for secession in the richer regions. But this logic suggests a possible problem in using the CH model to explain secession, as here we would expect richer states to want to secede. In one sense, the model still applies, as richer states should be better able to overcome the financial constraint of mounting an effective military campaign for secession. But the model's emphasis on the economic opportunity costs of violence is harder to apply here, as richer states have more to lose by a destructive civil war. Whether or not we will observe a war in reaction to a secessionist movement ultimately depends on the reaction by the Center, which has less to lose from war, so the opportunity cost argument now applies to the "government" (i.e., the Center) and not the "rebels" and can explain secession. But we still need to explain why richer states did not acquiesce when the Center decided to use force. A plausible explanation is that rich states weigh the long-term benefits of secession against the short term costs of war and find that their economic opportunity costs from war are actually low.

## Poverty and Unemployment

Bosnia was among the least-developed republics in Yugoslavia. The data on relative income in table 7.1 are instructive. Bosnia was poor and becoming poorer when the war started. Its relative income dropped from an index figure of 76.2 in 1988 to 67.76 in 1990, while Croatia's and Slovenia's income rose to 127.8 and 217.7, respectively. Kosovo was the only other region doing markedly worse in this two-year period and its per capita income amounted to only 24.4 of Yugoslavia's average income in 1990 (Montenegro and Macedonia were relatively unchanged, whereas Serbia's position was improving). Regional illiteracy rates confirm the regional disparities in development[23]: The Yugoslav average illiteracy rate was 13.7; it was 22.2 for Bosnia, 13.9 for Montenegro, 8.5 for Croatia, 14.8 for Macedonia, 1.4 for Slovenia, 15.2 for Serbia, 25.7 for Kosovo, and 8.4 for Vojvodina. Regional unemployment figures give a similar picture.

When we compare Bosnia's per capita income to the mean regional income in Yugoslavia, Bosnia is a poor state. The CH model fits very well in this regard. But when we compare Bosnia to the mean income for all countries in the CH data set, Bosnia is less poor: Its income is 21 percent lower than the average of $3,920, but it is well above the median income of $2,117.[24] This suggests that Bosnia does not fit neatly in the CH model. Yugoslavia, with a per capita income of $4,548 in 1990, is clearly a problem case for CH. But, once Yugoslavia fell apart, Bosnia's march to war fits the CH model's prediction, as does Kosovo, though Croatia in 1991 decidedly does not fit the model nor does Slovenia (there was no war there, but Slovenes seemed determined to go to war if Serbia tried to prevent them from seceding).

This all suggests a useful qualification to the CH model: In new states that emerge from dissolved federations, the risk of civil war is not independent of the war risk in other regions of the federation. The econometric analysis must account for this non-independence and the contagion effects of civil war must be properly modeled.[25]

This point about the dangers of political transition in dissolving federations implies that economic arguments have clear limits in explaining Bosnia. Economic arguments have also not been very popular in nonacademic analyses of the Bosnian war, which have generally favored the so-called ancient enmities explanation. Yugoslavia's history is seen as strewn with ethnic rivalry and the focus of these explanations is on the underlying motives for violence. But economic arguments offer a counterweight to the ancient hatreds approach and also speak to motives, as well as to the opportunity for war.

A prominent economic account that differs from the CH model is Susan Woodward's (1995), which focuses on the impact of economic crisis exacerbated by the austerity programs pushed by the International Monetary Fund (IMF). According to this view, rapid economic liberalization caused social stress, due to rising unemployment, a debt crisis, decline in real income per capita, and a dramatic drop in economic growth in the few years before the war's onset. The cause of the war was economic decline, mainly high debt and the consequences of programs to move quickly from a command and control economy to a market economy. The different republics' call for self-determination was the result of their desire to keep economic assets at home. The state was unable to modernize the economy and economic grievances that were generated during the 1980s were an important part of the story. Structural adjustment programs exacerbated these grievances.

Woodward provides a useful "top-down" economic explanation of the civil war's onset (by focusing on the foreign debt crisis) and downplays the bottom-up (e.g., ethnic) factors. She argues that Milosevic marshaled nationalism simply as a mobilization device to keep himself in power. Although the explanation does seem to capture some parts of the narrative we have offered above, Woodward's argument, like all other elite-centered accounts, does not explain why the masses would actually support violence if they did not share some of their leaders' nationalist ideas. The public cannot be treated as nonstrategic, simply yielding to elite manipulation. Successful nationalist mobilization must be consistent with facts or perceptions on the ground, and must reflect the public's fears and proclivities. Milosevic's decision not to fight a war to prevent Slovenia's secession must have been influenced by the fact that there were very few Serbs in Slovenia (2.3 percent in 1991), so he could not develop a credible nationalist argument for war. Thus, the fact that he allowed the richest republic to secede, whereas he fought to retain control of Kosovo—the poorest region of Yugoslavia, yet one with a significant historic and symbolic value for Serb nationalist history—suggests that elites' actions are themselves circumscribed by the boundaries of the ethnic group that they represent and largely reflect the preferences of that group. Economic accounts of war that emphasize the role of poverty, debt, negative growth, and unemployment must explain why the war was organized along ethnic lines and why nationalism was so easily cultivated by predatory elites.

## Natural Resources

What was the role of resource looting in Yugoslavia's wars? Yugoslavia had no natural resources of note. Some old lignite mines in Kosovo were of little economic value. Yet, despite the absence of natural resources, the CH model's focus on "looting" is applicable to this case. In the CH model, looting is a mechanism used to over-come the rebels' financial constraints. There was widespread looting during the Bosnian war; a large percentage of militia members or paramilitaries looted civilians as a way to sustain themselves. There is no evidence in case studies of the Bosnian war that looting was a motive for violence. But, as a means for irregular forces to sustain their insurgency, looting in Yugoslavia is consistent with the CH model's focus on predation.

That said, the resource-looting argument is not as relevant in this case because access to the weaponry of the JNA was pivotal in supporting the Serb rebellion in Bosnia and Croatia. Thus, this suggests another way in which the CH model might be modified when it is applied to war in former federal states. If the parties to the war are governments of former republics with access to trained soldiers and military equipment, access to natural resources may not be as significant a determinant of the parties' ability to fight an insurgency. Resources may still be a motive for secession (as in Aceh in Indonesia), but resource looting need not be a mechanism of over-coming the rebels' financial constraint if the parties have immediate access to the administrative and financial resources of the state. Slovenia, for example, had access to the arms-manufacturing industry; the Croats had access to tax revenues and could draft massive numbers of troops through conscription.

Could we perhaps reason by analogy to understand the role of looting in Yugoslavia? Could we argue that in Yugoslavia's deteriorating federal system, the most precious "natural resources" were Slovenia and Croatia—the richest republics that were sources of fiscal transfers to the poorest regions? This might be a plausible argument, though it is not directly analogous to the concept of looting in the CH model, because Slovenia and Croatia did not provide transfers to Serbia. The rich republics were important for the stability of Yugoslavia, in which Serbia had a dominant role, but if Serbia's wish was not to keep the federation intact, but rather to carve out as much land as possible from Yugoslavia to unite all Serbs and all historically Serb-controlled areas, then the looting analogy does not work. It may be the case that in nationalist conflicts, national symbols and memorials are just as valuable for mass mobilization as oil or diamonds or other "lootable" commodities in "greed"-driven conflicts.

## Diaspora Support

The CH argument about diaspora support is certainly relevant in this case, but the relationship between diaspora support and violence is complex. There was extensive diaspora support for all parties—not just the rebels—in all of Yugoslavia's civil wars. Diaspora support was not limited to financial assistance, but volunteers from other countries actually joined the fight. Ethnic associations abroad raised substantial amounts of funds for all parties. Perhaps the best example was Gojan Susak, the Croatian defense minister, who was a pizza place owner in Canada and was instrumental in the campaign to finance the Croatian movement through donations from Canada. There was also assistance from the regional diaspora, as was also the case in the Kosovo war, where ethnic brethren in neighboring countries were as important (if not more important) than the international diaspora. Support from the wider Islamic community was also available to the Bosnian Muslims (the Islamic lobby in the United States was crucial in efforts to lift the Bosnian arms embargo).The United Kingdom and France both had strong pro-Serb lobbies that were instrumental in putting in place the arms embargo, which ultimately helped the Serbs given the military status quo in Bosnia.The Croat lobby in Germany was extremely strong and was a major influence in Germany's decision to recognize Croatia in 1992 (see Woodward 1995). Given that all parties had substantial diaspora support, it is not clear in which direction we would expect diaspora support to influence the risk of civil war onset.[26] The CH model should consider diasporas in the neighborhood, not only in rich industrialized countries (which is the current focus of the model) and should factor in the potentially offsetting effects of diaspora support to both the rebels and the government.

## Terrain and Related Factors

Terrain variables—mountains and forests—are consistent with the model, as Bosnia is particularly mountainous and offered a good theater for guerrilla insurgency (the value for the mountainous terrain variable is 4.11 and the average for all countries is 2.17, with a maximum of 4.55). Croats, Serbs, and Bosniacs (Bosnian Muslims) were largely dispersed, with several small areas of concentrated majorities strewn across each region.Thus, demographic patterns in Bosnia seem consistent with the predictions of the CH model.

One potentially relevant variable that is not included in the CH model is population growth. Explanations of Bosnia's war sometimes mention the fact that the Muslims were growing much more rapidly than the other groups, threatening Serbian dominance.[27] This trend seems to have been particularly significant in Kosovo, because it was accompanied by growing Albanian control of the province and Serb out-migration. Indeed, the Serbian exodus from Kosovo is a counterexample for the Fearon and Laitin (2003) "sons of the soil" argument, which explains war onset as the result of friction between autochthonous populations and newly arrived migrants.

Another important dimension of the conflict that is not captured by the CH model is the rural/urban divide in Bosnia. Several analysts have observed a pattern of violence between the less-developed and less-educated (also Serb-dominated) rural areas against the more affluent (Muslim-dominated) urban areas.Thus, there is an urban-rural cleavage that maps on relatively well to the ethnoreligious cleavages along which the Bosnian war was fought.

## Democracy and Democratic Stability

The dissolution of Yugoslavia was an important shock that increased the risk of civil war onset. Collier and Hoeffler do not model the impact of a large regime transition, though other econometric studies have found this to be a significant correlate of war onset.[28]

The process of democratization in Yugoslavia was impeded by ethnic conflict in the constituent republics. With no civil society institutions to fall back on to sustain the process, the result of political liberalization was an incomplete democratization, which increases the risk of civil war (Snyder 2000). The effects of ethnic difference and ethnic dominance on democratization—like the effects of economic inequality, discussed earlier, on the probability of regime transition—are largely outside the CH model, which looks for independent linear effects on civil war (except with regard to natural resources, where the relationship is thought to be quadratic). The CH model could be extended to account for the indirect effects of ethnic difference and economic inequality on the process of democratization and, through that process, on civil war onset.[29]

Both ethnic cleavages and leadership loom large in most accounts of failed democratization in Yugoslavia. The eight-part (six republics and two provinces) presidency during Tito had created only an illusion of political decentralization. From 1987 to 1990, there was a marked change toward more centralization (or, rather, an effort to impose Serbian hegemony) and this might have incited fears of ethnic domination, consistent with theories of nationalism that highlight the negative effects of attempts to impose direct rule (cf. Hechter 2001). A series of constitutional amendments changed the status of the Republics. The Slovenia amendments were rejected and we witnessed an antibureaucratic revolution in Yugoslavia. The autonomy of regions (Kosovo, Voivodina) was taken away, suggesting that the Center was unwilling to use democratic governance and promote equal rights.

Growing centralization can fuel nationalisms (see above) and can cause security dilemmas as each ethnic group tries to defend itself during a period of emerging anarchy (Posen 1993). Consistent with this view, other analysts have focused on the role of opportunistic leaders in fanning these security dilemmas (De Figueiredo and Weingast 1999; Silber and Little 1997). According to these views, disastrous policy choices, nationalistic speeches, organization of paramilitary groups, and reluctance to compromise by exploitative politicians caused the war. Although this view could be correct, it cannot clearly distinguish the leaders' actions that resulted in their own preferences from those actions that were in response to rising nationalism in all the republics. Leadership arguments typically run into a sort of selection problem: Without explaining why the electorate would support a nationalist leader, it is hard to attribute all nationalist policies to elite preferences. Indeed, a reading of Yugoslav history does not give us a sense of social harmony that was suddenly disturbed by predatory elites. Rather, one can find clear evidence of ethnically organized social protest that, throughout Tito's era, was decisively and forcefully suppressed (Glenny 1999). Yugoslavia was a precariously balanced regime based on repression, and the ethnic contests in the 1990s had deep historical roots.

## Cold War

Finally, we should consider systemic influences. Collier and Hoeffler code a binary variable denoting the end of the Cold War as an indirect measure of the superpowers' interests in taming ethnic conflicts in their spheres of influence. Our narrative illustrates various other ways in which the international community can influence the risk of civil war onset. The obvious point is that multilateral peacekeeping intervention and mediation had an impact on patterns of violence and helped end the war with the Dayton peace accords in 1995.[30] A less apparent diffusion effect is discussed well by Woodward (1995), who places considerable emphasis on how the Yugoslav parties' behavior was shaped by international norms, especially norms regarding partition and self-determination. As she puts it, expectations of how the international community would react to events in Yugoslavia influenced the parties' decision to go to war. Woodward describes international norms as constraints that shifted suddenly as the European Community changed its position regarding recognition of Croatia and Slovenia. Related to this, Woodward offers a convincing account of how international irresponsibility and incoherence influenced events in Bosnia (looking the other way while the violence was intensifying; sending mixed signals by recognizing Croatia and Slovenia before deciding on how to handle demands for self-determination in Bosnia).

## Dynamics of Violence

The armies that fought in the Bosnian war were a mix of irregular and regular forces. At the one end of the spectrum were criminal and quasi-criminal elements, often freed from prison in order to take part in the fighting (Mueller 2000). At the other end were former career officers of the JNA who had defected to the various ethnic armies. In the middle were reservists and home guards, armed and trained by the JNA. They were mobilized locally by ethnic parties and ethnic entrepreneurs. The mobilization of civilians into militias was facilitated by the abundance of weapons (Maas 1996, 231; Sudetic 1998, 89). Paramilitary forces from outside Bosnia also actively participated. The degree of organization and discipline also varied widely, with quasi-criminal groups in one end and regular units in the other. Moreover, many of these units underwent an organizational transformation during the war, becoming more organized and centralized.

A key feature of the war was the combined numerical inferiority and (initial) military superiority of the Serb forces. Toward the end of the war, the two sides reached relative military parity. By the summer of 1994, the Bosnian government was able to eventually field 110,000 troops, including Croats, while Bosnian Serb forces reached 80,000. The initial military advantage of the Bosnian Serbs was offset by their demographic inferiority, the unwillingness of ordinary Serbs from the rump Yugoslav Federation to fight in Bosnia, and the multiform international support received by the Bosnian Muslims and Croats.

The Bosnian war can be described as a "symmetric nonconventional" war (Kalyvas 2005), a type of war characterized by a mix of regular and irregular forces fighting in territory defined by clear frontlines and a political context shaped by state collapse. These wars tend to generate high levels of violence.

The defining characteristic of violence in Bosnia was mass deportation of civilians along ethnic lines, commonly known as "ethnic cleansing." Mass deportation in Bosnia was initiated by the Serbs in April 1992 and became common practice throughout the war, practiced by all sides to varying degrees. It was first used in late summer 1991 in eastern Croatia but became most severe in Bosnia. Serb units from Serbia, many part of special paramilitary forces such as Arkan's Tigers, inaugurated this tactic in Bosnia. Eventually, the perpetrators included conscript soldiers, local policemen, and local villagers.

Though individual instances differed, a general pattern emerges. Initially, Serb forces would establish military control of an area, either from inside, relying on the local Serb population, or by attack or siege. This task was often carried out by Serb roving militias, though artillery support could be provided by regular units. In many cases, these outsiders were accompanied and helped by locals. In his description of the attack against his village, Pervanic (1999, 23) recalls that

> most of the faces came from the surrounding Serb villages, Maricka, Jelicka, Petrov Gaj, Gradina, Omarska, and Gornja Lamovita. But others were strangers speaking with an accent that could only be from some part of Serbia or Montenegro. Many of the local Chetniks were people who had gone to school with us, and with whom we socialised regularly.

These units would attack, and usually defeat, hastily organized "self-defense" units formed by Muslim villagers. Where complete control could not be achieved, for instance in some of Bosnia's larger cities, Serb forces lay the area under siege.

Once control was achieved, local non-Serbs met various fates. Some were killed immediately, some were imprisoned, and others were harassed, tortured, or forcibly deported. Thousands of men were taken to prison camps set up within Bosnia's borders, numbering close to 100. Possibly the worst was Omarska, where as many as 4,000 Bosnian men, primarily Muslim, were killed. In some places expulsion was immediate and violent, and sometimes safe passage was offered for those who voluntarily left an area. Many refugees were also coerced into signing over their property to the Serb forces before being allowed to leave. Property was frequently looted and destroyed. Although some of the violence was targeted, much of it was indiscriminate.

Where Serb control came early, coercive measures, such as restrictive security measures that set non-Serbs apart from other residents, were used against those who had not yet left. In the Banja Luka region, non-Serbs were put under curfew and were prohibited from meeting in public or in groups of more than three people, and prohibited from traveling by car and from visiting relatives out of town. Non-Serbs were also deprived of their livelihoods, their utilities were cut off, their houses often burned down, and many were beaten, raped, or killed. By the end of 1993, only 40,000 of the region's 350,000 Muslims remained.

Destroying a community's cohesion helped to break resistance. Community leaders—such as wealthy professionals, academics, and local clergy—were often eliminated. In the Kozarac area, prominent Muslims were identified, arrested, and earmarked for elimination based on existing blacklists. Sometimes, violence was accompanied with the victims' humiliation. In conquered areas, mosques and other religious and cultural relics were destroyed, often to the point where it was no longer possible to see that they had ever existed. Muslim clergymen were dispersed, imprisoned, or killed, and it is estimated that by September 1992 over half of Bosnia's mosques, historical monuments, and libraries were destroyed.

By the fall of 1992, ethnic cleansing had spread beyond Bosnia's villages to towns and cities. The publication by Western media, in August 1992, of extensive reports outlining the existence of concentration camps in Bosnia that housed thousands of Bosnian non-Serbs generated widespread outrage. In response, Serb leaders closed some of the worst camps and transferred their prisoners to other locations by the end of 1992. By November, there were approximately 1.5 million Bosnian refugees and at least 20,000 rapes had been committed.

## Polarization and Violence

In the following text, we address two questions. First, what is the relationship of ethnic polarization and ethnic violence? Second, how does one explain the prevalence of ethnic cleansing?

The Bosnian war is described as a case of "ethnic conflict." Most people sided with the ethnic group to which they belonged. Of course, this is a simplification. There were some high-profile instances of crossing ethnic lines. Best known is that of the Bosnian Muslim leader Fikret Abdic, who controlled a sizeable area of northwestern Bosnia (Bihac) and allied with the Serbs, fighting against the Bosnian government. Examples on a more minor scale are also numerous and include Serb commanders in the Bosnian Army, in Sarajevo and elsewhere, and Muslim soldiers in Serb units and even Serb prison camps (Human Rights Watch 1992, 77, 130). Overall, however, ethnic identity appears to be a good predictor of the side that an individual was likely to join. Whether it is also a good predictor of ethnically intolerant attitudes is a different issue (Massey, Hodson, and Seculić 1999).

There is evidence also suggesting that intragroup violence was not uncommon and served to police ethnic boundaries (Cohen 1998, 199; Human Rights Watch 1992, 15, 231; Silber and Little 1997, 137–44) and that most people wanted no part in the fighting (Claverie 2002, 48; Mueller 2000). It is often overlooked that many fighters were conscripts rather than volunteers (Maas 1996, 109). According to Loyd (2001, 85),

> many people found themselves carrying a gun whether they liked it or not. If you were of combat age, meaning only that you possessed the strength to fight, kill and possibly survive, then you were conscripted into whichever army represented your denomination, Muslim, Serb or Croat.

No systematic data are available about the motivations of the individuals who participated in ethnic cleansing. Initially at least, the war brought to the surface simmering tensions that had developed in the context of party politics during the period immediately preceding the advent of hostilities. However, the first to embrace the violence of the war were those who had embraced it in peace, including the most notorious one, the Serb warlord Arkan (Cohen 1998, 192; Sudetic 1998, 97). Some of the first leaders of the Bosnian army had criminal backgrounds. Ramiz Delic ("Celo") had served several years in prison for rape, while Jusuf Prazina ("Juka") was a "debt collector in peacetime" (Cohen 1998, 280; Maas 1996, 31). The men in charge of the Visegrad chapter of the Stranka Demokratski Akcije (SDA), the Sabanovic brothers, also had a criminal past (Sudetic 1998, 90). The influence of alcohol in the production of violence cannot be underestimated because it recurs in description upon description (e.g., Human Rights Watch 1992, 168; Sudetic 1998, 293). In other words, it appears that the war provided an opportunity for violent action to individuals with a propensity to violence, rather than turning most individuals into murderers (Mueller 2000).

Some of the violence took place between neighbors. Often the victims knew by name the perpetrators of violence (Human Rights Watch 1992, 67). However, the dominant form of violence appears to have been more of the "soldiers against civilians" rather than the "civilians against civilians" type that is more common in riots and pogroms (or the Rwandan genocide). Only small minorities of the various populations participated in the violence (Mueller 2000), and there is evidence that local deals were reached in several circumstances (Bougarel 1996). Often, the violence hid personal grudges rather than impersonal ethnic animosity. Pervanic (1999, 156–7) recalls that "many inmates" in the Omarska prison camp "were murdered for private reasons. Guards who had a grudge against somebody took their revenge. The visitors from outside often took advantage of the same opportunity."

It would be erroneous to assume that the ethnic divide was as deep as the violence suggests. Maas (1996, 149) writes of how

the airwaves came alive as men on both sides of the front line talked to each other, swore at each other and sang songs. A Bosnian soldier would chat over the airways with a Serb friend, now a solider on the other side, exchanging gossip about their families and mutual acquaintances.

The soldiers who found themselves 200 yards apart in trenches "traded in cigarettes and gasoline, at night there was banter about soccer teams or arguments about history. If somebody was injured, the person who shot him might even inquire later about his health" (Cohen 1998, 292). Often soldiers gave cigarettes and drinks to one another, had conversations, and warned each other against the most hostile units in their own forces; soldiers on both sides refrained from firing on one another and even arranged informal truces.

There are numerous examples of people's lives being spared precisely because they had the chance to see a friend on the opposite side. A Muslim tells how "one of my neighbors was taken into the house [to be killed] but a Serb friend spoke up so he was released." Another witness notes that "one of the soldiers wanted to kill us, but the soldier I knew didn't let them." Often having friends on the other side got one out of prison. Often people tried to cooperate with their friends in anticipation of the violence to come (Human Rights Watch 1992, 70, 72, 158, 260; Sudetic 1998, 109). In short, although people fought primarily along with their ethnic kin, their actual behavior was not always violent.

Disaggregating the cycle of polarization and violence is not easy given present data limitations. The available evidence suggests that the period prior to the war witnessed substantial polarization along ethnic lines. For example, the Muslim owner of a café in Rogatica recalls that while at first his clientele was mixed, during the course of 1991 Serbs stopped coming to his café. "There were now Serb cafes and Muslim cafes" (Cohen 1998, 195). Likewise, a Muslim school teacher from a town in northwestern Bosnia noted that "tensions between the various ethnic groups and discrimination against non-Serbs surfaced in Prijedor before fighting broke out in late May" (Human Rights Watch 1992, 43). The same situation prevailed in the villages of northeastern Bosnia.

> By late fall of 1991 Muslims from Zlijeb were no longer sending their children to the primary school in Odzak. Down in Visegrad, Muslim and Serb men were no longer sitting together in any café except for the bar hotel beside Mehmed Pasha's bridge. This café was Visegrad's illegal gun bazaar. (Sudetic 1998, 89)

In the eastern Bosnian town of Bijeljina, some of "the first violent incidents occurred in 1991 between the clients of the newly opened Istanbul and Serbia cafes" (Cohen 1998, 195). However, this polarization produced only limited violence.

## Conflict "Ethnification" as a Result of Violence

Rather than translating deep divisions into violent conflict, the anecdotal evidence suggests a situation of rapid "ethnification" of violence *once the war began.* Once the war began, it endogenously generated additional waves of violence and further polarization, through the mechanism of revenge; this process consolidated, magnified, and hardened ethnic identities. A soldier overlooking the hills of Sarajevo said that "he had volunteered because a relative was killed by Croatian forces near Derventa early in the war" (Cohen 1998, 137). "A Muslim soldier seeking revenge for the death of a relative, a military police chief killed near Skelani, had used the butt of a revolver to smash the skulls of a Serb man and his elderly mother" (Sudetic 1998, 172). The pace of killing accelerated in the Susica camp after a local Serb hero was killed in a Muslim ambush a few miles from Vlasenica (Cohen 1998, 214).

During the later years of the conflict, people who had witnessed the brutal deaths of their loved ones were driven to behave in a violent manner and became an important recruitment reservoir for the Bosnian Muslim forces. Some of them were known as *torbari* or "bag people." They were active around Srebrenica and were responsible for atrocities against Serbs in the villages of Podravnje, Grabovacka, and Kravica

(Sudetic 1998, 157). In Travnik, Muslim refugees formed the legendary 17th Krajiska Brigade commanded by Colonel Mehmet Alagic, himself a refugee from Sanski Most (Cohen 1998, 292). The Srebrenica massacre may have been driven, in part at least, by revenge. Philippe Morillon, the commander of the UN force in Bosnia, is quoted as saying a few days before the fall of Srebrenica that "the Serbs were not stopping their offensive in eastern Bosnia, not so much because they needed to capture the territory, but because they had become enraged after the discovery of a mass grave in Kamenica" (Sudetic 1998, 181).

The spirit of revenge could even subvert attempts to control it by the authorities, as in the town of Vares (Silber and Little 1997, 300). An armed Croat unit arrived from Kiseljak, the hard-line Croat stronghold to the south, and proceeded to imprison the local Croat mayor and police chief. Then, Muslim men were rounded up, and Muslim homes were raided and looted. Within days, almost the entire Muslim community had fled to the village of Dabravina to the south, where they waited and planned their return.

The anecdotal evidence suggests that the members of the more organized military forces tended to be more restrained and controlled in their behavior than their more loosely structured counterparts. In Herzegovina, witnesses reported that the jails of the Hrvatske Odbrambene Snage (HOS) were very much worse than those run by the Hrvatska Vojska Odbrane (Croatian Army of Defense), the official army of Bosnian Croats (Human Rights Watch 1992, 331). Likewise, the camps run by the regular Bosnian Serb army were more regulated than those run by Serb paramilitary groups (Gutman 1993, 29). And, although there were widespread allegations of the systematic use of rape as a weapon of war, there is evidence suggesting that the regular military and police units were actually the organizations to which raped women often turned to for assistance after their ordeals (Engelberg 1992, A8; Human Rights Watch 1992, 175). On the other hand, the worse single massacre of the war, in Srebrenica, was implemented mostly by regular forces, albeit with local assistance.

Why was ethnic cleansing so central to the war? By inferring the origins of the practice and the goals of those who used it from the actual outcome, one can conclude that the intention was to create ethnically homogeneous states. Another way to approach this issue is to examine the patterns of violence.

Although violence was depicted as uniform, it varied widely. This variation was both spatial and temporal: "In most regions of Bosnia the conflict retained a distinctly local character. Whole sectors of the front remained relative untouched by the war, loosely defended by local militia" (Burg and Shoup 1999, 138). Maas (1996, 20) reports that "it was one of the odd features of Serb controlled territory that while Muslims were being tortured at a prison camp a mile down the road others who had sworn their loyalty to the local Serb warlords remained at liberty." Yet, most descriptions come from the most violent parts of the country, indicating selection bias.

In general, violence tended to occur in areas that were of strategic or economic importance. The first outbreak of large-scale violence occurred in northwestern Bosnia, in the village of Hambarine which bordered the Croatian region of Krajina, where violence had already broken out in the Croatian war. Most importantly, northwestern Bosnia was strategic in that it linked Serb territory in Croatia and Bosnia. Hambarine itself lay in an important position connecting the larger town of Prijedor with the Ljubija mine. Northeastern Bosnia was another scene of intense fighting because it linked Serbia proper with the Serb-held areas of Croatia and eastern Bosnia.

Most notorious Bosnian Serb prison camps were also located in northeastern and northwestern Bosnia. Four of the largest camps (Omarska, Keraterm, Manjaca, and Trnopolje) were located in the northwest. Additionally, all of these camps were situated near the center of Serb power, Banja Luka. Likewise, the camps run by the Muslim and Croatian forces were also near their respective centers of power. The HOS operated a facility in Capljina (their stronghold of Herzegovina) and in Orasje in northern Bosnia, while the most notorious Muslim-run camp, Celibici, was near their stronghold of Konjic.

The concentration of violence in these particular areas emerges as well from a compilation of the data on human rights violations collected by various organizations. For the purposes of this chapter, we coded the evidence gathered by the UN, the U.S. State Department, and Human Rights Watch. Figure 7.1 shows a remarkable convergence in the evidence produced by these three bodies: Violence is clearly concentrated in northern Bosnia, and especially the northwest. Consistent with these results, figure 7.2, which graphs UN data on the size of mass graves, suggests that northwest Bosnia was the epicenter of violence.

Turning to temporal variation, we observe significant variation as well, which is consistent with the anecdotal evidence. Using the same data as above, we find that the violence is concentrated in the first months of the war, roughly the spring and summer of 1992, when the initial phase of territorial consolidation took place (figure 7.3).[31]

It has also been suggested that the impact of international diplomacy on violence was not negligible. Attempts to settle the conflict often led to military activities by the warring parties intended to consolidate or capture as much territory as they could prior to settlement. For example, the Bosnian Serb army undertook a major offensive in northeastern and southeastern Bosnia immediately after the United Nations proposed the division of Bosnia into largely autonomous provinces "in which an ethnic group would retain de facto control of designated areas" (Human Rights Watch 1992, 221). The anthropologist Tone Bringa (1993, 1995) recorded a similar outbreak of violence following the Vance-Owen plain in the Kiseljak area, northwest of Sarajevo.

Ethnic cleansing has been interpreted as an expression of ethnic hatred and intolerance. However, ethnic cleansing is hardly a constant feature of ethnic civil wars, even when ethnic polarization is high. Although the war in Chechnya has obvious ethnic characteristics, ethnic cleansing has not been used. Additionally, ethnic cleansing was not always implemented immediately after one warring side gained control over a certain territory. For instance, Serb forces entered the village of Hambarine on May 23 but its Muslims inhabitants remained until July 19. It was only on July 20 that the Serbs began to kill the inhabitants and take them to detention

*Figure 7.1* Spatial Variation of Reported Human Rights Abuse
Incidents and Mass Grave Locations

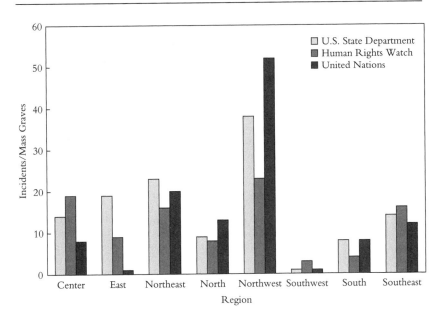

*Figure 7.2* Estimated Number of Bodies in Mass Graves
(1992–93)

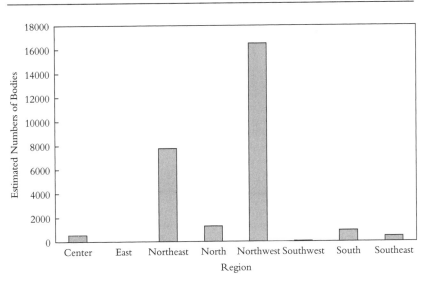

*Figure 7.3* Temporal Variation in Reported Incidents of
          Human Rights Abuses

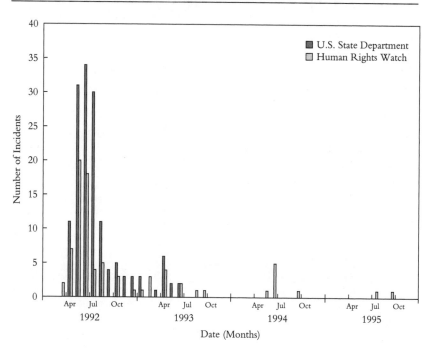

camps (Human Rights Watch 1993, 54). This was not the only case in which an army that overtook a city held it for weeks before engaging in mass violence and deportation.

A possible explanation is suggested in an interview given by a Croatian woman, who witnessed the takeover of the town of Prijedor by the Bosnian Serb forces, to Human Rights Watch. She claimed that "the takeover occurred without bloodshed because the Muslims and Croats did not resist with weapons at first" (Human Rights Watch 1993, 43). In Prijedor, the ethnic cleansing of the Muslim population began weeks after the Serbs took over, when the Muslim forces launched a counterattack. Likewise, the Serb forces began to cleanse the Muslims in the town of Kozarac only after the Muslim forces launched an attack on the town on May 26 (Human Rights Watch 1992, 44). Pervanic (1999) provides a similar account from the Bosnian Muslim point of view that also mentions sporadic guerrilla action and harassment by Muslim groups during the initial phase of the war.

The first move consisted of an announcement on radio or TV in which all the members of the opposing ethnic group were asked for their support. Support could be shown by handing over one's weapons or swearing an oath of loyalty. The inhabitants were then allotted a certain time period in which to make the decision on whether or not to give their support. Before they attacked Kozarac, Serb military leaders gave the village leaders seven days to consider signing an oath of loyalty to the Serb authorities, otherwise they would be considered a threat; the villagers of Grabska were also warned that they would be shelled unless they gave up their weapons by noon on May 10, 1992. The Serb forces announced to the people of Hambarine that they would be attacking the village the next day at 12:15 if they did not surrender their weapons (Human Rights Watch 1992, 53, 61, 216). Noncompliance led to large-scale violence. Conversely, there is evidence that people in villages that did not resist the Serbs were treated more leniently (Pervanic 1999, 78–80).

Overall, this pattern suggests that ethnic cleansing may have also been an answer to the problem of population control. Actors lacking the ability to control populations whose loyalty is questionable may choose to deport them instead in order to consolidate their defenses. The question is, why do strategies of population control vary so much across ethnic wars, from genocide, to ethnic cleansing, and to simple coercion?

## Conclusion

Our conclusion must begin with an overview of the CH model's fit to the case of Bosnia. Table 7.5 provides such an overview, summarizing our analysis in this chapter. Drawing on these lessons from Bosnia, how might we propose expanding or revising the CH model?

One suggestion is that the *peacetime* variable should not be the only variable used to capture the conflict-specific capital generated by prior conflict. Related to this, contagion and diffusion effects should not be ignored. The war in Croatia was decisive in shaping public opinion in Bosnia, as was the successful secession of Slovenia and Croatia, which pushed Bosnian Serbs and Krajina Serbs to demand independence and annexation to Serbia. Direct external intervention by Serbia in Croatia and Bosnia, by Montenegro in Croatia, and by Croatia in Bosnia had a clear effect on the duration of the civil war, and the expectation of such intervention might well have figured prominently in the parties' decision to go to war. To explore further the relationship between external intervention and civil war onset, one must endogenize intervention and model the effects of an expectation of partial intervention on the probability of civil war onset.

A second suggestion is to consider the effects of political institutions in greater depth. The lack of democratic institutions that could help sustain the democratic transition was important here. The CH model should control not only for the level of democracy, but also for the change in regime type. Leadership looms large as a factor in the Bosnian war, but it is hard to differentiate its effects from the effects of ethnic polarization, international shocks, and unresolved ethnic antipathies that were solidified during Tito's authoritarian rule.

Several improvements on the ethnic measures are also suggested by this case. First, polarization seems more significant than either fractionalization or dominance. Polarization should ideally be measured not simply in terms of the numerical size of

## Table 7.5 Checklist: CH Model "Fit" to the Bosnian Civil War

| Collier-Hoeffler variable | Association with war onset in CH model | Bosnia 1990–92; values for variable | Variable values consistent with war in Bosnia? |
|---|---|---|---|
| Primary commodity exports/GDP | Positive or inverted-U | No natural resources of note | Inconsistent (no resources); but logic of the argument seems to apply (other looting present) |
| GDP per capita | Negative | Yugoslavia's GDP high relative to other civil war countries; Bosnia is GDP higher than the median | Inconsistent (with respect to Yugoslavia); Bosnia closer to the CH model, though GDP was higher than the population median |
| Diaspora | Positive | All three groups (Croats, Serbs, Bosniacs) received diaspora support | Consistent (with respect to the effect of prolonging the war) |
| GDP growth | Negative | Large decline in Yugoslav rate of growth (15–20 percentage points) from 1988 to 1992 | Consistent (but growth likely affected by war in Croatia, so concern with endogeneity) |
| Mountainous terrain | Positive | Very mountainous, with a score of 4.11 (the average for all countries is 2.17 and maximum 4.55) | Consistent |
| Geographic dispersion | Positive | Croats, Serbs, and Bosniacs largely dispersed, with several small areas of concentrated majorities across the state | Consistent |
| Population size | Positive | Slightly lower than the average for all country-years (9.04) at 8.11 | Inconsistent—though there was only a small difference from the population mean |
| Social fractionalization | Negative | Interacting ELF and religious fractionalization gives Bosnia a very high index value | Inconsistent; yet consistent if we consider the modifications to ELF proposed in this chapter |

| | | | |
|---|---|---|---|
| Ethnic fractionalization | Negative, but nonsignificant | High fractionalization at 0.697 (population mean is 0.385, with 0.925 most fractionalized) | ELF is not significant in CH; ELF is lower if we consider coalitions among groups |
| Religious fractionalization | Negative, but nonsignificant | Very high 0.709 out of a population maximum of 0.78 (population mean is 0.367) | Consistent, but variable is not significant in CH |
| Ethnic dominance | Positive | Low: Bosniacs (Muslims) are the largest group with 43.7 percent of the population | Inconsistent; yet measure used by CH seems inappropriate |
| Income inequality | Negative, but nonsignificant | Fairly high—large rural-urban divide, corresponding to perceptions that Muslims were better off than Serbs | Variable not significant in CH; yet measure used by CH seems inappropriate; regional inequality is more relevant |
| Democracy | Negative, but nonsignificant | Nondemocratic regime (polity score = 0) | Consistent (low democracy); yet this is not a significant factor in CH and regime transition was more important than the "level" of democracy |
| Peace duration | Negative | Considering all Yugoslav wars as related, the Croatian war increased the risk of war in Bosnia | Consistent (if we code 0 months at peace prior to war onset, taking into account the Croatian war in 1991) |

the groups, but also in terms of their ideological opposition to each other. Second, ethnic and cultural differences between regions may be important in explaining violence in pursuit of self-determination in federal states.

Another suggestion is to consider the Sambanis-Milanovic interregional inequality hypothesis as well as the related hypothesis about interregional ethnic difference. This is consistent with Woodward's argument about the effects of international economic shocks, and Woodward's focus on external shocks offers another valuable, plausibly generalizable addition to the CH model. Shocks can prompt secessionist action, but interregional inequality provides the foundations for latent demand for self-determination. That demand was revealed at the time of weakness of the Communist regime at the Center. The effects of interregional economic inequality and ethnic difference suggest some potentially important differences in the causes of separatist violence as compared to other forms of violence and these differences deserve to be theorized better.[32]

Turning to the dynamics of violence, we inquired about the relationship between ethnic polarization and ethnic violence, and about the centrality of ethnic cleansing. The evidence indicates that although there was ethnic polarization before the outbreak of the hostilities, it was much enlarged by the war. This suggests that measures of ethnic polarization must be dynamic rather than static (as in the CH model), sensitive to the ways in which a conflict unfolds. It is also possible to suggest the logical strategy supporting the killing and ethnic cleansing, influenced by three factors: territorial control, the military balance of power, and the nature of the secession process in Yugoslavia. First, the imposition of full territorial control could be achieved only if the Serbs were able to invest superior military resources, which they were clearly lacking. Second, the initial Serb military superiority was certain to decline, thus placing a premium on rapid action at the very outset of the conflict in order to create facts on the ground, most obviously via mass deportation rather than the most costly and time-consuming policing of all potentially "disloyal" localities. Third, Yugoslavia's inability or unwillingness to prevent the secession of Bosnia created a geographical space to which Bosnian Muslims could be deported. It is telling that the Serbs were willing to contemplate the existence of a rump Bosnian state as opposed to try to control the entire territory of Bosnia. In a way, ethnic cleansing can be seen as the perverse effect of a process of "twin secession," where the Yugoslav state could not prevent the Bosnian Muslims and Croats from seceding from Yugoslavia, while the Bosnian Muslims and Croats could not prevent the Bosnian Serbs from seceding from Bosnia.

# Notes

We thank Branko Milanovic for very helpful comments on an earlier draft, Larisa Satara for input, and Samantha Green-Atchley, Zeynep Bulutgil, Gul Kurtoglu, and Paul Staniland for research assistance.

  1. The war is also dropped in Fearon and Laitin (2003), as data for gross domestic product (GDP) are missing for Bosnia. The other former Yugoslav republics are also missing data.

2. We could not find data on primary commodity exports for Bosnia, so we used data on primary commodity exports for Yugoslavia (0.032).

3. This problem is not addressed by any existing quantitative studies of civil war, which treat regime type as exogenous (except Elbadawi and Sambanis 2002). So, we do not consider the endogeneity problem further here, either.

4. The ELF is computed as follows: 100*{1 − [(0.437*0.437) + (0.314*0.314) + (0.173*0.173) + (0.076*0.076)]} = 67.473.

5. *Frac* is defined by Collier and Hoeffler as the product of *rf* and *elf*, but a slightly different figure is given in Collier and Hoeffler and the figure varies over time, although *rf* and *elf* do not vary.

6. We use the 1995 value for forest cover also for 1992.

7. The model was estimated as a pooled logit just as in the CH model. We regressed war onset on real income, growth rate, primary commodity exports and their square, fractionalization, democracy, peacetime, and log of population.

8. If we plotted the change in Pearson's $\chi^2$ by the predicted probability of war onset, and each observation is weighed by its relative influence on the estimation, we would find that Bosnia is one of four most influential observations. This figure is available from the authors. If we dropped three outliers—Cyprus, Bosnia, and Yugoslavia—the model fit increases dramatically: the pseudo-$R^2$ rises to 22.5 percent and all variables except democracy are highly significant.

9. The average change in Pearson $\chi^2$ statistic is 0.95. For Bosnia, this statistic is 66.41. The computed influence statistic has a mean value of 0.11 for the entire sample and the corresponding value for Bosnia in 1990 is 0.37. The most influential observation is the Congo in 1995 (0.45). Figures showing these results are available from the authors.

10. The within-sample prediction for Bosnia is 0.08 with *peacetime* coded 0; it drops to 0.0149 if we code *peacetime* equal to 532 (months at peace since 1960). The average probability for all country-years is 0.071.

11. For data on ethnic intermarriage in Yugoslavia, see Petrovic (1986) and Bromlei and Kashuba (1982).

12. If the intermarriage rate was a sign of interethnic affinity, then the relationship between that and separatism or war would run counter to expectations.

13. Rates in Kosovo dropped from 9.4 percent in 1962–64 to 4.7 in 1987–89; in Macedonia, they dropped from 13.5 percent to 7.8 percent in the same periods (Botev 1994, 469). By contrast, intermarriage rates increased from an already high rate of 22.5 percent to 28.4 percent in the same period.

14. Yugoslav was a political, not an ethnic identity. See Burg and Berbaum (1989, 536). Others (Botev 1994, 465) do not attribute any political significance to this category, because it includes people who simply do not wish to declare their own identity. However, the sharp changes in the percentages of Yugoslavs in different regions indicate that there is some significance to this identity as it responds to political events.

15. In 1971, there was another peak in nationalist conflict in Yugoslavia (Burg 1983), which might explain the shift away from the Yugoslav identity and toward the Muslim identity in Bosnia.

16. Note that all these ethnic percentages must be interpreted as approximate figures, because there is evidence of manipulation and pressure on small groups to declare

themselves part of the dominant group—Serbs during the time of the Federation. On this issue with reference to the 1953 census, see Botev 1994, 465.

17. That argument is developed in Sambanis and Milanovic (2004). They also provide data to code ethnic difference among all regions of all federal and politically decentralized countries.

18. Sambanis and Milanovic (2004) develop a theory of the demand for sovereignty that is based on the idea of a tradeoff between sovereignty and income. Both sovereignty and income are normal goods, but there are economies of scale for the provision of public goods that make the costs of sovereignty prohibitively high for some small states.

19. Even though these subsidies were small as percentages in GDP, the loans were never repaid and the political perception was one of heavy and unfair subsidization.

20. See Hechter (2001) for a discussion of a typology of nationalisms. The story presented here is consistent with Hechter's theory of the spread of nationalism. As control over a national minority becomes direct, overturning previously acquired rights during a period of indirect rule, Hechter argues that the minority would develop nationalist ideology. The Serbs' previously privileged position in Serb-dominated Yugoslavia was analogous to a shift from indirect to direct rule by a hegemonic, hostile ethnic group.

21. Bookman 1994, 181.

22. Murdoch and Sandler (2004) provide estimates of this neighborhood effect both for the short and long run using spatial econometric methods.

23. Percentage of people aged 15 or higher with no formal schooling in 1981. *Source:* Flere 1991, 189.

24. Fifteen war onsets are dropped in the CH analysis because of missing income data. Some of these countries were very poor when the war started (e.g., Afghanistan, Cambodia, Laos, Liberia, Sudan, Vietnam, and others). The mean income for the population of countries might have been lower if these countries were included, in which case Bosnia would have been closer to the mean.

25. The simplest way is to cluster on the predecessor country/federation, correcting the standard errors, as in Sambanis (2000). A more sophisticated correction would actually model the spatial dependence of civil war risk in the former Yugoslav and Soviet republics.

26. Perhaps this is why Collier and Hoeffler ultimately do not find a significant association between war onset and diaspora support, but they do find an association for war duration.

27. The threat was a political one with reference to the entire Yugoslavia. If the Muslim population eventually grew so large as to be clearly dominant over the Serbs, who were not dominant in Bosnia, then Serb power in Yugoslavia would be reduced. However, the Muslim population growth rate in Bosnia was lower than in Kosovo.

28. Hegre at al. (2001); Elbadawi and Sambanis (2002); Fearon and Laitin (2003). With respect to international war, see Snyder (2000) and Mansfield and Snyder (1995).

29. Sambanis (2005) shows in a cross-country regression that inequality is significantly associated with regime transition.

30. See Doyle and Sambanis (2006) for a case study of the effectiveness of UN peacekeeping in Brcko (Bosnia) and Eastern Slavonia (Croatia).

31. We code reported incidents of violence rather than the intensity of violence; as a result, the massacre of Srebrenica, arguably the largest single massacre of the war, is coded as one incident.
32. See Sambanis and Milanovic (2004) for a theory of the demand for self-determination.

# References

Bax, Mart. 2000. "Warlords, Priests and the Politics of Ethnic Cleansing: A Case Study from Rural Bosnia Hercegovina." *Ethnic and Racial Studies* 23 (1): 16–36.

Bookman, Milica Z. 1994. "War and Peace: The Divergent Breakups of Yugoslavia and Czechoslovakia." *Journal of Peace Research* 31 (2): 175–87.

Botev, Nikolai. 1994. "Where East Meats West: Ethnic Intermarriage in the Former Yugoslavia, 1962 to 1989." *American Sociological Review* 59: 461–80.

Bougarel, Xavier. 1996. *Bosnie, anatomie d' un conflit.* Paris: La Découverte.

Bringa, Tone. 1993. *We Are All Neighbors.* Videorecording produced and directed by Debbie Christie for Granada Television. Chicago: Public Media/Films Inc.

———. 1995. *Being Muslim the Bosnian Way: Identity and Community in a Central Bosnian Village.* Princeton, NJ: Princeton University Press.

Bromlei, Yu V., and M. S. Kashuba. 1982. *Brak I semia u narodov Yugoslavii* [Marriage and Family Among the Yugoslav People]. Moscow: Nauka.

Burg, Steven L. 1983. *Conflict and Cohesion in Socialist Yugoslavia.* Princeton, NJ: Princeton University Press.

Burg, Steven L., and Michael L. Berbaum. 1989. "Community, Integration, and Stability in Multinational Yugoslavia." *American Political Science Review* 83 (2): 535–54.

Burg, Steven L., and Paul S. Shoup. 1999. *The War in Bosnia-Herzegovina: Ethnic Conflict and International Intervention.* Armonk, NY: M. E. Sharp.

Claverie, Elisabeth. 2002. Apparition de la Vierge et "retour" des disparus. La constitution d'une identité à Medjugorje (Bosnie-Herzégovine). *Terrain* 38: 41–54.

Cohen, Roger. 1998. *Hearts Grown Brutal: Sagas of Sarajevo.* New York: Random House.

Collier, Paul, and Anke Hoeffler. 2001. "Greed and Grievance in Civil War." Policy Research Working Paper 2355, World Bank, Washington, DC.

De Figueiredo, Rui, and Barry Weingast. 1999. "The Rationality of Fear: Political Opportunism and Ethnic Conflict." In *Civil Wars, Insecurity, and Intervention,* ed. Barbara Walter and Jack Snyder. New York: Columbia University Press.

Doyle, Michael W., and Nicholas Sambanis. 2006. *Making War and Building Peace: United Nations Peace Operations.* Princeton, NJ: Princeton University Press.

Elbadawi, Ibrahim, and Nicholas Sambanis. 2000. "External Intervention and the Duration of Civil Wars." Policy Research Working Paper 2433, World Bank, Washington, DC.

———. 2002. "How Much War Will We See? Explaining the Prevalence of Civil War." *Journal of Conflict Resolution* 46 (3): 307–34.

Engelberg, Stephen. 1992. "Refugees from Camp Tell of Agony and Terror." *The New York Times,* August 7, A8.

Fearon, James, and David Laitin. 2003. "Ethnicity, Insurgency, and Civil War." *American Political Science Review* 97 (1): 75–90.

Flere, Sergej. 1991. "Explaining Ethnic Antagonism in Yugoslavia." *European Sociological Review* 7 (1): 183–93.

Glenny, Misha. 1999. *The Balkans: Nationalism, War, and the Great Powers, 1804–1999.* New York: Penguin Books.

Gurr, Ted Robert. 1970. *Why Men Rebel.* Princeton, NJ: Princeton University Press.

———. 2000. *Peoples Versus States: Minorities at Risk in the New Century.* Washington, DC: USIP.

Gutman, Roy. 1993. *A Witness to Genocide.* New York: Macmillan.

Hechter, Michael. 2001. *Containing Nationalism.* Oxford: Oxford University Press.

Hedges, Chris. 1997. "War Crime 'Victims' Are Alive, Embarrassing Bosnia." *International Herald Tribune,* March 3.

Hegre, Håvard, Tanja Ellingsen, Nils Petter Gleditsch, and Scott Gates. 2001. "Towards a Democratic Civil Peace? Opportunity, Grievance, and Civil War, 1816–1992." *American Political Science Review* 95 (March): 33–48.

Human Rights Watch. 1992. *War Crimes in Bosnia-Hercegovina: A Helsinki Watch Report.* New York, vols. 1–2.

———. 1993. *Abuses by Bosnian Croat and Muslim Forces in Central and South Western Bosnia-Herzegovina.* HRW Index No D518.

———. 1994a. *War Crimes in Bosnia Herzegovina: Bosanski Samac.* HRW Index No D605.

———. 1994b. *War Crimes in Bosnia Herzegovina: UN Cease-Fire Won't Help Banja Luka.* HRW Index No D608.

———. 1994c. *Bosnia-Herzegovina: Sarajevo.* HRW Index No D615.

———. 1994d. *Bosnia-Herzegovina: "Ethnic Cleansing" Continues in Northern Bosnia.* HRW Index No D616.

———. 1995. *Bosnia-Herzegovina: The Fall of Srebrenica and the Failure of UN Peacekeeping.* HRW Index No D713.

———. 1996a. *Bosnia-Herzegovina: A Failure in the Making.* HRW Index No D808.

———. 1996b. *Bosnia-Herzegovina: The continuing Influence of Bosnia's Warlords.* HRW Index No D817.

———. 1997. *Bosnia-Herzegovina: The Unindicted: Reaping the Rewards of Ethnic Cleansing.* HRW Index No D901.

———. 1998. *Bosnia-Herzegovina: "A Dark and Closed Place." Past & Present Human Rights Abuses in Foca.* HRW Index No D1006.

———. 2000. *Unfinished Business: Return of Displaced Persons and Other Human Rights Issues in Bijeljina.* HRW Index No D1207.

Kalyvas, Stathis N. 2005. "Warfare in Civil Wars." In *Rethinking the Nature of War,* ed. Jan Angstrom and Isabelle Duyvesteyn Abingdon, 88–108. Oxon: Frank Cass.

Loyd, Anthony. 2001. *My War Gone By, I Miss it So.* New York: Penguin.

Mansfield, Edward D., and Jack Snyder. 1995. "Democratization and the Danger of War." *International Security* 20 (1): 5–38.

Maas, Peter. 1996. *Love Thy Neighbor.* New York: Knopf.

Massey, Garth, Randy Hodson, and Duško Seculić. 1999. "Ethnic Enclaves and Intolerance: The Case of Yugoslavia." *Social Forces* 78 (2): 669–91.

Mueller, John. 2000. "The Banality of 'Ethnic War.'" *International Security* 25 (1): 42–70.

Murdoch, James C., and Todd Sandler. 2004. "Civil Wars and Economic Growth: Spatial Dispersion." *American Journal of Political Science* 48 (1): 138–51.

Pervanic, Kemal. 1999. *The Killing Days.* London: Blake.

Petrovic, Ruza. 1986. "Ethnically Mixed Marriages in Yugoslavia." *Sociologija* 28 (Suppl.): 229–39.

Posen, Barry. 1993. "The Security Dilemma and Ethnic Conflict." In *Ethnic Conflict and International Security,* ed. Michael Brown, 103–25. Princeton, NJ: Princeton University Press.

Ron, James. 2000. "Territoriality and Plausible Deniability: Serbian Paramilitaries in the Bosnian War." In *Death Squads in Global Perspective: Murder with Deniability,* ed. Bruce B. Campbell and Arthur D. Brenner, 287–312. New York: St. Martin's Press.

Sambanis, Nicholas. 2000. "Partition as a Solution to Ethnic War: an Empirical Critique of the Theoretical Literature." *World Politics* 52 (4), 437–83.

———. 2005. "Poverty and the Organization of Political Violence." *Brookings Trade Forum.*

Sambanis, Nicholas, and Branko Milanovic. 2004. "Explaining the Demand for Sovereignty." Unpublished paper, Yale University and World Bank, May 15.

Savezni Zavod za Statistiku. 1992. Nacionalni Sastav Stanovnistava Po Opstinama. Belgrade.

Silber Laura, and Allan Little. 1997. *Yugoslavia: Death of a Nation.* New York: Penguin. [Revised and updated edition.]

Sudetic, Chuck. 1998. *Blood and Vengeance: One Family's Story of the War in Bosnia.* New York: Norton.

Snyder, Jack. 2000. *From Voting to Violence: Democratization and Nationalist Conflict.* New York: Norton.

United Nations. 1994. *Final Report of the UN Commission of Experts established pursuant to Security Council Resolution of 780 (1992).* Doc S/1994/674/ Add 2 (vol.V), 28 December, Annex X, Mass Graves.

———. 1995. *Report of the Secretary General on Bosnia and Herzegovina.* November 27, 1995. Doc # S/1995/998.

U.S. Department of State. 1992a. *War Crimes in the Former Yugoslavia.* Dispatch, 9/28/92, Vol. 3, Issue 39.

———. 1992b. *Supplemental Report on War Crimes in the Former Yugoslavia.* Dispatch 11/2/92, Vol. 3, Issue 44.

———. 1992c. *Third Report on the War Crimes in the Former Yugoslavia.* Dispatch, 11/16/92, Vol. 3, Issue 46.

———. 1992d. *Fourth Report on the War Crimes in the Former Yugoslavia.* Dispatch, 12/28/92, Vol. 3, Issue 52.

———. 1993a. *Fifth Report on the War Crimes in the Former Yugoslavia.* Dispatch, 2/8/93b, Vol. 4, Issue 6.

———. 1993b. *Sixth Report on the War Crimes in the Former Yugoslavia.* Dispatch, 4/12/93, Vol. 4, Issue 15.

———. 1993c. *Seventh Report on the War Crimes in the Former Yugoslavia.* Dispatch, 4/19/93, Vol. 4, Issue 16.

Woodward, Susan L. 1995. *Balkan Tragedy: Chaos and Dissolution after the Cold War.* Washington, DC: Brookings Institution.

# Greed and Grievance Diverted

*How Macedonia Avoided Civil War, 1990–2001*

8

MICHAEL S. LUND

Macedonia was the only republic to secede from Yugoslavia without any shots fired.[1] Despite predictions in late 1991 that the young state would break apart as a result of external threats or internal strife, Macedonia to date has not experienced a civil war or war with any of its four neighbors. Instead, it has achieved a modicum of stability as a pluralist democracy. A small-scale insurgency occurred 10 years after independence, but hostilities ceased within six months and a negotiated settlement was reached.

What makes the Macedonia case intriguing is its abundance of risk factors that Collier and Hoeffler (CH) and others hypothesize are leading causes of civil war. While seeking to establish a democracy out of a legacy of authoritarianism and communism, Macedonia has ethnic dominance, a poor economy and high unemployment, minority grievances concerning discrimination, ethnic political entrepreneurs, diaspora funding for opposed ethnic communities, a mountainous terrain, weak security forces, and arms flows and other spillover from neighboring conflicts. Despite these risk factors, there was no civil war in Macedonia.[2]

This chapter seeks to unravel the puzzle of Macedonia's relative stability. There are three possible explanations: (a) the CH risk factors are nominally present, but not robust; (b) the risk factors are robust, but behaved differently than theories expect; or (c) they were robustly inducing conflict, but countervailing factors thwarted their impacts. In short, conflict might have been unlikely, redirected, or prevented.[3]

The third explanation has gained Macedonia considerable international attention. Because international actors introduced conflict-preventive measures very soon after its new nationhood, Macedonia has become a "poster child" for the assumed success of international preventive diplomacy.[4] Another claim is that Macedonia's pluralist political institutions enabled it to avoid the violent fate of its sister republics (Burg 1997). Thus, the Macedonia case allows a probe into whether timely international action or the country's own fledgling democratic processes helped avoid violent conflict.

This chapter assesses which of several CH and other plausible hypotheses are most consistent with Macedonia's relatively peaceful politics, focusing on the relationship between majority ethnic Macedonians and the republic's second largest group, ethnic Albanians, and the principal public controversies, players, and violent events in this relationship from 1990 to late 2001. At appropriate junctures, it weighs the evidence to determine whether CH's expected causal pathways are consistent with the actual course of events or other pathways are evident.

# Interethnic Tensions, 1990–2000: Why Not War?

Our first task is to determine whether CH and other conflict risk factors were significantly present in Macedonia, and if so, why they did not eventuate into armed conflict until 2001.

## Post-Communist Controversies, 1990–92

The specter of internal conflict arose in Macedonia as the Socialist Federal Republic of Yugoslavia (SFRY) disintegrated following the collapse of the Yugoslav Communist party in January 1990. The post-World War II Communist order was eroding, but what would replace it was unclear. Tito's nationalities policies had conferred on ethnic Macedonians a proprietary hold on that republic's territory and governmental apparatus. When the republic's government decided in September 1991 to declare independence, the question arose as to what would be the rights of the other ethnic groups living within its boundaries. Outside and inside observers feared these nationalist movements would tear the new country apart, for similar cross-pressures were leading the other seceding Yugoslav republics into war.

Interethnic issues and tensions erupted even as Macedonia was weighing independence. In February 1990, over 1,000 Albanians demonstrated against the discriminatory treatment that they received from the ethnic majority, declaring their desire for independence and unity with Albania. In the election campaign in November, Communists and Nationalists spoke approvingly of Albanian harassment, thus prompting Albanians to boycott the voting. In September 1991, the republic's Macedonian-dominated government held a referendum, in which 95 percent of the 72 percent of eligible voters, including ethnic Macedonians abroad, endorsed independence. Ethnic Albanians and Serbs boycotted the referendum.

The most salient controversy was the new constitution. Guaranteeing "full equality as citizens and permanent co-existence . . . for Albanians . . ." and other named minorities, it affirmed minority rights. But like most post-Communist constitutions, it conferred titular status on ethnic Macedonians by referring to the final realization of their quest for "a national state of the Macedonian people . . . ,"[5] thereby relegating Albanians and other groups to the secondary legal status of a national minority. The 25 Albanian parliament deputies absented themselves, and Albanians' boycotted the constitutional referendum. In January 1992, the Albanians own referendum attracted 93 percent participation from eligible voters and resulted in unanimous support for the autonomy of the Albanian areas in western Macedonia.

## Inherited Conflict Risk Factors

Despite these tensions, no large-scale violence broke out. The underlying CH risk factors of ethnic dominance, past conflict, and economic decline were in fact present. Out of a total population of 1,945,932, 66.5 percent are officially counted as ethnic Macedonian. The second largest group, Albanians, comprise 23 percent of the population.[6] Because of the restrictive citizenship requirements, Albanians claimed they actually constitute 30–45 percent of the population. Whatever the exact percentages, many ethnic Macedonians have expressed fear that the latter's higher birth rate will continue to increase the relative size of the Albanian minority.[7] Macedonian anxieties are also fed by the high proportion of Albanians in the Balkans as a whole.

According to the CH measure of ethnic fractionalization, Macedonia is more diverse than the average country and this should have reduced the risk of violence.[8] But this fails to recognize the reinforcing linguistic, religious, and social differences that separate Albanians and Macedonians. Although there are no serious income inequalities, there are few cross-cutting interests that might allow the two groups to build relationships. CH would predict that the risk of conflict is also reduced by the fact that ethnic Albanians are concentrated in the western and northern parts of the country and ethnic Macedonians live in the rest of the country.[9] However, because ethnic Macedonians predominate in the state structures that govern the Albanian areas, such concentration has not served to dissipate conflict but instead has provided a further political basis for intergroup resentment.

In addition, these cumulative ethnographic differences have long been politicized. The groups' consciousness of being ethnic nations began with the emergence of ethnic nationalist movements in the late 19th century. More recently, their identities were reinforced by well-known violent confrontations between Albanians and other groups under the SFRY, the Macedonians' predominance in the republic's government, and monopolization of the new nation's politics by ethnic-based political parties. Albanians and Macedonians participate in social and political life almost exclusively through separate ethnic-based organizations. Local and national organizations have heightened ethnic identities and defined individuals' interests in terms of stakes they share with the *ethnie*. Alternative channels for social and political mobilization are virtually nonexistent. Civil society is very weak; practically no indigenous nongovernmental organizations, such as women's groups, are multiethnic (Fraenkel and Broughton 2001, 6–7). In short, organizationally reinforced demographic, cultural, geographic, and political differences have created a sharp ethnic dualism that has polarized the two largest groups.

The CH model also hypothesizes that recent conflicts are another significant factor that puts a country at risk of civil war. Were factors related to the presence of prior armed conflict relevant in this case? Arms were widely available after the Croatian and Bosnian wars started in 1991 and 1992. Fears of the war spreading were prevalent. But, in contrast to the violence between Croatians and Serbs during World War II, in Macedonia, Albanians and Macedonians had not engaged in organized deadly conflict (Broughton and Fraenkel 2002, 265). In comparison with the harsh repression of Albanians in Kosovo by Serb authorities and the ethnic cleansing of Muslims in Bosnia, discrimination against Albanians was less severe.[10] However, both ethnic Macedonian and ethnic Albanian families in rural areas frequently associate each other with the ill treatment that their respective people had received from past regimes that occupied the country. Thus, Macedonia was not free from memories of past conflict.

A third CH predictor of conflict, economic decline, was also inherited, and it intensified in the new state. Under the Yugoslav Federation, Macedonia had one of the lowest levels of economic development in the Balkans and was one of the two poorest Yugoslav republics. To transition from a command economy, the government applied strict privatization and austerity measures. Macedonia became a member of the International Monetary Fund (IMF) in December 1992 and the World Bank in February 1993 and implemented structural adjustment programs. In addition, UN economic sanctions imposed on Yugoslavia during the Bosnian war (1992–95) caused Macedonia to lose more than US$3 billion in revenue by 1995 in relation to an annual government budget of $1.2 billion. An economic embargo by Greece further exacerbated the situation. From 1990 to 1994, real gross domestic product (GDP) fell nearly 35 percent, unemployment rose to 20–30 percent, and per capita income in 1994 was US$790.

In sum, three leading CH predictors of conflict pointed to a high risk of war, yet Macedonia became a "false positive" in terms of the CH model. As shown in the rest of this section, quasi-participatory institutions absorbed the impact of ethnic polarization. Memories of past conflicts were not stirred up by Macedonia's statesmanlike first president, Kiro Gligorov, and minority demands were addressed by successive governments, at least in part. The economic crisis did not affect the minority disproportionately. In the Communist era, ethnic Albanians had been excluded from state industries, so the privatizations hurt the ethnic Macedonians more. The economic decline did not reduce the Albanians' opportunity costs of violence. Overseas remittances sustained Albanian families and the sanctions, blockades, and austerity measures brought new income opportunities through smuggling, the black market, and other illegal enterprises (Hislope 2001, 2002). This growing shadow economy was to enable armed conflict, but not until years later.

## Minority Grievances and Violent Protest in the Mid-1990s

Representatives of the Albanians continued to articulate grievances through the mid- and late 1990s. In addition to the census and constitutional issues, they wanted greater administrative autonomy, Albanian to be recognized as an official language, education in Albanian to be available at all levels, and display of Albanian national symbols to be allowed. Although a few Albanians participated in the government and parliament, their leaders pressed for more jobs in the civil service, police, army, courts, and the state media. Ethnic political organizations organized boycotts, votes in the nonofficial referendums and official elections, and demonstrations. On balance, Albanian activists were more vocal than Macedonian activists. Nonelite

Albanians also reflected the political demands, so these grievances had the potential to lead to violence.[11]

Flare-ups occurred around some issues and resulted in a few deaths. The most explosive issue was education. In December 1994, Albanian leaders sought to create a parallel Albanian university in Tetovo. Kosovo's Albanian-dominated Prishtina University was closed in 1989, and the national universities in Skopje and Bitola taught only in Macedonian. A court rejected their request for recognition on constitutional grounds, but Albanian activists and students persevered. At a rally announcing the opening of classes in February 1995, the university's rector referred to possible resistance with guns and grenades if the police stopped the action. Arrests of the organizers led to a large street confrontation that left one Albanian student dead and about 20 injured.[12]

## Ambivalent Nationalisms, Partial Accommodation, and International Supports

The first feature of Macedonia's ethnic conflict that helps to explain why there was no escalation to war is that both ethnic groups were divided between wanting their own ethnic nations or pursuing group advantages through the existing state. Among most Albanians, the idea of a Greater Albania had considerable resonance. When, in the October 1996 local elections, the more nationalist Party of Democratic Prosperity (PDP) swept several municipalities in western Albanian areas, victorious officials were emboldened to declare a kind of de facto autonomy and provocatively raised Albanian flags. But few Albanians have been willing to die for nationalism (USIP 2001, 2). Neither of the two most nationalist parties could capture their respective ethnic constituencies but split apart.[13] Economic interests shared with other groups in the country also mitigated the conflict. For Albanians, after Albania descended into anarchy in March 1997, the idea of being annexed by Albania lost its attractiveness.[14]

Macedonia's representative institutions also helped defuse conflict by providing specific incentives to participate in processes for nonviolent conflict resolution. A mix of nationalist and more centrist parties competed in parliamentary elections. While voting follows ethnic lines, the voters from each group have at least two ethnic parties from which to choose, and parties compete for "swing" voters within their group. Party control of the presidency and the parliament has changed hands several times.[15] No single party has dominated the political scene and no ethnic Macedonian parties have governed alone. Except for the technocratic government immediately after independence, Macedonia has always been governed by multiethnic coalitions. Thus, Macedonia has been a democracy, albeit an imperfect one.[16]

Power sharing offered ways to meet Albanians' demands because they always held some share of parliamentary seats and ministerial posts.[17] Ironically, the political parties themselves are not internally democratic, and power is highly centralized in a charismatic leader and small cadre. But this makes it possible for parties that ostensibly represent the differing ethnic communities to bargain with each other to form a government, often crossing the ethnic divide out of political expediency. Being part of a governing coalition allows the ethnic parties to reward their supporters because government agencies can be used to advance a minister's personal agenda (ISPJR/SECOR 2000, 8–13, 134). Thus, Albanians secured jobs in the civil service, local government, police, military forces, and state enterprises, although in smaller proportions than their leaders enjoyed in the parliament and cabinet.[18] The elite governing coalitions thus co-opted mass-level social tensions.[19]

The security forces have contained the risk of escalating violence by not using excessive force against protesters, though exceptions have occurred.[20] Although playing the "ethnic card" often served the leaders' political interests, they were also very aware of how ethnic violence had led to bloody wars in Croatia in 1991 and Bosnia in 1992. Thus, in moments of crisis, prominent figures usually stopped short of inciting constituents to irregular action. The Democratic Party for Albanians' (DPA) leader, Arben Shaferi, and the VMRO's leader, Boris Trajkovski, have made conciliatory public statements to de-escalate interethnic conflict. When the Tetovo University demonstrations flared up, the chair of the PDP went on television to urge Albanians to stay off the streets, and Albanian leaders made efforts to keep the demonstrators peaceful.[21] Evidently, leaders believed they could gain more—both economically and politically—by supporting peace rather than war.

But these restraints were also influenced by several international incentives. From 1992 until the Kosovo refugee crisis in 1999, the OSCE spillover mission to Macedonia conducted constant monitoring both of the northern border and Macedonia's interethnic relations. The mission encouraged parties to avoid inflammatory actions and helped leaders to act quickly to defuse potentially volatile situations, such as the 1995 attempted assassination of President Gligorov and when some Albanian school children fell suddenly ill in circumstances that appeared at first like deliberate poisoning.

Because of the party-dominated bureaucratic patrimonies, dialogue among government officials was politically difficult for each side to initiate. But it could happen through "carrots and sticks" that major international actors could apply. The OSCE held roundtables to encourage dialogue among government officials and party leaders and to help conciliate specific legislative disputes over minority interests (Ackermann 2000; Leatherman et al. 2000). In particular, the OSCE office of the High Commissioner for National Minorities (HCNM), which was specifically designed to intervene in domestic ethnic relations of OSCE countries before they escalate, paid many visits to Macedonia, urged better employment and educational policies, and promoted a continuing roundtable between the government and minority groups. When the high commissioner proposed that the Tetovo University incidents be handled through a new law on education, parliament passed the law (Ackermann 2000; Leatherman et al. 2000).[22]

Especially significant was the visible presence in the small country of the United Nations' only preventive peacekeeping force. UNPREDEP and its American contingent were widely viewed as having a calming effect by signaling that the international community was watching and concerned. Its border patrolling may have discouraged insurgencies and its police component in those areas provided minorities with some protection against arbitrary government actions and help with social needs.

Because Macedonia was a poor and defenseless country, actual or prospective memberships in the UN, EU, OSCE, World Bank, IMF, and other international organizations were important to Macedonia's leaders and avidly pursued by Gligorov because they could protect its new sovereignty and unlock needed aid for its ministries. Immediately after it declared sovereignty in November 1991, the government requested EC recognition and UN membership. Although the 1991 government's quest for state status was initially spurned,[23] after Macedonia's parliament subsequently amended the constitution to pledge noninterference in the internal affairs of its neighbors, the country was admitted to the OSCE and the Council of Europe, and thus began receiving IMF and World Bank loans. The country was admitted to NATO's Partnership for Peace program in November 1995, and mention was made of eventual EU membership.

International benefits appealed to elites for they provided financial and symbolic resources that enabled the ministries to carry out their functions. The key to obtaining political support was patronage, the key to patronage was international assistance, the key to assistance was international recognition, and the key to recognition was responsiveness to international norms. Thus, a web of international conditionality helped maintain political stability.

## Resources for Rebellion: Diaspora and Arms

The absence of armed conflict in Macedonia up to 2001 was not due simply to the lack of sufficient or attractive resources for launching an armed rebellion; the ingredients were there. Macedonia did not possess valuable natural resources that could be plundered for revenue and support from neighboring governments was not forthcoming.[24] But by the mid-1990s, diaspora sources for financing, weapons, and a weak government army all made an armed challenge to the government possible.

With a diaspora estimated at over 700,000 worldwide, Albanians had sufficient funds coming from overseas.[25] More recent emigres were generally more receptive to militancy. Although a gun culture exists in rural Albania and Macedonia, individual gun ownership was relatively low.[26] But the end of the Croatian and Bosnian wars by 1995 created a flourishing small arms market in the Balkans. In Albania in 1997, around 500,000 to 1 million weapons were looted from police and army bases, many ending up in Macedonia. Macedonian armed services were so weak that would-be rebels could have not been easily controlled. Recruits for a rebel army could have been drawn from the many unemployed Albanians.[27]

However, Albanians' attention had been focused mainly on the plight of the oppressed Albanians in Kosovo. Until 1997, the Kosovo movement receiving diaspora support was the nonviolent Democratic League of Kosovo (LDK) party of Ibrahim Rugova. After the Albanian rebel group, the KLA, was organized in 1996 and 1997 and provoked the Serbian regime, the diaspora's resources were used to support its operations.

To sum up, during Macedonia's first decade, four leading CH factors and one non-CH factor would have predicted conflict: ethnic polarization, past conflict, economic decline, ethnic grievances, and resources for rebellion. But war did not materialize because of accommodative institutions, leaders who profited more from peace, carefully designed multilateral international intervention, and the focus of the Albanians on their cause in Kosovo.

## Armed Conflict in Early 2001: Why Then?

If CH and other risk factors suggested that the risk of civil war was high but these forces were diverted into nonviolent channels, why did armed conflict arise in 2001? On February 28, 2001 in Tanusevce, a remote mountain village north of Skopje and close to the Kosovo border, a state television film crew encountered 20–30 men in military uniforms with red arm patches of the KLA. Rumors that armed groups were operating in the area had prompted the crew to investigate. The soldiers detained them and police came to their aid. The first casualty of the conflict occurred when a police vehicle drove over a mine and the army began to shoot into the village.

Fighting quickly spread to nearby villages and east toward Kumanovo. On March 4, three policemen were killed by a newly announced National Liberation Army (NLA), sparking a military response by the Army of the Republic of Macedonia (ARM). In mid-March, the NLA began to lob mortar shells into Tetovo, west of Skopje. The ARM launched the first major military response by shelling the villages above Tetovo and advancing on them, but with little success. The NLA created a political party called the People's Democratic Party, appointed some political representatives, and issued demands that stressed that it did not want to break up the country in the name of a Greater Albania.[28]

In April, another surge in the fighting occurred after eight ARM soldiers were ambushed near Tanusevce, and the fighting shifted back to the northeast. A widely publicized ambush in May killed three soldiers. By this time, 11,000 people had been displaced. The rebels now controlled Vaksince and Shipcane, northeast of Skopje, which received more shelling and rocket fire from helicopter gunships. Though many villagers escaped the fighting by crossing the border into Serbia and Kosovo, thousands were trapped in their homes, prompting government accusations that the NLA was using them as civilian hostages. Fighting continued until August.

## Changed or New Risk Factors?

After 10 years of relative political stability, what had changed to bring about this armed conflict? The CH risk factors did not drastically worsen. Non-CH grievances did not increase ethnic tensions. The multiethnic power-sharing process did not deteriorate. Rebel challengers had not garnered new sources of financing. Nor had most of the international incentives to avoid armed conflict been removed. These trends stayed more or less the same, but new factors came into play.

It had long been feared that a possible influx of Albanian refugees into Macedonia from the volatile situation in Kosovo would have a destabilizing impact by shifting

Macedonia's ethnic balance. But surprisingly, when that actually happened, it did not have the predicted effect. From March to June, 1999, as a result of ethnic purging of Albanians by the Yugoslav regime, a virtual tidal wave of refugees numbering 355,000 crossed over from Kosovo into Macedonia, thus increasing the ethnic Albanian population by 76 percent. Constituting no less than 18.2 percent of Macedonia's total population,[29] this caused great anxiety, and the government abruptly expelled refugees to other countries. However, this crisis did not spark violent reactions on either side. Within a few months, the refugees had returned home, because of the quick conclusion of the Kosovo war.

Preceding the outbreak of armed conflict in 2001, CH would also expect continued economic decline and perhaps economic downturn, suggesting even fewer alternative sources of income to joining a rebellion. In fact, however, beginning in 1996, a second stage of economic transition saw some aggregate improvement in the economy, and no worsening of particular indicators.[30]

Still, some basis existed for popular grievances over the economy. Notwithstanding the positive upswing, almost 10 years after independence,[31] the standard of living was still worse than it had been under communism. In addition, illegal commerce and corruption were becoming more obvious. The 1994 governing coalition had been tarnished by a taxation scandal that closed a major bank in Bitola, with results for savers similar to Albania's collapsing pyramid scheme. After a series of publicized scandals, both ethnic groups voiced criticism of government agencies.[32] Opinion polls showed a low regard for all politicians, even causing postponement of parliamentary elections. Corruption was believed to be allowing leaders of the DPA or VMRO-Democratic Party for Macedonian National Unity (DPMNE) to benefit from privatization of state assets (USIP 2001, 3–4, 6).[33] In 1999, Transparency International ranked Macedonia with Romania, Bulgaria, Egypt, and Ghana in terms of perceived corruption (USIP 2001, 4).[34] In sum, even though unequal treatment of differing groups and interethnic distrust persisted (Petroska-Beska 2001), widespread cynicism toward government and politicians in general increased across *both* ethnic communities.

It is tempting to attribute the 2001 conflict to this growing public discontent. However, there is no evidence that popular grievances contributed directly to the organization of the NLA. First, rather than addressing the persisting economic problems, the chief demands stated by the NLA were almost identical to those long advocated by Albanian political leaders since independence.[35] The NLA did argue that the situation in the country was worsening to such an extent that the established politicians were inadequate for achieving the Albanian community's demands and thus only armed activity would be effective. As had the KLA vis-à-vis the nonviolent LDK movement in Kosovo, the NLA was seeking to "outbid" the established DPA and PDP Albanian parties for influence within the community. However, these statements did not animate a large number of Albanians to organize an insurgency or to join the NLA. The latter occurred only after the fighting was underway. Thus, the conflict did not break out because of large numbers of discontented Albanians feeling that they had no other choice than to resort to arms.[36] To the contrary, the cross-cutting negativism about government in general helped to *restrain* interethnic conflict by making citizens of all ethnic groups skeptical of *all* politicians, including the NLA (Focus group 2001).

Rather than any lessening of interethnic power sharing, in 1999, the two ethnic Macedonian and ethnic Albanian political parties that had been the most nationalistic in the early 1990s joined to form a coalition government. This further enhanced Macedonia's international reputation as an exemplar for interethnic peace. Nor can the emergence of the insurgency in 2001 be explained by the capture of new natural resources or new funding windfalls. Although chromium was mined in the territory that the rebels took over, there is no evidence that the rebels specifically intended or tried to capture and tap that source for revenue. Instead, the NLA drew from existing financial sources related in part to the Kosovo conflict. In descending order of size, these included: (1) contributions from the diaspora; (2) smuggling of cigarettes, drugs, and women; and (3) local stockbreeding.[37]

The Macedonian Albanian diaspora is smaller and less well organized than the Kosovar Albanians (Pettifer 2001, 138). But the members of the Albanian diaspora tended to identify themselves with all Albanians in the region, not only with those in their country of origin.[38] It was not until the outbreak of the conflict in Macedonia in particular that these funds supported the NLA. When the Kosovo theater no longer presented opportunity, Albanian militants turned their attention to Macedonia. The resources flowing through these channels were simply shifted to the Macedonia conflict arena.[39]

A large amount of the heroin traffic that comes from Central Asia runs by way of the "Balkan Route" through the southern part of the former Yugoslavia and Albania and across the Adriatic to Italy and on to the rest of Europe and the United States. This channel is estimated to be worth $400 billion a year in total (Cilluffo and Salmoiraghi 1999, 23). In Macedonia, organized crime is estimated at one-fifth of Macedonia's 2001 budget (Pendarovski 2002, 23). The amount of this illicit commerce that financed the NLA has not been conclusively determined.[40] NLA spokesman Ali Ahmeti claimed that the NLA tried to screen out contributions from tainted sources, but conceded that it had such a variety of sources that it was difficult to check.[41]

As seen earlier, arms were already plentiful from the recent wars and the 1997 assaults on Albania's police storehouses. As the demand for weapons grew in southern Serbia and northern Macedonia in 2000, many of these weapons were supplied to the NLA.[42] All told, the NLA was well equipped with thousands of old and new rifles and handguns, sniper rifles, heavy machine guns, mortars, and land mines, as well as sophisticated rocket-propelled grenades and heavier weapons.

## Low Opportunity Costs, Marginalized Areas, and Weakened Border Security

Although the armed group did not seek to capture economic resources, NLA local recruiting did benefit from the poor economy.[43] The areas of NLA activity were located a few kilometers north of Skopje in a string of ethnic Albanian villages and towns along the Vardar river valley. Macedonian police had no effective control of these villages and reportedly had not been in Tanusevce, where the fighting first erupted, for 10 years.[44] Moreover, during the spring and summer months, Macedonia's remote mountainous areas and forested terrain along the entire northern border with Albania and the Federal Republic of Yugoslavia (FRY) made it relatively easy to bring guns into Macedonia and operate an insurgency. Crucially, the NLA's incursions became even less detectable after UNPREDEP and its border patrols were terminated in 2000 so that only a weak Macedonian government presence existed along the largely porous border from Debar in the west to Kumanovo in the east. This afforded the NLA a largely secluded environment from which to launch and wage guerrilla-style warfare. They also acted during the winter, when it is especially difficult to travel in that area.[45]

## Rebel Leaders' Agenda: Old Cause, New Venue

The most direct explanation of the insurgency was the agenda and actions of the small group of individuals who had organized the KLA and the changes in Kosovo that prompted them to turn to Macedonia to pursue their agenda. The initial NLA group arrived over the border from southern Serbia to set up operations. Most had been born in Macedonia but had joined the KLA and fought in Kosovo. The NLA also included veterans of the other Balkan wars in Croatia and Bosnia, as well as a few foreign mercenaries. But this initial group of experienced fighters is estimated to have numbered only from 70 to 90.

For the NLA's top leaders, the NLA offered the prospect of ideological fulfillment and the possibility of leadership positions, having failed in those pursuits in Kosovo. The key individuals were originally from Macedonia but had not lived there for many years. The top four—Ali Ahmeti, Gezim Ostremi, Fazli Veliu, and Commander Hoxha—all had long been political activists who were associated with the ethnic Albanian political movement in the SFRY. Ali Ahmeti, the NLA's political spokesman, was born in a village in western Macedonia near Kicevo in 1959, but attended high school in Prishtina, Kosovo. He attended the Albanians' Prishtina University with several of the other future founders of the KLA, and, in 1981, became a protégé of the Albanian nationalist Ahmet Hoxhiu. Ahmeti participated in the Albanian demonstrations against the Belgrade government, which spread throughout Kosovo and were met by an extremely harsh government crackdown that killed a number of Albanians and jailed thousands. Moving to Switzerland, he was influenced by his expatriate uncle, Fazli Veliu, one of the most politically active persons in the Albanian diaspora in recent decades. In 1997 and 1998, both were instrumental in organizing the KLA when it took up arms against the Yugoslav regime under Milosevic.[46] Ahmeti fought with the KLA.[47] As Macedonians point out, Ahmeti never learned to speak Macedonian.

The NATO peace enforcement action in early 1999 led to a virtual UN protectorate in Kosovo in late 1999 and to the disbandment of the KLA. Ali Ahmeti then sought to enter politics by forming a political party called the "81 Movement," but it did not do well in the Kosovo elections. Younger men like Hashem Thaci, former head of the political directorate of the KLA, fared better. The opportunity to become a player in Kosovo declined further when Slobodan Milosevic fell from power in June 2000. A year later, the Kostunica-led Yugoslav government negotiated an agreement with the NATO Kosovo Force (KFOR) through which the Yugoslav army ( JNA) could re-occupy the 5-kilometer-wide Ground Security Zone (GSZ) that had been set up around Kosovo in order to keep the KLA and JNA from clashing. Between December 1999 and January 2001, former members of the KLA who had not given up their arms and reintegrated into Kosovo society following the NATO defeat of the Yugoslav army began to operate in the GSZ through an incursion into the Presevo Valley area of southern Serbia near Bujanovac. Seeking to take control by embracing local Albanian political grievances, they were forced to end their occupation when NATO allowed the Yugoslav army to reoccupy the GSZ starting in March 2001. Under the NATO agreement, NATO began to disarm the KLA in the Presevo area just a week or so after the Tanusevce incident.

In short, former KLA militants were being squeezed out of Kosovo as well as the Presevo Valley in southern Serbia to the east. Whether or not Ahmeti had intended in advance to return to Macedonia to enter politics, he seems to have turned to Macedonia as his last chance to become an Albanian leader. The NLA's leaders apparently saw an opening in Macedonia for achieving their political and personal agendas once Kosovo began to settle into a relatively stable period of competitive and internationally monitored elections in 1999–2000. But the NLA was a military organization, and only after its sixth public communiqué in mid-March 2001 were political demands announced. In short, the rising general unhappiness with the Macedonian government had not so much ". . . . intersected with the fallout from the Kosovo War . . ." as coincided with it, but without actually touching it (Broughton and Fraenkel 2002, 269).

## Ending Hostilities and Achieving Settlement, Mid-2001

If certain factors not found in the CH model explain why armed conflict broke out in 2001, why did that conflict not escalate into a civil war and instead ended rather quickly with a peace settlement?

### Cease-fires and Negotiations

In early June, the NLA boldly occupied the Albanian village of Aracinovo, within 10 kilometers of Skopje. Skopje's suburbs were within mortar range. This fighting caused 25 casualties and more refugees. Some guerrillas entered parts of Skopje itself without challenge. The guerrillas then cut off the water supply to Kumanovo to the northeast, Macedonia's third largest city, for two weeks. Reflecting increasing firepower supplied by Ukraine and other governments, government forces continued to shell NLA enclaves and used fighter planes to bomb them. But although better equipped than the NLA in heavy weaponry, the government was realizing little success against an agile guerrilla force and, in the process, was destroying Albanian villages, displacing thousands and seriously heightening interethnic tensions.[48]

The conflict began to flag by late June. The first of a number of cease-fires was negotiated, on the rationale of avoiding further damage to the villages. A stalemate developed in Aracinovo, where the ARM called off its campaign and NATO troops arranged to escort 200–350 NLA soldiers out of the village. The NLA and the government both began to recognize that their military effectiveness would be influenced by local attitudes and they took steps to win over the local populations.[49] From July through August, several cease-fires were reached and broken. From August 8 to 12, the fighting reached a final crescendo back in Tetovo, as peace negotiations were reaching agreement. All told, the armed combat had directly caused an estimated 150–200 deaths and displaced 137,000 persons and refugees.[50] Six months after the conflict ended, in March 2002, the leader of the rebel movement, Ahmeti, announced he would enter Macedonian politics. He formed a new political party and was elected in the 2002 elections to the National Assembly.

Did the fighting stop because the rebels "ran out of gas," met superior firepower, were restrained by the public, negotiated a compromise through Macedonia's vaunted democratic institutions, or were persuaded by international mediators? Several factors combined to reduce the rebels' military advantage and increase the attractiveness of the political options that rebel leaders were offered.

## *Balance of Power: Rebel Support and Government Firepower*

The rebels' military campaign was not waning because of declining funds, arms, or recruits. Fund raising continued, arms were easily bought, and more recruits came from several sources.[51] By the height of the conflict during the summer, the NLA claimed to have six brigades operating in various theaters of the conflict with a potential strength of 16,000. Analysts estimate there were between 2,000 and 2,500 full-time fighters, in addition to an echelon of suppliers of intelligence, communications, and logistics.[52]

But the insurgency was not riding a groundswell of Albanian resentment. Far from sparking any wider Albanian uprising, the NLA was initially met with curiosity, and only later attracted local recruits. Many ethnically mixed towns, including Ali Ahmeti's own hometown, Kicevo, remained peaceful (ESI 2002, 1). The rebel success had much to do with the weak government security forces. At the onset of the conflict, the ARM was unprepared and ineffective.[53] But after the summer offensive, having depleted its armaments and lost a helicopter, the ARM spent the equivalent of 5.4 percent of GDP to purchase more equipment and obtain some helicopter gunships and jet fighters. Yet Macedonia lacked a coherent security doctrine and even a functioning chain of command. The military effort was carried out with poor intelligence, and virtually no coordination among the police, army, and other branches of the security forces, or between the political and military offensives. Government security advisors state that the lack of preparedness arose from an implicit doctrine that assumed that Macedonia should rely primarily on its foreign relations and diplomatic means, and that political accommodation of the Albanian political leadership would be sufficient for defending against security threats (Pendarovski 2002, 8). Desperate, the government initiated a program of national conscription, issued assault rifles to the civilian population, and recruited several paramilitary groups, although the latter played little actual role in the fighting.

Because of these weaknesses, the ARM was essentially unable to contain the NLA, and the NLA could have brought the conflict into Skopje itself. There, ethnic Macedonians outnumbered Albanians, but were surrounded by predominantly ethnic Albanian villages. NLA control of the capital and its surrounding areas, the Albanian villages from Gostivar through Tetovo to Skopje, and the areas of western and northern Macedonia that it already controlled, would have constituted the de facto conquest of the country. But although the NLA had the upper hand, in the longer term a military stalemate was likely. On their part, the ARM realized that even if it could eventually repel the rebels, the conflict would result in a great amount of bloodshed, which would cost them the trust of the Albanian people and make coexistence in a unified Macedonia impossible.[54]

## Diminishing Returns: Military and Political Obstacles

Despite its military strength, the NLA advance gradually came to a halt by the end of the summer near Aracinovo. A military and political abyss opened up that made the NLA reluctant to pursue the conflict further. One clear barrier was that in order to advance further, it would have to move closer to the NATO KFOR forces stationed at Petrovec international airport and to the country's main oil refinery nearby. Also, the ARM could have put up considerable resistance (see the NLA's failure to take Tetovo in August) because the ARM had received some tanks and helicopter gunships. Finally, moving into the valley would have brought the NLA into Macedonian and Serb villages.

Also, if interethnic fighting broke out in the streets in Skopje, it would have resembled Sarajevo. Many people were already leaving the city and queuing up for visas to leave the country. This prospect was too drastic to contemplate even for the guerrillas and could have provoked intervention by international bodies. Were the NLA to take over, the ARM and the paramilitary groups formed by the government could still regroup and mount some kind of guerrilla activity, with or independently of the government. Taking advantage of the country's mountainous terrain to the south, they could make the country ungovernable for the NLA. This scenario suggested an immense amount of bloodshed from which it would have been difficult to recover the country in manageable shape.

These constraints explain the relatively early termination of the armed conflict in terms of military considerations such as the balance of power and lucid calculations of diminishing practical returns, despite the fog of war. Did political and international factors also restrain further conflict?

## *"Democratic" Politics: Managing or Exacerbating Conflict?*

In principle, Macedonia's democratic institutions also might have prevented escalation to interethnic war through engaging the competing communities in bargaining that achieved compromises. Public opinion polls during the crisis indicated divided views with respect to specific issues, but considerable overall disapproval across the ethnic groups of the conflict and criticism of how both government and rebels were behaving. The government, parliament, and the media did not draw on this sentiment to promote a peaceful resolution, however, and instead intensified the partisanship.

In May, a multiethnic "Government of National Unity" was formed among the mainstream ethnic Macedonian and Albanian parties to deal with the armed conflict.[55] Although expected to provide leadership in responding to the crisis, its members did not work together, and it only lost popular confidence. Its members tended to take individual or factional partisan actions unilaterally, which by grandstanding to particular constituencies just increased tensions. Facing choices between participating in multiethnic government actions toward the crisis or undertaking partisan responses, the high-level leaders differed considerably in their individual tactics and there were few actual face-to-face communications and negotiations among the leaders within the halls of the government.

The parliament was ineffective simply because it was not in session much of the time during the crisis or was distracted and largely overtaken by the military and political situation. Both opposition parties exploited the crisis (Fraenkel and Broughton 2001, 4). The DPA's Arben Shaferi first led an Albanian demonstration against the NLA. Political gains had required his keeping an active hand in Macedonia's mainstream national politics, and his interests were ill served by the new, possibly uncontrollable, more radical leaders or constituencies. But later, he endorsed the NLA demands. The opposition SDSM leader Branko Crvenkovski was more circumspect, reportedly because of his more methodical and professional advisers.[56]

There was no lack of expression of opinions during the crisis, and many opportunities for airing of views, but the discourse was dominated by the partisan media. Formerly independent newspapers such as *Dnevnik* now took sides. Although the two main ethnic groups' parties predictably differed in terms of positions that they took about the conflict, a broad segment of the public opposed the use of violence. But there is no evidence to suggest that such public opinion mattered. Protests expressed the most militant views on each side of the conflict. After NATO escorted the NLA soldiers out of Aracinovo, for example, ethnic Macedonians in Skopje rioted in protest. Their outcry for a harsh response to the "terrorists" generated so much anti-Western sentiment, some donor missions had to evacuate for security reasons. The parliament and the media acted as ventilators of partisan views, but they fueled the crisis rather than alleviated it.[57] Nor did executive or representative channels have a tempering effect and instead exacerbated the conflict. Party-instructed organizers of partisan demonstrations were in control.

Overall, the collective bodies and institutional channels of Macedonia's democratic political processes did not help to restrain the conflict. During the crisis, they proved incapable of embracing the contending parties and facilitating a common position so as to dampen tensions and reconcile competing views. Instead, democratic processes contributed to polarizing the unorganized general public.

## Regional Albanian Network

Surprisingly, another significant restraint came from Albanian political leaders in Kosovo as well as Macedonia. Within Macedonia, the leading mainstream Albanian leaders, DPA's Arben Shaferi and PDP's Imer Imeri, at first did not support the NLA and in fact initially condemned it for having no political program. In the first weeks of the fighting, Shaferi led a peace march in Skopje. But as the NLA continued to succeed on the battlefield, they shifted their approach and began to play the role of a political wing of the armed movement by agreeing to push within the system for constitutional reforms that favored Albanians. Shaferi tried to make the NLA's agenda his own, though it was close to that anyway. Whereas the politicians lacked the military power that Ahmeti had, he lacked the political legitimacy that they had.

However, the insurgents' challenge to the government and their leadership positions in Macedonia became too strong for Shaferi and Imeri alone to control. It took a wider set of ethnic Albanian political interests in Kosovo and their transnational communication to rein in the rebel movement and help end the fighting. All the older members of this network had attended Prishtina University and saw themselves as part of a regional Albanian ethnic community. In a telling instance of the influence of this wider network, the Kosovo Albanian leaders put pressure on Ahmeti to desist from pressing any further even when he was realizing his greatest tactical military successes. The leaders of the former KLA in Prishtina, Kosovo, which had voiced opposition to the NLA at an early stage, were crucial in ending the conflict by putting direct pressure on the NLA to slow down its efforts and to seek to negotiate an end to the war (Wood 2001). They were concerned that if Ahmeti's Macedonian insurgency were to destabilize that country further, the NLA's demands could endanger their own ultimate aspirations for an independent Kosovo by turning the major international actors, who were seeking to mediate the conflict and were already highly critical of the NLA, against the whole Albanian regional movement.[58]

In a crucial meeting held in Prizren, Kosovo in June, Shaferi met with Ali Ahmeti, the rebel leader, and worked out a common political program, which the Albanians eventually presented in the negotiations that were going on within the government. Some observers believe that this persuasion was possible in part because Ahmeti actually did not want to undertake a full-scale civil war, but simply sought to demonstrate that the NLA could win a war if it tried, and thereby to gain respect for and attention to the Albanian cause.

## International Pressure in the Peace Settlement and Implementation

On August 13, a framework agreement was signed by the two largest Albanian and Macedonian parties, respectively, in the southern city of Ohrid (ICG 2001a, 2). The

Ohrid agreement entailed government agreement to most of the Albanians' demands in exchange for a demobilized and disbanded NLA. Parliament was quite slow in ratifying Ohrid. Parliamentary debates were characterized by stalling tactics by hard-liners on both sides, the marginalization of moderate voices, and little interaction between political leaders and citizens about any changes being made.[59] But by November, Macedonia's parliament had agreed to constitutional amendments and legislation that gave broader rights to its Albanian minority. Ahmeti, the political leader of the rebel movement, formed a political party and was elected in the 2002 elections to the National Assembly.

The government and rebel leaders were influenced in their decisions by peace talks mediated by the United States and the European Union that provided targeted incentives and deterrents at certain moments to press the parties to reach a settlement. When the conflict first broke out in February, international bodies had done little more than denounce the insurgents. Because Macedonia was a multiethnic democracy, Western leaders at first viewed the insurgents as terrorists and extremists and the government as justified in protecting itself against a threat to its sovereignty. Starting in late March, however, the United States, EU, and UN took a more hands-on approach to stem the escalation of violence. Unwilling to provide troops directly to counter the insurgency, the United States and the EU sought to establish agreements and provide incentives to meet the demands of those protesting government policy, thus assuaging rebel grievances. They also pressed the government not to rely solely on a strictly military response by urging it to address the Albanians' political demands. When the government balked, the West became more sympathetic toward the Albanians, as they had in Kosovo against the Serbs. This stung the Macedonians, who felt they had met Albanian grievances already, had allowed NATO to use their soil during the conflict in Kosovo, and hosted thousands of Albanian refugees.[60]

In February 2001, despite the fact that the conflict had broken out, the EU deliberately signed an association agreement with the government in order to send a signal that the country could become a member if it weathered the crisis peacefully.[61] During May and June, representatives of the EU and the United States pressed the two sides to reach a solution and establish conditions for deployment of NATO troops once there was an agreement and cease-fire. A cease-fire was negotiated on July 5 through international facilitation. Special envoys Francois Leotard of the EU and James Pardew of the United States working closely together, along with NATO Representative Peter Feith, began negotiating a settlement that addressed many of the Albanian demands in exchange for cessation of hostilities. In May, the United States and the EU pressured the government and political parties to form the Government of National Unity. After a failed government offensive to remove the insurgents, NATO negotiated a face-saving withdrawal of government forces that escorted the rebels out of Aracinovo.

During the negotiations, the mediators promised that the World Bank would convene a donors' conference to provide postconflict reconstruction aid. Several visits to push things along were paid by top officials of the three organizations: NATO Secretary General Lord Robertson, EU External Affairs Minister Javier Solana, and

U.S. Secretary of State Colin Powell. In addition to public pressure, certain individuals around the negotiating table were reportedly given specific incentives. These included offers to help elevate the rebel leader Ahmeti to enter politics through running in the next election, suggestions to the prime minister that he could be exposed for corruption, and threats to both sides that the behavior of their troops might make them eligible for indictment for war crimes.[62] The prime minister was able to use the international community as a scapegoat, because the country was familiar with the idea that certain things had to be done under pressure.[63]

The Ohrid Framework Agreement signed in August called for meeting several demands of the rebels, in exchange for their turning over their weapons. These included the removal of the constitutional reference to Macedonia as the "national state of all Macedonian people," increasing the proportion of Albanians in the police force from 5 to 25 percent, equitable employment of minorities in state institutions, use of Albanian and other minority languages as official languages in areas with 20 percent minority populations, use of Albanian in parliament, and some devolution of authority to local institutions. These demands would be taken up by parliament when a certain number of NLA weapons were collected by NATO. In October, the president requested that the NATO contingent of about 1,000 be extended.

The implementation of Ohrid proceeded step by step, with international quids exchanged for domestic quos, as the EU and U.S. diplomats prodded and held out the promise of aid and/or threats of sanctions, and NATO maintained a continuous security presence while collecting weapons from the rebel side. By August 30, Operation Essential Harvest had collected more than one-third of the targeted amount of weapons, and parliamentary debate began. By September 26, NATO completed the planned turnover of weapons, receiving 3,850 guns, and the NLA disbanded.

Meanwhile, when the parliament alternately stalled and then edged toward progress in the debates in October 2001, a proposed IMF donors' conference was postponed. After a month of intense debate, the parliament approved by a slim majority tentative drafts of 15 constitutional amendments that accepted the Ohrid requirements. On November 15, 90 of the 120 MPs in parliament finally passed these amendments. The state is now described as made up of citizens of Macedonia, which includes the Macedonian people, Albanians, Turks, Vlachs, and Serbs residing in Macedonia.[64] Overall, several Macedonian and Albanian close observers believe that the peace settlement of the 2001 armed conflict would not have been reached without the leverage exerted by the international negotiators, or not nearly as soon as it was.[65] Once the parts of the agreement were ratified, the donors' conference was held in March 2002.

## Conclusion

Several of the factors that the CH model regards as risks of civil war were present in Macedonia after independence. But this study has identified reasons why those risk factors and others found in the literature did not result in civil war. This chapter has focused on a discussion of intervening variables that blunted or deflected the impact of those risk factors. The chapter also developed more general theoretical conclusions about the causes of civil war by drawing on the case of Macedonia.

Severe economic decline resulting from a loss of subsidies, markets, and privatization of state industries does not necessarily increase intergroup economic competition in ethnically divided, and even polarized, societies with ethnic dominance, nor does it have to lower the opportunity costs of rebellion for ethnic minorities. Whether this happens may depend on whether alternative sources of income, such as employment abroad and black markets, can provide temporary safety valves for violence. In addition, the political institutions in constitutionally regulated representative governments can co-opt ethnic elites and mollify their followers by securing some minority access to power and partial accommodation of their grievances, and by offering the minority group leaders private incentives for cooperation. Even low-level violent conflict will not always grow into large-scale violence if the groups' leaders see it in their interest to avoid the escalation of specific disputes into wider confrontations. Powerful international third parties can also influence these elites and leaders by offering them security assurance, monitoring and response to provocative events, ongoing informal mediation services, and individual inducements or constraints to support peace over war.

That said, even such relatively accommodative states remain vulnerable to conflict from the contagion effects of neighboring civil wars if they have porous borders and weak security forces. Cross-border flows of arms and a small determined and armed group presented the most immediate threat of civil war in Macedonia, especially once the capacity to police its borders eroded. Despite the lack of broad popular support behind the insurgents, and despite Macedonia's power sharing in a quasi-democratic political system, the armed conflict could have escalated into a larger civil war or it could have been sustained as a low-grade conflict for a long period. That threat was avoided due to a combination of belated but vigorous international security assurances, diplomatic mediation, and development incentives.

# Notes

1. Officially named the Former Yugoslav Republic of Macedonia (FYROM), but referred to here for convenience as Macedonia.
2. Including the armed conflict of 2001, the total number killed from all political violence over the entire decade fell far short of the 1,000 deaths per year that is the common threshold for a civil war. Leading up to the 2001 insurgency, not more than 20 people had been killed by political violence (compiled from data supplied by Bond 2003 and Gurr et al. 2002). The 2001 conflict resulted in fewer than 200 deaths.
3. Unless otherwise indicated, "conflict" is shorthand for violent conflict.
4. For example, see Ackermann (1996) and Sokalski (2003). Macedonia is unusual for the multiple international actors who have carried out diplomatic, defense, and development initiatives there since independence, to a great extent under an explicit conflict prevention rationale, including the United Nations, the United States, the European Union (EU), the Organization for Security and Cooperation in Europe (OSCE), and

other regional organizations, international financial institutions (IFIs), and Western governments.

5. Constitution of the Republic of Macedonia, Skopje, 1991.

6. The other ethnic groups are much smaller. There are 4 percent ethnic Turks, 2.2 percent Roma, 2.1 percent Serbs, 2 percent Macedonian Muslims, and 0.04 percent Vlachs and others. Because the country's total population is considerably smaller than the mean of 7.56 of the Development Economics Research Group (DECRG) sample, CH would predict a low risk of civil war (Sambanis 2003, 126). But relative group sizes may be more important (Sambanis 2003, 12, 26, 42).

7. The percentage of Albanians almost doubled from 13 percent in 1953 to 23 percent in the first two postindependence censuses, whereas Macedonians stayed about the same. By 2014, Albanians are predicted to increase to 27.8 percent (ISPJR/SECOR, 2000, 20–21).

8. Based on the ethnolinguistic fractionalization (ELF) index, ethnic fractionalization is 0.509, and thus higher than the population mean of 0.385. A similar index puts religious fractionalization at 0.46, and thus higher than the sample mean of 0.367 (Sambanis 2003, 126).

9. Seven of the country's 34 administrative districts have more Albanians than the national average, and these are concentrated in the north and west adjoining Albania itself and Kosovo in Serbia-Montenegro. The country's second and fourth largest cities, Tetovo and Gostivar, are more than 75 percent Albanian. Those districts that are Macedonian or mixed (e.g., Skopje) occupy the other 27 districts (ISPJR/SECOR 2000, 18).

10. During the early Tito years, Muslim institutions were repressed and Muslim property was destroyed (Pettifer 2001, 138). In the 1980s, Albanian-language secondary education was abolished, the use of Albanian in public life was restricted, and some Albanian customs were discouraged. Police have treated Albanian demonstrators roughly and several leaders have received stiff prison sentences for illegal political acts.

11. Survey data show that many Albanians feel that they are treated like second-class citizens. This is evident from replies to questions such as "Do equality and freedom exist for all in Macedonia?" Although 53 percent of Macedonians answered yes to that question, only 11 percent of Albanians did. Only 37 percent of Macedonians said no, whereas 73 percent of Albanians said no (ISPJR/SECOR 2000, 127–29; UNDP 2001, 3, 38, 107, 112, 122, 156).

12. In addition, when the government in the spring 1997 acted to accommodate Albanian educational demands by initiating instruction in Albanian at Skopje University's Pedagogical Institute for teacher training, ethnic Macedonian students started a hunger strike and demonstrations. In Gostivar in July 1997, after many Albanian candidates had won local elections, two demonstrators were killed when the police forcibly removed the Albanian flags from the city hall. Elections have also prompted some ethnic violence, as in the local elections of 2000 and 2002.

13. In February 1994, the largest Macedonian party, VMRO, split into two. The Internal Macedonian Revolutionary Organization—True Macedonian Reform Option (VMRO-VMRO) retained one seat in parliament, and a larger Internal Macedonian Revolutionary Organization—Democratic Party for Macedonian National Unity (VMRO-DPMNE) became the main extraparliamentary opposition party. In September 1993, the Albanian PDP also split into a moderate and more nationalist party.

14. See results of various polls: Transparency International (2001, 285–87); UNDP (2001); Williams and Associates (2001, 2–4); Penn, Schoen, and Berland Associates (2002); ISPJR/SECOR (2000, 134).

15. Kiro Gligorov of the Social Democratic Union of Macedonia (SDSM) party was president from 1991 until he retired in 1999, and Boris Trajkovski of the VMRO-DMPNE party occupied the office from November 1999 until his death in March 2004. Following a caretaker government of nonparty experts, Macedonia was governed by a succession of three different multiparty coalition governments: the New Alliance from 1992 to 1998; the VMRO-DMPNE-led coalition from 1998 to 2001, a Government of National Unity in 2001, and an SDSM-led coalition that took office in October 2001 and again in 2004. Power in municipal elections has tended to be more continuous, because they are located in areas where particular parties tend to retain influence. There have been no irregular transfers of executive power or threatened military or executive coups.

16. Freedom House ranked Macedonia higher in 2000 in terms of "advanced democratic development" than Albania, Bosnia-Hercegovina, Croatia, Yugoslavia, and Turkey (Freedom House 2000). World Audit (2000) ranked Macedonia higher than Bulgaria and Romania and just below Greece in terms of its democracy level.

17. In 1993, with 23 of 120 seats in parliament, the PDP obtained five of 24 ministerial posts in the coalition government and a number of vice-ministerial jobs. The main Albanian parties have always held between 10 and 22 seats in the 120-seat parliament, or between 8 and 18 percent, for a minority population estimated at 23 percent (Republic of Macedonia Statistical Office, October 1999). In 1997, there were four Albanian ministers out of 15 total, five deputy ministers, and one deputy secretary of the government. There also were 25 Albanian mayors, or about 20 percent of the 124. Four of 25 judges at the Supreme Court level were Albanian, as were eight of 88 judges in the Appellate Courts and 31 out of 551 at the basic court level (Management Systems International, Inc. 2000). In 2000, Albanians occupied six of 18 cabinet ministries.

18. The police force is heavily Macedonian even in predominantly Albanian areas. One estimate of the police and military force indicates that 3.1 percent are Albanian and 93.9 percent are Macedonian (ICG 2000, 18). In Tetovo and Gostiver, for example, Albanians are only 17 and 12 percent of the force, respectively. Minorities comprise 12 percent of the military, which includes 25 percent of the rank and file but much less in the officer corps. About 15 percent of military cadets are minorities. Although the deputy minister of defense and two of 10 general officers are ethnic Albanians, all minorities comprise 12 percent of the ministry's civilian employees. In overall state administration, Albanians are estimated to number very few and their proportions to be less than 10 percent (ICG 2000). Privatization of state industries, combined with the overall lower educational attainment of Albanians, might explain part of this record (ICG 2000, 18).

19. Interview, International Republican Institute, Skopje, October 24, 2002.

20. For example, the incarceration and sentencing of Gostivar's mayor and city council president over the flag incident and the declaring of martial law and a curfew were also widely considered by outside observers as overly harsh.

21. During the Kosovo crisis in 1999 caused by the influx of Albanians into the country, ethnic Albanian political leaders were clearly supportive of Macedonia's national interests by

helping to calm Albanian emotions, despite such provocations as rough treatment and even expulsions of the Kosovo refugees by the Macedonian army.

22. Similarly, in 1994, after the Security Council gave the United Nations Preventive Deployment Force (UNPREDEP) an explicit political mandate to focus also on internal issues, the resident Special Representative of the Secretary General (SRSG) used his good offices to foster political dialogue among the country authorities and monitor human rights. In November 1993, he publicly pushed the government to accommodate demands for Albanian language teaching at the Pedagogical Institute. The government did so soon thereafter.

23. In January 1992, the Badinter Commission of the EC had recommended that Macedonia's independence be recognized. Greece successfully pressed the consensus-governed European Community (renamed in January the European Union) to deny recognition. This action also blocked Macedonia's eligibility for IMF and other aid. The Macedonian government fell later that year in part because it failed to get recognition from more countries.

24. After the Bit Pazar riot and an arms smuggling episode, Albania's president Berisha exchanged assurances with President Gligorov. They met several times to pledge mutual respect for the two countries' borders. Berisha and other leaders of Albania have not encouraged aspirations of Albanians in Macedonia for unity with Albania.

25. Interview, Washington, DC, October 14, 2002.

26. Wolfgang-Christian Paes and Hans Risser, Bonn International Centre for Conversion, memo to author.

27. A few plots of planned political violence and armed activities by Albanian groups were discovered in Macedonia before the late 1990s, but those who pursued them were either ineffective or were focusing on Kosovo, not Macedonia. In November 1993, eight Albanians were arrested for plotting an irredentist movement. In June, 10 Albanians, including a deputy defense minister and a senior politician of the PDP, were convicted of plotting to organize an all-Albanian army in the Tetovo area. In 1995, an unsuccessful attempt was made by unknown assailants to assassinate the president, Kiro Gligorov. In 1998, a number of bombs exploded in Gostivar and Tetovo. Although responsibility was claimed by the Kosovo Liberation Army (KLA) based in Kosovo, the government and Albanian television dismissed that idea.

28. Its standard human rights demands were interpreted as a way to gain international support by allaying concerns that they were separatists (Wood 2001).

29. This external contingency was widely feared in the early 1990s, because the possibility was very threatening that if the former Yugoslavia were to clamp down hard on the ethnic Albanians living in Kosovo, the exodus of Albanian refugees into Macedonia might unsettle its uneasy ethnic balance. In 1995, large numbers of Bosnian refugees had been brought to Skopje and given housing. Ethnic Macedonians demonstrated against the idea of bringing more "Muslims" into the country, thus associating the Bosnians with Albanians. But a much more dramatic influx of "Muslims" occurred four years later.

30. GDP began to rise in 1997 and grew at an average annual rate from 1996 to 2000 of 2 percent. It fell in 2001 by 4.6 percent, but due largely to the armed conflict. From 1996 to 2000, the real GDP per capita growth rate increased from −0.1 percent to 5.1 percent.

Average annual GDP per capita growth rose from 2.1 percent in 1999 to 4.6 percent in 2000. GDP per capita itself increased during this period from $4,178 to $5,086. At the same time, unemployment was above 30 percent ever since 1994 according to official figures, but was unofficially estimated around 50 percent. "In 1999, only 53 percent of the working-age population was considered to be participating in the labor force . . . and more than 700,000 people of working age were neither working in the formal economy nor seeking work." During the Kosovo war in 1999, it rose to 70 percent (UNDP 2001, 123, 157, 160).

31. The average growth rate for the whole decade was −0.3. Official unemployment rose over the period from 15 percent to over 30 percent (UNDP 2001, 15). UNICEF reported an increase in poverty from 4 percent in 1991 to 22.3 percent in 2001. According to one estimate, 56 percent of the population was worse off in real income than they were 10 years before. "The real salary in 1997 was just 58 percent of that in 1990" (UNDP 1998).

32. This reflects both widespread corruption and cynicism and disillusionment with the government (USIP 2001, 3). Focus group results suggest that many people across the ethnic spectrum regarded the latest coalition government as a do-nothing collection of squabbling individuals from the four parties, whether moderate or hard-liners, with very different and often personal agendas (ISPJR/SECOR 2000, 134). Thus, some argued in favor of financial disclosures for political candidates and office holders and for greater transparency in procurement procedures (USIP 2001, 5).

33. Many suspected that foreign investors colluded with party supporters to benefit from privatization, and that foreign direct investment is more focused on gaining influence than on supporting productive activity.

34. Local government was seen as ineffective as well, largely because Macedonia's local governments divide its 2 million-plus people into 123 local government units (about 18,000 people each), thus prompting complaints that they lack sufficient population coverage to collect significant revenue and function as effective providers of public services. Thus, one focus group felt that a new proposed law on self-governance could achieve more governmental responsibility by encouraging more transparency (USIP 2001, 1, 4).

35. These included changing the constitutional status of Albanians, the right to use the Albanian language in parliament and teach it in schools, the decentralization of government, and the strengthening of municipal government.

36. The OSCE spillover mission's observers had closely monitored Macedonian domestic affairs since 1992. In the last half of 2000 and early 2001, some letters began appearing with Albanian political demands. But the OSCE noticed no rising discontent among the Albanian population directed at the government in the months preceding outbreak, nor any information that suggested that they even knew that opposition activity was in progress. Although bombs had exploded in Kicevo and Skopje in recent years, no group ever claimed responsibility for these incidents (Interview, OSCE, Skopje, October 24, 2002). In late January, Albanian armed groups had claimed responsibility for a rocket attack on a police station that killed one officer and wounded three other policemen. But when in the days following the outbreak in Tanusevce, OSCE observers visited a neighboring village, local young men did not know what was happening in Tanusevce. They asked the OSCE observers about it and, when told, asked their advice as to whether they

should join the movement (Interview, OSCE, Skopje, October 24, 2002). When the shooting was reported to be going on in Tanusevce, questions were circulating in Skopje on all sides about who this group in the mountains might be.

37. Interview, OSCE, Skopje, October 24, 2002.

38. Interview, National Albanian American Council, Washington, DC, October 13, 2002.

39. Money was collected for the KLA from the diaspora in the United States and Western Europe through the fund "Homeland Calling" and, later, through the "National Freedom Fund," which supported the NLA in Macedonia. Subscribers to the NLA were motivated by calls to help their oppressed ethnic kin (Interview, Washington, DC, October 14, 2002). The diaspora tended to be more nationalistic than Albanians in Macedonia or Kosovo. Although the NLA itself had stated that it supported the territorial integrity of Macedonia, some of its North American recruits sought the takeover of western Macedonia for the Albanians and the creation of Greater Albania (Hedges 2001).

40. Paes and Risser, memo to author; ICG 2001b. The KLA allowed areas under its control to be used for drug shipments and received up to half of its funds from this arrangement, but the extent to which drug money aided its successor, the NLA, is debated. Some observers believe it was a small percentage, whereas other analysts believe it was one of its major sources of revenue and weapons.

41. See note 26.

42. The government of Macedonia claims that as many as 300,000–350,000 small arms have come from Albania (Hans Risser, communication October, 18, 2002, drawing on a study of the Graduate Institute of International Studies). The highest concentrations are in the west and north of the country where the insurgency arose. But the NLA's weapons also came from other sources, including general suppliers in other parts of Eastern and Western Europe and Asia, who provided about 150,000 arms (Wolfgang-Christian Paes, communication, October 18, 2002).

43. A quarter of the population is 5–19 years old (ISPJR/SECOR 2000, 19). The unemployment rate in Macedonia for those under 30 years of age is 48 percent (UNDP 2001, 25). Unemployment rates of many of the small rural villages along the border with Kosovo were much higher.

44. Interview, OSCE, Skopje, October 24, 2002.

45. The weakened vigilance in peripheral areas may have stemmed in part from the power-sharing arrangements and government corruption. Power sharing under the VMRO-DPMNE/DPA coalition had led to the central government's administration of the country being effectively divided between the two parties. A de facto administrative division had occurred in not only the central government's institutions, but also in the local administration of the country. VMRO-DPMNE oversaw the eastern Macedonian areas, while DPA exerted virtual control over the western, Albanian-controlled areas. In effect, Macedonia had two parallel governments (Pettifer 2001; Interviews, Skopje, October 21–26, 2002).

46. The growing momentum to take up arms in Kosovo in 1996–97 arose from the growing sentiment, following the 1995 Dayton Accords regarding Bosnia, that though the nonviolent LDK had established parallel institutions in Kosovo, it was not achieving the aspirations of the Albanians there fast enough. Only guerrilla action would achieve that, possibly through provoking the intervention of international forces.

47. Other top officers, such as Commander Hoxha and Emrush Xhemajli, were also from ethnic Albanian or mixed towns in western Macedonia such as Debar. Some of its local commanders came from villages in northern Macedonia that the NLA occupied, such as Tanusevce and Arachinovo, and had criminal records (*Dnevnik,* June 12, 2001).

48. Because they were not under the effective control of a unified government, human rights abuses by the government police increased, as well as at the hands of the rebel forces. Human Rights Watch issued a warning that those responsible might be responsible for war crimes (Human Rights Watch 2001).

49. The ARM accused the NLA of holding civilians hostage and using them as a shield by hiding in Albanian villages, but the army's methods of indiscriminately shelling villages that were known to be Albanian in the hopes of killing insurgents antagonized the inhabitants and motivated many of their young men to join the NLA. Thus, after the NLA expanded into new villages in the initial stages of the fighting, the minister of the interior rushed to set up an electricity link with the nearby villages in an effort to retain their loyalty to the government (OSCE). Although the local population generally supported the NLA cause before the war spread, many villagers reportedly said afterwards that they would not invite them back, because of the suffering, displacement, and destruction that had occurred (Interview, OSCE, Skopje, October 24, 2002).

50. This description of the conflict is derived from numerous sources and BBC World News (e.g., "What Next for Ethnic Albanian Rebels?" May 25, 2001).

51. Some NLA rank and file were reportedly recruited through extortion. A family with two sons would be asked to contribute one of them or could pay money to be relieved of the obligation. But many others were attracted to the cause as the ARM indiscriminately shelled and destroyed Albanian homes and villages. The NLA included many unemployed, because unemployment in the villages, especially in the mountains, was sometimes almost 100 percent. However, other individuals left jobs or school to join the NLA, including doctors and teachers and students from the Albanian alternative Tetovo University. A number also joined from abroad, having been attracted to the cause by the special appeals organized in Europe and the United States (Hedges 2001).

52. Paes and Risser, memo to author. No evidence was uncovered that neighboring governments assisted the movement financially. The government of Albania was occupied with its own poor economy and other problems, and it was eager at this time to be accepted by the EU and NATO. Although it was unable to police its own borders, support for the NLA was not part of its political agenda and was beyond its capabilities.

53. The ARM's arsenal in 2000 comprised two or three old U.S. Howitzers, some East German armored personnel carriers, some lightly armed vehicles for protecting airports, some old and new U.S. jeeps, and an assortment of submachine guns, mortars, and Yugoslav rocket launchers (Wolfgang-Christian Paes, Bonn International Center, communication, October 18, 2002).

54. Interview, Skopje, Macedonia, October 25, 2002.

55. It was dominated by the four largest parties, the Social Democratic Alliance of Macedonia (SDSM), Internal Macedonian Revolutionary Organization-Democratic Party for Macedonian National Unity (VMRO-DPMNE), Democratic Party of Albanians (DPA), and the Party of Democratic Prosperity (PDP).

56. Interview, Skopje, October 23, 2002.
57. See note 56 above.
58. Interviews, Washington, June 2003.
59. Interview, Skopje, October 23, 2002.
60. Perry, Duncan, "Macedonia: Melting Pot or Meltdown?" *Current History,* November 2001, 362–65.
61. Interview, Skopje, October 26, 2002.
62. Interview, Washington, DC, October 15, 2002.
63. The former OSCE HCNM was designated the OSCE Special Representative and enlisted so he could provide the negotiating team with his expert knowledge of the Macedonia players to find them the best leverage points possible (Interview, OSCE, Skopje, October 25, 2002).
64. Interviews, Skopje, October 19–25, 2002.
65. Interviews, Skopje, October 19–25, 2002.

# References

Ackermann, Alice. 1996. "The Former Yugoslav Republic of Macedonia: A Relatively Successful Case of Conflict Prevention in Europe." *Security Dialogue* 27 (4): 409–24.
———. 2000. *Making Peace Prevail: Preventing Violent Conflict in Macedonia.* Syracuse, NY: Syracuse University Press.
*BBC World News.* 2001. "What Next for Ethnic Albanian Rebels?" May 25.
Bond, Douglas. 2003. *Protocol for the Assessment of Nonviolent Direct Action* (PANDA). Cambridge, MA: Program on Nonviolent Sanctions and Cultural Survival, Weatherhead Center for International Affairs, Harvard University.
Broughton, Sally, and Eran Fraenkel. 2002. "Macedonia: Extreme Challenges for the "Model" of Multi-culturalism." In *Searching for Peasce in Europe and Eurasia.* ed. Paul van Tongeren et al., 264–277. Boulder, CO: Lynne Rienner.
Burg, Steven R. 1997. "Nationalism and Civic Identity: Ethnic Models for Macedonia and Kosovo." In *Preventive Action: Cases and Strategies,* ed. Barnett R. Rubin. New York, NY: Center for Preventive Action, 23–45.
Cilluffo Frank, and George Salmoiraghi. 1999. "And the Winner Is . . . the Albanian Mafia." *The Washington Quarterly* Autumn, 23.
ESI (European Security Initiative). 2002. "Ahmeti's Village: The Political Economy of Interethnic Relations in Macedonia." ESI Macedonia Security Project, Skopje and Berlin, October.
Fraenkel, Eran, and Sally Broughton. 2001. "Macedonia: Extreme Challenges for the 'Model' of Multi-culturalism." Draft, May. http://www.euconflict.org/euconflict/guides/draftseurope/madeonia.htm.
Freedom House. 2000. *Freedom in the World: Country Rankings.* Washington, DC: Freedom House.
Gurr, Ted, et al. 2002. *Minorities at Risk.* College Park, MD: Center for International Development and Conflict Management, University of Maryland.
Hedges, Chris. 2001. "Rebel Ground in Staten Island: Albanians Recruited in Club." *New York Times,* March 19.

Hislope, Robert. 2001 "The Calm Before the Storm? The Influence of Cross-Border Networks, Corruption, and Contraband on Macedonian Stability and Regional Security." Paper prepared for Annual Meeting of the American Political Science Association, San Francisco.

———. 2002. "Organized Crime in a Disorganized State." *Problems of Post-Communism* 49 (3): 33–41.

Human Rights Watch. 2001. *Global Watch.*

ICG (International Crisis Group). 2000. "Macedonia's Ethnic Albanians: Bridging the Gulf." *Balkans Report 98,* International Crisis Group, Skopje/Brussels, August 2.

———. 2001a. "Macedonia: War on Hold." *Balkans Briefing,* International Crisis Group, Skopje/Brussels, August 15, 2.

———. 2001b. "Macedonia: Filling the Security Vacuum." *Briefing No. 23,* September 8.

ISPJR/SECOR (Institute for Sociological, Political, and Juridical Research and SECOR). 2000. *Strategic Management of Cultural and Ethnic Diversity in Public Administration.* Technical Report, ISPJR, Skopje, Macedonia, January.

Leatherman, Janie, William Demars, Patrick Gaffney, and Raimo Vayrynen. 2000. *Breaking Cycles of Violence: Conflict Prevention in Intrastate Crises.* Kumarian Press, Bloomfield, CT.

MSI (Management Systems International, Inc.). 2000. "An Assessment of Ethnic Relations in Macedonia." Management Systems International, Inc., Washington, DC.

Pendarovski, Stevo. 2002. "Contributions of the National Security System." Office of the President, Republic of Macedonia, Skopje, Macedonia, August, 23.

Penn, Schoen, and Berland Associates. 2002. "Attitudes Towards the Political, Social, and Economic Conditions in Macedonia: Results of Focus Group Research." Penn, Schoen, and Berland Associates, Washington, DC, January.

Petroska-Beska, Violeta. 2001. *Ethnic Stereotypes Among Future Pr-School and Primary School Teachers.* Skopje, Macedonia: Center for Ethnic Relations.

Pettifer, James. 2001. "The Albanians in Western Macedonia after FYROM Independence." In *The New Macedonian Question,* ed. James Pettifer. Houndsmill, Hampshire, UK: Palgrave, 137–47.

Republic of Macedonia Statistical Office. *Statistics of Macedonia.* 1999 (October).

Sambanis, Nicholas. 2003. "Using Case Studies to Expand the Theory of Civil War." *Conflict Prevention and Reconstruction Working Paper 5* (May). http://lnweb18.worldbank.org/ESSD/essd.nsf/CPR/WP5.

Sokalski, Henryk. 2003. *An Ounce of Prevention: Macedonia and the UN Experience in Preventive Diplomacy.* Washington, DC: United States Institute of Peace.

Transparency International. 2001. *Global Corruption Report.* Berlin, Germany: Transparency International.

UNDP (United Nations Development Programme). 2001. *Human Development Report.*

USIP (United States Institute of Peace). 2001. "Albanians in the Balkans." *Special Report.* United States Institute of Peace, Washington, DC, November.

Williams and Associates. 2001. *Focus Groups Conducted in the Republic of Macedonia.* Prepared for the International Republic Institute. Salem, MA: Williams and Associates.

Wood, Paul. 2001. "The Rebels' Agenda." *BBC World News,* March 11.

World Audit. 2000. *World Democracy Audit.* England: World Concern, www.worldaudit.org.

# Civil Wars in the Caucasus

9

CHRISTOPH ZÜRCHER, PAVEL BAEV, AND JAN KOEHLER

T̶he implosion of the Soviet Union was surprisingly peaceful. The Caucasus, Tajikistan, and Moldova were the exceptions and all had civil wars. The first war in the Caucasus erupted in 1988, between Armenians and Azerbaijanis over Nagorno-Karabakh, an autonomous province in Azerbaijan mainly populated by Armenians. Next, three civil wars took place in Georgia (1989–93), one over control of the state and two over self-determination in Abkhazia and South Ossetia. Two more wars took place in Chechnya in 1994–96 and 1999 to the present.

We focus on the wars in Georgia and Chechnya in this chapter, referring in passing to Nagorno-Karabakh. We also compare Chechnya to Dagestan, its neighbor to the east, which has managed to avoid war, and we compare South Ossetia and Abkhazia to Adjaria, an autonomous region in Georgia that has also avoided war. In a sense all these wars are inconclusive: None of the secessionist regions has gained international recognition, but the government has also not been able to win the war, so the end result is that South Ossetia, Abkhazia, and Nagorno Karabakh are de facto independent states.

Before we apply the Collier-Hoeffler (CH) model to see how much leverage it gives us to understand these cases, we discuss some peculiarities of the post-Soviet regions that are crucial for understanding the causes and dynamics of all these conflicts. We also point to some data problems that necessarily limit our ability to apply the CH model fully to the Caucasus conflicts. We will argue that the reason for these wars is partly state weakness and partly the emergence of "markets of violence" that favored the onset and continuation of armed conflict.

## The Soviet System and Post-Soviet Legacies

The civil wars in the Caucasus must be analyzed against the backdrop of the institutional legacy of the Soviet System, in particular Soviet ethnofederalism, which was critical in fueling movements for self-determination during a period of regime change in the Soviet Union.

## Ethnic Federalism

The fault lines of most violent conflicts in the Caucasus can be traced back to the system of ethnofederalism in the USSR. The Soviet Union was an asymmetric federation that consisted of territorial units with different status. On the first level, there were the 15 Union republics (SSR, *Sovetskaya Sotsialisticheskaya Respublika,* Soviet Socialist Republic). First-order units were, according to the Soviet constitution, sovereign states and possessed all the institutional prerequisites for statehood. They had the full set of political institutions and symbols, a constitution, borders, citizenship, and a titular nationality, as well as education and mass media in the language of this titular nationality. Legally, they had the right to have their own armed forces and to secede from the Union.

Within the Union republics were units of the second order, the ASSRs (*Avtonomnaya Sovetskaya Sotsialistecheskaya Respublika,* Autonomous Soviet Socialist Republics), defined as autonomous territories of national minorities. The ASSRs had political institutions, borders, a constitution, and titular nationality, among other privileges. ASSRs did not have the right to secede from the Union, but could be transferred to another SSR, provided that the center and both the relevant SSRs agreed.

One step down from the ASSR was the AO (*Avtonomnaya Oblast*), autonomous regions usually with a national minority. AOs had a high degree of control over local affairs but fewer privileges than ASSRs. The language of the titular nationality of an AO was considered to be an official language, but AOs did not have national universities, for example. AOs did not have an independent bureaucracy and key administrative positions were distributed centrally at the republican level.

All federal units were subordinated to the Communist party. However, the Soviet system of ethnofederalism granted the members of the titular nationality a high degree of control over local affairs, education, employment, and positions in the administration. Each federal unit had its own titular nationality. Ethnicity thus became "territorialized." Once central control weakened, this link between territory and ethnicity provided an excellent breeding ground for secessionism. Soviet ethnofederalism was a "subversive institution" (Bunce 1999), paving the way for the dissolution of the Soviet Union.

It is thus no coincidence that most cases of violent conflict in the Caucasus occurred in ethnoterritorial units subordinated to Union republics: Chechnya was an ASSR within Russia; Abkhazia was an ASSR and South-Ossetia was an AO in the Georgian SSR; and Nagorno-Karabakh was an AO in the SSR of Azerbaijan. However, as the cases of Adjaria and Dagestan show, not all second-level ethnofederal units experienced war. Our chapter explains why and how these two units avoided civil war.

## Perestroika, Democratization, and State Failure

In 1987, Mikhail Gorbachev launched his ambitious reform project, *perestroika.* In 1991, the Soviet Union imploded and left behind 15 successor states with very low state capacity, plagued by power struggles between the old elite and new nationalist challengers. Three aspects of Gorbachev's reforms account for the fall of the USSR: the creation of a public political space, the empowerment of republican and regional parliaments, and the dismantling of the vertical hierarchy of the Communist party.

Gorbachev's policy of *glasnost* created a public sphere where political ambitions could be voiced and favored the formation of national movements in many of the Union republics. By 1989, national movements advocated radical positions, including secession. Among the first secessionist movements were the popular fronts of the Baltic states, followed by less organized popular fronts of Armenia, Azerbaijan, and Georgia.

Popular movements were aided by the first partly free elections to republican and local parliaments (Soviets). Between February and October 1990, these elections led to victories of popular movements in Estonia, Latvia, Lithuania, Armenia, Georgia, and Russia. Local leaders were forced to change their point of political reference from Moscow to the republican level. Soviet parliaments became a locus of real power.

Gorbachev undermined the political authority of the Communist party and supported new institutions such as the presidency and parliament to prevent party interference with his reforms. On March 6, 1990, a multiparty system was established. With the collapse of the "vertical hierarchy" of the USSR, the Union and Autonomous republics grasped as much sovereignty as they could. By early 1990, all the SSRs had passed declarations of sovereignty, and in summer 1990 most ASSRs followed suit. For most republics, sovereignty meant control over resources, property rights, taxation, and legislation. Some republics went further: Lithuania declared independence on March 11, Estonia and Latvia followed shortly thereafter, and Armenia followed in August.

In Moscow these changes created a power struggle. Gorbachev was maneuvering between the conservative *nomenklatura,* which wanted to preserve the old system, and the democratic opposition, which pressed for more radical reforms. In the republics, nationalist opposition challenged the Communist *nomenklatura.* In many republics where the parliaments were still controlled by the old *nomenklatura,* as in Chechnya and Azerbaijan, the nationalist opposition organized into popular mass movements.

In March 1991, a referendum over the "Union treaty," which would allow decentralization within a federal state, resulted in 70 percent of the electorate voting in favor of the Union, but the Baltic states and Georgia boycotted the vote. The strong support for the Union did not curb the move toward more self-determination in the republics and the Soviet system was de facto dismantled. The Russian republic under Boris Yeltsin was a leader in this trend, inviting opposition from conservatives. On August 19, an emergency committee headed by Vice President Yanaev, Prime Minister Pavlov, Chairman of the KGB Kriuchkov, Defense Minister Yazov, and Minister of Internal Affairs Pugo staged a coup in Moscow to prevent the signing of the Union treaty. Yeltsin resisted, the coup failed, republican leaders gained even more strength, and the Soviet Union collapsed.

Despite the collapse of the Soviet state, which generated uncertainty, opportunity, and incentives for political entrepreneurs to incite violence, violence was the exception and not the rule. In the Caucasus, there was violence, partly because the stakes for state claimants were high and partly because the opportunity to organize a rebellion was low.

## Economic Fundamentals

The CH model measures opportunity cost of violence, but to apply the model to the Caucasus we need hard data that are not available. Soviet gross domestic product (GDP) is hard to measure accurately, even retrospectively.[1] GDP measures for the constituent republics are even less meaningful. We need GDP data for the period from 1985 to 1988 to apply the CH model to explain the wars of 1988–92, but this was a period of weakening of all government capacity, including official statistics collection and analysis.

Another related problem involves the growth of the "shadow economy" in the 1980s, for which there are no reliable estimates, but all observers consider as a huge part of the Russian economy. The shadow economy can be defined as the sum of economic activities related to production (small-scale manufacturing and agriculture beyond the subsistence level), trade, and services that are unregistered by official statistics but do not violate the key norms of criminal law (such as drug trafficking or extortion). In the Caucasus, the shadow economy coexisted with and penetrated official government structures and permeated the society with its own special norms and rules of behavior. In the three South Caucasus states, the most conservative estimates of the shadow economy currently are 40–50 percent of GDP. Its size was probably similar in the mid-1980s.

## Caucasian Peculiarities: "Testability" of CH Indicators

Given these data problems, we focus on a subset of the variables from the CH model and cover economic, demographic, geographic, and historical variables. For the USSR as a whole, economic growth slowed in the first half of the 1980s and turned negative in 1990–92. In the Caucasus, however, the slow growth of the early and mid-1980s was compensated by the blossoming of the shadow economy. Semilegal cooperative markets offered employment and supported household incomes until the outbreak of violent conflicts in 1989. We argue that these conflicts were not caused by the overall economic decline, but rather that they accelerated the collapse of the most productive and profitable sectors of the economy.

Other development indicators in the CH model are also hard to quantify for the Caucasus. For example, data on male secondary school enrollment are not available, but in the USSR secondary schooling was generally free and mandatory. We do not have estimates of differences in land distribution or income distribution across countries in the region. Private ownership of land was limited and, although some regions suffered from unemployment (e.g., Dagestan, Nagorno-Karabakh, and South

Ossetia), before the wars there were labor market opportunities. Unemployment surged as a result of the wars.

The CH indicator of dependence on primary commodity export can be used with caution. Of all the Caucasian regions, only Azerbaijan (and to a lesser degree Chechnya) has significant resources of oil and gas. In the late 1980s, profits from such exports were, however, concentrated in Moscow, while deliveries to other Soviet republics were not generating any real profits. Expectations of future exports profits from control of these resources might have been a factor in war onset in Azerbaijan and Chechnya, but we do not have evidence that there were such motives.

Geographic and ethnodemographic indicators are easier to measure for the Caucasus and they do appear relevant (more below), but the history of previous civil war is not applicable because there were no large-scale civil wars in the Soviet Caucasus after 1922. At the same time, distant memories and traumas caused by events such as the deportation of Chechens in 1944 and the Armenian genocide of 1915–17 played a crucial role in mass mobilization. The CH variable measuring the peacetime since the last civil war is in principle relevant, but it must be reoperationalized to capture other past conflicts.

Measuring religious fractionalization is also difficult. The Soviet system suppressed religion, so it is hard to find official data on religious fractionalization. However, our study identifies a role for religious "fault lines," particularly given the religious extremism of Islamist fighters in Chechnya.

## Markets of Violence

Conflict escalation and de-escalation are components of a dynamic process in which the rationales of the conflicting parties and their incentive structures undergo changes. The underlying causes of a conflict may be different from what actually triggers the conflict and from factors that lead either to conflict resolution or to violent escalation. We argue that, regardless of its underlying causes, sustained organized violence becomes self-sustaining by creating "markets of violence: . . . economic areas dominated by civil wars, warlords or robbery, in which a self-perpetuating system emerges which links non-violent commodity markets with the violent acquisition of goods" (Elwert 2003, 221).

Although at their core civil wars have roots in sociopolitical conflict, the strategic actions of war entrepreneurs are mostly governed by short-term economic gain by interest or necessity to sustain the insurgency. A war economy can involve both legal and illegal activities, including trade and investment, or drug trafficking, kidnapping, extortion, or taxing the shadow economy. Government officials may also benefit from the market of violence. Thus, sustaining low-level violence with low risks of overturning that status quo can be a rational objective of both the rebels and the state. Neither side will want to commit substantial resources to win the war. This argument contradicts the view of prolonged war as a communication problem.

All violent conflicts in the Caucasus developed markets of violence for a period. In Georgia, these markets did not last long. In Chechnya, the market has been successful.The links between these markets of violence and the shadow economy can explain the lack of progress in resolving the Caucasian conflicts.We turn to the cases next.

## Civil Wars in Georgia: Causes and Duration

Georgia descended into a short-lived civil war immediately after independence.The state nearly collapsed in 1992, but by the end of 1993 all major hostilities had ended. The conflicts underlying the violence are still alive.There has been a 10-year pause in the fighting, punctuated by occasional skirmishes, but there is significant uncertainty regarding the survivability of Georgia as an independent state.

The first question we address is why there were so many wars in Georgia. Some data sets only code a single war. But there were three distinct conflicts: the violent struggle for power at the state level, the secession of South Ossetia, and the secession of Abkhazia. In addition to applying the CH model to this case, we advance two arguments: (a) civil war onset was directly linked to a significant drop in opportunity costs, and (b) the wars were short because the economic "prize" of war was quickly exhausted.

### *Background*[2]

Georgia is a relatively small country (with an area of 69,700 km$^2$, including Abkhazia with 8,600 km$^2$ and South Ossetia with 3,900 km$^2$) squeezed between the Black Sea to the west, the Greater Caucasian mountain range to the north, and the Lesser Caucasian range to the south. It is mountainous (65 percent of its territory is above 800 m) with high peaks (above 1,500 m). Georgia has no high-value extractable natural resources and no reserves of hydrocarbons.The subtropical climate and fertile soils are favorable for agriculture, allowing cultivation of citrus fruits and tobacco in the coastal areas, grapes and tea in the lower mountain slopes, wheat and maize in the valleys, and sheep farming in the alpine pastures. According to the last Soviet census of 1989, Georgia's population was around 5.4 million (4.7 million without Abkhazia and South Ossetia).About 45 percent of the population lives in rural areas, but the country has a rich urban culture, and the capital Tbilisi has over 1 million inhabitants.Abkhazia has a population of 150,000–300,000 and South Ossetia has around 50,000–60,000.

Georgians are the dominant majority, accounting for up to 70 percent of the population (see table 9.1).[3] Georgians were also the largest nationality in Abkhazia, comprising about 45.5 percent of its 525,000 inhabitants, whereas the Abkhazians made up only 18 percent (in the 1989 census), and the Russians and Armenians made up about 14.5 percent each. In South Ossetia, Georgians made up only about 30 percent of a population of 100,000, whereas Ossetians accounted for 66 percent. About 100,000 Ossetians lived in Georgia proper.The wars of the early 1990s resulted in a drastic shift in the ethnic compositions of Abkhazia, South Ossetia, and Georgia proper, largely due to population displacements. Significant emigration and a falling

Table 9.1 Georgian Ethnic Composition (Main Groups)

| Region | Abkhazi | Armenian | Azeri | Byelorussian | Georgian | Greek | Jewish | Kurds | Ossetian | Russian | Ukrainian | Other | Total |
|---|---|---|---|---|---|---|---|---|---|---|---|---|---|
| **Georgia** | | | | | | | | | | | | | |
| 1989 | 1.8% | 8.1% | 5.7% | 0.2% | 70.1% | 1.8% | 0.5% | 0.6% | 3.0% | 6.3% | 1.0% | 0.9% | |
| | 95,900 | 437,200 | 307,600 | 8,600 | 3,787,400 | 100,300 | 24,600 | 33,300 | 164,100 | 341,200 | 52,400 | 48,200 | 5,400,800 |
| (*) | 0.1% | 7.5% | 6.4% | 0.1% | 73.7% | 1.8% | 0.5% | 0.7% | 2.0% | 5.5% | 0.9% | 0.1% | |
| (*) | 2,600 | 359,700 | 307,600 | 6,500 | 3,519,000 | 85,600 | 23,200 | 33,300 | 97,700 | 264,200 | 40,700 | 37,100 | 4,777,200 |
| 2001 (*) | 0.1% | 5.5% | 5.0% | 0.1% | 84.2% | 0.5% | 0.1% | 0.4% | 0.9% | 2.1% | 0.4% | 0.8% | |
| (*) | 2,000 | 220,000 | 200,000 | 2,000 | 3,398,000 | 21,000 | 2,000 | 18,000 | 38,000 | 85,000 | 15,000 | 32,275 | 4,033,275 |
| **South Ossetia** | | | | | | | | | | | | | |
| 1989 | — | 1.0% | 0.1% | — | 29.3% | 2.8% | 0.3% | — | 66.0% | 1.9% | — | — | |
| | — | 985 | 53 | — | 28,868 | 1,470 | 157 | — | 65,028 | 1,971 | — | — | 98,532 |
| **Abkhazia** | | | | | | | | | | | | | |
| 1989 | 17.8% | 14.6% | 0.1% | — | 45.7% | 2.8% | 0.3% | — | 0.2% | 14.8% | — | 3.7% | |
| | 93,461 | 76,659 | 525 | — | 239,953 | 14,702 | 1,575 | — | 1,050 | 77,709 | — | 19,427 | 525,061 |

Note: (*) = without Abkhazi and South Ossetian population.

birth rate has led to a steady decline in Georgia's population. The total number of refugees and internally displaced persons is estimated at 250,000.

The fundamental problem with economic data for the period immediately preceding Georgia's wars (1985–89) is that the only source is Soviet statistics with all their known deficiencies. Another part of the problem is that the 1980s were a decade in which Georgia's shadow economy grew rapidly; while official figures were showing a slow growth of the so-called net material product (NMP) and per capita income, in reality, more wealth was generated "informally" than was registered by the accounts. The real level of income and the standard of living in Georgia were significantly higher than the average for the USSR.[4] The collapse of that economic prosperity was unprecedented, even in comparison with the rest of the former USSR. In 1990, NMP declined by 11.1 percent, in 1991 by 20.6 percent, in 1992 by 43.4 percent, and in 1994 by a further 40.0 percent; the GDP estimates (corrected retrospectively) give a decline of 44.8 percent in 1994 and a total decline in 1989–94 of 76 percent. These figures give a picture of massive economic contraction.

## Struggle for Power in Georgia

In these chaotic conditions, three distinct political crises unfolded.[5] A demonstration in central Tbilisi was met with violence in April 9, 1989, killing 20 people. This event resonated in Georgian society, and eroded the authority of the Communist party, encouraging wide resistance to any political control from Moscow. In March 1990, the Georgian Supreme Soviet declared Georgia to be an "annexed and occupied country" and set parliamentary elections for the autumn. Those brought a clear victory to a loose coalition of opposition groupings called "Round Table–Free Georgia"; its leader, the well-known dissident Zviad Gamsakhurdia, duly became the chairman of the parliament.

From that point, the unraveling of institutional structures of power acquired such a catastrophic speed that, unlike in other republics and regions of the USSR, the middle-rank Communist *nomenklatura* was unable to convert its political resources into economic assets (Solnick 1998). In March 1991, Georgia refused to participate in the Soviet referendum on preserving the Union (Abkhazia and South Ossetia did take part and voted in favor) and held its own referendum on independence (Abkhazia and South Ossetia did not participate) with an overwhelming vote in favor. On April 9, 1991, the Georgian parliament approved the formal restoration of independence. The next month, Gamsakhurdia was elected Georgia's president, receiving some 85.5 percent of the vote. He immediately launched a thorough cadre sweep in the state apparatus seeking to replace the Soviet *nomenklatura* with a new elite and emphasizing loyalty far above competence. His power base, however, remained very uncertain, as was his control over two major paramilitary structures: the National Guard, led by Tengiz Kitovani, and the *Mkhedrioni* (the Knights), led by Dzhaba Ioseliani.

The turning point was the coup attempt in Moscow (August 19–21, 1991). Gamsakhurdia was so alarmed that he ordered the National Guard to disarm.

Kitovani refused to comply and moved his forces (some 2,000 men) outside Tbilisi, setting up a military camp that became a base for the opposition. The decisive escalation of the crisis came in late December 1991, when Kitovani led his forces (perhaps only 500 men) into Tbilisi and besieged the parliament buildings, receiving support from the *Mkhedrioni*. Gamsakhurdia could not fight for more than a week and fled the country (Fuller 1991).

The coup brought a significant change in the character of the struggle for power: It became confined mainly to western Georgia (Mingrelia), where support for Gamsakhurdia was high. In Tbilisi, the victorious opposition sought to resolve the problem of legitimizing its power by inviting Eduard Shevardnadze from Moscow to chair the newly created State Council. Shevardnadze was initially squeezed between the two warlords (Kitovani and Ioseliani) and focused his agenda on the parliamentary elections scheduled for October 1992. It is still unclear to what degree Shevardnadze was in charge of the National Guard that advanced into Abkhazia in August 1992 and engaged in high-intensity fighting. Despite that emergency, Shevardnadze moved forward with the elections, which produced a divided parliament but, most importantly for him, a strong personal mandate for his leadership.

The unsuccessful war in Abkhazia gave Shevardnadze a chance to replace Kitovani as defense minister with the energetic Giorgi Karkarashvili. But the devastating defeat in Abkhazia in September 1993 led to a pro-Gamsakhurdia uprising in western Georgia, which neither the demoralized National Guard nor the disorganized *Mkhedrioni* was able to check. Shevardnadze had to appeal to Russia for help, and in the final tragicomic act of the war in October 1993, a rebel force of about 800 Zviadists that threatened to conquer the whole country was miraculously dispersed by an intervention involving a couple of Russian battalions (Baranovsky 1994, 195). That, essentially, was the end of Georgia's civil wars. Gamsakhurdia died in late December 1993 and several subsequent small uprisings in Mingrelia posed little threat.

Internal stabilization initially brought economic recovery, but by the end of the 1990s, rampant corruption had stifled growth. Unnerved by the rise of opposition, Shevardnadze resorted to blatant cheating in the parliamentary elections of November 2, 2003. This brought a massive public discontent; the opposition found a leader in Mikhail Saakashvily, who on November 22 stormed the parliament building, forcing Shevardnadze's resignation. In the January 2004 elections, Saakashvily was overwhelmingly elected president, securing also solid support in the reconstituted parliament. Further trajectory of this nonviolent "rose revolution" is impossible to predict because economic development depends too heavily upon Western support, and the culture of corruption has penetrated deep into the societal fabric (Derluguian 2004).

## The War in South Ossetia

The conflict in South Ossetia escalated into violence quickly and unexpectedly. There was no history of conflict between Tbilisi and South Ossetia.

The conflict arose out of the contest among nationalist parties fighting for power in Georgia. The essentially symbolic decision of the Georgian parliament in August 1989 to strengthen the status of the Georgian language (intended primarily to challenge Moscow) triggered a public campaign in South Ossetia in favor of upgrading the region's autonomous status from the third level (AO) to the second level (ASSR). A unilateral decision by the South Ossetian parliament on this matter on November 10 sparked a public protest in Tbilisi, which provided Zviad Gamsakhurdia with his first opportunity to make a mark on Georgian politics. He led a "peaceful" march on Tskhinvali with some 20,000–30,000 protesters. After marching about 120 km, the column was blocked by several hundred Soviet Interior troops but not without a few casualties.

In the next summer, the South Ossetian parliament, claiming that the format of the parliamentary elections in Georgia was discriminatory against the regions, decided to boycott them and, on September 30, 1990, declared independence from Georgia. The new Georgian parliament reacted by revoking South Ossetian's autonomy. Moscow intervened and a state of emergency was declared in South Ossetia. The Gamsakhurdia government imposed an economic blockade on South Ossetia and, in early January 1991, made an attempt to gain control over Tskhinvali with paramilitary forces, which were repelled by fierce street fighting. The blockade was maintained throughout the winter, with only sporadic clashes and looting of a few villages. In early March, Gamsakhurdia reduced South Ossetia's status to "cultural autonomy." South Ossetians were outraged and refused to participate in the March 31 referendum on Georgia's independence.

The level of hostilities remained low through the summer. In September, Gamsakhurdia ordered the National Guard yet again to advance into South Ossetia. He sought a victory to defeat his political opposition and save his presidency, but the National Guard had little interest in a protracted warfare in a province with no lootable resources. Only a few detachments attacked and were repelled by the Ossetian militia.

The New Year coup in Tbilisi created an opportunity to de-escalate the conflict. Indeed, Shevardnadze initiated negotiations, seeking to put the blame for the violence squarely on Gamsakhurdia. The attack on Tskhinvali in early June, when the National Guard burned and destroyed up to 80 percent of dwellings in the city, was therefore particularly unexpected. The aim of that "last push" was perhaps not to achieve a decisive victory but to assert a position of strength in the final round of negotiations resulting in an agreement, which was signed on June 24 by Shevardnadze, Yeltsin, and representatives from South and North Ossetia. The agreement marked the end of open hostilities and established a cease-fire that was to be monitored by a joint peacekeeping force for which Russia contributed a battalion of 700 lightly armed troops.[6] Neither serious incidents nor much progress at the follow-up negotiations were registered in the next 12 years, and South Ossetia saw a modest economic development based primarily on smuggling. The fragility of this arrangement in the post-"rose revolution" situation became apparent in summer 2004 when occasional shooting quickly escalated to serious fighting at the outskirts of Tskhinvali with the use of artillery, while Russian peacekeepers had few doubts on taking sides with the Ossetians.

## The War in Abkhazia

Tensions around Abkhazia had been evident long before the eruption of violence. The strongest warning sign was the violent clash in Sukhumi in July 1989, provoked by an attempt by the Georgian authorities to divide the University of Sukhumi in two parts, one of which was to become a branch of the Tbilisi University. Despite these tensions, Abkhazia managed to stay out of the war in South Ossetia and kept "neutrality" during the internal struggle in Georgia. Having effectively abstained from the March 1991 Georgian referendum on independence, Abkhazia reached a compromise with the Gamsakhurdia government and held its own parliamentary elections in October 1991, on the basis of a de facto quota system (28 seats to be given to Abkhazis, 26 to Georgians, and 11 to other ethnic groups).

On July 23, 1992, the Abkhazian parliament (all 26 Georgian members boycotted the vote) restored the republican constitution of 1925 and so effectively proclaimed Abkhazia an independent state. Three weeks later, some 5,000 National Guard troops moved into Abkhazia and entered Sukhumi; another 1,000 guardsmen landed in Gagra, blocking Abkhazia's border with Russia. The Abkhazian parliament retreated to Gudauta and declared mobilization against Georgia's "invasion." Its paramilitary forces (no stronger than 1,000) took defensive positions along the River Gumista approximately 20 km north of Sukhumi, with the Russian airbase in their immediate rear.

For the first week of the war, Georgian troops were busy looting Sukhumi and Gagra, but then they discovered that the enemy was serious about protracted resistance. By the end of September, up to 1,000 armed volunteers arrived from the Russian North Caucasus via mountain passes to support the Abkhazians. On October 2–3, a surprise attack was launched toward Gagra, where an isolated Georgian grouping was soundly defeated. After restoring the main line of communications with Russia, the Abkhazian de facto government started to build up its forces.

One of the most serious controversies in the Abkhazian war involves the role of Russia. Officially the Russian government tried to mediate the cessation of hostilities, though Russian forces in Abkhazia supported the rebels. The Abkhazians launched a decisive attack on Sukhumi in mid-September, breaking the cease-fire agreement of July 27, guaranteed by Russia. Despite Shevardnadze's desperate efforts, Sukhumi fell on September 27 and by the end of the month Abkhazian forces had driven the demoralized National Guard south of the River Inguri, establishing control over the whole territory of Abkhazia and forcing some 200,000 Georgians to flee.

That was the end of the war, which was consolidated by the deployment of 3,000 Russian peacekeepers in July 1994 under a Commonwealth of Independent States (CIS) mandate and UN monitoring performed by its 100-strong Observer Mission in Georgia (UNOMIG). This external protection of the Abkhazian victory has not helped in setting an effective framework for the peace process; negotiations on resolving the conflict remain deadlocked, while fighting occasionally resumes; the most serious clashes occurred in May 1997 and October 2001. Abkhazia's internal development has remained affected by the war legacies, and the controversial presidential elections in October 2004 revealed the sharpness of societal fragmentation (Novikov 2004).

We have mapped out Georgia's three civil wars, but it is also interesting to consider the wars that could have happened but did not. A good comparison to Abkhazia is Adjaria, an autonomous republic that remained stable despite wars in other Georgian regions. The reason for this stability, we find, is that a single clan, led by Aslan Abashidze, an able and authoritative leader, managed to establish complete control over the local structures of power. Abashidze reached a compromise first with Gamsakhurdia and then with Shevardnadze, promising not to advance any separatist claims in exchange for letting him rule as he saw fit. While the center was preoccupied with Abkhazia in 1992–93 and was weakened by war, Abashidze was not threatened and saw no need for a nationalist mobilization of Adjarians.[7] The collapse of Shevardnadze's regime undermined Abashidze's authority, so in the spring of 2004 President Saakashvily took a calculated risk and decided to remove him from power (Mitchell 2004). Enforcing an economic blockade and moving troops to Adjaria's borders, he brought Georgia to the brink of another civil war. His gamble, however, paid off. Facing massive public protests in Batumi, Abashidze fled the country in June 2004, granting Saakashvily the opportunity to transfer power to new "hungrier" groupings of elite.

## Organization of Violence

The three Georgian wars had remarkably different patterns of organization, but in all three the paramilitary forces were built from scratch, because the military structures of the Trans-Caucasus Military District remained under Russian control. Although the spontaneous meltdown of Soviet law-and-order institutions created tempting opportunities for political actors to get access to yet-to-be-built instruments of power, the rapid growth of militias can be explained only by a sharp decrease in recruitment costs. These costs were determined by the wide availability of young men as recruits, the availability of weapons, and the availability of financing for the war.

At the starting point of these "troubles" in early April 1989, we could see mass-level protest in Tbilisi, but not much organization. The use of force against unarmed protesters gave a strong mobilizational impulse to the opposition. In late November 1989, we see a greater degree of organization, when a column of 20,000–30,000 made a march from Tbilisi to Tskhinvali, marking the start of the first war. The opposition took most of the credit, but the organizational resources for the march came from a different source: It was the newly appointed leader of Georgian Communist party, Givi Gumbaridze, who led the column together with Gamsakhurdia and also provided for logistics.

Repression from Tbilisi mobilized the organization *Adamon Nykhas* (People's Assembly) to demand more autonomy. This organization was hard pressed to build a paramilitary structure. The main source of small arms was the Soviet Army helicopter regiment based in Tskhinvali. In response to that mobilization, in the neighboring Georgian villages a self-defense force known as the Merab Kostava Society began to grow, and engaged in sporadic low-profile clashes.

In early 1990, South Ossetian forces had only 300–400 poorly armed fighters, who were able to hold the second line of defense behind some 500 Soviet Interior troops. But in just six months, that force grew to about 1,500 full-time fighters plus some 3,500 "minuteman" volunteers; it was able to resist more determined attacks without any direct help from Moscow. Although defending against an attack is always a more cost-efficient form of warfare, the better organization of forces on the South Ossetian side was to a large degree the result of direct material support from North Ossetia (a part of the Russian Federation). Some 320,000 Ossetians lived there (out of a total population of 630,000) and the arrival of a few hundred volunteers made a big difference when the fighting around Tskhinvali came to a head. North Ossetia had several large Soviet Army garrisons, which were "leaking" arms to local militias who then delivered them to the conflict area. It should be noted that for South Ossetia the costs of mobilizing the force were further lowered by the flow of Ossetian refugees from Georgia.

In Georgia in the autumn of 1990, one of the first laws adopted by the new parliament declared the conscription of Georgians into the Soviet Armed Forces to be illegal, and this provided a potential pool of young men for a proto-army, the National Guard. The corresponding legislation was approved in January 1991 and authorized the buildup of a 12,000-strong force on the basis of conscription. Moscow drastically reduced its financial transfers to the mutinous republic, so the Georgian government was unable to support its National Guard with meaningful resources. Instead of conscription, it had to rely on volunteers who had to rely on their own weapons in order to feed themselves.[8] The commander of the National Guard, Tengiz Kitovani, a power-thirsty man with no military experience, engaged in targeted taxation of various shadow businesses, thus building his forces through a soft extortion racket. Another paramilitary organization was growing alongside (and, perhaps, one step ahead of) the National Guard: the *Mkhedrioni* led by the prominent former criminal authority Dzhaba Ioseliani. This organization had no connections whatsoever to the new government but was built as a combination of old criminal groupings and urban teenage gangs. It relied entirely on illegal sources of income (particularly targeting gasoline supplies) and exploited connections with the Georgian underworld in Moscow. By mid-1991, the National Guard and the *Mkhedrioni* each had about 1,000 fighters and 10,000 associate members and focused their efforts on buying arms or seizing them from Soviet military garrisons.

When the government attempted to establish firmer control over the National Guard and suppress the *Mkhedrioni,* the struggle for power in Georgia degenerated into civil war. The warlords opted to seize political power directly, seeing the need to secure their monopoly on the extortion racket in order to sustain their paramilitary structures; they also recognized the need to find new loot. The greed-driven nature of the coup explains why the scale of the decisive battle was so miniscule (perhaps 500 people were fighting in Tbilisi on both sides) and why the number of casualties was so low (not more than 200 people were killed in the initial phase of the civil war).

The successful coup still left the National Guard and the *Mkhedrioni* with the problem of a rapidly shrinking resource base that undermined their sustainability. It was a no small achievement that a brewing clash between them was avoided by carefully dividing the spheres of control, so that the *Mkhedrioni* got the monopoly over the distribution of fuel, while the National Guard sought to profit from the arms trade. Neither organization managed to find stable sources of income, but both remained loyal to their leaders. When these leaders agreed to bring Shevardnadze back from exile, they also opted for connecting their militias to the state. The National Guard became the "official army" (with Kitovani as the defense minister), and the *Mkhedrioni* became the interior forces (Temur Khachishvili, one of Ioseliani's lieutenants, became the interior minister). In July 1992, the National Guard received a large amount of heavy armaments, including some 50 tanks, from the former Soviet arsenals in Georgia, controlled by Russia.[9] But it was the *Mkhedrioni* that had the task of maintaining order in western Georgia, where it duly looted and burned several villages. Kitovani became confident that his forces were ready to claim new loot, and in mid-August the National Guard deployed its newly acquired tanks into Abkhazia.

In Abkhazia, the newly elected parliament approved the creation of its own National Guard in response to Georgian aggression, especially after mid-August 1992. The Abkhazian government declared from Gudauta a mandatory mobilization, aware that there were not nearly enough Abkhazians with even elementary military training. Support was sought from the recently created Confederation of Caucasian Mountain Peoples, which called for volunteers from the North Caucasus and raised about 1,500 fighters in the space of a month, perhaps half of them from Chechnya.

The reinforcements from the North Caucasus kept arriving in Abkhazia during the first half of 1993, so the balance of forces was gradually shifting away from the Georgians, particularly because many of their part-time combatants were increasingly reluctant to return to the battlefield, while the permanent fighters lost their motivation to serve because of the lack of material rewards. The key factors determining the outcome of the war were to be found outside Abkhazia, and the most controversial of those was the position of Russia.[10] One part of the Russian military, particularly the Command of the Trans-Caucasus MD, supplied Georgia with heavy weapons and ammunition. As for the Russian forces based in Abkhazia, they directly supported the Abkhazian side, perhaps with the implicit consent of the defense ministry in Moscow. There were several air strikes from Gudauta on Sukhumi, which had a mainly psychological impact, but the few dozen artillery guns that became available for the rebels perhaps decided the outcome of the battle for Sukhumi. The motley force assembled on the Abkhazian side, where Chechens were fighting alongside Cossacks, had very little organization and was only able to win the war because of the complete demoralization of the Georgian forces.

The defeat in Abkhazia provided Shevardnadze with a chance to eliminate the warlords from Georgia's politics. In late 1993, relying on assistance from Russia, Shevardnadze started to build a new security force answerable to State Security Minister Igor Giorgadze. In February 1994, the weakened *Mkhedrioni* was formally transformed into a Rescue Corps and after the August 1995 assassination attempt on Shevardnadze, it was disbanded and its leadership was arrested. Before that, in February 1995, Kitovani had been provoked into attempting a new march on Abkhazia, which was presented as a mutiny and suppressed by the security forces. In autumn 1995, relying on rehabilitated police and Interior Minister Shota Kviraia (a former KGB general), Shevardnadze also managed to get rid of Giorgadze, which left him as the undisputed leader of Georgia's armed agencies. It could also be mentioned that Abashidze saw little need in building an Adjarian "army" (except for a small unit of bodyguards), expecting that in an emergency situation hundreds of armed volunteers would raise to defend Batumi, with the help from a Russian military base. Shevardnadze never dared to challenge this assumption, but Saakashvily in spring 2004 staged a convincing demonstration of force with a couple of U.S.-trained battalions and scored a bloodless victory.

The market of violence in Georgia was more or less closed in 1995. Crucial for the organization of violence in the early 1990s was the availability of arms and financing. The case of financing these wars fits uncomfortably within the CH model, where financing comes from natural resources or diasporas. In the South Ossetian war, the secessionists obtained material support from North Ossetia, which, strictly speaking, does not constitute a diaspora, but is rather the larger part of an ethnic group across the border. This is more clearly an example of irredentist nationalism than an ethnic diaspora as thought of by CH.[11] But support from the Ossetian diaspora in Moscow fits better with the CH model. In the Abkhazian war, secessionists recruited mostly volunteers from several republics of the North Caucasus, including Chechnya. None of these peoples are ethnically related to the Abkhazians, but their imagined ethnic solidarity sufficed for a short-term mobilization. This nationalist and ideological motivation is outside the scope of economic models such as the CH model.

## Causes of Georgia's Wars

The causes of the three Georgian wars shared some similarities. Institutional weakness was a shared element in all three. Emotions also were important and these are squarely outside the CH model.

How did geography matter? According to the CH model, Georgian rugged terrain would make insurgency easier to sustain. But geography obviously did not matter much at the start of the struggle for power, which centered on the capital Tbilisi. Terrain became important only when Mingrelia became the key theater of violence. Terrain was also not particularly relevant in South Ossetia, where the war was fought primarily around Tskhinvali. In fact, high mountains were more of a problem for the rebels, because their vital connection with North Ossetia was blocked during winter. Even the war in Abkhazia was not influenced that much by the mountains and forests, because it was fought primarily in the narrow corridor along the coast, with very little guerrilla activity.

A geographic factor with a heavy impact is the neighborhood: The Caucasus in the late 1980s and early 1990s was extremely unstable, with several wars, coup attempts, and protests. Although there were only limited spillovers from one conflict to another,[12] the concentration of these conflicts implied a greater availability of arms and an overall unease generated by widespread violence.

For a small state with a small population, Georgia had more than its share of civil war (recall that in the CH model, population size is positively correlated with civil war risk). But Georgia's population was highly dispersed and the key ethnic minorities in Abkhazia and South Ossetia had been empowered by Soviet ethnofederalism, which fueled their capacity and interest in secession.

History, as measured by the CH model, did not matter, because Georgia had not had a civil war in recent memory. Moreover, the fact that civil war was avoided during the rose revolution runs contrary to the CH model. Our narrative suggests that the war outbreak in Abkhazia in the summer of 1992 was aggravated by the two other wars. Although this is consistent with the CH *peacetime* variable, the effect is not captured by the model because overlapping wars in the same country are not coded in the CH data set. Collier and Hoeffler look only to prior civil wars in the preceding five-year period to measure the effects of history on the risk of a new civil war. This does not allow them to consider risks associated with nearby insurgencies or chronologically overlapping wars or low-violent conflict.

Our narrative also points to a significant role of ethnic fractionalization in South Ossetia and Abkhazia. On the surface, both wars seem to conform to the CH arguments about ethnic dominance. But in South Ossetia, the Ossetians were dominant in their region and this was more relevant than Georgian countrywide dominance. Abkhazia fits the CH model uncomfortably, because this was an example of a struggle for ethnic dominance by a minority group with titular status in its region. Ethnic dominance was not relevant to the war over control of the center. The lack of war in Adjaria cannot easily be explained by this variable either, because the Adjarians are not recognized as an ethnic group and Abashidze refrained from building a new ethnic identity.

One political factor that had a heavy impact on all three wars is democratization.[13] This impact cannot be fully captured by measuring the correlation between the gradual "softening" of the USSR and occurrence of violent conflicts across its vast territory; the multiple effects of institutional erosion on the cohesion of society and its resistance to violence are not easily quantifiable. Mobilization of antisystemic forces in Georgia advanced so quickly precisely because their leaders combined democratic and nationalistic discourses. The key points in the trajectory of every war were elections and referenda; typically, it was a decision of a recently elected parliament that triggered a violent escalation. On the contrary, the curtailing of democratic processes in Georgia by the Shevardnadze regime noticeably contributed to the relative stabilization of the conflict situations (Aves 1996). A new wave of democratization set off by the rose revolution of November 2003 has already brought new escalation of tensions, first around Adjaria and then in South Ossetia.

A different explanation focuses on competition among elites during the period of transition. Indeed, the struggle for power in Georgia turned violent when the new semidemocratic regime, snatching power from the old Communist *nomenklatura,* antagonized the warlords. Although the personal qualities of the leadership did play a role (ambitious Gamsakhurdia quickly alienated his key political allies), retrospectively, the new regime's most serious failure was its inability to incorporate the entrepreneurs from the shadow economy. When the warlords seized power in January 1992, they, in turn, also failed to win the confidence of this elite group. In the end, it was an alliance between parts of the old political elite and those figures in the entrepreneurial elite that had managed to preserve their fortunes that stabilized the country. The war in Abkhazia also fits well into such a causal explanation. Local clans with strong connections to the blossoming shadow economy were eager to grasp more direct executive power, but Tbilisi was equally eager to claim more control over the lucrative businesses.

Turning to economic factors, Georgia was by no means poor by Soviet standards, despite falling into the lowest 20 percent of the countries in the CH data set. Prewar GDP per capita is probably in the range of $1,100–1,300 per capita (in 1995 US$). This certainly appears close to poverty but the shadow economy was creating perhaps an equal amount of income. Although the Soviet economy in the 1980s experienced declining growth, this mostly affected heavy industry, so Georgia's economy, based on light industry and tourism, was growing comparatively strongly. The struggle for power in Georgia, therefore, cannot be explained by economic stagnation. However, the arrival of the Gamsakhurdia government caused a sharp decline in economic performance, and this sudden downturn was quite possibly a significant variable. The war in South Ossetia (where the average income was perhaps 30–40 percent lower than the average for Georgia) could to some degree be explained by irritation over perceived "discrimination," but on balance the impact of economic factors here was insignificant. As for the war in Abkhazia, by the time it started in the autumn of 1992, Georgia's GDP had declined by as much as 40 percent, with a corresponding shrinkage of the shadow economy. Although this decline was perhaps not as sharp in Abkhazia itself, this war definitely shows a clear correlation with the drastic downturn in economic performance.

The problem with one of the key risk factors in the CH model—export of primary commodities—is that although Georgia produced plenty of high-value agricultural products (tea, wine, tobacco, fruit, flowers) for the USSR, they were not, in the strict sense, exported, and had little, if any, market value outside the Soviet Union. By the start of the war in Abkhazia, Georgia had become an independent state, so the trade in these commodities with Russia was indeed real export. However, the volume of that trade had declined drastically, because Russia was flooded by cheap imports from Turkey, Eastern Europe, and other markets. Therefore, Georgia's civil wars generally defy this correlation.

Overall, economic factors do not provide a sufficient explanation for Georgia's civil wars, and neither do geographic or historical factors. Ethnic dominance was partly relevant for both secessionist wars and the perils of democratization and elite competition were strong driving forces that are not accounted for by the CH model.

In the end, the wars ended quickly because of a lack of a sufficiently significant economic prize worth fighting for. The role of economic factors in limiting the duration of war is particularly evident in South Ossetia. That war had the weakest local resource base, because South Ossetia had always been one of the poorest regions in Georgia. The war escalated and de-escalated according to the political struggle in Tbilisi. Georgians never attempted to deploy forces capable of controlling the hostile population, and for the South Ossetians it would been impossible to organize serious resistance over a prolonged period given the small size of the population. As soon as it became obvious for Tbilisi that the war would bring no more political dividends, the war was brought to an end.

Similarly, the internal struggle for power lost steam with the rapid exhaustion of the resource base. The need to "feed" the greed-driven National Guard and the criminalized *Mkhedrioni* helped push the war into Abkhazia, and the government's defeat there totally exhausted the potential for a long struggle. The war destroyed the sectors of the shadow economy with highest profits, further removing any incentives for more loot-driven war. The logic of the CH model seems useful here in explaining why the wars ran out of steam when the resource base was exhausted. But Georgia's wars also suggest some modifications and expansions to the CH model, particularly the focus on the risks of democratic transition, elite competition, and manipulation of ethnicity.

## Chechnya and Dagestan: a Tale of War and Peace

Chechnya and Dagestan share many similarities, but war is not one of them. In autumn 1991, Chechnya declared its independence from the Russian Federation. Moscow fought two wars to prevent Chechnya's secession, losing the first army (1994–96) and currently fighting the other (1999–ongoing). These are by far the bloodiest conflicts in the post-Soviet territories. Dagestan remained within the Russian Federation and its multiethnic society was able to resist war despite the breakup of the Soviet Union and spillovers of other Caucasian wars.

Within the CH set of variables, the most striking differences between Chechnya and Dagestan are, first, that Chechnya possesses considerable oil reserves, whereas Dagestan does not. Second, Dagestan is highly ethnically fractionalized, whereas Chechnya is dominated by Chechens (73 percent) and has a large Russian minority (26 percent). We argue that one of the main factors contributing to stability in Dagestan is its ethnic fractionalization, which has led Dagestani society to develop a set of flexible political institutions that allowed it to respond to the external shock of the collapse of the USSR. Dagestan is a good test case for the CH argument that high ethnic fractionalization *reduces* war risk.

## Background

Chechnya spans over 15,677 km² of rugged terrain. All major settlements (Argun, Gudermes, Shali, Urus-Martan, and the capital Grozny) are in the middle part of Chechnya, between the mountains and northern plains. Most of the fighting has taken place exactly in this middle part, although the rebels have bases in the mountains. Dagestan, to the east, measures 50,300 km². Its northern part, the Caspian basin, is a plain, and mountains cover the southern part.

The population of Chechnya in 1989 was around 836,000. Dagestan's population was 1,802,188. Chechnya derives its name from the titular ethnic group, whereas the term "Dagestan" does not refer to an ethnic group, but only to a territory. More than 30 distinct ethnic groups live there speaking more than 80 languages. The four largest groups are: Avars (28.0 percent of the population), Dargins (15.8 percent), Kumyks (13.1 percent), and Lezgins (11.5 percent). The Soviet policy of ethnic "balancing" involved a careful distribution of the key posts in the administration among these four groups.

Chechnya and Dagestan have always been two of the poorest regions of the Soviet Union and have been heavily subsidized by the center. Already in the 1980s both regions suffered from high unemployment, and in 1991, it was as high as 30 percent (Vasil'eva and Muzaev 1994, 58). Neither region had much industry, while agriculture suffered from a shortage of arable land. However, Chechnya possesses oil reserves, which, however, seem to be dwindling (in 1993, the reserves were estimated to be only 30 million tons) (Holoboff 1995). Dagestan's oil revenues are minuscule: in the 1990s the oil extracted from the Caspian shelf was approximately 300,000 tons per year (Biygishev and Abdullaev 1998).

## Chain of Events: The Dagestan Transition and the Chechen Revolution

During the later days of *perestroika* and *glasnost,* powerful national movements emerged in both Chechnya and Dagestan. In Chechnya, the Congress of the Chechen people was founded in November 1990 and grew into an aggressive nationalist movement led by General Dzokhar Dudaev, declaring independence in June 1991. The coup in Moscow fuelled the revolution in Chechnya. In early September, Dudaev forced the Chechen-Ingush Supreme Soviet, the main bulwark of the Soviet political system, to dissolve. Dudaev and his followers took control of the police and seized a large part of the weapons belonging to the local units of the Soviet troops. On October 27, Dudaev won 90 percent of the vote in presidential elections.

Dagestan also had a movement for national independence. But unlike Chechnya, this movement utilized existing Soviet institutions, mainly the regional parliaments

(Soviets), as a means for mobilization. In April 1991, 39 out of 54 regional Soviets supported a resolution to create a sovereign Dagestan republic, independent from the Russian Federation. National groups that wished to secede from Dagestan dominated the 15 Soviets that opposed this resolution. The political leadership of Dagestan came to understand that the price of secession from the Russian Federation might be the secession of some of the ethnonational groups of Dagestan. From that time on, Dagestan's secession from the Russian Federation was no longer on the political agenda.

The political leadership in Dagestan, largely made up of the former Communist *nomenklatura,* integrated the nationalist challengers. This avoided the escalation of political power struggles—another big difference from Chechnya, Georgia, or Azerbaijan.

Also contributing to stability is the fact that old Communist elites traditionally represented all major clans and ethnic groups. Thus there was no deficit in political representation of ethnic interests and the multinational elite of Dagestan is aware of the importance of maintaining ethnic balance. This was reflected in the new constitution of July 1994, which established a complicated electoral system guaranteeing the fair representation of ethnic groups in parliament and the executive (Ware and Kisriev 2001).

By contrast, Chechnya's new nationalist leaders failed in their state-building efforts. When Chechnya became de facto independent, there was hardly any Chechen state per se. Crime, organized violence, and endemic power struggles destroyed the few remnants of state institutions. President Dudaev grew dependent on armed gangs to retain control and Chechnya became a safe haven for crime.

Why is Chechnya so different from other potential conflicts in the former Soviet Union? Why did the CH risk factors actually result in violence here? A comparison with the Baltic states provides helpful insights. In Estonia, Latvia, and Lithuania, nationalist mobilization was as rapid and widespread as in the Caucasus. All three Baltic nations were deeply traumatized by the Soviet annexation and the consequent Stalinist purges and deportations. There were also massive tensions between the titular nationality and the Russian part of the population, which had grown rapidly because of the influx of a Russian workforce into the industries that were built in the 1960s–70s. It was not hard to predict that ethnic violence would go hand in hand with the Balts' struggles for independence. But it did not.

Three factors may account for the lack of violence in the Baltics. First, the political choices of Baltic elites. In 1988, the *nomenklatura* in all three Baltic republics swiftly abandoned the Communist ideology and formed a de facto coalition with the national-democratic opposition. Although these coalition partners continued to argue about tactical issues, they nevertheless shared a common goal of reestablishing independent and democratic states with market economies. This political choice was facilitated by the fact that all three Baltic nations had memories of a successful period of independence and a market economy before World War II, and there was overwhelming public support for such a transition from the Balts, but also from a clear majority of the Russian population living in the Baltics.

Second, Russia's policy was accommodating. Gorbachev made it clear after the January 1991 clash in Vilnius that he would not use force to discipline breakaway republics. After the coup of August 1991, Yeltsin recognized the Baltic states' independence, making clear Russia was not interested in restoring its empire.

Third, the Baltic states had a clear European option. The prospect of gaining access to the security system and economy of the European Union (EU) facilitated a quick transition to market institutions and tempered the attitudes of nationalist elites, which became much less threatening to the Russian minority. Despite many legitimate grievances, the Russian population has not mobilized against their new Baltic masters.

The strategic coalition of old and new elites, the relatively balanced and cautious Russian policy, and incentives for peaceful economic development were all crucial in keeping the peace in the Baltics. None of these factors existed in Chechnya.

## The First War: 1994–96

In December 1994, more than three years after the declaration of Checnhya's independence, the Russian army invaded Chechnya. Why, and why then? It was first and foremost Russian domestic politics that triggered military action. Yeltsin and his inner circle hoped for domestic political dividends from a short and successful military campaign. Hard-liners in the Kremlin also hoped to gain political capital from a victory.[14] The growth of organized crime in Chechnya was also a source of concern for the Kremlin. Finally, political elites in Russia were afraid of the precedent that Chechnya's secession would set for other potential breakaway territories.

The war turned into a humiliating disaster for the Russian army. The invasion had the effect of unifying the various Chechen factions and population. Thousands of Chechens took up arms and on August 6, 1996, the Chechen forces recaptured Grozny. After 18 months of fighting, 40,000 civilians and 7,500 Russian servicemen were killed and Moscow decided to end the war with the Khasavyurt agreement. The parties agreed to resolve the question of the future status of Chechnya prior to December 31, 2001.

## The Interwar Period

After the Russian withdrawal, parliamentary and presidential elections were held in Chechnya on January 27, 1997. The Organization for Security Cooperation in Europe (OSCE) provided organizational and financial aid and sent election observers. Aslan Maskhadov (the Chechen commander who had signed the Khasavyurt agreement) won 59.3 percent of the vote in the first round, well ahead of the popular field commander Shamil Basaev (25.3 percent) and the incumbent president Yandarbiev (10.1 percent). But, this democratic ritual did not conceal for long the fact that Chechen statehood was virtually absent. After 1996, the state in Chechnya was made up of a coalition of commanders who had been effective in the war, but proved utterly unwilling to establish governance institutions.

Soon, the coalition began to break down. Attempts to make a government out of these armed groups and subordinate them to democratic control failed. Different governmental and administrative branches had control of their own troops. The President had the National Guard and an antiterrorist unit at his disposal; the ministry of State Security commanded the *Sharia* Guard and the so-called Islamic regiment. The National Security Service controlled the border troops. These armed units were in effect the personal armies of their respective field commanders.

Chechen warlords increasingly exploited the market of violence that had emerged in Chechnya during the war. Profits from the extracted oil were supplemented by proceeds from the kidnapping "business" and racketeering, as well as funds which flowed from the diaspora.[15] In postwar Chechnya, the rationales of the key actors were increasingly dominated by short-term economic gains; weak statehood was not only a result of the war, it became an objective of the warlords.

Increasingly, Islamic fundamentalism spread among segments of society and the more radical warlords. Radical Islamism (or *Wahabism,* as it is called in the Caucasus and in Central Asia) was not a cause of the Chechen war, but added to the fragmentation and was used as a tool in the struggle between the warlords and Maskhadov.

In December 1998, a broad coalition of warlords opposed to President Maskhadov formed a state *Shura* (Arabic for consultation or council). This was a consultative body to which the president and the parliament (which were dubbed "un-Islamic institutions") should transfer their powers (Isayev 1998). President Maskhadov, trying to counter this coup d'état by outflanking the opposition, stripped the parliament of its legislative power, called for his own *Shura,* abandoned the constitution, and gave the order to begin working on an "Islamic" constitution ("Dual Power in Chechnya" 1999). In the spring of 1999, the dismantling of the Chechen state was complete: The President and parliament had no power, there was no constitution, no constitutional court, and two opposing *Shuras.*

## The Second War

In this climate of state collapse, in August 1999, several hundred Chechen fighters led by maverick field commanders Basaev and Khattab invaded Dagestan to "liberate" it and unite it with Chechnya to form an Islamic republic. Chechen Islamists encountered fierce resistance from locals, who were supported by the Russian security forces. The Russian army drove the Islamists back into Chechnya, but this action quickly escalated into a large-scale war against Chechnya. The Russian army took this opportunity to reinvade Chechnya with a large force of 100,000 men.

There has been much speculation about the motives of Basaev and Khattab. What is clear is that they overestimated the strength of the Islamic movement in Dagestan. The overwhelming majority of Dagestan's population were against it. They also underestimated the willingness of the Russian army to launch such a massive counteroffensive. Despite these miscalculations, these leaders had rational motives if they are seen in the context of Chechnya's state collapse. The position of warlords is threatened if there is no war; Basaev and Khattab had both built their fortunes through war. Maskhadov's efforts to undercut the influence of warlords threatened Basaev and

Khattab. Furthermore, by mid-1999, Basaev and Khattab had been receiving donations from Islamist fund raisers outside Chechnya. It is plausible that the raid into Dagestan was meant as a "return" on the investment by these financial backers.

## *Organization of Violence*

RECRUITMENT. It is surprising how few men were needed to mount a rebellion. A former police officer and successful entrepreneur of the shadow economy, Bislan Gantenmirov, organized the first paramilitary group in Chechnya. His organization became the core of Dudaev's "National Guard," which in August and September 1991 added muscle to the Chechen revolution. In 1994, just before the Russian attack, this National Guard numbered barely more than 500 men. According to Maskhadov, the chief of staff of the rebels, the total number of trained fighters under his command did not exceed 1,000 when the war started. Only 200 of them, the so-called Abkhazian battalion of Shamil Basaev, had gained combat experience from fighting with the Abkhazians against Georgia (Gall and De Waal 1997, 207). However, the pool of recruits in Chechnya was relatively large. Once the war started, volunteers from every village filled the ranks of the rebels. In January 1995, the rebels already had 5,000–7,000 fighters in town (Gall and De Waal 1997, 208).

The recruitment and financing of permanent units were decentralized. Each field commander recruited his own unit and took care of financing. Nonpermanent units were formed mostly on the basis of village communities and extended families. Most Chechen units were ethnically homogeneous and most fighters knew each other before the war.

Three groups of fighters can be distinguished. First there are the well-equipped, disciplined, and experienced fighters, belonging to the well-known field commanders. Some of these organized groups employ their capacities partially or even predominantly in the gray zone between war economy and organized crime. These groups dispose of sufficient financial resources to fund a long-term guerrilla war. A second group comprises occasional fighters, who join a group for a period of time or form their own small independent unit. The surprising ability of the Chechen rebels to swell their ranks very quickly can be attributed to this group. A third group consists of the self-defense militias, which have been formed in almost every village to protect the inhabitants. In some cases such militias have forbidden the rebels from quartering themselves in their village, lest they provoke Russian retaliatory strikes. With the end of large-scale Russian offensive operations in the spring of 2000, only the first group is still active in fighting.

WEAPONS PROCUREMENT. Chechen rebels looted the armories of the Soviet army. In June 1992 the Russian authorities withdrew their military from Chechnya, leaving behind most of their arms and equipment.[16] Although artillery, tanks, and airplanes were most likely not operational, the Kalashnikovs and RPG-7 (a portable, shoulder-fired rocket-propelled grenade launcher) made the Chechen guerrilla warfare possible.

Finding sources of new arms has been easy. The borders with Georgia and, via Dagestan, with Azerbaijan are porous and the post-Soviet arms markets in those countries are easily accessible. Large quantities of military supplies were acquired from the Russian army, either from Russian garrisons in Georgia and Armenia, or directly from the Russians in Chechnya. Corrupt Russian troops and officers regularly sell weapons to the Chechens. The price of a Kalashnikov from the Russian army starts at US$100; in the summer of 2001 the same weapon was sold for six times that price at the Grozny market.[17] Thus, the presence of the Russian army has reduced the price of weapons!

## Financing of the Rebellion

For obvious reasons, it is impossible to obtain accurate figures on the financing of the Chechen rebellion. Some data have been disseminated by the Russian secret service (FSB), but they must be treated with caution, as the FSB had operational command over the Russian forces in Chechnya for part of the war. The FSB also engages in propaganda. Since 9/11, it has made continuous attempts to link the Chechen rebels with international terrorism, downplaying the Chechen nationalist demands.

According to a popular Russian saying, control over a kilometer of the Russian border suffices to make one a millionaire. Between 1991 and 1993, breakaway Chechnya controlled more than 300 km of the Russian border, making it a profitable "free-trade" zone. From 1991, with de facto independence, Chechnya possessed an international airport and utilized its border with Georgia, which was still fully integrated in the Russian economic zone, to gain access to cheap and exportable Russian natural resources and supplied the Russian consumer goods markets. Chechnya was a key part of the shadow economy and profits from illegal trade financed Dudaev's regime and the war. Chechnya's position as a hub between world markets and Russian markets proved to be extremely lucrative. Consumer goods were imported duty-free via Chechnya, while natural resources and weapons were exported to world markets without any regulation. A class of *biznesmen-patrioty*[18] was created, with deep financial interests in an independent Chechnya, which would be out of the reach of the Russian state, but maintain access to Russian and world markets. For that new entrepreneurial class, a weak Chechen state was also desirable, to allow them freedom in their dealings in the shadow economy.

The oil business also fed the illegal trade in Chechnya. Despite the economic blockade which Russia imposed on Chechnya after 1991, oil continued to flow from Siberia to Chechnya. Officially, 23 million tons were exported via Grozny between 1991 and 1994 (Gall and De Waal 1997, 127), but the real figures are undoubtedly higher. Russian oil barons used Grozny as an outlet for illegally pumping cheap Russian oil onto the world market. Most of these profits returned to Russia, but some remained in Chechnya. Conservative estimates the share of the oil profits in this period at US$300 million. Other sources put it at up to $900 million ("Put Dzhokhara—kuda on privel" 1998).

During and after the first war, the profits from the shadow economy collapsed, and Chechnya adapted to an economy of war. However, local oil production was never completely halted and started up again after the end of the first war in 1996. This was the single most important source of income in interwar Chechnya. A further source of income was the systematic tapping of the pipeline which carried oil through Chechnya to the Russian Black Sea port of Novorossisk. In July 1997 the pipeline management put losses for the first half of the year at 22,000 tons (*Chechnya: The White Paper* 2001).

Another source of income was kidnapping, especially in the interwar period. In fact, since 1996, hundreds of people in Chechnya and in the neighboring republics, especially Dagestan, have been kidnapped. According to the Russian Interior Ministry, from 1994 until 2000 there were 1,811 persons kidnapped in the North Caucasus, most of them in Chechnya.[19] It is worth noting that the Russian army is also involved in this trade. It is common practice for the Russian army to sell the bodies of dead Chechens to their relatives and to obtain ransom for the return of Chechen prisoners.

The most important source of funding for Chechen rebels is both legal and illegal economic activity in Russia. According to statistics of the Main Directorate for the Struggle Against Organized Crime, in 2000, up to 4,000 enterprises in Russia were under the control of so-called ethnic mafias. Chechen diaspora, donating part of their profits to the rebels, controlled a substantial number of these businesses (Borisov 2001, 7). The 300,000-strong Chechen diaspora in Russia supports the struggle for independence with voluntary donations and "war taxes" have been gathered, comparable to taxes raised by the Albanian, Kurdish, and Tamil diasporas to finance the civil war in their homelands. Larger sums of money from abroad began to come in after the first war. Russian intelligence points to a number of source countries: the Arab Emirates, Egypt, Libya, Kuwait, Qatar, Afghanistan and Saudi Arabia, Turkey, and Azerbaijan. According to the FSB, these donations amounted to US$6 million per month for the year 2000.

## Causes of War

Our narrative has suggested that the war over Chechnya was triggered by the Chechen secession and facilitated by state failure in Chechnya. Crime, corruption, and internal power struggles were all highly relevant factors. Other variables in the CH model were also relevant.

Let us consider the CH argument about resource dependence first. Chechnya's economy collapsed when the Soviet Union dissolved. The decline in industrial production in Chechnya in 1992 was 30 percent (Hill 1995, 3) and Chechnya grew dependent on oil extraction and illegal activities (Gall and De Waal 1997, 127). But oil does not explain the initial organization of violence. Oil reserves could have been easily tapped into by corrupt political elites without a civil war. Dudaev did not need to mount a struggle for independence to appropriate profits from Chechnya's mineral wealth. Oil did not create motives for the war.

Likewise, oil cannot explain the Russian intervention. Chechnya's oil yield in 1993 was less than 1 percent of Russia's oil production, so it was of little value to explain such a massive investment in fighting Chechnya's independence. We suggested that Chechnya is important as an oil transit country (between the Caspian oil fields and the Russian export port of Novorossisk). But it would have been easy to choose another transit route. A pipeline circumventing Chechnya was planned in 1996 and was built in 2000–2001 without great difficulties. Thus, the CH model does not apply here. Though in terms of sustaining the war once the war started, we have suggested that oil and other "looting" (i.e., illegal trade, etc.) were a key factor.

Geography also had little impact on the outbreak of violence. During the first war, all the heavy fighting that occurred was aimed at controlling the few larger cities. The decisive battle that ended the first round of the war was the recapturing of Grozny by Chechen rebels in August 1996. However, the existence of mountainous and forest-covered terrain explains the durability of the Chechen resistance. The rebels' fallback positions are in the mountains, a large part of their supplies are delivered via mountain paths, and Chechen units encounter little difficulty crossing the borders into neighboring Georgia, Dagestan, and Ingushetia, where they can supply, regroup, and rest.

Ethnic fractionalization also seems irrelevant. Conflict lines did not occur between the Chechens and the Russians in Chechnya, but between the Russian state and the newly founded secessionist Chechen state. However, the clear ethnic dominance of the Chechens (73 percent) versus the Russian minority (23 percent) significantly reduced the cost for the Chechen revolution, as it provided a source of willing recruits in the first war. The Russian minority never was a political actor, and the masses of the Chechen population supported Dudaev's nationalist aspirations.

The history of violent colonization by the Russian Empire and brutal deportation under Stalin has scarred the Chechens. This has been critical in mobilizing support for the rebellion. It should be noted, however, that the Chechens and Russians had lived after World War II without major clashes in the same state, and that the level of intercommunal violence even after the first Chechen war had begun remained extremely low. The outbreak of the second Chechen war is a textbook example of the hypothesis that violence is likely when the cost of organizing violence is low, because the war stocks and the organizational structures for waging war are still functional. It was the opportunity of an inexpensive war that tempted Chechen warlords to carry the war to Dagestan.

The single most important factor in the Chechen revolution was the rapid demise of the Soviet state. The implosion of the Soviet state cleared Dudaev's way to a swift takeover of power. The minor resistance he met came only from the Soviet parliament (in Chechnya), which was still controlled by the Communist leader Doku Zavgaev. The police, the security forces of the ministry of the interior, the KGB, and the dissolving Soviet army, lacking leadership and having lost the state they served, did not resist. Most of them even handed over their weapons. The Chechen revolution was easy.

The internal fragmentation and state-building failure in Chechnya can be explained by a somewhat different set of factors. First, regime transition in Chechnya occurred through revolution, rather than through evolution. In the Soviet context this is a rather rare exception. In Dagestan, as in most other SSSRs and ASSRs, regime transition was managed by old elites, which used the political institutions of the Soviet Union, most often the parliaments, as a nucleus around which to reconstruct their statehood. In Chechnya, the newcomer Dudaev radically dismantled the old Soviet structures and tried to build a new state from scratch.[20] As a result, Dudaev was dependent on the muscle of his gunmen, many of them criminals with long working experience in the Soviet Chechen mafia, and therefore more interested in short-term economic gains than in state building. In addition, Dudaev played extensively on the theme of the Chechen nation threatened from Russian imperialism, a strategy that proved to be a self-fulfilling prophecy.

Second, the Dudaev regime was mainly financed by semilegal or outright criminal operations, such as the trade of nontaxed goods or the profits made from exporting cheap Russian oil to international markets. A market economy flourished with an interest in keeping the Chechen state weak and keeping Russia away. Diaspora support, donations from Islamic donor organizations, and locally extracted oil also helped fund the war. But Chechen leaders after 1996 were unable to centralize illegal oil profits. Instead everyone tried to grab a piece of the pie. Household refineries became, after 1996, a branch of the economy, in which a number of groups and single households participated in the extraction and trade of oil. After the second Russian invasion, Russian commanders allegedly also shared in the profits from illegally extracted and refined oil. This increased the army's incentive to prolong the war.

Third, competition over oil profits caused factional conflict, which contributed to state failure. The internal fragmentation of Chechen rebels has actually increased the duration of the war. Russia has no negotiating partner, particularly because Russian policy since 1999 has sidelined President Maskhadov. The lack of a central authority and the dependence on the market of violence for illegal profits means that all actors prioritize short-term gain, which makes it harder to think about how to establish a credible long-term solution to the conflict. War entrepreneurs and organized crime gain from a prolonged war.

## Explaining Stability in Dagestan

In sharp contrast to Chechnya's political factionalism and state failure, Dagestan kept its political institutions intact and had substantial elite continuity. It also was not reliant on natural resources. Dagestan's political elite was sustained by transfers from the Russian federal budget, which gave the coalition of ethnopolitical clans in Dagestan incentives to maintain stability.

However, these two factors alone might not have been sufficient to explain Dagestan's stability. Another crucial factor is that in Dagestan, there was a cost to breaking the rules largely because of the region's diversity. Collier and Hoeffler posit two mechanisms for their argument that highly fragmented societies are more stable than homogeneous societies: First, in highly fragmented societies the aspirations of individual groups can be blocked by an alliance among other groups; and second, there is a relatively smaller pool of ethnic recruits for an ethnically based civil war.

Both mechanisms are potentially relevant, but they miss the importance of political institutions that this case brings out. Political institutions can facilitate the formation of coalitions and can foster consensus building. In Dagestan, we cannot understand the effects of ethnic fractionalization without considering the institutional mechanisms that supported such diversity. At the core of Dagestan's stability are two interlocking institutions: the traditional, informal system of the *dzhamaats* (cross-ethnic communities based on neighborhood), and the formal institution of the 1994 Dagestani constitution (Kisriev 2003; Ware et al. 2001).

The Arab term *dzhamaat* denotes in Dagestan a political community within a given territory that usually includes one or several villages. Each *dzhamaat* thus consists of several extended families. The elders of these families form the council of elders of a *dzhamaat*. Russian explorers of the 19th century described the *dzhamaat* as a sort of republic. It is governed by customary (or in many cases also written) law (*adat*), which regulates political, economic, and social affairs. Since *dzhamaats* are based on neighborhood and families, ethnicity is not a significant structuring factor. Owing to ethnic patterns of settlement, in many cases a *dzhamaat* consists of members of only one ethnic group. However, what is important is that in Dagestan the loyalty of the individual, including political loyalty, belongs to the *dzhamaat* rather than to the ethnonational group (Ware et al. 2001). The *dzhamaat* is a concrete solidarity group with internal rules that structure coordination and preferences.

The *dzhamaat* is the traditional *nucleus* of political life in Dagestan. It is the most important political organization and the primary political actor. The *dzhamaat* system can be described as a large number of mostly monoethnic, political entities. They compete with each other at regional or local level for scarce resources (land or votes). This system nurtures stability for two reasons. The *dzhamaats* constitute small, flexible "particles" in the political system, which can rapidly form coalitions if the ethnic balance is threatened. In addition, *dzhamaats* belonging to the same ethnic group often compete with each other. In this way, the emergence of monoethnic coalitions is prevented. Both mechanisms, the built-in "balancing capacity" and the built-in competition within an ethnic group, increase the costs for mobilization of an ethnic group. On account of the built-in balancing effect, a mobilizing group must expect the resistance of a coalition of other groups. The incentive for mobilization weakens correspondingly. The built-in competition within an ethnic group increases the costs of coordination within the entire group. The incentive for mobilization is weakened here as well.

The efficiency of the system of *dzhamaat* was strengthened with the 1994 constitution, which favored the regionalization of politics (Kisriev 2003). Deputies are elected by constituencies in which only one predetermined ethnic group presents candidates but everyone can vote. Thus, by virtue of the strict majority voting system in regional constituencies, there are no ethnic coalitions at the republican (country) level and no pan-Dagestani ethnic parties. Also, intraethnic competition is encouraged in regional constituencies. Because all candidates must belong to the same ethnic group, they have to canvas for voters from other ethnic groups. Under these conditions, the *dzhamaat* is the ideal organizational structure given Dagestan's ethnic composition.

The most important lesson we draw from the case of Dagestan is that we have to consider the interactive effects of informal and formal institutions to understand how political conflicts can be resolved peacefully in multiethnic states.

# Conclusion: Is the CH Model Applicable to the Caucasus?

Each of the Caucasian civil wars shows some uniqueness, but they also share some commonalities. Together, the cases we considered pose challenges for the CH model. All Caucasian cases were related to some degree to the legacies of the Soviet system and were affected by its collapse. This may set those cases apart from other cases of civil war in the CH data set.

Soviet social engineering was successful at creating a secular society with narrow gaps in income distribution and widely available education. Given that these characteristics applied to most Soviet regions and republics, they cannot explain civil wars in the Caucasus and peace in other ex-Soviet regions.

## Ethnic Federalism and National Mobilization

Another legacy of the Soviet Union was the system of ethnofederalism, which provided minority groups with institutions and organizational capacities that made them better able to pursue a struggle for independence. It is not a surprise that all the wars in the Caucasus, with the exception of the power struggle among the Georgian elite, were fought over the status of ethnic homelands. The CH model does not consider nationalism or the institutional incentives for nationalist violence. We have argued that there was a causal link between civil war in South Ossetia, Chechnya, and Abkhazia (also Nagorno Karabakh) and their status as ethnofederal units of the second and third levels under the USSR. However, this is not a complete explanation. Two other cases that we have considered—Adjaria and Dagestan—had the same institutional capacities and ethnofederal legacy, but avoided war. Thus ethnofederalism can turn violent only under some circumstances.

Mark Beissinger, in his seminal work on nationalist mobilization in the Soviet Union (Beissinger 2002), compares the likelihood of violence for 47 ethnic groups within the Soviet Union between 1987 and 1992. Among other variables, he looks into the effect of size of population, relative proportion of population within the ethnoterritorial unit (which broadly fits the CH concept of ethic dominance), extent of urbanization, and linguistic assimilation. He finds support for the hypothesis that ethnofederal units tend to be prone to violence, especially when the percentage of the titular group is high. However, in no case are the results very robust and demonstrably not endogenous (Beissinger 2002, 281).

Which conditions make ethnofederalism a risk for violence during transition? One condition is the interdependencies and power relation between the center and breakaway units. Compare, for example, the breakup of the Soviet Union and Yugoslavia, where during the 1980s the most powerful of the republics, Serbia, tried to usurp the position of the dwindling federal center. This alienated the other republics, which feared Serbian-hegemony. Thus, they intensified their struggle for secession, while the Serbian dominated center tried to hold the federation together by force. When this became apparently impossible, Milosevic tried to secure a "greater Serbia"—at the expense of the territorial integrity of Croatia and later Bosnia-Herzegovina.

By contrast, in the USSR, the most powerful of the republics, Russia, opposed the Soviet center. It was the democratic movement in Russia that prevented the center from holding the Union together by force. Russia was, until 1992, an ally of the secessionist Union Republics. Russia became by far the most powerful of the successor states and had the strength to protect its vital interests, as well as Russian minorities living outside Russia. Russia thus, by and large, avoided ethnopolitical violence within its territory and refrained from major interventions outside its territory. The war in Chechnya is an exception. By contrast, in Yugoslavia, Serbia and Croatia emerged as two states with relatively similar capacities and neither had the means to scare off the other or decisively win, which resulted in the Croatian and Bosnian wars (Koehler and Zürcher 2003a).

The Yugoslavian case resembles Georgia: South Ossetia and Abkhazia both feared rightly that a nationalist, dominant Georgia would curb their privileges. Thus, they opted for independence, which led to war. Likewise, Nagorno-Karabakh feared dominance by Azerbaijan and opted for union with the Republic of Armenia, which full-heartedly supported this move, leading to a war between Azerbaijan and Karabakh.

Another condition that makes ethnofederalism a risk for violence during transition is the degree of institutional cohesiveness in ethnofederal units. Related to this, the demographic balance of the population is critically important, as are elite cleavages and conflict. In Chechnya, nationalist opposition staged a successful revolution against the Communist incumbents, but then destroyed all state institutions. Chechen leadership was factionalized and could not control renegades and this situation was aggravated by an illicit economy that benefited from the absence of statehood. These factors provoked the Russian invasion. In Abkhazia, the demographic structure helps explain why the Abkhaz opted for confrontation: They were a minority within their region, but profited from an overrepresentation in the administration, education, and business. They feared a change of status quo within a nationalizing Georgia and opted for independence.

In contrast, the local elites in Dagestan and Adjaria avoided confrontation. In Dagestan, leaders of the major ethnic groups, aided by Russia, were cautious not to upset a delicate ethnopolitical balance. A low elite turnover and the co-optation of potential challengers resulted in political stability, because the high ethnic fractionalization of that region led to a system that does not reward ethnic competition at the national level.

In Adjaria, stability was achieved by a "gentlemen's agreement" between Georgian leader Shevardnadze and local leader Abashidze. According to this agreement, Adjaria would not challenge Georgia's territorial integrity and would politically support Shevardnadze. In return, Abashidze was given a free hand to consolidate his fiefdom and to use for that the considerable revenues generated by trade from the Batumi port. There were also no tensions between the Adjarian majority and the Georgian minority within Adjaria because Adjarian identity is not ethnically defined. Abashidze thus reigned unchallenged until the fall of Shevardnadze in November 2003.

## State Weakness, Regime Transition, and Democratization

These conditions for stability of ethnofederal units are outside the purview of the CH model. So is the generalized risk of war due to the collapse of the USSR. Defining an operational proxy for state failure is, in our opinion, a task that has still not been satisfactorily resolved by the research community. State failure is certainly not adequately grasped by low GDP. The state was arguably quite strong in all former Soviet Republics before 1988, although their GDP was rather low compared to non-Soviet states. Variables such as democratization or political instability as measured in the quantitative literature on comparative politics (using the Polity scale) do not reflect the rapid deterioration of state capacities throughout the Soviet Union since 1989. In the USSR, rapid democratization went hand in hand with a rapid reduction in state capacity (except for the Baltics).

What actually triggered violence in the Caucasus was not democratization per se, but rather the fact that the new states had miniscule capacities to resolve conflicts and fight back insurgencies. State collapse dramatically reduced the opportunity cost of rebellion. This mechanism was crucial in the rebellions in Chechnya, Abkhazia, and South Ossetia, and it also fueled the power struggle in Georgia. The fact that the Caucasus after 1991 was virtually flooded with weapons from the storehouses of the Soviet army forces further reduced the costs of organizing violence. Democratization is only a problem when it takes place simultaneously with national mobilization and state weakness or state collapse. The democratization of the Soviet Union enabled the expression of national projects and forced the successor states to rebuild their state institutions. Not surprisingly, in the competition over power in the new states, ethnic nationalism proved to be a major asset. Unregulated elite competition and nationalistic outbidding led to a quick erosion of what little statehood was left (especially in Georgia and in Chechnya). Popular elections threatened ethnic minorities, who were also forced to mobilize. Not surprisingly, the Abkhaz and the Ossetians opted for independence and the Armenians of Karabakh opted for union with Armenia.

Thus, what we learn from our cases is that democratization in ethnically mixed environments poses a high risk for violence, when state capacities are low and institutions that guarantee minority representation are not yet in place. This discussion of the effects of state failure relates to commitment problems as explanations of civil war (Fearon 1998). Commitment problems arise when the state or rebels do not believe each other's promises. Corruption, weak institutions, and war economy incentives all exacerbate the problem of credible commitment, because they incite the parties to renege on their promises. The Chechen and Abkhazian wars can be attributed partly to commitment problems. As we have demonstrated, the emergence of war entrepreneurs operating outside the control of the state made it very difficult to negotiate a settlement.

Commitment problems also arise between a minority group and the state, if the state's commitment to provide safety for the group is not credible. In Nagorno Karabakh, the secessionist aspirations of its Armenian population might have been defused by credible guarantees from the Soviet state. Likewise, credible security guarantees to the Ossetians and Abkhaz might have led them to soften their stance on independence. This was, however, impossible in view of the political situation during the transition of 1988–91. Russia was weak and unstable and any guarantees would have to come from the new nationalists in the republics—all of them unlikely sources of credible guarantees to minorities. Abashidze in Adjaria had reasons to trust the security guarantees offered by Shevardnadze who needed his support.

## Loot Seeking

The narrative we have offered suggests that the motivations of organizers of violence in the Caucasus are too complex to be reduced to "greed" or "grievance," or to any simple combination of the two (Collier and Hoeffler 2001). In the case of Chechnya, it was the dramatic change in the incentive and opportunity structure caused by the collapse of the Soviet Union that made possible the nationalist-ideological revolution. In addition to overwhelming support by the public, the revolution was also supported by private economic interests and organized crime. The new elites were unable to build working state institutions, largely because of the sources they had to rely on for their power. Thus, the dismantling of state structures was a crucial factor leading to violence.

In contrast to the consistently strong role of "greedy" war entrepreneurs in Chechnya, "greed" played different roles in Georgia's three wars. The weakest connection to greed is found in the South Ossetian war, in which the "prize" was indeed quite insignificant. The internal struggle for power within Georgia, on the contrary, can be interpreted as entirely greed-driven, with the democratic discourse used as a cover. The Abkhazian war combined greed with nationalist grievance.

Although looting was present in all wars, particularly in the relatively affluent Abkhazia, by and large warfare was not profitable in Georgia and "loot seeking" cannot explain the outbreak of war in Georgia. The strongest connection between the outbreak of war and pure loot seeking was observed in the attack on Sukhumi by the Georgian National Guard in August 1992. However, looting ultimately hurt the war, as it alienated the local population and destroyed the business that the looters wanted to control.

Our analysis indicates that loot seeking increases with the duration of the war. We found that organized violence has a high probability of stabilizing for a certain period as so-called markets of violence become established. Although the core of the conflict may be sociopolitical, the strategic actions of the entrepreneurs of violence are influenced by the need for short-term economic gain. War entrepreneurs engage in activities that combine legal business, organized crime, and warfare. Gradually, short-term economic interests replace long-term political ones, and entrepreneurs of violence become interested in sustaining profit and avoiding battles. Each of the internal wars in the Caucasus, during some period of conflict, can be modeled as profitable quasi-criminal activity.

We agree with the CH model that shifts in opportunity structures have more explanatory value than models that focus on grievances. However, grievances do play a role, in that they explain how social mobilization can take hold. This is especially true if grievance is connected to fear, as in Nagorno-Karabakh. Armenian fears of victimization by Azerbaijanis are connected to the region's history (memories of the Armenian genocide at the hands of "the Turks"). Fear fueled nationalism and was the single most important organizational advantage of the Armenians, lowering the cost of recruitment, disciplining the elites, and encouraging diaspora support (Koehler and Zürcher 2003b).

Such intense fear is rare. More common are fears of political elites or minority groups who want to maintain their privileges. The Ossetians and Abkhaz clearly feared that in a nationalizing Georgia they would lose their privileged access to scarce resources, which had been guaranteed by Soviet-style affirmative action in eth-nofederal policy. The fear of likely future discrimination, together with low opportunity costs, accounts for the national-secessionist mobilization that occurred in Ossetia and Abkhazia.

The insights that we gained from these cases into the importance of natural resources are not easy to generalize. In our cases, including Nagorno-Karabakh and Adjaria, only Chechnya had significant natural resources and there looting was a key source of income for the rebels. Power struggles between rival warlords over oil profits promoted internal fragmentation and hindered state building. In this regard, natural resources proved to be highly relevant for explaining the dynamics of the Chechen war. But we found no evidence that oil caused either the Chechen revolution or the Russia's military response to it and the invasions of 1994 and 1999 (Baev 2003b; Zürcher 1997).

## Terrain

The CH model has identified a significant correlation between mountainous terrain/forest cover and civil wars. Because the Caucasus is a very mountainous region, our cases certainly fit the mold. However, our analytical narratives indicate that there is no causal link between the outbreak of war and these features of physical geography. We found no evidence that mountains facilitated the rebellion. For that matter, Adjaria and Dagestan remained peaceful despite their mountains and forests.

In Chechnya, mountainous terrain has had some impact on war duration, because rebels were able to retreat into the mountains and war supplies were brought in across mountain paths. However, the most decisive fighting has taken place in urban surroundings. Likewise, the character of the terrain did not matter much for the start of the struggle for power in Georgia, because it was concentrated mainly around the capital Tbilisi; it only acquired importance when the western province of Mingrelia became the key theater of action. Terrain was also not particularly relevant in the South Ossetian war, which was fought primarily around the capital Tskhinvali. Finally, the war in Abkhazia was not influenced much by the mountains and forests either, because it was fought primarily in the narrow corridor along the sea, with very little guerrilla activity.

## Ethnic Fractionalization

The level of ethnic fractionalization proved to be of high importance. As predicted by the CH model, high fractionalization reduced the risk of conflict. The highly fractionalized Dagestani society has preserved its stability under extremely difficult circumstances. As we have shown, this stability has depended on formal (first of all, the constitution) and informal (the *dzhamaat*) institutions. This is not to say that Dagestan's stability can be attributed solely to its ethnic composition. Among other factors that contributed to preventing conflict are a high institutional and elite continuity in the post-Soviet period and the successful incorporation of new elites. Subsidies from the Russian federal budget, particularly since 1999, have been an additional incentive for the multinational elite to preserve the status quo.

We also saw that the CH hypothesis that ethnic dominance increases the risk of violence applies to our cases. In Chechnya, Chechen dominance was a necessary condition for the secessionist movement and subsequent national "homogenization" of Chechnya. It is noteworthy that there was never any intercommunal conflict between Chechens and Russians in Chechnya, but after the war the Russian community has shrunk as Russians fled from the war zone. Likewise, ethnic dominance in Georgia influenced the discourse of both the Abkhazian and Ossetian secessionists. But here we have two different types of dominance. In South Ossetia, the Ossetians were the dominant group, mounting a nationalist struggle. In Abkhazia, the Abkhazians were not in the majority and we saw a rebellion by a minority ethnic group with titular status.

## Diaspora and Past Wars

We also presented evidence for the impact of ethnic diasporas, but we had to relax the CH definition of a diaspora. We considered Chechens living outside Chechnya, but still within the Russian Federation, as a diaspora. We have also treated the Ossetians living in North Ossetia as a diaspora. The more broadly we define this term, the more diasporas appear to be relevant in explaining war duration, but not in explaining onset. In the cases of Chechnya, Ossetia, and Abkhazia (and also Nagorno-Karabakh), the diaspora provided substantial help in terms of volunteers and finance. Support took the form of donations from households, voluntary war taxes, and profits from the legal or illegal businesses of entrepreneurs operating in the Russian economic space or abroad. However, diasporas were clearly mobilized only after the wars had started.

Finally, the CH model considers past wars as a risk factor. We find support for this in Chechnya, but not in Georgia. There were exactly three years between the end of the first Chechen war (August 1996) and the outbreak of the second one (August 1999). Past conflict operated not through generating desires for vengeance, but by increasing war-specific capital in the region. Georgia had no history of civil war prior to the 1990s and has managed to remain relatively peaceful since 1994. The struggle for power at the state level in Georgia was certainly intricately connected with both wars in South Ossetia and Abkhazia and the war in Abkhazia started just two months after the war in South Ossetia came to the end. But the CH model cannot capture these complex temporal and spatial interdependencies.

Overall, the wars in the Caucasus support the main insights of the CH model, but also suggest ways to expand and revise the model. Research focused on the interplay between their political economy and institutional setting is ultimately more promising than analysis focused on historical grievances, ethnic incompatibilities, and conspiracy theories.

# Notes

We gratefully acknowledge the cooperation of our colleagues in the Caucasus in the difficult task of gathering the data: in Armenia, Gayane Novikova, Center for Strategic Analysis, Yerevan; in Azerbaijan, Arif Yunusov, Institute of Peace and Democracy, Baku; in Georgia, Georgi Nizheradze, ICCN, Tbilisi, and Gia Zirakishvili, GRID Geoinformation, Tbilisi. The comments of Jonathan Wheatley and two anonymous referees helped us in revising our earlier drafts.

1. For example, even CIA experts could not measure the size of the USSR's economy (see http://www.foia.cia.gov/princeton_intelligence.asp). Anders Åslund (2001, 20) suggested that estimates of Soviet GDP should be cut by at least 20 percent because of the production of unmarketable final goods.

2. The main source of data for this study was the articles on "Georgia" in *Eastern Europe and the Commonwealth of Independent States* (1994, 1997, 1999) and *Eastern Europe, Russian and Central Asia* (2001, 2003). For the economy, these were supplemented by World Bank data from "Georgia Data Profile" (http://devdata.worldbank.org/external/CPProfile.asp?SelectedCountry=GEO&CCODE=GEO&CNAME=Georgia&PTYPE=CP).

3. It should be pointed out that the Adjarians are not counted as a separate ethnic group. The ethnic diversity is accentuated by the language gap: the Georgian, Abkhazian, and Ossetian languages (as well as Armenian and Azeri) belong to different families, so in the 1990s the Russian language still played the role of *lingua franca*.

4. One estimate of the "underground economy" based on electricity consumption (Åslund 2002, 123) puts it at 24.9 percent of official Georgia's GDP in 1990 (higher than in other republics). But most of Georgia's shadow economy was in agriculture, trade, and tourism (i.e., sectors that cannot be measured by this indicator).

5. On the Georgian wars, see Baev 2003a, Cohen 1999, Herzig 1999, Nodia 1996, Ozhiganov 1997, and Zverev 1996.

6. It is essential to emphasize that it was not the intervention from Russia that terminated the fighting; Russian peacekeepers constituted a symbolic force not even backed by any military grouping. Throughout the war, the 34th Army Corps of Soviet/Russian Armed Forces based in Georgia remained "neutral" and did not perform a single operation either toward South Ossetia or in the struggle for power in Georgia.

7. Adjaria has a relatively large population (380,000), but Adjarians were never officially recognized, perhaps because of religious differences (the Christian-Muslim divide). An insightful comparison of the Adjarian and Abkhazian cases is discussed in Derluguian (1995).

8. In 1993, in the vicinity of the zones of conflict, an AK-47 assault rifle was offered for US$100; in Tbilisi, volunteers for the Abkhazian war had to pay $200.

9. That delivery was a result of the formal agreement between Soviet successor states on dividing the USSR's limit on heavy armaments as fixed in the CFE treaty; details of this intrigue can be found in Baev (1996, 81–90).

10. In neither of these wars did Russia have a consistent and comprehensible position, but the zigzags in its policy were often interpreted in the region as maneuvers in a complicated strategy. The legacy of Russia's interference in Georgia's wars is linked directly to the fact that in 2002–2004 Georgia was the only country with which Moscow had conflictual and at times hostile relations (Baev 2002).

11. In the initial stage of the Nagorno-Karabakh (NK) conflict, Armenia played a similar role in helping Armenians in NK.

12. The connection between Chechnya and Abkhazia had been strong only before the start of the Chechen war. Since the early 2000s, some Chechen groups have turned against Abkhazia. There was also an implicit link between the war in South Ossetia and the clash between North Ossetia and Ingushetiya in the Prigorodny district in October–November 1992; although that violence occurred after the war, it involved Ossetian refugees from Georgia (Osipova 1997).

13. Conceptualization of this factor remains ambivalent. Although the explanation that political power in that fledgling democracy was sufficiently consolidated to make it a prize worth fighting for (as developed by Hegre et al. 2001) appears sound, it is also possible to make an argument about the endogenous nature of the relationship between institutional inconsistency, political instability, and civil war (Gates et al. 2001).

14. See Gall and De Waal (1997), Lieven (1998, 86), McFaul (1995, 149–166), Zürcher (1997).

15. Around 230,000 Chechens lived in Moscow, Petersburg and other parts of Russia. We treat them in the same way that Collier and Hoeffler treat a diaspora in foreign countries.

16. This included, according to semiofficial estimates: 42 tanks (T-62M and T-72); 66 armored combat vehicles (ACVs), BMP-1, BMP-2, BTP-70, BRDM-2; 30 122-mm towed howitzers D-30; 58 120-mm PM-38 mortars; 18 B-21 Grad MRLs; 523 RPG-7 antitank grenade launchers and 77 ATGW (Concurs, Fagot, and Metis); 18,832 AK-74, 9307 AK-47 (AKM); 533 sniper rifles; 1,160 machine guns; 4 ZCU-23-4 Shilka, 6 ZU-23 and an unspecified number of Igla portable SAMs; 152 Czech-made L-39 trainer-bomber jets and 94 L-29s; several Mig-15, Mig-17, and An-2 airplanes; and 2 Mi-8 helicopters (Felgenhauer 1995).

17. This is based on our observation from Grozny, September 1996. See also Lagnado (2000), cited according to *Johnson's Russia List* #4069, January 26, 2000; Gall and De Waal (1997, 192) put the price of an AK-74 on the market in Grozny at US$600 before the war and US$200 during the war.

18. This is a term coined by Emir Kusturica in his post-Socialist Balkan movie "Black Cat, White Cat." The term denotes a social class that emerged all over the socialist region in the late 1980s. This class was extremely successful at combining the two key resources of post-socialist areas, nationalism and shadow entrepreneurship.

19. These figures were given in the memo from Russia's Interior Ministry, "On the State of Struggle Against Kidnapping and Hostage Taking in the North Caucasian Region." Quoted from: *Chechnya: The White Paper* 2001.

20. There are sociocultural reasons for the Chechen preference for revolution over evolution. Among these are the superficial institutionalization of the Soviet system, a lack of a Soviet (Chechen) national elite, and a widespread, traditional Chechen mistrust of state structures in general.

# References

Åslund, Anders. 2001. "Russia." *Foreign Policy* July/August: 20–25.

———. 2002. *Building Capitalism: The Transformation of the Former Soviet Bloc.* Cambridge, MA: Cambridge University Press.

Aves, Jonathan. 1996. *Georgia: From Chaos to Stability?* London: Chameleon Press.

Baev, Pavel K. 1996. *The Russian Army in a Time of Troubles.* London: SAGE.

———. 2002. "Russia's Virtual War Against Georgia: Risks of a PR Offensive." *PONARS Report 251.* Washington, DC: CSIS.

———. 2003a. "Civil Wars in Georgia: Corruption Breeds Violence." In *Potentials of (Dis)Order: Explaining Violence in the Caucasus and in the Balkan,* ed. J. Koehler and C. Zürcher, 127–45. Manchester: Manchester University Press.

———. 2003b. "Examining the 'Terrorism-War' Dichotomy in the 'Russia-Chechnya' Case." *Contemporary Security Policy* 24 (2): 29–46.

Baranovsky, Vladimir. 1994. "Conflict Developments on the Territory of the Former Soviet Union." In *SIPRI Yearbook 1994,* 169–203. Oxford: OUP for SIPRI.

Beissinger, Mark R. 2002. *Nationalist Mobilization and the Collapse of the Soviet State.* Cambridge: Cambridge University Press.

Biygishev, Marat, and Nabi Abdullaev. 1998. "Dagestan Holds Tender for Exploration of Caspian Shelf." *IEWS Russian Regional Report 02.07.1998,* 3: 26, Internet Edition.

Borisov, Timofey. 2001. "Na chi dengi voyuyut chechnskie boeviki? [With what money are the Chechen fighters fighting?]." *Rossiyskaya Gazeta,* June 16 (in cooperation with the Main Directorate for the Struggle against Organized Crime and the Press Service of the FSB).

Bunce, Valerie. 1999. *Subversive Institutions. The Design and the Destruction of Socialism and the State.* Cambridge: Cambridge University Press.

*Chechnya: The White Paper.* 2001. Second edition. Moscow: Russian Information Centre and RIA Novosti. http://www.infocentre.ru/eng_user/index.cfm?page=10 (accessed September 14, 2001).

Cohen, Jonathan (ed.). 1999. *A Question of Sovereignty: The Georgia-Abkhazia Peace Process,* Accord 7. London: Reconciliation Resources.

Collier, Paul, and Anke Hoeffler. 2001. "Greed and Grievance in Civil War" (Revised Version-October 2001), DECRG Project Paper. http://www.worldbank.org/research/conflict/papers/greedandgrievance.htm (accessed May 14, 2002).

Derluguian, Georgi. 1995. "The Tale of Two Resorts: Abkhazia and Ajaria Before and Since the Soviet Collapse." Working Paper of the UC Berkley Center for German and East European Studies, 6 (2).

———. 2004. *Georgia's Return of the King.* Working Paper 22, Center for Security and International Studies, Washington, DC, February.

"Dual Power in Chechnya?" 1999. *RFE/RL Caucasus Report,* February 9, 2 (6).

Elwert, Georg. 2003. "Intervention in Markets of Violence." In *Potentials of (Dis)Order: Explaining Violence in the Caucasus and in the Balkan,* ed. J. Koehler and C. Zürcher, 219–43. Manchester: Manchester University Press.

Fearon, J. D. (1998). "Commitment Problems and the Spread of Ethnic Conflict." In *The International Spread of Ethnic Conflict, Fear Diffusion, and Escalation,* ed. D. A. Lake and D. Rothchild, 107–27. Princeton, NJ: Princeton University Press.

Felgenhauer, Pavel. 1995. "The Chechen Campaign." In Proceedings of a conference sponsored by the Department of National Security Affairs, Naval Postgraduate School Monterey, CA, November 7–8. http://nsa.nps.navy.mil/Publications/Tsypkin/Chechnya/fel.html (accessed February 26, 2002).

Fuller, Elizabeth. 1993. "Paramilitary Forces Dominate Fighting in Transcaucasus." *RFE/RL Research Report* 2 (25): June 18, 74–82.

Gall, Carlotta, and Thomas De Waal. 1997. *Chechnya: A Small Victorious War.* London and Basingstoke: Pan Original.

Gates, Scott, Hegre Håvard, M. P. Jones, and Strand Håvard. 2001. "Institutional Inconsistency and Political Instability: Persistence and Change in Political Systems Revisited, 1800–1998." Paper presented at the annual meeting of International Studies Association, Chicago, February 20–21.

"Georgia." 1994. In *Eastern Europe and the Commonwealth of Independent States,* 305–22. London: Europa Publications.

———. 1997. In *Eastern Europe and the Commonwealth of Independent States,* 343–64. London: Europa Publications.

———. 1999. In *Eastern Europe and the Commonwealth of Independent States,* 353–73. London: Europa Publications.

———. 2001. In *Eastern Europe, Russia and Central Asia 2002,* 166–94. London: Europa Publications.

———. 2003. In *Eastern Europe, Russia and Central Asia 2004,* 175–210. London: Europa Publications.

Gurr, Ted R., Barbara Harff, and Monty G. Marshall. 1997. *Codebook: Internal Wars and Failures of Governance, 1954–1996.* State Failure Task Force. http://www.bsos.umd.edu/cidcm/stfail/index.htm (accessed March 12, 2001).

Hegre, Håvard, Tanja Ellingsen, Scott Gates, and Nils Petter Gleditsch. 2001. "Toward a Democratic Civil Peace? Democracy, Political Change, and Civil War, 1816–1992." *American Political Science Review* 95: 33–48.

Herzig, Edmund. 1999. *The New Caucasus: Armenia, Azerbaijan and Georgia.* London: The Royal Institute for International Affairs.

Hill, Fiona. 1995. *Russia's Tinderbox: Conflict in the North Caucasus and Its Implications for the Future of the Russian Federation.* Report of the Strengthening Democratic Institutions Project. Boston: Harvard University.

Holoboff, Elaine. 1995. "Oil and the Battle of Grozny." *Jane's Intelligence Review* 7 (6): 253–57.

Isayev, Said. 1998. "Opposed Chechen MPs 130 to Debate ARSANOV'S Motion on New Body." *Itar Tass,* December 21.

Kisriev, Enver. 2003. "Why Is Dagestan Stable and Chechnya Not?" In *Potentials of (Dis)Order: Explaining Violence in the Caucasus and in the Balkan,* ed. J. Koehler and C. Zürcher, 103–27. Manchester: Manchester University Press.

Koehler, Jan, and Christoph Zürcher. 2003a. "The Art of Losing the State: From Weak Empire to Weak Nation State Around Nagorno-Karabakh." In *Potentials of (Dis)Order: Explaining Violence in the Caucasus and in the Balkan,* ed. J. Koehler and C. Zürcher, 145–74. Manchester: Manchester University Press.

Koehler, Jan, and Christoph Zürcher (eds). 2003b. *Potentials of (Dis)Order: Explaining Violence in the Caucasus and in the Balkan.* Manchester: Manchester University Press.

Lagnado, Alice. 2000. "Russians Try to Bar Rebels' Escape Route." *The Times,* January 26.

Lieven, Anatol. 1998. *Chechnya: Tombstone of Russian Power.* New Haven and London: Yale University Press.

McFaul, Michael. 1995. "Eurasia Letter: Russian Politics After Chechnya." *Foreign Policy* 99 (Summer): 149–66.

Mitchell, Lincoln. 2004. "Georgia's Rose Revolution." *Current History* 103 (675): 342–48.

Nodia, Ghia. 1996. "Political Turmoil in Georgia and the Ethnic Policies of Zviad Gamsakhurdia." In *Contested Borders in the Caucasus,* ed. B. Coppieters, 70–90. Brussels: VUB University Press.

Novikov, Vladimir. 2004. "Presidential Campaign in Abkhazia Evolves into a Civil War." *Kommersant,* October 13.

Osipova, Olga. 1997. "North Ossetia and Ingushetia: The First Clash." In *Managing Conflict in the Former Soviet Union,* ed. A. Arbatov, A. Chayes, and A. J. Chayes, 27–76. Cambridge, MA: MIT Press.

Ozhiganov, Edward. 1997. "The Republic of Georgia: Conflicts in Abkhazia and South Ossetia." In *Managing Conflict in the Former Soviet Union,* ed. A. Arbatov, A. Chayes, and A. Handler Chayes, 341–400. Cambridge, MA: MIT Press.

"Put Dzhokhara—kuda on privel? (The path of Dzhokhar—where did it lead to?)." 1998. *Trud,* December 8.

Solnick, Steven L. 1998. *Stealing the State: Control and Collapse in Soviet Institutions.* Cambridge, MA: Harvard University Press.

Vasil'eva, Ol'ga, and Timur Muzaev. 1994. *Severnii Kavkaz v poiskakh regional'noi ideologii (The North Caucasus in Search of a Regional Ideology).* Moscow: Progress.

Ware, R. Bruce, and Enver Kisriev. 2001. "Ethnic Parity and Political Stability in Dagestan: A Consociational Approach." *Europe and Asia Studies* 53 (1): 105–33.

Ware, R. Bruce, Enver Kisriev, Werner J. Patzelt, et al. 2001. "Democratization in Dagestan." Paper presented at the Annual Meeting of the American Political Science Association, San Francisco, CA, September 1.

Zürcher, Christoph. 1997. "Krieg und Frieden in Tschetschenien: Ursachen, Symbole, Interessen." *Arbeitspapiere des Osteuropa-Instituts der Freien Universität Berlin:* 2, http://user-page.fu-berlin.de/~segbers/wp/wp.htm (accessed February 15, 2002).

Zverev, Alexei. 1996. "Ethnic Conflicts in the Caucasus 1988–1994." In *Contested Borders in the Caucasus,* ed. B. Coppieters, 13–72. Brussels: VUB University Press.

# Conclusion

## Using Case Studies to Refine and Expand the Theory of Civil War

# 10

NICHOLAS SAMBANIS

T he previous chapters have offered rich historical narratives of civil war onset and avoidance, explaining the organization of rebellion and analyzing the dynamics of violence in several countries. They have evaluated the fit between the cases and the core economic model of civil war that we used to structure each case. In this chapter, I try to synthesize the many lessons and insights that we can draw from the cases. I use those insights to suggest possible revisions and refinements to the Collier-Hoeffler (CH) model and to identify a number of ways in which we can expand the theory of civil war.

## Measurement and Theory Refinement

One of the main functions of the case study project was to analyze the usefulness of empirical proxies used in the quantitative analysis of civil war. Many of our cases suggest better ways to code explanatory variables so that there is a closer connection between the theoretically significant variables in the CH model and the proxies used in empirical testing. Improving the selection and coding of such proxies can reduce the uncertainty associated with our causal inferences from the CH model.[1]

## Have We Coded All the Wars and Can We Predict Their Occurrence?

One source of measurement error is lack of clarity in the definition of civil war and difficulties in coding war onset and termination (see Sambanis 2004b).[2] Some of the case studies in our project suggest revisions to the CH list of civil wars. Accurate coding of the dependent variable should improve the accuracy of the model's predictions.

Many of the predictions of the CH model seem accurate: some of the country-years (five-year periods) with the highest estimated risk of civil war were actually periods when war occurred (e.g., the Democratic Republic of Congo [DRC]/Zaire in 1995–99). The tables with statistical results included in the introduction can be used to make predictions for the cases included in our project. Case study authors have looked at those predictions to figure out if the model "fits" their case. By looking at "wrong" predictions, we can explore if and how problems with the measurement of the dependent variable reduce the predictive accuracy of the CH model.

There are several problems with the model and the data. First, the CH data set sometimes codes no war in country-periods in which the cases indicate that a war did occur. Thus, if the model predicted a high risk of civil war in that country-period, then we would think that the prediction was wrong, when it was in fact accurate. This seems to be the case in Burundi in 1965–69.

Second, it is frequently the case that country-periods that are coded as being "at peace" are in fact experiencing significant political violence that does not meet the definition of civil war. In those cases, if the predicted probability of civil war in the CH model is high, the model would appear to be making an inaccurate prediction, when in fact it is correctly predicting the occurrence of political violence. The model cannot distinguish between predictions of civil war and predictions of other violence, because the theory underlying the CH model could potentially apply to lower-level insurgencies, terrorism, coups, and other violence, including organized crime. I return to this point later and argue that we need to develop a model that attempts to explain the organization of violence into different forms and the transition from one form to the other.

Third, the flipside of the problem that I just raised is that several cases of civil war in the CH data set are not necessarily civil wars. For example, both the death toll in Romania in 1989 and the level of organization of the opposition do not meet the CH definition of civil war. Several other cases of war in the CH data set are coded in countries that were not yet sovereign states, like Angola before 1975 or Guinea-Bissau in the 1970s. These are better characterized as extra-state wars or civil wars in the territory of the colonial metropole.[3]

Classifying an armed conflict as a civil war is not straightforward. Ross (volume 2, chapter 2), for example, argues that Indonesia has had only one civil war with two phases (Aceh in 1990–91 and 1999). This war is not coded in the CH data set. Other armed conflicts in Indonesia that are often considered civil wars in commonly used data sets are not classified as civil wars according to Ross (e.g., East Timor, 1975–99). Similarly, Collier and Hoeffler do not code a civil war in several of the countries in which chapter authors argue that a civil war has occurred (e.g., in Senegal and the United Kingdom). Case studies can help us establish with greater certainty if an armed conflict meets the definition of civil war.

The lack of many time-sensitive variables in the CH model, combined with errors in coding the dependent variable, may result in poor predictions of civil war risk because of the overwhelming importance of the "peace-time" variable in the model. (Remember that, the longer a country has been at peace, the lower is its estimated risk of a new war.) In Burundi, the fact that Collier and Hoeffler do not code a civil war in 1965 leads them to underestimate the risk of a civil war just before war broke out in 1972. In Algeria, the predicted probability of civil war is heavily influenced by the peace-time variable and declines steadily from 45 percent in 1965 (high because of the proximity of the postindependence strife in 1962) to 30 percent in 1975, and 17 percent in 1990. Although at 17 percent this point estimate is almost three times the population average (0.067, with a standard deviation of .08), the model still produces a declining trend in the risk of civil war in Algeria and war actually occurred in a period of relatively low risk (as compared to previous periods).

The CH model cannot make accurate predictions of the timing of civil war onset and this is partly due to coding errors in the data. A case that illustrates this point is the DRC. The fact that several wars in the DRC are not coded in the CH data set (e.g., the Kisangani mutiny of 1967 and the Shabba wars of 1977–78) decreases the accuracy of probability estimates derived from the model (the standard errors of point estimates will be very large). Collier and Hoeffler predicted probabilities of civil war for the Congo ranging from 8 percent for 1975–79 to 77 percent for 1995–99. At 8 percent the estimated risk of civil war is only marginally higher than the mean risk for the population (but it is within the bounds of the confidence interval for the average probability). These estimates for the DRC should have been much higher: The DRC has lower income, lower growth, higher dependence on natural resources, and a larger and more highly dispersed population—all of which increase war risk. What pulls probability estimates downward is the peace-time variable, which is coded with error in this case.

In Nigeria, the model runs into similar problems. We have both false-positive and false-negative predictions in this case. The model predicts a high risk of civil war in the 1990s, when a war did not occur. The economy was deteriorating and oil production was declining, while expansion of the oil pipeline allowed even more regions to claim a piece of the oil resources. But, although the model is technically incorrect here, it does capture something important, given that several episodes of intercommunal fighting have caused thousands of deaths in that period (Zinn, volume 1, chapter 4). What distinguishes these events from civil war is that the state was generally not involved directly in the fighting and the death toll was sometimes low in individual events. Thus, the model actually predicts violence accurately; and part of the problem with predicting war is related to the rather arbitrary ways we distinguish civil war from other political violence. Zinn (volume 1, chapter 4) identifies up to 60 violent conflicts in Nigeria from 1985 to 1989, during a time when the country is coded as being "at peace" in the CH data set. The operationalization of the peace-time variable in the CH model (years at peace since the previous war) does not allow us to capture the consequences of such ethnic violence and turmoil in Nigeria. If a different version of "peace time" is coded that can capture the history of all organized domestic political violence, the model's predictions of war onset in Nigeria and other countries should improve.

## *Economic Variables: Gross Domestic Product, Growth, and Education*

The key proxies used to test the CH opportunity cost hypothesis are gross domestic product (GDP) per capita, secondary education, and economic growth. Collier and Hoeffler find that high values of these variables reduce the risk of civil war.

Consistent with this result, many countries included in our project had low and declining income and low education levels in the years leading up to the war. Although the CH hypothesis is consistent with these cases, there can be different ways to interpret the association between civil war and these economic variables. The case studies help us sort out the mechanisms underlying this correlation.

GDP per capita is also a proxy for Fearon and Laitin's (2003) state weakness hypothesis, and they argue that state weakness leads to civil war. If this measure (GDP) can be used as a proxy for two competing hypotheses, then we cannot easily distinguish among these hypotheses with statistical analysis. Given the lack of clarity about what exactly GDP measures, one wonders why we do not use more direct measures of the potential rebel supply (which should be affected by the opportunity cost of violence in a metaphorical "labor market" for insurgents). Unemployment, especially among young men, should be a better measure of potential rebel supply. In Mali and Senegal, local unemployment was greater in Azawad and Casamance—the two regions where the insurgency took place (Humphreys and ag Mohamed, volume 1, chapter 9). In prewar Yugoslavia, while income per capita was two or three times the average for civil war countries (thereby lowering estimates of relative risk in Yugoslavia), unemployment had surged and in some regions reached 40 percent of the adult population (Kalyvas and Sambanis, volume 2, chapter 7).

Turning to education, our case studies suggest that the relationship between schooling and war are complex and might vary across regions. While African cases seem broadly consistent with the CH hypothesis that low secondary school enrollment is found in countries with civil war, Eastern European and Middle Eastern cases pose a problem for the hypothesis. There, high levels of education are found in civil war countries (e.g., Yugoslavia, Georgia, Russia, Lebanon). Lebanon's civil war was among the longest in the region, but its education levels are also among the highest in the Arab world with a 60 percent adult literacy rate (Makdisi and Sadaka, volume 2, chapter 3). In Saudi Arabia, by contrast, the secondary schooling rate was low (4 percent), but there was no civil war.

What is missing here is an explanation of *how* schooling influences civil war risk. The CH interpretation is that schooling increases the opportunity costs of violence because educated people face higher economic opportunity costs if they join a rebellion. Although this seems like a reasonable argument, it does not consider interactive effects: How do educated people behave if the political economy of their countries does not provide them with opportunities for productive activity? The case studies of civil wars in Lebanon or in countries in the Caucasus pose particular problems for this argument. In those countries, the curriculum has been the primary mechanism of inculcating children with nationalist ideology, and education may, therefore, encourage violence. It is not surprising that this mechanism is absent from Collier and Hoeffler's thinking about schooling, because nationalism plays no role in the CH model and is dismissed as rhetoric. But others (Darden 2002) show that there is a close correlation between nationalist education and the persistence of nationalist ideology. Darden's argument about the galvanizing effect of mass schooling in forging and hardening a national identity that can be used to mobilize support for conflict—

including violent conflict—can go a long way toward explaining cases such as Lebanon, where education was as sectarian as the country's politics. (The flipside of this argument is that a strong and widespread national identity can dampen support for secession and violence against the state.)

Several of the case studies are consistent with the CH argument that economic growth, the third proxy for the opportunity cost model, reduces the risk of civil war. Growth was negative before a war started in Senegal, Mali, Bosnia, Azerbaijan, and other countries among our cases. However, this relationship, too, may be complicated with potentially two-way causal effects. First, something that all quantitative studies miss is that low-level violence typically precedes civil war and this should reduce both income and growth by reducing investment and encouraging capital flight. Second, once violence reaches the level of civil war, it further undermines economic activity, reducing growth. Civil wars in the Caucasus caused massive drops in income (Zürcher, Baev, and Koehler, volume 2, chapter 9), as they did in the DRC, Burundi, and in all countries with recurrent or long wars. If some of the decline in growth is influenced by previous values of the dependent variable (war), then we have a feedback effect that has not yet been properly modeled in empirical tests of the CH model or other studies.

Third, in some cases, rapid growth may actually increase the risk of civil war. In Lebanon, growth averaged 7.5 percent for the 1950s, 6–6.6 percent for the 1960s; and 7 percent for 1970–74 (Makdisi and Sadaka, volume 2, chapter 3). In Indonesia, rapid growth indirectly reinvigorated the Acehenese rebel movement (GAM) because it led to the expansion of the extractive resource industry and an increase in the number of migrants, leading to land seizures in Aceh (Ross, volume 2, chapter 2). Thus, while it was not growth per se that increased the risk of war, there seems to have been a positive correlation between growth and war in Aceh, as a result of government policies during high-growth periods. The government aimed at increasing migration into Aceh and its policies favored migrants at the expense of the autochthonous population. This is a mechanism that increases the potential for violence. But migration was part of a deliberate government policy of repression. So, without placing migration in the context of a deliberate policy of repression, it is hard to argue that migration *caused* the violence any more than high economic growth did.

The difficulties associated with distinguishing between rival mechanisms on the basis of limited quantitative results are becoming clearer. Consider what the CH model would predict as a result of declining income per capita. If the opportunity cost argument is correct, then the risk of civil war should increase. But, if we had interpreted GDP per capita as a measure of state strength, as Fearon and Laitin (2003) do, then the same empirical result would have led us to different inferences that support a different theory. Indeed, several of our case studies seem to support the hypothesis that state strength reduces the risk of war. Woodwell's (volume 2, chapter 6) study of the war in Northern Ireland is explicit in arguing that the violence there stayed protracted, but of low intensity, largely because it was taking place in a highly developed country.[4] The "Troubles" and their aftermath were the worst political violence in Western Europe, causing 3,281 deaths and dozens of thousands of injured (Smith 1999).[5] According to Woodwell, part of the reason that the conflict did not escalate into a larger war had to do with the strength of the British state, which forced the insurgents from the "Troubles" of 1969 until 1994 into a strategy of low-level urban violence and terrorism.[6]

Woodwell is explicit in his discussion of the strength of the British army, which deterred conflict escalation. (The strength of the army as a measure of state strength is not something that either Collier and Hoeffler or Fearon and Laitin explore in their studies.) What this explanation probably leaves out is the role of civil society and public opinion in the United Kingdom and neighboring Ireland. A more intense war campaign by the IRA and a more decisive response from the British army could have backfired, causing protest from civil society institutions. In an established democracy like Britain, war-fighting tactics like the ones that Russia has used in the second Chechen war (e.g., bombing Chechnya's capital, Grozny) are not viable— indeed they are unthinkable. In other words, the state strength argument may be conflated with the liberal-democratic characteristics of the British state.[7]

An example that helps disentangle the complicated relationship between GDP and state strength is Kenya, because there we have a weak economy and a strong authoritarian state (strong in terms of the state's penetration of society and its ability to defend itself against challenges). The absence of war in Kenya may be a consequence of the state's strength (Kimenyi and Ndung'u, volume 1, chapter 5). Despite intense ethnic antagonisms, electoral violence, and a coup attempt in August 1982, no civil war has occurred in Kenya.[8] However, in this case GDP per capita is low. The state has exercised control over Kenyan territory through corruption. Local police violently repress those opposition groups that could not be bought off with gifts of public land. The problem here is that a low GDP is not a good measure of the Kenyan state's capacity to prevent a civil war. Although the case study helps identify this problem, it introduces another: We now cannot distinguish between the effects of state strength and the consequences of weak civil society institutions. Clearly, to sort out the relative significance of these explanations, we must return to large-$N$ data analysis. But case studies help us identify plausible candidates for large-$N$ analysis.

On the whole, the cases support the CH hypothesis about the negative association between economic development and civil war onset. But they also indicate that the CH model does less well in proposing theoretically consistent mechanisms that explain these correlations.

## Natural Resources

The resource predation hypothesis is central to the CH model, which argues that looting of natural resources is a way in which rebels can finance their insurgency. This is certainly a plausible argument, and it seems to apply well to several cases. But some cases do highlight problems both with the argument and the empirical measures used to test it. First, the CH model is unclear if resource predation is a motive for violence, and it cannot distinguish between looting as a motive and looting as a means to sustain rebellion. Second, empirical tests of the hypothesis are weakened by the fact that Collier and Hoeffler measure resource dependence as the ratio of primary commodity exports over GDP. Using this very broad measure, they find that the risk of civil war onset is maximized when the share of primary commodity exports to GDP is around 25–32 percent.

Although this is a useful result, it is obvious that the proxy includes agricultural commodities that are not easily looted unless the rebels gain control of the state. Some case studies suggest that the correlation between dependence on primary commodities and civil war may be spurious. In several resource-dependent countries with civil wars (e.g., Nigeria, Mali, Senegal, Azerbaijan), the occurrence of civil war seems to justify the CH model's predictions, but the narratives in this volume show that those natural resources were neither a motive for the war nor a means to sustain rebellion. (In the case of the Biafran rebellion, the prospect of control of oil reserves might have been a factor, according to Zinn, but it was not in the Maitatsine rebellion.) A more targeted test of the resource predation hypothesis would, first, disaggregate the components of the primary commodity exports, focusing on easily lootable resources,[9] and, second, establish whether the civil war actually took place in resource-rich regions. Most of our case studies suggest that primary commodity exports do not influence decision making about civil war onset, though many cases did identify a link between war and oil, diamonds, or other high-value lootable commodities.

The DRC is a good example, suggesting a refinement of the resource predation hypothesis. According to Ndikumana and Emizet (volume 1, chapter 3) most of the Congolese rebellions originated in the resource-rich regions of Katanga, Kivu, and Kasai. The DRC has massive mineral deposits, including diamonds and gold, and most of them are concentrated in the east. The authors argue that it is not resource dependence per se that increased the risk of war, but rather the territorial concentration of these resources. Dominant ethnic groups in resource-rich regions demanded secession and the government, which could not afford to lose control over this natural wealth, responded violently. By contrast, if resources had been evenly distributed across the country's territory, the government's response might have been different.

The mechanisms that link natural resources to civil war also become clearer in the case studies. Some chapters have argued that natural resources were unimportant as both motives for rebellion and sources of rebel financing once the war had begun. But in several of those cases, we see a lot of looting of other assets to finance the insurgency (e.g., Bosnia, Lebanon, Burundi, Georgia, and Mozambique). Looting in resource-poor countries takes the form of small theft, looting houses and businesses, car-jackings, extortion, and kidnappings. Looting, therefore, seems to be a mechanism to sustain rebellion in the absence of external support for insurgency. If they are available, natural resources will also be looted. Thus, the cases suggest that looting is a mechanism to sustain rebellion even where resource predation is not a motive for war. This is not to say that resources never create incentives for violence. In Indonesia and Nigeria—two countries with sizable oil and natural gas reserves—natural resources provided motives for rebellion. But what ultimately determines whether claims on natural resources will lead to war is the state's response to those claims. An accommodative state may prevent conflict escalation into war (more on escalation later). But the state's reaction is a function of its dependence on the resources and this, in turn, is a function of the territorial concentration of resources (see Sambanis and Milanovic 2004). Thus, government response may be a mechanism that can connect resource dependence and war outbreak.

Four other data and measurement issues confound the interpretation of the CH empirical results on resource predation. First, sometimes natural resources can create motives for war even when the country's dependence on primary commodity exports is low. This is the case of Nigeria in 1967 (with primary commodity exports at 9 percent of GDP), where exploitation of recently discovered oil deposits was a key motive for the Biafran rebellion (Zinn, volume 1, chapter 4).[10] Second, in some cases, no war is coded by the CH model in a country with high levels of primary commodity exports (as in Nigeria in the 1980s). This results in underestimating the effect of resource dependence on civil war risk. Third, large fluctuations to a country's ratio of primary commodity exports over GDP can be due to international economic conditions and price shocks. These shocks would affect the coefficient for the resource/GDP ratio in the civil war regression, but they do not make the country any less dependent on resources, nor do they make resource predation any less useful in supporting insurgency. (A drop in the price of coffee in a country like Burundi may actually increase the available pool of rebel labor by increasing the pool of unemployed young men.) Controls for trade flows might capture these international or regional price shocks.[11] Finally, dependence on certain commodities, such as oil, may influence civil war risk through its effects on regime type. Many oil exporters have autocratic systems (Ross 2000; Wantchekon and Neeman 2000) and can use oil revenues to repress political opposition violently.

Thus, we need to pay more attention to the mechanisms through which resource dependence influences war risk. The difficulty in sorting out several plausible mechanisms in quantitative studies demonstrates the usefulness of the case studies, which have suggested that the CH model would benefit from considering interactions between resource dependence and other covariates (e.g., regime type, level of development, trade).

## Population, Dispersion, and Terrain

Population size is one of the most significant variables in the CH model with a large positive coefficient. The CH hypothesis is that the larger the population, the easier it should be to find a group that wants to challenge the state, *ceteris paribus*. Although the quantitative evidence shows a correlation, several cases pose a challenge to the logic underlying the CH hypothesis. Many civil war countries are small: Burundi, Rwanda, Georgia, Azerbaijan, Cyprus, Lebanon, Mali, and Senegal all have small populations. Moreover, the argument clashes with some of the policy recommendations that flow from the CH model. The authors are reluctant to propose partition as a solution to secessionist war, although in principle a state divided into smaller parts would contain smaller ethnic majorities, thereby reducing the risk of civil war by the logic of their argument.

It would be useful to consider ways to refine the theoretical links between population size and war. A potentially significant variable that the CH model does not consider is population growth. Changes to the demographic balance of antagonistic populations may increase a country's propensity to war and such changes might be more common in very populous countries. But, in this case, the mechanism through which population size is linked to violence is ethnic mobilization of groups whose relative size decreases vis-à-vis other groups that are perceived as hostile. The absolute size of each group need not matter much in this case.

Related to population (but also to income level), urbanization may be an important variable in tempering the prevalence of civil war. Several insurgency scholars have pointed out the difficulty in sustaining urban warfare.[12] Urbanization is, of course, a function of GDP per capita, but it also provides an additional explanation for the fact that most long civil wars tend to occur in peripheral areas of relatively sparsely populated countries (as predicted by the CH model). Thus, population density—not just population size—is important in identifying where a civil war might break out.

Density (or rather, dispersion) is crudely measured by Collier and Hoeffler, but it is nonetheless part of the model. But many of our case studies are ambivalent about this variable. In some cases, high dispersion works to facilitate insurgency because a country with large unpopulated regions may offer hideouts to the rebels. But, in other cases, the same condition can have the opposite effect: High dispersion reduces the effectiveness of rebellion because the rebels cannot establish control over a population large enough to hide them or support them through material or other contributions.

Rough terrain (mountainous and/or forested terrain) is related to population dispersion. Mountains and forests offer hideouts to the rebels. Yet, again, our cases point to the need to refine the argument, because rough terrain is more likely to be associated with war duration than with onset. In expectation, perhaps rough terrain does influence war onset, if rebels plan on hiding in mountains once the insurgency is under way. But a study using several different definitions of civil war has found that the CH results on rough terrain are not robust and that this variable is not statistically significant (Sambanis 2004b). Indeed, even in areas without rough terrain, rebels can find sanctuary across the border if foreign governments are sympathetic to their cause. So, rough terrain (as measured in the CH model) is not necessarily a critically important determinant of the technology of insurgency.

## *Diasporas*

One of the key variables in the CH model, measuring international assistance to the organization of rebellion, is the size of the ethnic diaspora, measured as the ratio of nationals of the war-affected country living in the United States as a proportion of the national population at home. The larger the diaspora, the greater should be the ability to organize and finance a rebellion. (Collier and Hoeffler use a statistical correction to account for the endogeneity of the diaspora variable.) There are several cases that motivate this hypothesis, including Irish American support of the IRA, Canadian Tamil support of the LTTE, German Albanian support to the KLA, and financing of the Chechen rebellion from Chechens living in Russia, but outside Chechnya.

Many case studies suggest that we must broaden the definition of diaspora and refine its measurement. In most cases, it is the presence of migrants in neighboring countries (not in the United States or in countries of the Organization for Economic Co-operation and Development, OECD) that increases the risk of civil war onset. Diaspora communities can also include refugees living in camps across the border. Having ethnic kin across the border is likely to nurture irredentist and unification nationalisms, fueling secessionist movements (Hechter 2001; see also Woodwell 2004).

Diasporas can not only finance rebels at home, but they can also influence the foreign policies of their host countries. In the case of the Yugoslav conflict, the Croatians were the big winners of the diaspora influence, as their large lobby in Germany decidedly influenced the German government's decision to recognize Croatia's bid for independence in 1991–92 (see Woodward 1995). Ethnic lobbies play a significant role in influencing the foreign policies of developed, multicultural countries such as the United States and the United Kingdom. Moreover, a complication that is hard to accommodate in the CH model is that diasporas do not constitute a unified entity that supports a single party to a war. Multiethnic states could have multiethnic diasporas, each supporting a different party, including the government. In Yugoslavia's wars, all three groups (Croats, Serbs, and Bosniacs) received diaspora support (Kalyvas and Sambanis, volume 2, chapter 7).

Finally, perhaps we should consider a broader concept of diaspora, one that incorporates all shared transnational networks and cultural communities that can influence the pattern of civil war. In some of our cases, Islamist militants joined Muslim groups fighting wars in the Balkans and Central Asia (see Zürcher et al., volume 2, chapter 9). Such transnational networks are becoming increasingly important in world politics.

## Ethnicity, Social Fragmentation, and Polarization

One of the key findings of the CH model is that ethnic diversity does not increase the risk of civil war. This result counters widely held assumptions about the causes of civil war in the popular press and scholarly literature. Several of our case studies illustrate why Collier and Hoeffler might be right. The primary mechanism through which social (ethnic and religious) fractionalization contributes to peace is by increasing the costs of coordinating a rebellion against the government (see the Nigeria chapter, as an example).

While higher fractionalization need not make civil war more likely, Collier and Hoeffler argue that ethnic dominance raises the risk of civil war. Several case studies agree with this hypothesis. There are several plausible mechanisms. Perhaps the most important is that dominance raises the minority's fears of victimization or exclusion, particularly when ethnic divisions overlap with class cleavages. The case of Northern Ireland suggests that the mechanisms through which ethnic dominance influences the risk of civil war are economic and political.

In two of our cases of war avoidance, Macedonia and Côte d'Ivoire, we also had ethnic dominance.[13] But in both cases, war was avoided by virtue of strong political institutions that, in the case of Macedonia, allowed a policy of cultural accommodation vis-à-vis the Albanian minority. In the Côte d'Ivoire, a system of fiscal transfers (often informal) to northern regions that were not well-represented in the government reduced the minority's fears of exploitation by the ethnic majority. Here, again, institutions are an important intervening variable in the process of ethnic competition.

In other cases, we find indirect evidence of the CH hypothesis about ethnic dominance. Collier and Hoeffler measure dominance by the index of ethnolinguistic fractionalization (ELF) and characterize ethnic dominance as occurring when the majority group is between 45 and 90 percent of the population. But in some cases, even when the ELF index suggests a high degree of fractionalization (i.e., when it does not fit the "dominance" scenario), the country may well be deeply polarized. In Mali, despite high fractionalization (the ELF is equal to 78/100), there is deep polarization between the Tuareg and Arabs in the north, each fearing domination at the hands of the other (Humphreys and ag Mohamed, volume 1, chapter 9). Similarly, in the Sudan, the Arab North has dominated political life and sought to limit the cultural autonomy of Christian and Animist South, and this cleavage has dominated the country's political life and has been centrally associated with the civil war (Ali, Elbadawi, and el-Battahani, volume 1, chapter 7). These cases point to deficiencies in the way in which ethnic dominance is measured in the CH model.

Several case studies discuss at length problems associated with ethnic dominance and ethnic fractionalization and explain that domestic political institutions are an important variable to consider in interaction with ethnic dominance. But the cases also suggest that, to understand the role of political institutions, we must look beyond the blanket measures of democracy currently used in quantitative studies and we must consider, for example, how different electoral systems and constitutional arrangements might influence the risk of civil war in multiethnic states.

## Political Institutions—Which Ones Matter, When and How?

The message from the CH model is that grievances do not matter once we control for the opportunity to rebel. Collier and Hoeffler show that democracy does not reduce the risk of civil war significantly (see the results of their "combined" model in chapter 1). This negates theories about the positive effects of democratic institutions and contradicts the empirical evidence that has been presented to support those theories (Esty et al. 1995; Gurr 1993, 2000; Hegre et al. 2001). The impact of democratic institutions on the probability of civil war is still heavily debated in the literature. The case studies suggest several ways in which we could qualify the statement that "democracy does not matter" and modify the specification of the CH model to better capture the effects of political institutions.

ESTABLISHED VERSUS NEW DEMOCRACIES. Gurr's (2000) distinction between established democracies and new democracies is an important one. Newly established democratic institutions may not be credible or effective in resolving social conflicts. Ross's chapter (volume 2) offers an example from Indonesia: Trying to respond to demands for greater autonomy in Aceh, the newly elected democratic government in Indonesia implemented three legislative changes in late 1999, passing decentralization laws that would increase Aceh's administrative and cultural autonomy. Decentralization should have reduced the risk of violent conflict according to theories of nationalist conflict (e.g., Gurr 2000; Hechter 2001). However, these changes were noncredible, given the previous governments' track record in Aceh and the government's apparent inability to prevent attacks on civilians by the military. Government *credibility* and *legitimacy* are crucial components of democratic regimes that cannot easily be coded in quantitative studies. But they are important dimensions that differentiate new (and unstable) democracies from old (and stable) ones.

Beyond the question of institutional stability, we must also contend with the degree of institutional openness and social inclusion. A country may be coded as democratic on the basis of the criteria in the "Polity" database used by Collier and Hoeffler, while not being truly inclusive. In some countries, a relatively high democracy "score" implies that the government will accommodate its ethnic minorities, averting the escalation of ethnic conflict, as was the case in Macedonia (Lund, volume 2, chapter 8). But in other countries, democracy is shallow. In Lebanon, electoral democracy was based on sectarianism, restricting the operation of the parliamentary system (Makdisi and Sadaka, volume 2, chapter 3).

The concentration of power is another important dimension. Federal institutions have been offered as a solution to ethnic competition. But they do not always work. In Nigeria, federalism failed to control ethnic competition over resources. Colonial legacies intensified ethnoregional conflict, as British rule had pitted the northern and southern protectorates against each other. Just as in the case of Cyprus (Sambanis 1999), which inherited a consociational system from the British colonial rulers in 1960, so in Nigeria the system endogenized ethnic conflict; it did not resolve it. Thus, although on paper a federal system might appear as a balanced solution to ethnic competition over the distribution of resources, the central government might not be able to offer credible guarantees about minority rights and regional institutions can be manipulated by local elites to demand more autonomy and secession.

In addition to the fact that the CH concept of democracy does not distinguish between new and old, liberal and illiberal, and federal and centralized democracies, the CH model may also suffer from important selection effects, which may explain the nonsignificance of democracy. Democratic institutions may be endogenous to previous war outcomes (Elbadawi and Sambanis 2002) and/or to levels of economic development (Przeworski et al. 2000). To date, these complex relationships have not been studied adequately, with the possible exception of Hegre (2003), who argues that we should study the risk of civil war in poor and rich democracies separately. Since poor democracies tend to be unstable, they cannot provide effective conflict resolution mechanisms to prevent the onset of war. But more stable democracies in richer countries will be more effective in managing conflict. Tilly (2003) also pursues a similar argument as he considers how high-capacity democratic regimes differ from low-capacity regimes with respect to the type and intensity of political violence that we are likely to see in each of these regime types. Other selection effects or non-linearities in the data may also be present. For example, some of the variables (democracy, in particular) may have different effects on civil war risk before and after the end of the Cold War, perhaps because several new, unstable democracies were established with the end of the Cold War (see Sambanis 2003 for some preliminary results).

POLITICAL INSTABILITY AND POLITICAL SYSTEMS. Moving from levels of democracy to the process of democratic change, the case studies make clear that there are dangers associated with failed democratization. In Burundi, challenges to Tutsi elites from the Bururi region during democratization was causally linked to the onset of the civil war of 1993 (Ngaruko and Nkurunziza, volume 1, chapter 2). Other cases offer similar evidence. A massive political transition to independence and Marxist revolution in Mozambique added to the burdens of a young and weak state and gave way to infighting in various regions of the country in 1976 (Weinstein and Francisco, volume 1, chapter 6). In Bosnia, state failure as a result of the crumbling Communist Party apparatus gave way to nationalist violence in Croatia, Bosnia, and later Kosovo (Kalyvas and Sambanis, volume 2, chapter 7). None of the conflicts in the Caucasus can be understood outside of the context of the collapse of the Soviet state (Zürcher et al., volume 2, chapter 9). In Kenya, ethnic violence started as a result of a political transition to a multiparty system in 1991 (Kimenyi and Ndung'u, volume 1, chapter 5). And the failed democratic transition of Zaire in 1960 is an example of how ethnic competition, compounded by external intervention, can undermine the peace (Ndikumana and Emizet, volume 1, chapter 3).

Quantitative studies of civil war have also identified a risk of war associated with regime transition. What these studies do not capture, however, is the increased risk of political violence that can result from a *power transition* even without a *regime transition*.[14] Consider the case of a change in leadership in a dictatorial regime. The Polity database would still code the country as autocratic, if the institutions of dictatorial exclusion are preserved through the leadership change. But disaffected elites with access to war-making capital may strike at the new leadership and a civil war can occur from a military coup, particularly if the military splits, each supporting a faction of elites. All this could happen without a substantive change in the underlying "polity" score. Indeed, violence in authoritarian regimes can occur precisely in an effort to prevent such leadership change, as in the case of Kenya during the Rift Valley riots.

The risks associated with political instability seem to be magnified with economic transition. Declining growth in the early 1990s and negative growth since the mid-to-late 1990s exacerbated the political conflict in Kenya's Rift Valley. In Azerbaijan, Chechnya, and Georgia, it was not only the disintegration of the USSR, but also the transition to a free market that magnified the political conflict between titular nations and ethnic minorities. The selection effects mentioned previously are relevant again here, as economic decline weakens political institutions and makes them even less able to respond to crisis.

Several cases, particularly the wars in the Caucasus, suggest that broad-ranging political instability is a necessary but not sufficient condition for violence. Of all the former Soviet Republics, only a small number actually descended into violence. We learn three important lessons from careful case studies of that region. First, not all regions had the same level of latent nationalist sentiment, and the potential for nationalist mobilization and conflict differed according to the level of nationalist education that they had received in the pre-Soviet period (Darden 2002). Second, in several former Soviet and former Yugoslav Republics, the collapse of the USSR spelled conflict between ethnic minorities and politically dominant titular nations that were previously forced to coexist by an authoritarian and repressive central administration (Glenny 1999; Zürcher et al., volume 2, chapter 9). Third, these latent ethnic conflicts were likely to escalate to civil war because of external interference or political failure of the dominant elites to assuage the fears of ethnic minorities. In Georgia, Russian interference took the form of bussing Chechen fighters to support Abkhazian demands for self-determination. In Chechnya, collapse of the USSR meant a chance to pursue a long-held desire for national independence. In all these places, we had civil wars.

But in other areas of the former USSR, political instability and economic strain did not translate into civil war partly because of the strength of local institutions. The comparison between Chechnya and Dagestan (Zürcher et al., volume 2, chapter 9) is instructive. The 1994 constitution and the informal *dzhamaat* system fostered stability in Dagestan, despite the tensions that might have otherwise emerged due to Dagestan's high ethnic fractionalization. By contrast, no political institution was left standing after 1991 in Chechnya and there was no continuity in political elites— both of these developments made the state-building challenge harder in Chechnya.[15]

Less democratic solutions to political conflict may eventually yield democratic outcomes, though the transition may be difficult and long. State oppression can certainly result in (a perhaps unjust) peace and in the long run it may lead the way to a more open political system. This was the case of the Greek civil war, where oppression of leftists in the 1950s and 1960s gave way to a successful democratic transition in the mid-1970s and 1980s (Iatrides 1993). But, although authoritarianism can work in some cases to prevent war onset or war recurrence, it is not always straightforward that supporting local warlords will eventually lead to representative government. A recent finding that autocracies are less stable than democracies (Hegre et al. 2001), in conjunction with other findings that regime change increases the risk of civil war and that this risk is even greater in states that transition out of nondemocratic regimes (Elbadawi and Sambanis 2002), suggests that the strategy of supporting authoritarian governance after civil war need not yield stable polities or peaceful societies.

Civil wars frequently result in patterns of minority exclusion if postwar institutions reify old (prewar) identities (Rothchild 2002, 118). If the war ends in a negotiated settlement and not a decisive victory, then there can be a number of group-based mechanisms to design an equitable polity, three of which are "proportional distribution," "proportional representation in electoral systems," and "cultural and social protections." To negotiate postwar institutions, the first hurdle is that all parties must be included for a stable power-sharing system to be established. In Cambodia, even the homicidal Khmer Rouge leadership was included in the Paris Agreements (Doyle 1997).

Proportional distribution of political power is one way to manage multicultural societies after civil war. Consociationalism (proportional representation and a minority veto) can in theory at least be good solutions to manage ethnic conflict,[16] but in reality these institutions are difficult to create and credibly maintain as mechanisms of adjudicating ethnic antagonisms (Horowitz 1991). That is why the empirical record of proportional distribution of power in postwar systems is mixed (Rothchild 2002).

Another way to manage multiculturalism is through parliamentarianism. Parliamentary systems may be better than presidential systems in managing conflict because of dispersion of political authority, which makes minority exclusion harder (Linz 1996; Sisk 1996). This is not yet a fully tested hypothesis, but some preliminary statistical evidence demonstrates the peace "dividend" of parliamentary systems (Reynal-Querol 2002). Another solution at the level of electoral rules in a centralized political system is to foster multiethnic proportionality in the central government and reward leaders for "interethnic moderation" (Horowitz 1991). The advantage of such a system is that it could be self-enforcing, if voter preferences and electoral districts are not organized in such a way as to create powerful ethnic majorities. But caution is needed in advocating the adoption of multiparty democracy. First, statistical studies have not necessarily demonstrated an effect of proportional representation systems as compared to presidential systems, while taking into account the factors that explain the prevalence of those systems in the first place. Second, multiparty elections alone are an insufficient inducement for cooperation because democratic institutions in postwar situations can be hijacked by warlords (Walter, 2002, 29). Power-sharing agreements can help in implementing the terms of civil war settlements. The difficulty in estimating the effects of such agreements is in controlling for the fact that the power-sharing systems themselves are likely to be the consequence of previous war, thus making it hard to identify their impact using quantitative analysis.

It is difficult to apply insights from the literature on political institutions (consociationalism, parliamentarianism, etc.) to the question of how to prevent civil war and to do so in the context of the CH model, because the model does not consider political grievance as a significant cause of civil war. Thus, effective political institutions in multiethnic states need not influence the risk of civil war, if that risk depends more on organizational capacity and on the "technology" of insurgency. But the case studies and the brief analysis presented here suggest that the CH model might have produced different empirical results if it had taken into account those dimensions of political institutions that I have mentioned here: how new/old the regime is; how liberal and open it is; and what electoral mechanisms it has instituted to manage multi-culturalism. Interaction effects between political institutions and the different "structural" characteristics of countries (such as their ethnic diversity or their growth patterns) must also be considered carefully.

To address these complicated questions on the link between political institutions and civil war, the CH model must be revised and expanded, and different econometric techniques must be used to estimate a model that accounts for interaction and selection effects. This brief review of how the CH model fits the case studies offers insights into how the model might be revised and expanded. I make some suggestions below.

# Drawing on the Case Studies to Expand the Theory of Civil War

A number of theoretical extensions to the CH model are suggested by the case studies. This section outlines some of them.

First, we must take better account of escalation dynamics and government repression to explain the outbreak of war. Second, we must reconceptualize the relationship between ethnicity and violence. Third, we must model the regional and international dimensions of civil war. Fourth, we must consider violence as a recurring phenomenon and rethink the meaning and definition of civil war and the similarities between civil war and other forms of political violence. Fifth, we must account for case heterogeneity; the model's fit to the data might be influenced by variables such as the rebels' ideology and war aims or the type of warfare. Sixth, we need to understand better the role of elite preferences and the organization and growth of rebel movements. And, finally, we need more nuanced analyses of the impact of different kinds of inequality; regional inequalities, for example, may matter more for secessionist war than for popular revolutions. I take up each of these topics briefly.[17]

## Escalation Dynamics

Case studies can describe social protest and low-level violence leading up to civil war and can give us a view of the sequence of protest events. Several of the case studies in our project focused on the government's reactions to nonviolent protest as a key variable influencing conflict escalation and civil war outbreak. This dynamic perspective is missing from the CH model and other quantitative studies of civil war onset.

In Nigeria, what triggered the war in the 1960s was the demand for independence by the leadership of the Biafra region. Faced with such a demand, the government could have responded with repression, accommodation at the center, increased independence (regional autonomy, or de facto independence as in the cases of the regions of Somaliland, Abkhazia, and Trans-Dniestria). State capacity is what largely decided the approach to be used. Strong states have the capacity to either accommodate or suppress demands for self-determination at low cost (Gurr 2000, 82). It is easier to gain concessions from the government by pursuing non-violent movements that do not threaten state security.

One of the main insights from the case study project is that government repression increases opposition and, if repression is incomplete, it can lead to violence.[18] It may be the case that there is a causal link between regime type and ability to repress effectively and this link may explain the higher risk of war in so-called anocracies: Democratizing states lose the ability to use their repressive apparatus with impunity and open the door to protest and rebellion. Several of our case studies (e.g., Burundi, Nigeria, Indonesia) suggest that the lack of government legitimacy and loss of control over the military and police (especially in periods of transition) undermine the government's ability to provide credible guarantees that satisfy the demands of minority groups.

This raises an interesting question: Under what conditions will governments be accommodative? And when will policies of accommodation be credible and effective in reducing the threat of war? These questions have not yet been answered in the literature and suggest fruitful ways to expand the CH model so as to link the economic theory of war onset that it provides to political theories about the uses of institutions to reduce social conflict and violence.

## *Ethnic Fractionalization, Dominance, and Polarization*

Whereas the CH model seems to be correct in identifying the increased civil war risk associated with ethnic dominance, the case studies suggest several ways in which we must reconceptualize the relationship between ethnicity and violence. The ELF index used by Collier and Hoeffler and others is a very crude measure if what we care about is politically relevant fractionalization.[19] For example, Côte d' Ivoire has more than 70 ethnic groups and, according to its ELF score, is highly fractionalized. However, natural aggregations of these groups result in three or four major ethnic groups, the largest of which, the Akan, makes up 42 percent of the population and has been politically dominant by controlling the state since independence (Azam and Koidou 2003). Similarly, most of the 40 large tribes of Kenya were excluded from government after Kenyatta's postindependence government instilled ethnic favoritism and this is not captured by the ELF index. In Nigeria, we have a nominally highly fractionalized country that includes more than 250 ethnic groups. Yet, the country is effectively polarized along the Muslim North versus the Christian and Animist South (Zinn, volume 1, chapter 4). In these and other cases, the ELF index often does not allow us to identify the political dominance of an ethnic group.

The ELF index also does not allow us to account for the role of race or religion in shaping ethnopolitical action.[20] Several case studies in our project indicate that this is a mistake. In the case of Lebanon, religious fractionalization was more salient that other forms of ethnic division. Christians and Muslims constituted around 45–55 percent of the population; but each group within each cleavage was not larger than

20–25 percent of the population, which would suggest no ethnic dominance even though, on the basis of religious affiliation, we had an intensely polarized society. In Mali, Tuareg and Arab groups are racially and ethnically similar, but a pattern of cultural-political discrimination has imposed a divide between those groups, which have come to consider themselves as racially distinct.

Regional concentration of ethnicities matters more than the ethnic fragmentation of the entire country.[21] In Nigeria, despite having more than 200 ethnic groups and an ELF score of 87/100 (which places the country above the 95th percentile of fractionalization for all countries in the world), there is significant ethnic dominance in the regions where conflict has occurred. If we used the subnational region rather than the entire country as our unit of analysis, we would find a different relationship between ethnic fragmentation and violence. In Russia, the Chechens are only a small minority of the population, but they are a majority (73 percent) in Chechnya. In Indonesia, 90 percent of the population is Muslim, which might lead one to argue that religion is not a politically relevant cleavage. However, the distribution of Muslim population in various islands makes religious affiliation politically salient in some of the Indonesian conflicts. In Kenya, Kimenyi and Ndung'u (volume 1, chapter 5) find that of the 13 most ethnically diverse districts in Kenya, 12 have had violent conflicts of one type or another, whereas of the eight most ethnically homogenous districts, only Kisii experienced violence.

At the same time, the concept of ethnic dominance used by Collier and Hoeffler is shallow and focuses exclusively on the size of the largest group. This brings us back to an earlier point, on the need to recognize politically salient ethnic cleavages. The CH definition leads the authors to code Bosnia, United Kingdom (Northern Ireland), and Lebanon as not ethnically dominated, so the model predicts a low risk of civil war in these countries. But this coding rule does not capture the full potential for ethnic conflict that can be created with polarization. Knowing the size of the second largest group is critically important in understanding ethnic violence in each of the three cases above. Improper measurement of ethnic dominance contributed to a false-negative prediction in the case of the Biafran war in Nigeria. According to Zinn (volume 1, chapter 4), Collier and Hoeffler code Nigeria as not ethnically dominated, but in practice, each of the three semiautonomous regions is dominated by a single group. Northern dominance has been a constant source of conflict in Nigerian politics. We also have ethnic dominance in Mozambique, as the Macua-Lowme tribe is larger than most other sizable minority groups (Weinstein and Francisco, volume 1, chapter 6). This establishes a good fit with the CH model, although Weinstein and Francisco never focus on this aspect of Mozambican society to explain the war.

Finally, currently available measures of ethnic fragmentation do not tell us anything about the degree to which ethnic, religious, racial, or other identity cleavages are cross-cutting. How many of the 250 ethnic groups in the DRC share one or more cultural characteristics that might lead to them to forge alliances? We do not yet know the answer to this question for a large enough number of countries. Theorists of ethnic conflict have argued convincingly that conflict potential is maximized when ethnicity overlaps with class, resulting in so-called "ranked" systems

(Horowitz 1985). But we do not have the data necessary to classify systems into ranked and unranked cross-nationally; and perhaps this concept would be better at describing the power relationships between pairs of groups, rather than characterize entire societies. Several of our cases, however, highlight the explosive potential of ranked systems. Northern Ireland is one of them. The divide between Catholics and Protestants was reinforced by a pattern of socioeconomic stratification that overlapped with religious cleavages (Woodwell, volume 2, chapter 6).

These insights from the case studies suggest ways in which the CH model must be respecified to test better the hypothesized relationship between ethnicity and civil war. We do not simply need better measures, but also measures that correspond better to our theories about the ways in which ethnic affiliation leads to political violence.

## Neighborhood and Spillover Effects of Civil Wars

Another largely neglected dimension of civil wars in the quantitative literature is the regional dimension. If civil wars are caused by military, economic, or diplomatic interference by major powers or neighboring states, then the CH model must be respecified to capture that dimension. One promising direction for further research is to explore the contagion and diffusion effects of civil war.[22]

Demonstration (diffusion) effects were clear in several of the cases. A good example was the rebellion in Indonesia's Aceh province, where an independence movement had been simmering for decades, after the revocation of Aceh's "special region" status in 1968 by the Suharto government. A brief civil war in 1991 quieted down in the mid-1990s and re-ignited in 1999 when, in a climate of political instability and economic recession due to the East Asian financial crisis, East Timor's referendum on independence emboldened Acehnese resistance. Ross (volume 2, chapter 2) traces the onset of mass protest in favor of independence in Aceh in November 1999, following soon after the September 1999 referendum in East Timor. In Senegal, Humphreys and ag Mohamed (volume 1, chapter 9) argue that the Casamance movement was influenced by the ideology of the independence struggle in Guinea-Bissau. This influence became more tangible as war broke out in Casamance and Guinea-Bissau was used as a location for cross-border bases, a market for goods, and a source for arms.

Examples of regional contagion are even more common. Yugoslavia's wars, in Croatia in 1991, Bosnia in 1992–95, Croatia again in 1995, and Kosovo in 1998–99, all shared similar characteristics and were influenced by the ideology of greater Serbia and greater Croatia. In the former Soviet Republics, wars clustered in the Caucasus in the early 1990s, taking advantage of war-specific physical and human capital in the region (Zürcher et al., volume 2, chapter 9). Sierra Leone's civil war was sustained by international crime networks that were engaged in arms-for-diamonds trade and the Sierra Leone rebels received direct assistance and sanctuary from Liberia's Charles Taylor (Davies and Fofana 2002). The civil wars in the African Great Lakes region are perfect examples of contagion as recurrent wars in Burundi and Rwanda spilled over their borders and influenced each other as well as the DRC and involved Uganda and Zimbabwe in international military interventions in the Congo.

There is substantial cross-national evidence in quantitative studies that highlights these neighborhood effects, but these studies do not distinguish between diffusion and contagion mechanisms. Sambanis (2001) analyzed ethnic civil wars from 1945 until 1999 and found that living in "bad" neighborhoods (i.e., neighborhoods with undemocratic countries and countries experiencing ethnic wars of their own) increases a country's risk of having a civil war threefold. Recent empirical work at the dyadic level suggests that the presence of common ethnic groups across national borders influences the patterns of external involvement in civil war and the spread and internationalization of these wars. The risk of a violent conflict increases if two countries share an ethnic group and one of them has an ethnic majority composed of that group (Woodwell 2004). The presence of ethnic kin across the border may be one of the principal mechanisms that transmit civil war across borders. In Macedonia, Lund's study makes clear that the main risk of civil war in the 1990s came from eth-nic Albanians who were actively supporting independence in neighboring Kosovo and moved across the border when their movement in Kosovo was blocked by the international intervention. Another possible mechanism of contagion occurs through the accumulation of war-specific capital (e.g., small arms) in regions experiencing wars, making it easier for other wars to start.

This argument has two implications. First, civil wars in neighboring countries may be regional phenomena. If the war in Burundi or Rwanda is really a war between Hutus and Tutsis in the Great Lakes region and not one specifically between Burundi Hutus and Burundi Tutsis or Rwandan Tutsis against Rwandan Hutus, then the country-year is not the appropriate unit of observation to analyze such civil wars. Instead, it would be more appropriate to focus on the ethnic group or we should analyze patterns of violence in a geographical region that does not necessarily cor-respond to predefined national boundaries. With current data limitations, however, it may not be feasible to adjust this unit of analysis problem.[23] Second, civil wars are affected significantly by wars in neighboring states or by nonstate actors in neigh-boring states. These influences must be modeled and properly analyzed. Gurr (2000, 92), for example, argues that the presence of politically mobilized ethnic kin across the border increases the opportunity for rebellion. This implies the need for the implementation of methods from spatial econometrics that control for the non-independence of cross-sections (countries) in our panel data sets (see Sanchez, Solimano, and Formisano, volume 2, chapter 5). For these relationships to be prop-erly modeled, we must identify some of the diffusion and contagion mechanisms that underlie these trans-border influences.

Our case studies identify two contagion mechanisms: refugee movements and external intervention. First, refugee flows contribute to the risk of civil war by sup-porting cross-border movements by insurgents with access to refugee camps (see the chapter on Burundi); and by changing the demographic balance in conflict-prone neighboring regions (see Ndikumana and Emizet's discussion of the consequences of refugee inflows from Burundi and Rwanda to the Kivu region). Second, external military and economic intervention can increase the length of civil war by influencing the military balance between the state and rebels (Elbadawi and Sambanis 2000; Regan 2000, 2002) and may also be critical in helping potential insurgents organize their rebellion and start a civil war, as illustrated by the case studies on Mozambique, the DRC, Burundi, Georgia (Abkhazia), Bosnia, Sierra Leone, and Lebanon.

Questions that still need to be addressed include: Can negotiated settlements be achieved without external intervention and, if intervention prolongs civil war, how do we weigh the pros and cons of such interventions? If unilateral interventions are more effective in ending the violence and multilateral interventions are more effective in keeping the peace, how can the international community develop appropriate mechanisms to address the different challenges of war and peace?[24] The impact of refugees on civil war risk has also not been sufficiently studied in quantitative analyses. Analyzing the effects of refugee movements on political stability and economic growth can be a first cut at this question, since the effects of refugee problems on civil war risk may work through those two channels (instability and growth).

## Civil War as Part of a Cycle of Violence

The CH model accounts for the temporal association between episodes of civil war in the same country over time by controlling for "peace time"—the number of years at peace since the last war. Several case studies have pointed to problems with this variable. One of the problems is that the temporal dependence of violence is complex and cannot be captured only by a variable measuring time since the last civil war. Rather, this measure should account for linkages across several forms of organized political violence over time. Additionally, temporal dependence should be considered together with spatial dependence (see the earlier discussion on regional effects).

There is currently no overarching theory of political violence that explains how societies transition from one form of violence to another (see Sambanis 2004a for an outline of such a theory; and Tilly 2003 for a related discussion). But such a theory may be necessary, particularly given the difficulty in clearly distinguishing civil war from other types of violence. The quantitative studies assume that civil war is a clearly defined and coded category of violence, but several case studies cast doubt on this assumption. Very bloody coups are often classified as civil wars (e.g., Costa Rica in 1948, Bolivia in 1952, Argentina in 1955), whereas genocides or politicides are not, given that a theoretical distinction is made in the literature between one-sided and reciprocal political violence. This distinction may well be valid, but which of the variables in the CH model can account for the conditions under which violence will be one-sided as opposed to reciprocal? Perhaps the "terrain" variable or variables currently outside the model (such as external intervention, or level of prewar political organization) could explain such differences. But, in its current formulation, the CH model and the related empirical tests assume—they do not explain—why violence will take the form of a civil war.

Civil wars can degenerate into organized crime, as in the case of Russia or Colombia. State weakness favors both insurgency and organized crime. Looting, which can sustain insurgency, is also the primary function of organized crime. Another function shared by rebel groups and criminal networks is the provision of security to local populations in areas beyond the control of the state. Crime and insurgency create production externalities for each other and work together to undermine state authority and capacity. Violence is the by-product of both crime and insurgency and the form that violence will take is determined by, among other factors, the type of available "loot" and the way that it can be appropriated.

Terrorism can also feed from civil war and vice versa. In Egypt, terrorism against Western tourists was the direct result of government suppression of and armed struggle against the Gamaat Islamiya, an insurgent group. The Israeli-Palestinian civil war (since the first Intifada of 1987) has been at the heart of international terrorism, certainly during the period of PLO's involvement in supporting such activities (before the Oslo accords of 1997). Kidnappings in Colombia are a direct consequence of the civil war and a means for the rebels to finance their insurgency (Sanchez et al., volume 2, chapter 5). Chechen terrorism in Russia today is the outgrowth of the Russo-Chechen war (Andrienko and Shelley, volume 2, chapter 4).

These interrelationships among various forms of violence (civil war, coups, terrorism, and organized crime) are outside the purview of the CH model and are also not considered by other prominent models of civil war (e.g., Fearon and Laitin 2003). A quick "fix" for the CH model would be to revise the definition and measurement of the peace-time variable so that it could account for time since the last incident of a broader set of violent events. But a fuller treatment of the organization of violence is needed before we can explain why some countries experience civil war as opposed to other forms of violence or crime.

## Unit Heterogeneity: Ideology, Ethnicity, and Types of Civil War

This discussion of a taxonomy of violence suggests another question: should we distinguish between different categories of civil war and does the CH model explain each category equally well (or equally poorly)? Rich and poor countries seem to have very different structures of risk; indeed, the inclusion of highly industrialized countries in the data set might well account for the strong results on education and income variables in the CH model. Another possible source of heterogeneity in the data might be uncovered by looking at the organization of rebellion. In ethnically organized rebellions, the CH model's economic opportunity cost argument need not be as central as in loot-driven or class-based rebellions, where private or class-based economic interests are driving rebellion (Sambanis 2001). In pure "ethnic" conflicts, such as conflicts over self-determination—understood as conflicts between ethnic groups over issues that are at the core of ethnicity—ethnic solidarity and ideology may compensate for the lack of financial motives ("loot") and the causes of separatist war may be different than the causes of popular revolutions (Sambanis 2004c).

In most of our case studies, we saw that violence was "ethnicized." Some authors downplayed the ethnoreligious dimension of the violence (e.g., Lowi, volume 1, chapter 8). But it is an open question whether this ethnicization is unimportant for understanding the origins of the violence. In Algeria, Lowi argues that economic decline and demographic pressures led to the emergence of Islamist protest. But she also points to more than one period of serious economic decline in that country. Under Boumedienne (1965–78), Algerian society saw rapidly declining economic growth and increasing unemployment and corruption, yet there was no Islamist backlash. What was the impact of a "bankrupt" political system on Algerian society during successive periods of economic decline? Might an explanation for Islamist protest be found in political, not economic, failure in Algeria? And, if religion is not causally linked to civil war, why was protest organized along religious cleavages? The same question should be asked with reference to several of our case studies, where rebel groups were organized along ethnoreligious lines, as in Burundi, Lebanon, the DRC, or Georgia and Chechnya.

Some scholars argue that ethnicity is used as a cover for economic motives (Collier and Hoeffler 2001), personal animosities (Kalyvas 2003), criminality (Mueller 2001), or an assortment of other motives that are not truly ethnonationalist at their core (Brubaker and Laitin 1998). But, even if many conflicts can become "ethnicized" after they start for a variety of reasons, the empirical regularity that some wars are organized along ethnic lines while others are not cannot be explained away simply because of the presence of other competing motives for war. A large literature on nationalism has taught us that ethnic identities are not always salient and that they can change over time. Some social systems can encourage pathological patterns of identity evolution, leading to the outbreak of civil violence (Anderson 1983; Brubaker 1995). Given that the salience of ethnic identity is malleable, the focus of much research on civil violence has been on the role of elites in manipulating ethnic, religious, or class identity to pursue private goals (e.g., Brass 1985, 1997; Chandra 2000; Darden 2002; Kasfir 1979). But that literature cannot explain why groups define themselves along ethnic lines in the first place (as opposed to other identity categories) or why membership in such a group draws upon a set of perceived objective, ascriptive characteristics that resemble kinship ties. If there is something special about ethnic ties, then wars that are aimed to preserve those ties may be different from wars that are unrelated to ethnicity. (It should not be the case that ethnicity can always be relied on as a source of mass mobilization for violence.) To address properly the question of differences across war types, we must disaggregate the concept of civil war and systematically test for differences between ethnic wars (e.g., wars over secession) and nonethnic wars (e.g., revolutions), just as we should test for differences across various other forms of violence, such as coups, genocides, and riots.

## Leadership and the Roots of Ethnic Violence

This discussion of social mobilization reveals that the CH model is silent on the role of political elites. Many case studies in this volume have pointed to the importance of political leadership in mobilizing support for violence (e.g., Indonesia, Nigeria, Burundi, Bosnia) or, less frequently, in reducing social tensions and helping prevent a war (e.g., Macedonia). The case studies have used terms such as "charismatic leadership," "cleptocracy," and government "legitimacy" to describe the ways in which leaders matter. These terms are hard to quantify, so it is not surprising that quantitative studies have been unable to test the effects of leadership, though few authors would argue that elites have no role in organizing and sustaining a rebellion.

But even where narratives of elite-driven mobilization seem entirely plausible, we still need to explain which groups are likely to be mobilized and why? What type of person chooses to commit violence and why? Bosnia has been a case to which authors have applied the mobilization explanation, blaming the war on Milosevic and other elites. A closer look at the pattern of violence reveals that most of the violence (particularly against civilians) was in fact perpetrated by organized militias, which were composed of criminal elements and paramilitaries (Kalyvas and Sambanis, volume 2, chapter 7). Those are groups that derive tangible benefits from their actions and we would not expect their motives for being mobilized to war to be the same as the motives of the general population. The mass mobilization perspective should not have to rely on cases where most of the killing is done by a few criminals.

There is a considerably large literature on the risks associated with elite manipulation of ethnicity. Such mobilization is easier when ethnocultural identity is already more salient than other socioeconomic identities, and when actual or expected group-level grievance increases groups' interest in political protest and forces groups to become more cohesive in the face of an external threat (Brass 1997; Gurr 2000; Hardin 1995). This literature, which has been influenced by constructivist theory on identity formation, differs from so-called primordial perspectives because it does not view ethnic identity as inherently conflictual and focuses on social interactions and patterns of identity evolution to explain violence (Anderson 1983; Brubaker 1995). However, the mobilization perspective (see De Figueiredo and Weingast 1999 for an application to Bosnia) must also explain why followers are not as strategic as leaders and why they allow themselves to be manipulated.

If people are prone to being manipulated, we must understand the root of their fear and distrust which allow them to be manipulated. If rebellion is "easy" to motivate, then the distinction between the leaders' influence and the people's proclivities becomes smaller and is, at best, a distinction between proximate and permissive causes of violence. Therefore, elite-driven explanations of wars such as the Bosnian war must be interpreted within the context of a history of ethnic violence and prior conflict. Without the historical memory of violent conflict between the Ustashe and Chetnicks during World War II, how would Serbs have been mobilized by their elites to preempt another round of victimization by the Croats? It is the mixture of a perception of ethnic difference, combined with memories of old group-level conflicts and new manipulation by elites, that best explains how groups can be mobilized to use violence.

## Formation and Growth of the Rebel Organization

The question of who fights and why leads me to consider how rebel organizations grow. An important contribution of the case study project is that it provides us with systematically collected evidence on the formation and growth of insurgent groups in several countries. We see clearly that most insurgencies start small—very small—and grow into civil wars only under certain conditions. The CH model's focus on "opportunity cost" gives only part of the answer to the question of how do rebel groups grow. Frequently, insurgent groups grow if and when they receive external assistance (through alliances with foreign actors or financial support from diasporas) and this is consistent with the CH model. But they also grow through several other mechanisms. Ethnically based rebellions grow by tapping into ethnic networks, or as a result of anger, hatred, resentment, or fear of victimization at the hands of a hostile ethnic majority. Ideologues join rebellions as a result of their beliefs. Criminals may join to maximize their profits. Rebel leaders can coerce participation by threatening civilians or by abducting children and turning them into fighters. Secessionist parties can benefit from manipulating the administrative capacities of regional governments and they can utilize ethnic parties and preexisting political organizations to mobilize support for rebellion.

Thus, while Collier and Hoeffler are certainly correct in emphasizing the importance of opportunity structures in explaining civil war occurrence, the case studies have illustrated several mechanisms that influence the organization of rebellion that the CH model has not considered.

## Inequality: Interpersonal vs. Interregional Inequality and War

Inequality is another variable that keeps coming up in the case studies, but it is dismissed as nonsignificant in most quantitative analyses of civil war. How can inequality be nonsignificant in the CH model and yet be so much a part of the narratives? There can be several explanations. The authors may have been misled by discourses of inequality by the rebels, whereas the true motives of the rebellion lay hidden. It could also be a selection problem: The cases in this book may not be representative of the population of cases, and inequality may not be significant in the population of cases.

Alternatively, the problem may lie with the quantitative studies. It could be that Collier and Hoeffler are looking at the wrong kind of inequality. Their focus is on economic interpersonal inequality, measured by the well-known Gini coefficient. This is known as "vertical" inequality in the literature. Some authors have argued that it is horizontal inequality that increases the risk of war.[25] Others distinguish between income and asset inequality and find disputes over land rights to be a salient cause of ethnic violence (Bates 1989; Humphreys and Mohamed, volume 1, chapter 9; Kimenyi and Ndung'u, volume 1, chapter 5).

Several case studies suggest that the Gini coefficient may be poorly measured and that it does not measure the sort of inequality that is relevant to civil war. This should not surprise us, because it is not clear how interpersonal inequality would influence the ability to organize a civil war. There may exist a relationship between inequality and popular revolutions or class conflict, which is another reason to consider disaggregating the cases of civil war. But ethnic or secessionist wars should, in theory, be driven more by group-based inequality (which I refer to here as horizontal inequality) than by interpersonal inequality. High levels of interpersonal inequality in all ethnic groups may actually reduce the ability to coordinate an ethnic rebellion as they can erode group solidarity. Thus, if group-level data on inequality are not available, a useful measure of inequality to consider should be regional inequality, measured in terms of the differences between mean levels of per capita income across subnational units (such as provinces or republics).[26] Several of our case studies point to the need to consider the regional concentration of resources as an explanation of war (see chapters on Burundi, Senegal, Lebanon, and the DRC, among others). Interregional inequality could motivate the demand for more autonomy, or even secession. Thus, a potentially useful modification of the CH model would be to incorporate such a measure of inequality and see if it can explain ethnopolitical rebellion in subnational units rather than in entire countries.

## Conclusion

This book has demonstrated one way in which a comparative case study project can be combined with large-$N$ quantitative analysis to produce better theory and better empirical results about an important social problem. The case studies have all applied the Collier-Hoeffler economic model of civil war as a way to structure their analyses and they have suggested several improvements to the model. One gain from reading these cases is a better understanding of the process leading to civil war. The cases help us understand the complex interactions among variables in the formal/quantitative model and illustrate several different ways in which the same variable can operate in different contexts. Case narratives also help establish if empirical proxies used in the quantitative analysis are measured accurately and if they are good operationalizations of the theoretically significant variables. Case studies illuminate the mechanisms that underlie the Collier-Hoeffler theory but are not always distinguishable in the quantitative analysis. Finally, case studies help us formulate hypotheses about the role of variables that are omitted from the theoretical model, but should perhaps be added to the model so as to obtain better predictions and reduce the risk of omitted variable bias.

Taken as a whole, the case studies in this book suggest that we need to refine the economic model of civil war and improve the basic measures used to test the model. Drawing on the case studies, I have argued that we need to define and measure civil war better; that the relationship between ethnicity and political violence is still not well-understood, despite many empirical results on this topic; that we must consider regional dimensions of civil war; that country-, region-, and period-specific effects must be further explored; that the unit heterogeneity assumption that underlies the Collier-Hoeffler model must be tested; and that the relationship between different forms of violence must be the subject of new theorizing and new empirical tests.

Although the case study project has helped improve our intuitions about civil war and could help improve the Collier-Hoeffler model, it is also clear that the research design that guided these case studies would not have been possible without Collier and Hoeffler's theory and empirical results. Their model has made a seminal contribution to the field and was used here to provide an analytical framework within which qualitative analysis could help theory building that could then feed back into more empirical testing. The case studies were thus a secondary line of inquiry designed to illuminate the pathways through which independent variables influence the dependent variable and to explore interactions among the independent variables.

The Collier-Hoeffler model fits most of our cases quite well. But the improved understanding of the causal mechanisms that underlie the model should help us take civil war theory further. After reading these complex narratives, it becomes harder to see "greed" and "grievance" as competitive explanations of rebellion. Greed and grievance are often alternative interpretations of the same phenomenon; they are shades of the same problem. Indeed, we often see more political greed and economic grievance than the other way around. If political institutions can reduce grievances and if economic variables can influence the stability of political institutions, then economic variables will indirectly affect "grievance" factors in the Collier-Hoeffler model. And if state failure or government illegitimacy turns domestic politics into a near-anarchic world, then what Collier and Hoeffler call "greed" is really synonymous to the pursuit of survival. Civil war may be a response to either greed or grievance, but most often it is the result of both. We must now move beyond the greed-grievance distinction to explain why civil war occurs. Moreover, if it is civil war that we want to explain, our theories must be able to explain not only which countries are more likely to experience violence in general, but more specifically why violence takes the form of a civil war as opposed to other forms, such as genocide, coups, riots, or organized crime.

## Notes

1. "Quantitative indixes [sic] that do not relate closely to the concepts or events that we purport to measure can lead to serious measurement error and problems for causal inference" (King, Keohane, and Verba 1994, 44). These measurement errors do not introduce bias in the analysis, but they may decrease the efficiency of the results (King et al. 1994, 155).

2. For example, Fearon's (2001) and Licklider's (1995) coding of civil wars correlates only up to the range of 50–56 percent with civil war dates included in the Correlates of War 2 project (Sarkees and Singer 2001; see also Singer and Small 1994 for an earlier version of the COW list).

3. The coding of right-hand-side variables becomes more complicated in these cases, as the variables refer to entire empires.

4. This is one potential explanation. We cannot say with certainty that any single factor caused an outcome of war or peace in a single case, because within each case study, there is little variation on which to base such a claim. Yet, the narratives in the case studies take into account over-time variation in the explanatory variables, so there is a basis for Woodwell's (and others') causal arguments.

5. That death toll qualifies the cases as a civil war according to most criteria, but Collier and Hoeffler code no civil war in the United Kingdom.

6. Woodwell (volume 2, chapter 6) also notes the deterrent effect of the Royal Ulster Constabulary's strength of 13,500 members.

7. The same is true in quantitative tests of the CH model, because they include no controls for civil society or the government's degree of liberalism.

8. Here coding wars is an issue that complicates the analysis. The Shifta war in the 1960s against Somali secessionists probably qualifies as a civil war. And some data sets (e.g., Doyle and Sambanis 2005) code a civil war in Kenya in 1991–93 because of the extensive involvement of the state in organizing and financing the violence. For a discussion of these cases, see Sambanis (2004b).

9. Indeed, subsequent versions of the CH model have performed such a test.

10. This may explain the CH model's false-negative prediction for the Biafran war. Nigeria's primary commodity export share of GDP increased to 38 percent in 1990–94.

11. Esty et al. (1995) include a trade variable in their models of state failure; so does Gleditsch (2003).

12. See, for example, Mao Tse-Tung's (1954) own writing (he was more than a "scholar" of insurgency). See, also, Kocher (2003) for a quantitative analysis. Other cases, however, do not fit this mold. In the Algerian war of the 1990s, the violence has been concentrated in regions with the greatest population density and highest rate of urbanization.

13. A civil war broke out in the Côte d'Ivoire after the end of our analysis period (the CH data set goes up to 1999). The chapter on the Côte d'Ivoire is not included in the volume, but is available online.

14. I thank Keith Darden for pointing this out.

15. See Jones-Luong (2002) for an argument of the impact of constitutional design in preventing violent conflict in Central Asian Republics in the period of post-Soviet transition.

16. Horowitz 1985; Lake and Rothchild 1996; Lijphart 1977, 1984.

17. I develop each of these topics further in several papers (Sambanis 2002; 2003; 2004a, 2004b, 2004c) and Sambanis and Zinn (2004).

18. Theoretical works and large-N studies have also suggested this. An important paper is Lichbach (1987). See, also, White (1989) on the escalation of the Northern Irish conflict.

19. For a conceptual discussion of this point, see Laitin and Posner 2001.

20. Some authors do not consider race as part of ethnicity, because a racial group need not share a belief in common descent. Horowitz (1985) considers ethnic identity to derive from all ascriptive characteristics.

21. Sambanis and Milanovic (2004) have developed a theory of secession that focuses on, among other variables, the impact of ethnic difference across regions of a country. See, also, Fearon and Laitin (2002) and Toft (2003).

22. On contagion and diffusion, see Lake and Rothchild (1998).

23. The Minorities at Risk (MAR) data set is a good source of data at the group level. But it currently does not have sufficient data on groups not "at risk" so it cannot be used to predict war onset. The MAR is moving to expand its data collection to address this issue.

24. See Doyle and Sambanis (2005) for a book-length discussion of the impact of multilateral United Nations interventions on postwar peace building and the risk of civil war recurrence.

25. A comparative case study by Frances Stewart argues that complex humanitarian emergencies occur where group identity coincides with horizontal inequality that is widening, over a number of dimensions.
26. See Sambanis and Milanovic (2004) for such a measure.

# References

Anderson, Benedict. 1983. *Imagined Communities: Reflections on the Origins and Spread of Nationalism.* London:Verso.

Azam, Jean-Paul, and Constant Koidou. 2003. "Rising Threats: Containing Political Violence in Côte d'Ivoire." World Bank-Yale University Case Study.

Bates, Robert H. 1989. *Beyond the Miracle of Markets: The Political Economy of Agrarian Development in Kenya.* Cambridge, UK: Cambridge University Press.

Brass, Paul R. 1985. *Ethnic Groups and the State.* London: Croom-Helm.

———. 1997. *Theft of an Idol: Text and Context in the Representation of Collective Violence.* Princeton, NJ: Princeton University Press.

Brubaker, R. 1995. "National Minorities, Nationalizing States, and External National Homelands in the New Europe." *Daedalus* 124 (2): 107–32.

Brubaker, Rogers, and David D. Laitin. 1998. "Ethnic and Nationalist Violence." *Annual Review of Sociology* 24: 423–52.

Chandra, Kanchan. 2000. "Why Ethnic Parties Succeed." Ph.D. Dissertation, Harvard University.

Collier, Paul, and Anke Hoeffler. 2001. "Greed and Grievance in Civil War," World Bank Policy Research Working Paper 2355, World Bank, Washington, DC.

Darden, Keith. 2002. "The Scholastic Revolution." Mimeo, Yale University.

Davies, Victor A. B., and Abie Fofana. 2002. "Diamonds, Crime and Civil War in Sierra Leone." Paper prepared for the Yale University-World Bank Case Study Project on the Political Economy of Civil Wars.

De Figueiredo, Rui, and Barry Weingast. 1999. "The Rationality of Fear: Political Opportunism and Ethnic Conflict." In *Civil Wars, Insecurity, and Intervention,* ed. Barbara Walter and Jack Snyder, 261–302. New York: Columbia University Press.

Doyle, Michael W. 1997. "Authority and Elections in Cambodia." In *Keeping the Peace,* ed. Michael W. Doyle, Ian Johnstone, and Robert Orr, 134–64. Cambridge, UK: Cambridge University Press.

Doyle, Michael W., and Nicholas Sambanis. 2005. *Making War and Building Peace: The United Nations in the 1990s.* Princeton, NJ: Princeton University Press.

Elbadawi, Ibrahim A., and Nicholas Sambanis. 2000. "External Intervention and the Duration of Civil Wars." Policy Research Working Paper 2433, World Bank, Washington, DC.

———. 2002. "How Much War Will We See? Explaining the Prevalence of Civil War." *Journal of Conflict Resolution* 46 (3): 307–34.

Esty, Daniel C., Jack Goldstone, Ted Robert Gurr, Pamela T. Surko, and Alan N. Unger. 1995. *Working Papers: State Failure Task Force Report.* McLean, VA: Science Applications International Corporation.

Fearon, James D. 2001. "Why Do Some Civil Wars Last Longer Than Others?" Paper presented at the World Bank Conference on "Civil Wars and Post-War Transitions," University of California, Irvine, May 18–20.

Fearon, James D., and David Laitin. 2002. "Group Concentration and War." Unpublished manuscript, Stanford University.

———. 2003. "Ethnicity, Insurgency, and Civil War." *American Political Science Review* 97 (1): 91–106.

Gleditsch, Kristian. 2003. "Transnational Dimensions of Civil War." Unpublished manuscript, University of California, San Diego.

Glenny, Misha. 1999. *The Balkans: Nationalism, War, and the Great Powers, 1804–1999.* Penguin Books.

Gurr, Ted Robert. 1970. *Why Men Rebel.* Princeton, NJ: Princeton University Press.

———. 1993. *Minorities at Risk.* Washington, DC: U.S. Institute of Peace.

———. 2000. Peoples Versus States: Minorities at Risk in the New Century. Washington, DC: U.S. Institute of Peace.

Hardin, Russell. 1995. *One for All: The Logic of Group Conflict.* Princeton, NJ: Princeton University Press.

Hechter, Michael. 2001. *Containing Nationalism.* Oxford: Oxford University Press.

Hegre, Håvard. 2003. "Disentangling Democracy and Development as Determinants of Armed Conflict." Paper presented at the Annual Meeting of International Studies Association, Portland, OR, February 27.

Hegre, Håvard, T. Ellingsen, S. Gates, and N.-P. Gleditsch. 2001. "Toward a Democratic Civil Peace? Democracy, Political Change, and Civil War, 1816–1992." *American Political Science Review* 95: 33–48.

Horowitz, Donald, L. 1985. *Ethnic Groups in Conflict.* Berkeley and Los Angeles: University of California Press.

———. 1991. "Self-Determination: Politics, Philosophy, and Law." In *NOMOS XXXIX,* ed. Ian Shapiro and Will Kymlicka. New York: NYU Press.

Iatrides, John O. 1993. "The Doomed Revolution: Communist Insurgency in Postwar Greece." In *Stopping the Killing: How Civil Wars End,* ed. Roy Licklider. New York: NYU Press.

Jones-Luong, Pauline. 2002. *Institutional Change and Political Continuity in Post-Soviet Central Asia: Power, Perceptions, and Pacts.* Cambridge, UK/New York: Cambridge University Press.

Kalyvas, Stathis N. 2003. "What Is Political Violence? On the Ontology of Civil War." *Perspectives on Politics* 1 (3): 475–94.

Kasfir, Nelson. 1979. "Explaining Ethnic Political Participation." *World Politics* 31 (3): 365–88.

King, Gary, Robert O. Keohane, and Sidney Verba. 1994. *Designing Social Inquiry: Scientific Inference in Qualitative Research.* Princeton, NJ: Princeton University Press.

Kocher, Matthew. 2003. "Human Ecology and Civil War." Ph.D. Dissertation, University of Chicago.

Laitin, David D., and Dan Posner. 2001. "The Implications of Constructivism for Constructing Ethnic Fractionalization Indices." Mimeo.

Lake, David A., and Donald Rothchild. 1996. "Containing Fear: The Origins and Management of Ethnic Conflict." *International Security* 21 (2): 41–75.

———. eds. 1998. *The International Spread of Ethnic Conflict: Fear, Diffusion, and Escalation.* Princeton, NJ: Princeton University Press.

Lichbach, M. I. 1987. "Deterrence or escalation? The puzzle of aggregate studies of repression and dissent." *Journal of Conflict Resolution* 31 (2): 266–97.

Licklider, Roy. 1995. "The Consequences of Negotiated Settlements in Civil Wars, 1945–1993." *American Political Science Review* 89 (3): 681–90.

Lijphart, Arend. 1977. *Democracy in Plural Societies.* New Haven, CT: Yale University Press.

———. 1984. *Democracies: Patterns of Majoritarian and Consensus Government in Twenty-One Countries.* New Haven, CT: Yale University Press.

Linz, Juan. 1996. "The Perils of Presidentialism." In *Global Resurgence of Democracy,* 2nd ed., ed. Larry Diamond and Marcg F. Plattner. Baltimore: Johns Hopkins University Press.

Mueller, John. 2001. "The Remnants of War: Thugs as Residual Combatants." Mimeo. Ohio State University.

Przeworski, A., M. E. Alvarez, J. A. Cheibub, and F. Limongi. 2000. *Democracy and Development: Political Institutions and Well-Being in the World, 1950–1990.* Cambridge, UK: Cambridge University Press.

Regan, Patrick M. 2000. *Civil Wars and Foreign Powers.* Ann Arbor, MI: Michigan University Press.

———. 2002. "Third Party Interventions and the Duration of Intrastate Conflicts." *Journal of Conflict Resolution* 46 (1): 55–73.

Reynal-Querol, Marta. 2002. "Ethnicity, Political Systems, and Civil War." *Journal of Conflict Resolution* 46 (1): 29–54.

Ross, Michael L. 2000. "Does Oil Hinder Democracy?" *World Politics* 53: 325–61.

Rothchild, Donald. 2002. "Settlement Terms and Post-agreement Stability." In *Ending Civil Wars,* ed. Stephen Stedman, Donald Rothchild, and Elizabeth Cousens. Boulder, CO: Lynne Rienner.

Sambanis, Nicholas. 1999. "United Nations Peacekeeping in Theory and in Cyprus." Ph.D. Dissertation, Princeton University.

———. 2001. "Do Ethnic and Non-Ethnic Civil Wars Have the Same Causes? A Theoretical and Empirical Inquiry" (Part 1). *Journal of Conflict Resolution.* 45 (3): 259–82.

———. 2002. "A Review of Recent Advances and Future Directions in the Literature on Civil War." *Defense and Peace Economics* 13 (2): 215–43.

———. 2003. "The Causes of Genocide and Civil War: Are They More Similar Than We Thought?" Unpublished manuscript, Yale University.

———. 2004a. "Expanding Economic Models of Civil War Using Case Studies." *Perspectives on Politics* 2 (2): 259–80.

———. 2004b. "What Is a Civil War? Conceptual and Empirical Complexities of an Operational Definition." *Journal of Conflict Resolution* 48 (6): 814–58.

———. 2004c. "What Is an 'Ethnic' War? Organization and Interests in Ethnic Insurgency." Unpublished manuscript, Yale University.

Sambanis, Nicholas, and Branko Milanovic. 2004. "Explaining the Demand for Sovereignty." Paper presented at the Carnegie Corporation-YCIAS Conference on Self-Determination, May 15–16.

Sambanis, Nicholas, and Annalisa Zinn. 2004. "The Escalation of Self-Determination Movements: From Protest to Violence." Paper presented at the Carnegie Corporation-YCIAS Conference on Self-Determination, May 15–16.

Sarkees, Meredith Reid, and J. David Singer. 2001. "The Correlates of War Data sets: The Totality of War." Paper prepared for the 42nd Annual Convention of the International Studies Association, Chicago, IL, February 20–24.

Singer, David J., and Melvin Small. 1994. *Correlates of War Project: International and Civil War Data, 1816–1992.* Inter-University Consortium for Political and Social Research, Ann Arbor, MI.

Sisk, Timothy. 1996. *Power Sharing and International Mediation in Ethnic Conflict.* Washington, DC: United States Institute of Peace.

Smith, M. L. R. 1999. "The Intellectual Internment of a Conflict: The Forgotten War in Northern Ireland." *International Affairs* 75 (1): 77–98.

Tilly, Charles. 2003. *The Politics of Collective Violence.* Cambridge, MA: Cambridge University Press.

Toft, Monica. 2003. *The Geography of Fear.* Princeton, NJ: Princeton University Press.

Tse-Tung, Mao. 1954. *The Chinese Revolution and the Chinese Communist Party.* Peking: Foreign Languages Press.

Walter, Barbara F. 2002. *Committing to Peace.* Princeton, NJ: Princeton University Press.

Wantchekon, Leonard, and Zviika Neeman. 2000. "A Theory of Post-Civil War Democratization." Mimeo, July 28.

White, Robert W. 1989. "From Peaceful Protest to Guerilla War: Micromobilization of the Provisional Irish Republican Army." *American Journal of Sociology* 94 (May): 1277–1302.

Woodward, Susan. 1995. *Balkan Tragedy: Chaos and Dissolution After the Cold War.* Washington, DC: The Brookings Institution.

Woodwell, Douglas. 2004. "Unwelcome Neighbors: Shared Ethnicity and International Conflict During the Cold War." *International Studies Quarterly* 48 (1): 197–223.

# Contributors

YURI ANDRIENKO earned a degree in mathematics at Moscow State University in 1993, an M.A. in economics at the New Economic School in 1998, and a Ph.D. (candidate degree) in economics in 2004. He has worked at the Russian European Center for Economic Policy from 1999 to 2000, and has been working as an economist at the Centre for Economic and Financial Research in Moscow.

PAVEL BAEV is a senior researcher and the head of the Foreign and Security Policy program at the International Peace Research Institute, Oslo (PRIO). He also leads a working group at the newly created Centre for the Study of Civil War at PRIO. After graduating from the Moscow State University (M.A. in Political Geography, 1979), he worked in a research institute in the USSR Defence Ministry and Institute of Europe, Moscow. From 1995 to 2001 he was a co-editor of PRIO's quarterly *Security Dialogue*.

PAUL COLLIER is Professor of Economics and Director of the Centre for the Study of African Economies at Oxford University. During 1998–2003, he was on leave at the World Bank as Director of the Development Research Group. He has specialized on Africa, being a founding editor of the *Journal of African Economies*, and a coauthor of the *Journal of Economic Literature* survey article on African economic performance (1999). Much of his recent research has been on conflict, including coauthorship of "Greed and Grievance in Civil War" (*Oxford Economic Papers*, 2004) and *Breaking the Conflict Trap* (Oxford University Press, 2003). In 2004 he gave a keynote address on "conflict and development" to the General Assembly of the United Nations.

MICHEL FORMISANO is an economist from Bogotá, Colombia. He works as a junior researcher at the Research Center for Economic Development at Universidad de Los Andes, in Bogotá. As a graduate student, he became interested in the economics of violence, a topic that he pursued during his studies through work as a research assistant, and through subsequent publications.

Understanding Civil War

**ANKE HOEFFLER** is a research economist at the Centre for the Study of African Economies at Oxford University and has worked as a consultant to the World Bank's Development Economics Research Group. Her research interests are focused on economic growth and the economics of conflict. She is the coauthor (with Paul Collier) of "Greed and Grievance in Civil Wars," published in *Oxford Economic Papers*.

**STATHIS N. KALYVAS** is Arnold Wolfers Professor of Political Science and Director of the Program on Order, Conflict, and Violence at Yale University. He has previously taught at the University of Chicago (2000–2003), New York University (1994–2000), and Ohio State University (1993). His current research includes the dynamics of polarization and civil war, ethnic and nonethnic violence, and the formation of cleavages and identities. He is the author of *The Rise of Christian Democracy in Europe* (Cornell University Press, 1996) and *The Logic of Violence in Civil War* (forthcoming in 2006 from Cambridge University Press).

**JAN KOEHLER** received a Masters degree from the Freie Universität Berlin in Social Anthropology. At present he is codirector of the interdisciplinary research project on state building and conflict in Central Asia and the Caucasus region at the Freie Universität Berlin. He has worked as the assistant of the personal representative of the chairperson in the Office of the OSCE on the Nagorno-Karabakh conflict until November 2000 and has accomplished extensive fieldwork in the former Soviet Union over the past 10 years and focused his interest on informal organization of violence and justice in the South Caucasus. The results of his empirical work are accessible in various publications. He is, together with Christoph Zürcher, the editor of *Potentials of (Dis)Order: Conflict and Stability in the Caucasus and in Former Yugoslavia*, Manchester University Press (forthcoming), and, together with Sonja Heyer, editor of *Anthropologie der Gewalt. Chancen und Grenzen der sozialwissenschaftlichen Forschung* (Berlin, VWF, 1998).

**MICHAEL S. LUND** is Senior Specialist for Conflict and Peacebuilding, Management Systems International, Inc., and a professorial lecturer, the School of Advanced International Studies, Johns Hopkins University, in Washington, D.C. He is author of *Preventing Violent Conflicts* (USIP Press, 1996) and has researched conflicts and evaluated the effectiveness of conflict interventions for the UN, World Bank, USAID, European Union, and other organizations in the Balkans, Africa, Central Asia, and other regions. Lund received his Ph.D. in political science from the University of Chicago.

**SAMIR MAKDISI** is Professor of Economics and Director of the Institute of Financial Economics at the American University of Beirut and is a member of the Governing Board of the Global Development Network (Washington, DC). He was Deputy President of the American University Beirut, 1993–1998 and Minister of the National Economy for Lebanon in 1992. From 1993 to 2001, he was Chair of the Board of Trustees of the Economic Research Forum for the Arab Countries,

Iran, and Turkey. He is author of the recently published, *The Lessons of Lebanon, the Economics of War and Development* (London, I.B. Tauris, 2004).

**MICHAEL L. ROSS** is Associate Professor of Political Science at the University of California, Los Angeles (UCLA). His book *Timber Booms and Institutional Breakdown in Southeast Asia* was published in 2001 by Cambridge University Press. Most of his publications and working papers are available at www.polisci.ucla.edu/faculty/ross.

**RICHARD SADAKA** is a Professor of Economics at the American University of Beirut, Lebanon.

**NICHOLAS SAMBANIS** is Associate Professor of Political Science at Yale University. He received his Ph.D. from Princeton University's Woodrow Wilson School in June 1999. From 1999 to 2001, he held the position of economist at the World Bank's Development Economics Research Group, where he was part of the core research team for the project on "The Economics of Political and Criminal Violence." He has researched several topics on ethnic conflict and political violence. He is coauthor of *Making War and Building Peace: United Nations Peace Operations*, a book evaluating the effectiveness of UN peacekeeping and peacebuilding after civil wars.

**FABIO SÁNCHEZ** has a Ph.D. in economics from Rutgers University. He is Professor of Economics and current Director of the Center of Studies on Economic Development of the Economics Department at the Universidad de Los Andes, Bogotá-Colombia. He is the author of several studies on Colombian violence and conflict, including *Illicit Crops and Conflict in Colombia, Determinants of Violent Crime in Colombia, and Political Polarization and Violence during La Violencia.*

**LOUISE SHELLEY** is the founder and Director of the Transnational Crime and Corruption Center (TraCCC), and a leading United States expert on organized crime and corruption in the former Soviet Union. Dr. Shelley is a Professor in the Department of Justice, Law and Society (School of Public Affairs) and the School of International Service at American University. She is the author of *Policing Soviet Society* (Routledge, 1996), *Lawyers in Soviet Worklife,* and *Crime and Modernization,* as well as numerous articles and book chapters on all aspects of transnational crime and corruption.

**ANDRÉS SOLIMANO** is a regional advisor at the United Nations Economic Commission for Latin America and the Caribbean. He was previously Country Director at the World Bank and Executive Director at the InterAmerican Development Bank. He is the editor of the series, *Development and Inequality in the Market Economy,* by University of Michigan Press. He holds a Ph.D. in economics from MIT.

DOUGLAS WOODWELL is a Ph.D. candidate in the Department of Political Science at Yale University. His research interests include ethnic conflict, quantitative methodologies, and the synthesis of international relations and comparative politics.

CHRISTOPH ZÜRCHER is Assistant Professor at the Institute of East European Studies, Free University Berlin. He holds the chair for conflict studies. He received his Ph.D. from the University of Bern. His research interests include political transition in the Former Soviet Union, ethnopolitical conflict, and international relations. He is the editor of *Potentials of (Dis)Order: Explaining Violence in the Caucasus and in the Former Yugoslavia*, published by Manchester University Press in 2003.

# Index

# 338

Colombia, 119–57. *see also* FARC
(Revolutionary Armed Forces of
Colombia)
armed groups in, illegal, 121–24, 147, 148
Catholic Church in, 120
cocaine in, 125, 126–28, 127*f*
in Collier-Hoeffler model, 119, 154–55
Communist party in, 123
dates of civil war in, 4*t*
FARC (Revolutionary Armed Forces of
Colombia) in, 119, 121, 123, 127,
127*f*, 131*f*, 134, 135, 137*f*, 140,
143*t*–146*t*, 147, 155n4
*Frente Nacional* in, 120, 125
gross domestic product of, 127
*haciendas* in, 120
homicide in, 121, 122*t*, 125–26, 125*f*,
129–30, 131*f*, 132*f*, 136*f*, 137*f*,
138*f*, 139*f*, 140–53, 143*t*–146*t*, 152*t*
kidnapping in, 124, 126, 126*f*,
143*t*–146*t*, 148, 153*t*
*La Violencia* in, 119, 120, 121, 142, 146*t*,
154
liberation of, from Spain, 120
modernization in, 120
National Liberation Army (ELN) in,
123–24, 128, 132*f*, 135, 138*f*, 140,
143*t*–146*t*, 147, 155n4
paramilitary organizations in, 124
property crimes in, 128, 128*f*, 148, 149*t*,
154
road piracy in, 128, 128*f*, 148, 149*t*, 154
Southern Block in, 123
taxes levied by guerillas in, 127
war of the Supremes in, 120
Communist Action Organization, in
Lebanon, 65*t*
Communist Party, 64, 65*t*, 123. *see also*
Soviet Union
concentration camps, in Bosnia, 213–14
Congo, Democratic Republic of, dates of
civil war in, 4*t*
Conservative party (Colombia), 120, 121
Côte d'Ivoire, 309, 326n13
crime. *see also* drug(s)
in Collier-Hoeffler model, 95
contagious diffusion of, 130, 134*f*
diffusion of, 130

economics and, 108–9
and education level, 107–8
growth of, and prisons, 108
hierarchical diffusion of, 130, 135*f*
property, in Colombia, 128, 128*f*
relocation of, 130
in Russia, 91–92
in Soviet Union, 88–91, 90*f*
Croatia, 192–93, 196*t*, 201*t*, 207, 209. *see
also* Yugoslavia
Croatian Democratic Union, 192
Crvenkovski, Branko, 245
Cuban revolution, and Colombia, 123
Cyprus, dates of civil war in, 4*t*

## D

Dagestan
in Collier-Hoeffler model, 285–86
ethnic fractionalization in, 276, 292
ethnic fractionalization of, 276
language in, 277
oil in, 276, 277
political organization in, 286–87
population of, 277
size of, 277
stability in, 285–87
transition of, 277–78
unemployment in, 277
*vs.* Chechnya, 276–77
Darul Islam rebellion, 54n8
Delic, Ramiz, 215
democracy
and civil conflict, 166
as Collier-Hoeffler variable, 6*t*
established *vs.* new, 310–11
in ethnically mixed environments, 289–90
in Indonesia, 52
in Lebanon, 72
in Macedonia, 245–46
partial, 45, 51
in Yugoslavia, 210–11
Democratic League of Kosovo (LDK),
237, 239, 254n46
Democratic Party for Albanians (DPA),
236, 239, 255n55
Democratic Party for Macedonian
National Unity (DPMNE), 239. *see
also* Macedonia

ethnicity *(Continued)*
  of Chechnya, 276
  and civil war risk, 54n6
  in Collier-Hoeffler model, 308–09
  diversity of, 6*t*, 7–8, 15*t*
  in Georgia, 264–65, 265*t*
  hatred over, and grievance proxy, 8
  in Indonesia, 36–37
  in Lebanon, 69
  manipulation of, by elites, 322
  mobilization by, 23–24
  in Russia, polarization of, 99*t*
  in Soviet Union organizational policy, 260
ethnification, after the fact, in Yugoslavia,
  216–18, 220–21
ethnolinguistic fractionalization, 114n6
exclusion, political, and grievance proxy, 8
exogamy, 199, 225n11–13
exports, 6*t*, 9, 10*t*–11*t*
external intervention
  in Collier-Hoeffler (CH) model, 71,
  318–19
  in Lebanon, 62–63, 67, 71, 73
  in Northern Ireland, 181–82
ExxonMobil, 48, 55n25. *see also* Mobil Oil

**F**

FARC (Revolutionary Armed Forces of
  Colombia), 119, 121, 123, 127, 127*f*,
  131*f*, 134, 135, 137*f*, 140, 143*t*–146*t*,
  147, 155n4. *see also* Colombia
Faulkner, William (Prime Minister), 172,
  175, 180, 186n35
Feith, Peter, 247
financing, of rebellions, 6–7, 17
Firqat an Nasr, 65*t*
Fitzgerald, Garrett, 176
forest cover, 6*t*, 174
France, 67, 82n11, 194, 210
Frangieh, Sulieman, 82n6
*Frente Nacional*, 120, 121, 125. *see also*
  Colombia

**G**

Gaitán, Jorge Eliécer, 120
GAM. *see* Aceh Freedom Movement
Gamsakhurdia, Zviad, 266, 267, 268, 275
Gantenmirov, Bislan, 281

Gemeyel, Amin, 67–68, 68
Gemeyel, Bashir, 67
General Method of Moments (GMM), 101,
  102, 103*t*–105*t*
Georgia, 264–76
  Abkhazia war in, 269–70, 272, 274, 275
  *Adamon Nykhas* (People's Assembly) in,
  271
  Adjaria republic in, 270
  causes of war in, 273–76
  climate of, 264
  in Collier-Hoeffler model, 273–76
  dates of civil war in, 4*t*
  economy of, 266, 293n4
  elections in, 261
  ethnicity in, 264–65, 265*t*
  exports of, 275
  GDP of, 275
  markets of violence in, 263
  organization of violence in, 270–73
  population of, 264
  size of, 264
  South Ossetia war in, 267–69, 271, 274,
  275
  terrain of, 264, 273–74
Germany, 54n3, 193, 308
Gini coefficient. *see also* income
  of Colombia, 147–48
  definition of, 108
  of Indonesia, 37
  problems with, 323–24
  of Russia, 100*t*
  of Yugoslavia, 196*t*
Giorgadze, Igor, 273
*glasnost*, 90–91, 96, 261, 277
Gligorov, Kiro, 234, 237, 251n15
GMM. *see* General Method of Moments
  (GMM)
Gómez, Laureano, 120
Gorbachev, Mikhail, 90, 91, 96, 260–61, 279
Government of Ireland Act (1920), 163
Greece, civil war in, 312
greed, 2, 3, 170
grievance, 8, 53
gross domestic product (GDP)
  of Aceh province, Indonesia, 38, 45
  in Collier-Hoeffler model, 302
  as Collier-Hoeffler variable, 6*t*

348                                                    *Understanding Civil War*

Taylor, Charles, 317
terrain, 6*t*, 10*t*, 14*t*, 210, 291–92, 307
Territorial Defence Force, 204
terrorism, 93, 94–95, 282, 320
Thaci, Hashem, 242
Thailand, 38, 44–45, 48
Thatcher, Margaret, 176
Tito, Josip, 192, 211, 232, 250n10
Tone, Wolfe, 163
topography, as CH variable, 6*t*
Torres, Camilo, 155n2
Trajkowski, Boris, 236, 251n15
Trimble, David, 179
Tripartite Agreement, 78
"troika rule," 79–80
Tudjman, Franjo, 192
Turkey, dates of civil war in, 5*t*

**U**

Uganda, dates of civil war in, 5*t*
Ulster Special Constabulary, 164, 167
Ulster Volunteer Force (UVF), 184n16
Ulster Worker's Council (UWC), 175
unemployment
  in Chechnya, 277
  and conflict, 110
  in Dagestan, 277
  in Macedonia, 253n31
  in Northern Ireland, 163, 165
  in Yugoslavia, 207–8
United Irishmen, 163. *see also* Northern
    Ireland
United Kingdom. *see also* Northern Ireland
  in Bosnian conflict, 194
  in Collier-Hoeffler model, 170
  education in, 184n20
  population of, 170
  security forces of, 168
  Serbian lobby in, 210
  urbanization in, 186n32
United Nations (UN), 193
United Self Defense of Colombia (AUC),
    124, 127
United States
  attacks on soldiers of, in Lebanon, 82n11
  GDP and ethnic power dynamics in, 164
  and Irish Republican Army, 171
  and Lebanese civil war, 67

Lebanese diaspora in, 60
liberation of Kuwait by, 78
and Macedonia, 247
mediation of Bosnian conflict by, 194
trip to, by Gerry Adams, 178
urbanization
  in Bosnia, 210
  as Collier-Hoeffler variable, 6*t*, 307
  in Northern Ireland, 174, 186n32
  in Soviet Union, 89–90
  in United Kingdom, 186n32
  and violence, 110
UWC. *see* Ulster Worker's Council (UWC)

**V**

Veliu, Fazli, 241
Vietnam, dates of civil war in, 5*t*
Vojvodina, 196*t*, 202*t*, 207

**W**

Waad Party, 65*t*
*Wahabism,* 280
Wahid, Abdurrahman, 45, 46
Wilson, Harold, 166
Wiranto, 45, 46
women, as criminals, in Russia, 89
World War I, II, Russia in, 88

**X**

Xhemmajli, Emrush, 255n47

**Y**

Yanaev, Gennady, 261
Yandarbiev, Zelimkhan, 279
Yazov, Dmitriy, 261
Yeltsin, Boris, 261, 279
Yemen, dates of civil war in, 5*t*
Yugoslavia. *see also* Bosnia; Croatia; Jugoslav
    National Army (JNA); Kosovo;
    Macedonia; Montenegro; Serbia;
    Slovenia
  alcohol in, 215
  areas of greatest violence in, 217–18
  census of, 200
  Cold War and, 211–12
  collective presidency in, 192
  in Collier-Hoeffler model, 194–212,
    221, 222*t*–223*t*, 224